Studies in Regional and Local History

General Editor Jane Whittle

Previous titles in this series
Founding Editor Nigel Goose

Volume 1: *A Hertfordshire demesne of Westminster Abbey: Profits, productivity and weather* by Derek Vincent Stern (edited and with an introduction by Christopher Thornton)

Volume 2: *From Hellgill to Bridge End: Aspects of economic and social change in the Upper Eden Valley, 1840–95* by Margaret Shepherd

Volume 3: *Cambridge and its Economic Region, 1450–1560* by John S. Lee

Volume 4: *Cultural Transition in the Chilterns and Essex Region, 350 AD to 650 AD* by John T. Baker

Volume 5: *A Pleasing Prospect: Society and culture in eighteenth-century Colchester* by Shani D'Cruze

Volume 6: *Agriculture and Rural Society after the Black Death: Common themes and regional variations* by Ben Dodds and Richard Britnell

Volume 7: *A Lost Frontier Revealed: Regional separation in the East Midlands* by Alan Fox

Volume 8: *Land and Family: Trends and local variations in the peasant land market on the Winchester bishopric estates, 1263–1415* by John Mullan and Richard Britnell

Volume 9: *Out of the Hay and into the Hops: Hop cultivation in Wealden Kent and hop marketing in Southwark, 1744–2000* by Celia Cordle

Volume 10: *A Prospering Society: Wiltshire in the later Middle Ages* by John Hare

Volume 11: *Bread and Ale for the Brethren: The provisioning of Norwich Cathedral Priory, 1260–1536* by Philip Slavin

Volume 12: *Poor Relief and Community in Hadleigh, Suffolk, 1547–1600* by Marjorie Keniston McIntosh

Volume 13: *Rethinking Ancient Woodland: The archaeology and history of woods in Norfolk* by Gerry Barnes and Tom Williamson

Volume 14: *Custom and Commercialisation in English Rural Society: Revisiting Tawney and Postan* edited by J.P. Bowen and A.T. Brown

Volume 15: *The World of the Small Farmer: Tenure, profit and politics in the early modern Somerset Levels* by Patricia Croot

Volume 16: *Communities in Contrast: Doncaster and its rural hinterland, c.1830–1870* by Sarah Holland

Volume 17: *Peasant Perspectives on the Medieval Landscape: A study of three communities* by Susan Kilby

Volume 18: *Shaping the Past: Theme, time and place in local history – essays in honour of David Dymond* by Evelyn Lord and Nicholas R. Amor

Lichfield and the Lands of St Chad

Creating community
in early medieval Mercia

Andrew Sargent

University of Hertfordshire Press
Studies in Regional and Local History

Volume 19

First published in Great Britain in 2020 by
University of Hertfordshire Press
College Lane
Hatfield
Hertfordshire
AL10 9AB
UK

© Andrew Sargent 2020

The right of Andrew Sargent to be identified as the author of this work has been asserted by him in accordance with the Copyright, Designs and Patents Act 1988.

All rights reserved. No part of this book may be reproduced or utilised in any form or by any means, electronic or mechanical, including photocopying, recording or by any information storage and retrieval system, without permission in writing from the publisher.

British Library Cataloguing in Publication Data
A catalogue record for this book is available from the British Library

ISBN 978-1-912260-24-9 hardback
ISBN 978-1-912260-25-6 paperback

Design by Arthouse Publishing Solutions
Printed in Great Britain by Charlesworth Press

Contents

List of illustrations	vii
General Editor's preface	ix
Acknowledgements	xi
Abbreviations	xii

	Introduction	**1**
	Early medieval communities	2
	The communities of the lands of St Chad	9
1	**Lichfield and the English Church**	**11**
	The episcopal list tradition	12
	Theodore's church	19
	Church and kingdom	21
	The division of the Mercian see	26
	The English Church and the Mercian kingdom	33
	The English Church from the late ninth century	40
	Conclusions	44
2	**The Church of Lichfield**	**48**
	The Lastingham narrative	48
	Bishop Chad and Bishop Wilfrid	54
	The diocesan community	60
	The Church of Lichfield and the diocesan community	80
3	**The cathedral and the minsters**	**86**
	Hunting for minsters	87
	Lichfield cathedral	110
	Minsters attested by pre-*c.*1050 hagiography	123
	Minsters attested by post-*c.*1050 hagiography	137
	Minsters securely attested by stone sculpture	141
	Minsters less securely attested	146
	Minsters and communities	150
4	**The bishop and the lords of minsters**	**156**
	Ecclesiastical tribute	157
	Episcopal authority over the lords of minsters	166
	Conclusions	175
5	**The people**	**177**
	Agricultural communities and the historic landscape	177
	Domainal communities and the possession of land	186
	Brythonic place-names	190

	Old English place-names	195
	Eccles place-names	203
	Agricultural and domainal communities in the diocese of Lichfield	206
6	**The parish**	**216**
	Churches and parishes	217
	Churches, estates and 'regnal territories'	225
	Regnal territories and the regnal community	240
	A parochial transformation	244

Conclusion   **253**

Bibliography   261
Index   273

Illustrations

Figures
1. Bounds of the diocese of Lichfield in the late thirteenth century — 3
2. Layout of the Mercian episcopal lists — 15
3. Distribution of estates of the bishop of Lichfield in 1066 — 63
4. Distribution of stone sculpture dated to the late eighth and early ninth centuries — 95
5. Examples of stone sculpture dated to the late eighth and early ninth centuries — 98
6. Distribution of stone sculpture dated to the mid- to late ninth and early tenth centuries — 102
7. Examples of stone sculpture dated to the mid- to late ninth and early tenth centuries — 104
8. Composite plan of the archaeological evidence beneath Lichfield cathedral — 113
9. Hypothetical reconstruction of the church and chapel at Lichfield — 118
10. Distribution of minsters probably established in or before the early tenth century — 149
11. Distribution of various soil types amenable to cultivation across the diocese of Lichfield — 184
12. Distribution of sizes of estates with place-names containing Brythonic elements — 193
13. Distribution of sizes of estates with place-names containing *dūn* — 197
14. Distribution of sizes of estates with place-names containing *ēg* — 197
15. Distribution of sizes of estates with place-names containing *hām* — 198
16. Distribution of sizes of estates with place-names containing *burh* — 199
17. Distribution of sizes of estates with place-names containing *feld* — 201
18. Distribution of place-names overlain on the distribution of different soil types — 210
19. Reconstruction of the early twelfth-century parochial geography of the diocese — 226
20. The thirteenth-century fee of Leek — 236
21. Cheshire fees of six barons recorded in *Domesday Book* — 238

Tables
1. The estates of the bishop of Lichfield in 1066 represented in Domesday Book — 66
2. 'Superior churches' identified in Domesday Book within the diocese of Lichfield — 220

Studies in Regional and Local History

General Editor's preface

For those of us who work on later periods of history there is an inescapable romance to early medieval England. The exact contours of historical change in this period are elusive, but many institutions which still influence our lives in the early twenty-first century have their origins in this era: the county, the parish, and the English church. This book focuses on the bishopric of Lichfield within the kingdom of Mercia, which encompassed the Midland counties of Staffordshire, Derbyshire, Cheshire and parts of Shropshire and Warwickshire. Lichfield's importance to early English Christianity explains the presence today of a grand medieval cathedral in what has remained a small market town. Andrew Sargent's innovative new study explores the emergence of different types of community centred on the diocese of Lichfield between the seventh and eleventh centuries. These include the establishment of a community of the English church, to which the Bishop of Lichfield contributed; the diocesan community centred on Lichfield; liturgical communities within the cathedral and local minsters; hierarchical relationships of spiritual lordship that funnelled ecclesiastical tributes to the bishop and his clergy; agricultural communities and their lords; and the interaction of secular lordship, ecclesiastical lordship and royal lordship to create something we might now label a system of government. In doing so, the idea of community is interrogated and developed. Communities are considered not just as groups of people who lived close to one another, but as networks of interaction which allowed 'the creation and renewal of shared norms'. As such, individuals such as Lichfield's first bishop, Chad, were members of multiple communities in which they had different roles. Communities encompassed both horizontal bonds of shared interest, and vertical bonds of tribute, protection and rule. The importance of this period lies in the fact many of these relationships were being developed for the first time, creating institutions which were at first fluid, but later solidified into durable structures which shaped religious, social and political life into the high medieval period and beyond. Sargent's careful consideration of the meaning and nature of communities is also a model that could helpfully be followed by historians of later periods.

A second, other distinctive feature of this study is its focus on the history of what has been described as the 'Mercian hole': a region for which relatively little written or archaeological evidence survives for before the tenth century. This requires ingenuity and skill, with the careful but creative use of available evidence. It necessarily makes the study inter-disciplinary, relying on evidence of material culture (buildings and sculpture) as well as written texts, and using topographical and toponymical evidence to locate lost buildings and boundaries. In doing so it makes what might some regard as an obscure period of English history surprisingly accessible. On a rainy summer's day in the Peak District near Dovedale – a day of luminous greenery and overflowing waterways – I stumbled across the church at Ilam, now part of a National Trust property. This small and rather odd-looking church has been heavily restored and little remains of its original fabric, but the presence of two early medieval decorated stone cross shafts in the graveyard indicate its early importance. Sargent identifies this church as a centre of the Mercian cult of St Beorhthelm, later St Bertram. A late-medieval Life of the saint, reputedly the son of a king, relates how he went to Ireland, fell in love with another King's daughter, and eloped with her back to England. She went into labour in a forest, and tragically she and the newborn child were killed by a wolf while Bertram went to seek help. In response Bertram became a hermit. Ilam church contains his reputed tomb and the associated shrine dates to the thirteenth century, while the twelfth century font in Ilam church appears to depict his story, with an image of a wolf consuming two human heads. This striking story need not be more than a pious fable, but the presence of Bertram's shrine points to the likely importance of the church in the Mercian kingdom. Accounts such as this connect the local and the physical, not just with semi-mythical elements of the distant past, but with genuine struggles of the seventh to eleventh centuries: establishing a new belief system, creating an organised church, and balancing power between religious and secular lords in this new cultural landscape.

Jane Whittle
March 2020

Acknowledgements

This book is the result of a twelve-year journey that began with a PhD at Keele University, and with a project conceived by my supervisor Philip Morgan, to whom I owe a great deal (including the title). His friendship and encouragement, and that of other Keele colleagues, notably Kate Cushing and Nigel Tringham, has sustained me throughout my degree and on my subsequent career path. My PhD was funded by an AHRC collaborative award, and I am very grateful to the external partner, Lichfield Cathedral, and in particular to Pete Wilcox, then the Canon Chancellor, and Catherine Fox, who welcomed me warmly to the community there. I owe a profound thanks to members of the congregation at Lichfield, whose patience with my earliest attempts at public speaking and constant interest in the project buoyed me through the otherwise rather solitary process of research and writing. The publication of this book was aided by generous grants from Keele University and from the Jack Leighton Trust, a charity that encourages research into the history of Staffordshire and its region; both have my sincere thanks.

Any intellectual journey is always the product of innumerable encounters and conversations, and mine is no exception. Those to whom I owe sparks of insight or challenging critique are too numerous to list, and must forgive me for naming only a few here. Bob and Jean Meeson have given me constant friendship and support over the years, and possess a depth of knowledge on the history and archaeology of the region that is second to none. Matthew Blake has encouraged me to get out into the landscape and think through ideas on the ground. Charles Insley, my external examiner, prompted me to go further, and has since followed my career with interest. To these, and many others, I owe the wellspring of my enthusiasm for early medieval studies, and I look forward to encountering them again on the journeys ahead.

Finally, I owe thanks and more than thanks to those who care for me the most. Among these I must count my cat, Hazel, whose constant attention marks my memories of writing both my thesis and this book. Yet I give my greatest thanks to my mother, Janet Sargent, and my father, Ken Sargent, who have always shown a conviction in my choices, even when I lacked it myself, and especially when I gave up the possibility of a career in astrophysics to become an archaeologist; and to my wife, Clare, and my children Athena and Aneirin, who arrived partway along this journey, who carry me through the mental and emotional thickets on the way and who give me a life to live when the writing is done.

Abbreviations

Alcuin ep. E. Dümmler (ed.), *Alcuin epistolae*, Monumenta Germaniae historica, epistolae Carolini aevi 4 (Berlin, 1895); references are given by letter number.

ASC *Anglo-Saxon Chronicle:* the version is given in parentheses, and translations are taken from M. Swanton, *The Anglo-Saxon Chronicles* (London, 2000).

DB *Domesday Book:* references are taken from J. Morris *et al.* (ed.), *Domesday Book*, Phillimore, 34 volumes (Chichester, 1974–86); volumes are indicated by abbreviated county, and references given according to section and entry annotations given therein.

EEE Bede's letter to Bishop Ecgberht: Bede, 'Epistola Bede ad Ecgbertum Episcopum', in C. Plummer, *Venerabilis Baedae opera historica* (Oxford, 1896), 405–23.

EHD 1 D. Whitelock (ed.), *English Historical Documents c. 500–1042*, vol. 1 (London, 1955).

HE Bede's *Historia Ecclesiastica gentis Anglorum*: B. Colgrave and R.A.B. Mynors (eds), *Bede's Ecclesiastical History of the English People* (Oxford, 1969). References are given by book and chapter numbers.

S P.H. Sawyer, *Anglo-Saxon charters; an annotated list and bibliography* (London, 1968); charters are referenced by the number assigned to them.

SHC Staffordshire Historical Collections: Volumes of *Collections for a History of Staffordshire* have been published by the Staffordshire Record Society in four series, of which two are referenced herein; the first series is denoted by volume number and the third series by year of publication.

VG Felix's *Vita Sancti Guthlaci*: B. Colgrave, *Felix's Life of Saint Guthlac* (Cambridge, 1956).

VMM Geoffrey's *Vita et miracula Sancte Modwenne*: R. Bartlett (ed.), *Geoffrey of Burton: Life and miracles of St Modwenna* (Oxford, 2002).

VSW *Vita Sanctae Werburgae*: R.C. Love, *Goscelin of Saint-Bertin: the hagiography of the female saints of Ely* (Oxford, 2004).

VW *Vita Wilfridi*: B. Colgrave, *The life of Bishop Wilfrid by Eddius Stephanus. Text, translation, and notes* (Cambridge, 1927).

Introduction

This book explores a hole at the heart of Mercia, the great Midland kingdom of early medieval England. Chad, the kingdom's fifth bishop (669–72), had fixed his cathedral at Lichfield in 669 and, by 737, after the creation of four further Mercian bishoprics, the territory of the diocese had been confined to the north-west part of the Midlands (now Staffordshire, Derbyshire, Cheshire and parts of Shropshire and Warwickshire). When compared with other regions of early medieval England the diocese of Lichfield is bereft of the kinds of evidence that typically inform histories of this period.[1] The region has no parallel to the voluminous corpus of land charters, surviving from the seventh century, preserved in the archive of the see of Worcester in the south-west Midlands, while the textual exuberance associated with the English Benedictine monasteries of the tenth and eleventh centuries concerns places to the south and east, with only a single north-western outlier in Burton-on-Trent.[2] Turning to archaeological evidence, the distribution of furnished burials dated to the fifth, sixth and seventh centuries, long thought to be characteristic of 'Anglo-Saxon' culture, tails off at the eastern edges of the diocese, excepting only the enigmatic barrow burials of the Peak District.[3] Special burials of the seventh and later centuries – local saints with Old English names – occupy a similar distribution.[4] Even Bede, whose *Historia Ecclesiastica* has provided so much material to those who would attempt to construct a narrative of seventh- and early eighth-century English history, has scarcely anything to say about the region apart from his tribute to Bishop Chad.[5] This book tackles the challenge offered by this 'Mercian hole' in the north-west Midlands by synthesising evidence from a number of different sources – archaeological, textual, topographical and toponymical – and comparing it with other regions where evidence is more plentiful. In doing so it seeks to realise the promise of the best kinds of local and regional history: those that define and explain distinctiveness within the context of a wider world.

---

1 Regional studies in Britain and beyond have relied overwhelmingly on more plentiful textual evidence; examples include N. Brooks, *The early history of the church of Canterbury* (Leicester, 1984); P. Sims-Williams, *Religion and literature in western England 600–800* (Cambridge, 1990); W. Davies, *An early Welsh microcosm: studies in the Llandaff charters* (London, 1978); M. Innes, *State and society in the early Middle Ages: the middle Rhine valley, 400–1000* (London, 2000); H.J. Hummer, *Politics and power in early medieval Europe. Alsace and the Frankish realm, 600–1000* (Cambridge, 2005).
2 P.H. Sawyer, *The charters of Burton Abbey, Anglo-Saxon Charters 2* (Oxford, 1979).
3 A. Ozanne, 'The Peak dwellers', *Medieval Archaeology*, 6/7 (1962/3), pp. 15–52.
4 J. Blair, 'A saint for every minster? Local cults in Anglo-Saxon England', in A. Thacker and R. Sharpe (eds), *Local saints and local churches in the early medieval West* (Oxford, 2002), pp. 455–94, at pp. 457–8.
5 *HE*, iv.3.

The north-west Midlands region has appeared in previous studies primarily as a locus of conflict, a borderland contested by Mercians, Welsh and Vikings. Scholars have made use of martial allusions in early Welsh poetry and annals marking battles between Mercian kings and their Welsh and Viking counterparts, and have undertaken archaeological and topographical analyses of that striking epitome of the Anglo-Welsh border, Offa's Dyke.[6] The region has also been viewed through the prism of clashing polities and cultures within a wider 'Irish Sea province'.[7] There is much to appreciate in these studies, and a recent contribution on the 'Anglo-Welsh borderland' has demonstrated that territorial divisions need not always imply conflict.[8] Nonetheless, a broad-based consideration of the Mercian side of this borderland has not yet been attempted. Indeed, excepting relations with the Welsh, the excellent collections of essays on Mercia published in 1977 and 2001 hardly mention the region, focusing instead on the more plentiful evidence to the south and east, and particularly on the sculptural and archaeological riches of the east Midlands.[9] In this book the bounds of the diocese of Lichfield, at least as they can be reconstructed from late thirteenth-century evidence, are used to delimit a study of this neglected region (see Figure 1).[10] In particular, the persistence of this episcopal territory throughout the medieval period raises questions concerning the creation, development and transformation of communities in the region.

Early medieval communities

Concepts of 'community' are central to the following study, and thus require careful consideration here. The word has often been used in relation to ecclesiastical

---

[6] D.P. Kirby, 'Welsh bards and the border', in A. Dornier (ed.), *Mercian studies* (Leicester, 1977), pp. 31–42; T.M. Charles-Edwards, 'Wales and Mercia, 613–918', in M.P. Brown and C.A. Farr (eds), *Mercia: an Anglo-Saxon kingdom in Europe* (London, 2001), pp. 89–105; D. Hill, 'Mercians: the dwellers on the boundary', in M.P. Brown and C.A. Farr (eds), *Mercia: an Anglo-Saxon kingdom in Europe* (London, 2001), pp. 173–82; D. Hill and M. Worthington, *Offa's Dyke: history and guide* (Stroud, 2003); K. Ray and I. Bapty, *Offa's Dyke: landscape and hegemony in eighth century Britain* (Oxford, 2016).

[7] D.W. Griffiths, 'Anglo-Saxon England and the Irish Sea region AD 800–1100: an archaeological study of the lower Dee and Mersey as a border area', PhD thesis (Durham, 1991).

[8] L. Brady, *Writing the Welsh borderland in Anglo-Saxon England* (Manchester, 2017).

[9] A. Dornier (ed.), *Mercian studies* (Leicester, 1977); M.P. Brown and C.A. Farr (eds), *Mercia: an Anglo-Saxon kingdom in Europe* (London, 2001); exceptions to this neglect in the latter include Jane Hawkes' exploration of the Sandbach crosses (J. Hawkes, 'Constructing iconographies: questions of identity in Mercian sculpture', in M.P. Brown and C.A. Farr (eds), *Mercia: an Anglo-Saxon kingdom in Europe* (London, 2001), pp. 230–45) and Michelle Brown's consideration of the possibilities offered by the cathedral at Lichfield as a centre of Mercian manuscript production in the eighth and ninth centuries (M.P. Brown, 'Mercian manuscripts? The "Tiberius" group and its historical context', in M.P. Brown and C.A. Farr (eds), *Mercia: an Anglo-Saxon kingdom in Europe* (London, 2001), pp. 278–91).

[10] The papal taxation of 1291 enables the diocesan allegiance of individual parishes to be determined, although the earliest delineation of their boundaries must be sought in nineteenth-century tithe maps; for useful searchable access to the taxation see the following webpage hosted by the Humanities Research Institute at the University of Sheffield: https://www.dhi.ac.uk/taxatio/.

Introduction

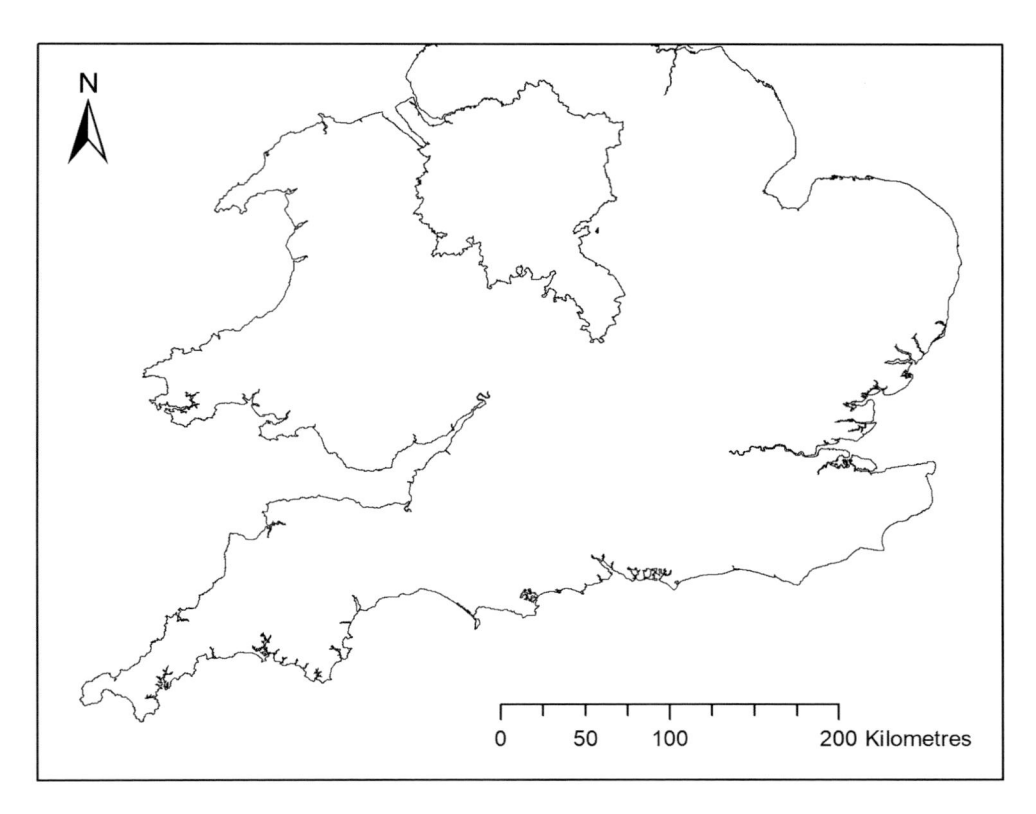

Figure 1 Bounds of the diocese of Lichfield in the late thirteenth century, excluding a northern extension between the rivers Mersey and Ribble probably added to the diocese in the tenth century.

organisations during the medieval period; in particular, monastic life was lived 'in community'.[11] This has particular relevance to early medieval England owing to the dominance of such communal institutions in the early English Church, which were established in great numbers between the seventh and ninth centuries. Scholars often call these 'minsters' – a modernised form of Old English *mynster*, itself borrowed from Latin *monasterium* – and the promotion of the term has been boosted by John Blair's definitive study *The Church in Anglo-Saxon Society*.[12] Blair's definition of the minster deserves full quotation:

> A complex ecclesiastical settlement which is headed by an abbess, abbot, or man in priest's orders; which contains nuns, monks, priests, or laity in a variety of possible combinations, and is united to a greater or lesser extent by their liturgy

---

11 A good synthetic study is provided by S. Foot, *Monastic life in Anglo-Saxon England, c.600–900* (Cambridge, 2006).
12 J. Blair, *The church in Anglo-Saxon society* (Oxford, 2005).

and devotions; which may perform or supervise pastoral care to the laity, perhaps receiving dues and exerting parochial authority; and which may sometimes act as a bishop's seat, while not depending for its existence or importance on that function.[13]

The inclusive scope of this passage emphasises the variety observable in minsters, in terms of both their scale and the numerical proportions of monks and nuns (people living under religious vows) to clergy (formally ordained members of the church hierarchy) living within them. Nevertheless, despite such flexibility, Blair is clear that minsters were institutions, and his book presents what we might label a 'minster narrative', in which 'the evolution of institutions through the whole period is a central argument'.[14] Approaching the study of early medieval religious life through an institutional framework such as this has borne much fruit, but the elision of minsters as institutions with minsters as communities of people sharing specific approaches to their lives has obscured broader perspectives. This book recognises a more complex meshwork of communities, including, for example, those formed from among the elite members of minsters' inhabitants who attended provincial synods, or those outside the minsters altogether, whether the highest of the lay elite who attended the royal court or those whose significance extended no further than a local assembly drawn from a handful of settlements. Communities can be defined and observed in many varied contexts, at different scales, nested, overlapping and interacting, and encompassing different segments and groups within the population.

The predominantly institutional appearance of the church and of individual churches (including minsters) may well have encouraged scholars interested in questions concerning the malleability and intersection of different forms of community to focus on other sectors of medieval society. Susan Reynolds' seminal work, *Kingdoms and Communities in Western Europe 900–1300*, focuses specifically on lay communities, but otherwise ranges extremely widely over different kinds of community across western Europe, such as villages, towns, principalities and kingdoms.[15] By considering Reynolds' treatment of such communities, we can begin to formulate a definition of 'community' to act as a useful tool of historical analysis. It should be stated initially that the communities discussed here are primarily those that can be defined by historical analysis (i.e. observable comings-together of people acting in some collective fashion), and not necessarily by contemporary discourse (i.e. contemporary ideas *about* communities), although the two may overlap to varying degrees and must often be considered together. Reynolds largely recognises this distinction in her methodology, prioritising evidence for communal activity over its written representation in law codes and custumals, and analysing the ways labels for various kinds of community were used rather than any meaning 'intrinsic' to the label itself. Reynolds' own definition of community is to some extent ambiguous, but she is explicit about her focus, setting her work against historians who 'have concentrated on kingship and the vertical bonds of society', and focusing instead on what she identifies as 'horizontal bonds' and the creation of a community,

---

13 Blair, *Church*, p. 3.
14 Blair, *Church*, p. 7.
15 S. Reynolds, *Kingdoms and communities in Western Europe 900–1300* (Oxford, 1984).

which defines itself by engaging in collective activities – activities which are characteristically determined and controlled less by formal regulations than by shared values and norms, while the relationships between members of the community are characteristically reciprocal, many-sided, and direct, rather than being mediated through officials or rulers.[16]

The terminology of 'vertical' and 'horizontal' relations is unfortunate to the extent that it might imply the role of hierarchy as the distinguishing issue. In fact, Reynolds' distinction is much closer to that between 'Gesellschaft' (formal association within social institutions) and 'Gemeinschaft' (a more spontaneous communalism within an 'organic' community) proposed by Ferdinand Tönnies in 1887, which still retains a dominant position at the historiographical root of work on community and society, even if criticised, nuanced and often superseded in practice.[17] Reynolds takes pains to criticise Tönnies' formulation when used as the basis of periodisation within a progressive notion of social development, and makes the fundamental point that all societies are likely to manifest both forms of socialisation simultaneously, rather than moving from one to the other.[18] Nevertheless, while she describes greater and lesser degrees of formal association within the 'horizontal' communities that she identifies, Reynolds' own distinction between the results of 'horizontal' and 'vertical' relations appears to impose a distinction similar to that advocated by Tönnies; her definition of 'vertical' relations as 'formal regulations … mediated through officials or rulers' appears very close to the accepted meaning of 'Gesellschaft'.

In fact, Reynolds' realm of 'vertical' relations is better understood as a straw man illustrating an opposing scholarly tendency, rather than a description in itself of any kind of society that actually existed, for she effectively demonstrates that *all* lay communities, from village to kingdom, were articulated around forms of collective activity informed by 'shared values and norms'. In this sense her work does provide an important corrective to those who have been overly concerned with kings, lords and vassals, and the development of 'feudal' relationships. Instead, rather than forming the 'vertical' half of a polarity with 'horizontal' relations, 'feudal' hierarchy needs to be seen as one element informing relations *within* communities. Indeed, the shared norms and values that Reynolds identifies as common to much collective activity in western Europe are frequently characterised by various hierarchical relationships. For example, while many of her communities shared 'an inheritance and tradition of collective judgement and law, of fraternal and neighbourly solidarity', they were nevertheless also characterised by 'respectful, voluntary submission to wealth and status'.[19] Moreover, 'collective judgement' frequently prioritised 'local landowners who ought to know the law and custom of their country and could therefore judge on its behalf', involving the creation of consensus over 'the issues to be proved and the

---

16   Reynolds, *Kingdoms and communities*, pp. 1–2.
17   F. Tönnies, *Gemeinschaft und gesellschaft* [1887], trans. and ed. J. Harris and M. Hollis, *Community and civil society* (Cambridge, 2001).
18   Reynolds, *Kingdoms and communities*, pp. 333–6.
19   Reynolds, *Kingdoms and communities*, p. 215.

method of proof – generally oaths, ordeals of water or hot iron, or battle – which should apply'.[20] Moreover, Reynolds makes the presence of hierarchical norms within such communities explicit, suggesting that 'the successful exercise of any sort of authority required collective activity and that created solidarity'.[21] Such arguments make collective activity within community the context for *all* social life, from the informal neighbourly association of adjacent peasant farmers to the strict hierarchy fossilised in the governing institutions of later medieval royal courts.

There is, however, a difficulty created by focusing on the normative values or ideology that supported collective activity: precisely because they are normative, these values appear to exist prior to the communities they created, and any clear sense of the agency and motivation of those creating and maintaining those communities is therefore lost. Instructive examples of this deficiency are furnished by explicitly hierarchical norms; indeed, much of the collective activity in the communal fora analysed by Reynolds was conceived in relation to some kind of superior, whether this was the king or a group of the 'better men' of the neighbourhood. Reynolds emphasises the 'representative' quality of these superiors: 'the bishops and nobles of a kingdom, like the senior and richer landowners of a province or village, were, in the terms of the time, those who were qualified to speak on behalf of the collectivity of which they were the most solid, respectable, and responsible members.'[22] 'In the terms of the time', perhaps, but in accepting the normative value of these terms Reynolds overlooks the fact that they had to be constantly *recreated*; power had to be *imposed*, and might be accepted or resisted. The 'better men' were keen to present consensus, but this was itself an attractive norm, and the process of achieving it was not necessarily consensual; we must recognise the creation of communities as political acts. Ultimately, Reynolds' analysis identifies and describes an ideology but does not explain its creation, reproduction or transformation. If we return to minsters for a moment, we can suggest in much the same way that John Blair is happy to accept the pre-existence of the regulated community ruled by an abbot, abbess or bishop that lies behind his definition of the minster as an institution. Both rely on common assumptions about the hierarchical nature of medieval society to fill the explanatory deficiency.

We thus reach an impasse in the use of 'community' as an analytical tool; on the one hand it offers an attractive holism, encompassing both 'horizontal' and 'vertical' relations within collective activity, but on the other hand scholars often obscure the impact of the latter relations by focusing on the former. Community thus remains under-theorised in medieval studies, although Gervase Rosser's study of *The Art of Solidarity in the Middle Ages* provides an inspiring exception that offers a way forward.[23] Rosser's study focuses on later medieval guilds, but is informed by a thorough historiographical and theoretical analysis of broader notions of community and solidarity. In particular, Rosser suggests that the distinction made by Tönnies between 'Gesellschaft' and 'Gemeinschaft', in representing a polarity between the open informality and closed

---

20 Reynolds, *Kingdoms and communities*, pp. 23 and 25.
21 Reynolds, *Kingdoms and communities*, p. 221.
22 Reynolds, *Kingdoms and communities*, p. 22.
23 G. Rosser, *The art of solidarity in the Middle Ages* (Oxford, 2015).

regulated formality of different societies, is analogous to a dialectic explored at the psychological level by subsequent authors within the humanities and social sciences: a flux between a 'subject', socially embedded and defined through open relation to others, and a 'person' or a 'self', constituted as an act of closure or claim to a specific personhood within society.[24] A similar dyad has been asserted in anthropological studies, comprising the relational 'dividual' and the autonomous 'individual', argued to represent a universal human psychology.[25] The fundamentally connective nature of the subject is crucial here, enmeshed in the shared symbolically structured space of a single moment, open to possibilities; the creation of the person or self is a movement, closing down possibilities and apprehending a specific form, but in doing so it opens new possibilities, repositioning the subject in the next moment. This cyclical dialectic essentially defines human experience.

Rosser argues that over the last two and a half centuries this dynamic has been informed in the West by forms of socialisation that produce a particularly autonomous form of selfhood, which emphasises norms of personal over collective experience, individual over society, and represses apprehension of its own rootedness in collective subjectivity; such a self is often allied with the concept of 'liberal individualism'.[26] In the realm of political thought Rosser points to Thomas Hobbes, whose *Leviathan* of 1651, with its isolated individuals prevented from any kind of association by an authoritarian state, prefigured this mode of being.[27] Jeremy Gilbert has recently made a similar point, adding that hierarchy becomes the only mode of relation within communities of such individual persons, as all relations between them are mediated through the authority of the ruler of the state.[28] Decentring the 'liberal individual' of the modern condition allows us to recognise the possibility of a whole spectrum of historic expressions of the 'subject/person' dialectic. This has two important implications for our understanding of historic (and contemporary) communities. First, community must be defined not as just a collection of autonomous individuals but as the common ground of all social life, which permeates subjectivity and acts as the sole source of all claims to personhood. Second, the fundamentally dynamic nature of the subject/person dialectic must be acknowledged. It must be studied as a process, a constant re-presentation of personhood within a symbolically structured mesh or field of relations; people seek constantly to anchor their own selfhood by reaching for 'values and norms', enrolling them into their own personal life courses, but in doing so reveal such norms to be imaginary stabilities, subject to a constant process of re-creation and renewal, dissolution and transformation.[29]

The study of historic communities thus becomes the study of how people, as subjects/persons, created and inhabited the social fields that existed in different

---

24　Rosser, *Art of solidarity*, pp. 23–8.
25　For a recent review, see K. Smith, 'From dividual and individual selves to porous subjects', *The Australian Journal of Anthropology*, 23 (2012), pp. 50–64.
26　Rosser, *Art of solidarity*, pp. 13–19.
27　T. Hobbes, *Leviathan* [1651], trans. and ed. N. Malcolm, *Thomas Hobbes: Leviathan* (Oxford, 2012).
28　J. Gilbert, *Common ground: democracy and collectivity in an age of individualism* (London, 2014), pp. 49–68.
29　On this process see Gilbert, *Common ground*, pp. 143–71.

times and places. In part, this can be undertaken by a focus on the kinds of norms that Reynolds elucidates, but this is not enough by itself, because the reasons for the generation of such norms – apprehended as qualities or properties of personhood, such as the 'better' men, the 'consenting' individual – remain to be explained. We must seek the processes of normalisation by which they became attractive attributes of personhood. Here Rosser points to the utility of Pierre Bourdieu's concept of the *habitus*: 'a culturally conditioned and conditioning environment' analogous to the social fields described above, which 'may be modified and renewed, not by individuals acting alone but through the collective agency of regular and repetitious practice by the group'.[30] Such 'environments' comprise the material bodies and multi-sensory spaces that define communities; they confer particular qualities or properties on those producing and inhabiting them through movement, gesture and speech. This process has been explored by some early medievalists in the context of ritualised behaviour, notably within Frankish contexts, in particular Ottonian and Salian Germany, although some recent contributions have applied such ideas to English contexts.[31] While such studies have tended to focus on the creation of an affective consensus for government within elite sections of early medieval societies, the basic framework is more widely applicable to any context in which communal repetition enables subjects to create and renew social norms in order to produce their personhood.

Consequently, this book uses 'community' as a very specific tool, intended to identify groups of people who formed relationships mediated by specific forms of encounter and to understand how these worked materially, often through repeated activities, enabling these people to inhabit social worlds defined through the creation and renewal of shared norms. Such communities must be understood as open-ended entities, and a certain degree of flexibility in their identification and description is essential. Defined according to the collective material practices through which they were created, communities coexisted at different scales and overlapped to varying degrees, possessing different rhythms of activity, operating at different intensities of focus and dispersion. Individual lives were therefore defined by membership of many such communities. A focus on the creation of these communities allows us to

---

30 Rosser, *Art of solidarity*, p. 33.
31 Much of the early scholarship on this topic is in German, but the following Anglophone contributions are notable: J. Barrow, 'Playing by the rules: conflict management in tenth- and eleventh-century Germany', *Early Medieval Europe*, 11 (2002), pp. 389–96; P. Depreux, 'Gestures and comportment at the Carolingian court: between practice and perception', *Past and Present*, 203, supplement 4 (2009), pp. 57–79; C. Pössel, 'The magic of early medieval ritual', *Early Medieval Europe*, 17 (2009), pp. 111–25; D.A. Warner, 'Rituals, kingship and rebellion in medieval Germany', *History Compass*, 8 (2010), pp. 1209–20. For studies of English contexts, see: J.N. Nelson, 'England and the continent in the ninth century: III, rights and rituals', *Transactions of the Riyal Historical Society*, 6th series, 14 (2004), pp. 1–24; J. Barrow, 'Demonstrative behaviour and political communication in later Anglo-Saxon England', *Anglo-Saxon England*, 36 (2007), pp. 127–50; L. Roach, *Kingship and consent in Anglo-Saxon England, 871–978* (Cambridge, 2013); C. Insley, '"Ottonians with pipe rolls"? Political culture and performance in the kingdom of the English, c.900–c.1050', *History*, 102 (2017), pp. 772–86.

understand historically important routes to personification manifest in the attraction of particular norms in specific material circumstances, such as those studied by Reynolds. Crucially, the dialectical relationship of such phenomena with a fundamentally collective subjectivity also allows us to understand historical change and assertions of power and resistance. Communities did not simply coalesce organically around pre-existing norms, but had to be created and continually maintained by the promotion and defence of such norms; they might also be threatened or even dissolved by the contestation and abandonment of these norms. Some norms became very attractive to many people, providing a sense of stability as long as they were adhered to. However, none were completely hegemonic, ultimately because all historical moments can be represented by the intersection of a variety of communities, creating unique personal experiences that embodied tensions and contradictions between competing norms. Collective subjectivity always offered cracks through which alternative possibilities might be glimpsed, old communities resisted and new ones created.

The communities of the lands of St Chad

These ideas about community are used in the following chapters to explore the creation, inhabitation and development of a number of different kinds of community within the early medieval diocese of Lichfield, in particular those of which the bishop was a member. The study begins with ecclesiastical communities before expanding to incorporate lay communities within the diocese. Chapter 1 explores the incorporation of the north-west Midlands within the nascent 'English ecclesiastical community', articulated around the idea of an English Church, which coalesced in the later seventh century, and particularly during the episcopate of Theodore, archbishop of Canterbury (668–90). Analysis of textual material reveals the development of an extensive multi-centred community of men and women who often defined themselves according to an emerging field of spiritual imperatives and maintained a dispersed connectivity through the regular production of texts. Within this network a distinctive 'spiritual lordship' mediated discourse within the wider community and affected the relations of its individual members with others in their localities. The diocese of Lichfield crystallised within this context as one element within the broader ecclesiastical community of the English Church.

Chapter 2 focuses on the diocese and considers the extended 'diocesan community' centred on Lichfield cathedral, but incorporating other clerical and monastic communities across the diocese, articulated around the idea of a Church of the Mercians. Chad's significance is explored, both as a focal member of overlapping communities that transcended individual places, built around norms of kinship, friendship and spiritual lordship, and as a sanctified totem enabling the maintenance of such communities after his death. The development of Lichfield's diocesan community over subsequent centuries is then approached through an analysis of the episcopal holdings recorded in the Domesday survey of 1086, illustrating the desire of successive bishops to govern the spiritual life of the diocese.

Chapter 3 explores the notion of churches as 'liturgical communities' in their own right, focusing on Lichfield cathedral and the minsters of the diocese. The importance of saints' cults as focal points of ritualised behaviour within these place-centred communities is emphasised here, but analysis of stone sculpture within the diocese hints at their intersection with larger 'associative fields' of connection and encounter with which these communities interacted dialectically.

Chapter 4 builds on the role of spiritual lordship, analysing in greater detail the nature of the hierarchical relations established between the bishop and the churches of the diocese and tackling, in particular, current debates around the implications of ecclesiastical tributes for the nature of episcopal authority. The contours of the latter are explored in more detail through a consideration of an interesting set of churches in the diocese of Lichfield that emerged as 'royal free chapels' in the later medieval period.

Chapters 5 and 6 broaden the study to consider lay communities within the diocese and their interaction with the ecclesiastical communities explored in earlier chapters. Chapter 5 focuses on the diocese's population more broadly, beginning with the 'agricultural communities' responsible for much of the overall development of the historic landscape during the period. Topographic and toponymic analyses are used to define and understand communities centred on the evolving settlements of the region, and the evidence of the Domesday survey is harnessed to explore communities of landholders: 'domainal communities'. In Chapter 6 'domainal lordship' is explored alongside spiritual lordship and the 'regnal lordship' asserted by the king and other members of his regnal community, within contexts that move on from the ecclesiastical communities of the seventh, eighth and ninth centuries to focus on the establishment of 'mother churches' and an associated parochial network during the tenth and eleventh centuries. This chapter uses an analysis of parochial morphology to argue that an elite of kings, ealdormen and paramount thegns began to stake their own claims to a degree of spiritual lordship during a period when ecclesiastical, regnal and domainal communities became increasingly closely integrated. These represented a significant evolution of the religious and lay communities of earlier centuries, amounting to a considerable expansion of the field of spiritual imperatives among much of the population of the diocese during this period, most of whom belonged to discrete 'parochial communities' by the end of the eleventh century.

Chapter 6 begins to present the merits of viewing the region as an evolving set of overlapping and intersecting communities, a view that is promoted more generally in the Conclusion. This narrative possesses advantages over the homogeneity and monolithic institutionalism of the dominant minster narrative presented by John Blair, which emphasises a 'golden age' in the seventh and eighth centuries and a decline thereafter characterised by secularisation and fragmentation. In contrast, the later period is characterised here by the 'spiritualisation' of many relations formerly secular in nature, and notions of fragmentation are criticised, as they assume an earlier simplicity belied by the complex interconnections between communities that had existed in one form or another since at least the seventh century. Furthermore, against Blair, the significance of the role of the bishop within many of these communities is argued to be pivotal here, although, crucially, the spiritual lordship that bishops and others wielded is viewed as a collective creation, generated through the cultivation and alignment of the interests and motives of members of different communities across the landscape of the north-west Midlands, which reached an apogee in the tenth and eleventh centuries. The period thus has a distinctive shape that is, perhaps paradoxically, revealed by this book's exploration of the relatively meagre evidence within the Mercian hole.

Chapter 1

Lichfield and the English Church

The diocese of Lichfield was the first bishopric to be founded in the kingdom of Mercia, in 654, although its seat at Lichfield was not established until 669. It appears to have retained some status as *the* Mercian bishopric, but four other dioceses were also considered to be in some sense 'Mercian' by the end of the eighth century. These were the dioceses of the Hwicce (at Worcester), the Magonsæte (at Hereford), the Middle Angles (at Leicester) and the people of Lindsey (probably at Lincoln), and their Mercian identity derived from their locations in territories that were brought within the direct rulership of the Mercian kings in the later seventh and eighth centuries. The entanglement of royal and episcopal governance is one of the key foci of this book, and this chapter is concerned with the ways in which bishoprics and kingdoms were formed within communities that spanned the English kingdoms and beyond. The main purposes of the analysis are twofold: first, to detach the diocese of Lichfield and its fellows from an institutional view of history in which such organisations act as simple frameworks within (or against) which historical activity occurs, rather than forming part of that activity; and, second, to illuminate the place of the diocese within the ideological project that became known as the Church of the English.

In the 1320s a scrivener named Alan of Ashbourne, one of the staff in Lichfield cathedral's newly established scriptorium, produced a chronicle that has survived the tests of time and is now known as the Lichfield Chronicle.[1] Its content is varied, but Alan was obviously very interested in the early history of Lichfield, and included a list of the bishops of the 'bishopric of the Mercians' or the 'Church of the people of Lichfield', two phrases that he appears to have considered synonymous.[2] Alan's fourteenth-century chronicle is the earliest surviving work to build a sense of institutional continuity for the diocese of Lichfield, but a long-lived textual discourse promoting the institutional identity of the 'English Church' as a whole had first emerged in the seventh century; this chapter explores its early stages, which Alan was later to draw upon. This discourse

---

1   It was initially labelled the 'Book of Alan of Ashbourne, Vicar of Lichfield', a title written at the top of the first folio (British Library MS Cotton Cleopatra D IX (hereafter BL Cott. Cleo. D IX), f.5r); a fine copy of the chronicle was produced by Canon Thomas Chesterfield towards the middle of the fifteenth century, and it was to him that Henry Wharton accredited the chronicle in his *Anglia Sacra*, Part 1 (London, 1691), p. 423, a mistake thereafter perpetuated and rectified only in the early twentieth century by H.E. Savage, *Book of Alan Asseborn: an address given on the festival of St. Chad* (Lichfield, 1922), p. 21. On the scriptorium and the chronicle see also: H.E. Savage, *The Lichfield Chronicle: an address given on the festival of St. Chad* (Lichfield, 1915) and H.E. Savage (ed.), 'The Great Register of Lichfield cathedral known as Magnum Registrum Album', *SHC* 1924, pp. xi–404, at pp. xv–xxii.

2   BL Cott. Cleo. D IX, ff. 71v–75.

was produced, reproduced, changed and developed by several different 'textual communities' over succeeding centuries, each with different motivations. Analysing this process serves to make fluid the solidity of an institutional vision of the Church by demonstrating how the very idea of an institution as such proved useful – vital, even – to the ecclesiastical communities of the early medieval north-west Midlands and beyond.

This chapter begins with an analysis of the tradition of episcopal lists that Alan was later to draw upon, providing crucial insights into a number of conjunctions that were important in shaping the English Church as an imagined community. An 'English ecclesiastical community' is defined by reference to the regular assembly of bishops and their clergy from the late seventh century onwards and by the community's considered use of textual instruments to define its own nature and powers. These ritualising contexts enabled the promotion and maintenance of the English Church across several centuries, and the chapter explores elements of this phenomenon within the conjunctions outlined in the analysis of the episcopal lists. Particular attention is paid to the Mercian elements within the discourse of the English Church, and emphasis is placed on the close entanglement of the English ecclesiastical community with various 'regnal communities' across the period, and in particular on the role of the former in stabilising the latter. The later parts of the chapter explore these dynamics in the late eighth and early ninth centuries, when an archdiocese of Lichfield enjoyed a brief existence, and during the tenth and eleventh centuries, when the English ecclesiastical and regnal communities became more closely integrated.

The episcopal list tradition

Alan's list of bishops is a later medieval example of a significant tradition of such lists, which were employed in and after the late eleventh century by chroniclers such as John of Worcester and William of Malmesbury to provide a chronological framework for the early centuries of diocesan history. However, the earliest textual sources of this episcopal list tradition (hereafter ELT), upon which all of these later authors drew, were produced in contexts within the first half of the ninth century. The earliest manuscripts representing the ELT have been edited by Raymond Page, and work on many of the same manuscripts has been undertaken by David Dumville for his edition of the so-called 'Anglian Genealogies' concerning several of the early English royal dynasties, which are found beside the episcopal lists in these early manuscripts.[3] The episcopal lists are simply lists of names marking the passage of time, and can easily be subsumed within institutional histories, wherein the succession of bishop after bishop is a testament to the unchanging concreteness of his diocese. However, the texts do not give us a linear, evolving history but express a set of historical moments, which may not relate to one another at all, in which the (re)creation or updating of the lists expressed a specific view of the episcopal past. These moments were connected by the use of similar material, but in some cases the creation of this material in one

---

3   R.I. Page, 'Anglo-Saxon episcopal lists', *Nottingham Medieval Studies*, 9 (1965), pp. 71–95, and 10 (1966), pp. 2–24; D.N. Dumville, 'The Anglian collection of royal genealogies and regnal lists', *Anglo-Saxon England*, 5 (1976), pp. 23–50.

context, with one meaning, can be shown to have been recycled in another and given a new meaning. The following section employs a close analysis of the Mercian lists to outline the date and nature of these contexts.

Assigning a precise date to the origin of the ELT is problematic. In his study, David Dumville has traced the earliest existing manuscript versions of the royal genealogies to a single hypothetical archetype that he labels α, a collection that also contained the episcopal lists.[4] He suggests that the collection was compiled in 796 on the evidence of two regnal lists included with the genealogies for the Mercians and Northumbrians:[5] the final entry in the Northumbrian list is the second reign of King Æthelred (790–6), and the final entry in the Mercian list to include a reign length is King Ecgfrith (796); the Mercian list extends in its earliest manuscript witness through subsequent kings to King Beorhtwulf (840–52), but all these kings are without reign lengths, and were almost certainly added to the manuscript's exemplar.[6] There is a problem with Dumville's date, however, as, although they died in the same year, Æthelred and Ecgfrith were not contemporary kings. According to the northern annals included in the *Historia Regum*, Æthelred was murdered on 18 April and his successor Eardwulf was consecrated on 26 May; Ecgfrith succeeded to the Mercian kingdom after the death of his father Offa on 26 July, and his reign of 141 days recorded in the regnal list takes us to 14 December (perhaps slightly later if his succession was not immediate, although Ecgfrith was certainly dead by the end of the year).[7] Thus one could only draw up a Mercian list ending with Ecgfrith's reign at least seven months into the reign of the Northumbrian king Eardwulf.

Several different sets of assumptions might be invoked to move beyond this point and establish the date range within which the regnal lists were produced. None of these assumptions is decisively superior to the others, and it suffices here to note the plausible possibility that regnal lists conventionally featured only kings whose reigns had concluded, for which a length could be given, and that these two lists were thus produced during the reigns of the successors to Æthelred and Ecgfrith, respectively Eardwulf of Northumbria, who was driven from his kingdom in 808, and Cœnwulf of Mercia, who died in 821. Turning to the dating of the episcopal lists, Raymond Page dated the earliest manuscript witness to the ELT to 805×814, a period during which

---

4   Dumville, 'Anglian collection', pp. 38–41; the earliest witnesses of the ELT comprise the British Museum MS Cotton Vespasian B VI (hereafter BM Cott. Vesp. B VI; early ninth century) and the Corpus Christi College Cambridge MS 183 (hereafter CCCC 183; early tenth century), which, according to Dumville's analysis of the genealogies therein, were derived from hypothetical exemplars that he labels β and ε respectively, which were both probably of Mercian origin and copied directly from α during the reign of king Cœnwulf (796–821).
5   The genealogies do not appear in all early versions of the collection, but Dumville ('Anglian collection', pp. 39–41) argues that they were included in the archetype α, though perhaps not in the position they currently occupy in the surviving versions, and his conclusion is accepted here.
6   Following convention, surviving manuscript versions of the ELT are referred to here as 'witnesses' to the tradition. Dumville, 'Anglian collection', p. 40: the earliest witness to the regnal lists is CCCC 183, as they are not present in BM Cott. Vesp. B VI.
7   *EHD* 1, p. 248 (*Historia Regum*, s.a. 796).

all thirteen of the most recent bishops of sees south of the Humber recorded in the text were alive; however, he was forced to exclude from his reckoning the most recent bishop in the list for the see of Lindisfarne, Hygebald, who died in 802 or 803, and to acknowledge that the obits of the latest bishops in the other two Northumbrian dioceses, York and Whithorn, are not known.[8] There was thus no single moment at which all the bishops at the ends of the lists in this manuscript were alive together, and it can be suggested that this witness represents an updated version of a set of up-to-date lists in the collection α, produced at a time when all listed bishops were alive, with subsequent updates confined to sees within the metropolitan province of Canterbury (usually labelled the 'Southumbrian' province by historians); the compilation of α might therefore be dated before Hygebald's death in 802/3, but after 796, as discussed above in relation to the regnal lists.

However, it may be significant that the earliest manuscript witness presents a set of lists in which the information on at least one Northumbrian see was out of date. The collection α was almost certainly put together in a Southumbrian context, and it is worth noting in this regard that the diocese of York appears in the lists as a simple bishopric, rather than as a metropolitan see, a status it had enjoyed since 735. The compiler was plausibly well informed on the contemporary incumbents of Southumbrian sees, who came together at regular synods at this time (see further below); but concerning the Northumbrian kingdom and its sees, whose bishops were within the metropolitan authority of York and held their own councils, the compiler may have made use of the most recent textual information in his or her possession, lacking the knowledge (or perhaps the will) to update it. The same may have been true of the compiler's access to a Northumbrian regnal list, which after 808 would presumably have featured Eardwulf. If we assume that the Northumbrian material was somewhat out of date in this way, it is possible that the episcopal lists of α itself were identical to those in the earliest manuscript witness, and that its compilation dates to 805×814. Allowing for both possibilities discussed here, it is possible to state only that the collection α must have been assembled within the dating bracket 796×814.

Although the archetypal form of the ELT in α cannot be reconstructed entirely, there is enough close correspondence between various manuscript witnesses to make several claims with confidence. Some of the lists are grouped together to correspond with the English kingdoms in which they lay, including the five bishoprics of the Mercian kingdom, whose lists follow the heading 'Names of the bishops of the provinces of the Mercians'. Figure 2 shows the overall layout of the Mercian lists in the earliest witness of the text, and divides it into two sections. The first section encompasses the episcopates of Diuma, the first Mercian bishop, to Seaxwulf, the seventh in succession.[9] The second section contains several separate lists, the first of which begins with an explanatory rubric intended as a continuation of the first section, followed by two parallel lists representing the episcopal successions of the

---

[8] Page, 'Episcopal lists', pp. 74–5; this manuscript, BM Cott. Vesp. B VI, was copied from the hypothetical exemplar that Dumville labelled β ('Anglian collection', pp. 38–9).

[9] BM Cott. Vesp. B VI, f. 108v, col. 2 (Page, 'Episcopal lists', p. 5). The same rubric in CCCC 183 contains minor variations in orthography and layout that do not affect the following discussion.

Lichfield and the English Church

Names of the bishops of the provinces [*provinciae*] of the Mercians   **Heading**

The first bishop in the province [*provincia*] of the Mercians and the people of Lindsey and the Middle Angles [was] 1) Diuma, 2) Ceollach, both from Ireland [*Scottia*], 3) Trumhere of the nation of the English, 4) Jaruman, 5) Chad, 6) Winfrith, 7) Seaxwulf.   **Section 1**

After that however it was divided into five dioceses [*parrochiae*]:

After Seaxwulf the province of the Mercians had two bishops, Headda and Wilfrid.

Later, Wilfrid was banished, and the aforesaid Headda ruled both dioceses [*parrochiae*], then Ealdwine, who was also called Wor

A second time it was divided into two dioceses.

[Leicester]	[Lichfield]
Torhthelm	Hwita
…	…

Section 2

Name of the bishops of Lindsey after Seaxwulf

…

Name of the bishops of the Hwicce after Seaxwulf

…

Name of the bishops of the Magonsæte after Seaxwulf

…

Figure 2 Layout of the Mercian episcopal lists in the British Library manuscript Cotton Vespasian B VI, including a partial translation.

two dioceses of 'the province of the Mercians', Leicester on the left and Lichfield on the right.[10] After these, the second section continues with three further lists, each identified by a heading containing the name of the diocese and informing the reader that its list of bishops should be placed 'after Seaxwulf', again connecting it to the first section. The following analysis explains the rationale for understanding the Mercian lists to be divided into these two sections, and demonstrates that the first section had an earlier history before it was enrolled in the compilation of α in 796×814.

A striking difference between the two sections concerns the concept of Mercian territory expressed by each. The first section introduces the bishop of the singular province (*prouincia*) of the Mercians, the people of Lindsey and the Middle Angles, while the dioceses (*parrochiae*) of the second section, after the division into five, comprise the plural provinces (*prouinciae*) of the Mercians (two bishops), Lindsey, Hwicce and 'Uestor E[...]'; the last province is identifiable with a group Bede characterised as the 'people who dwell beyond the River Severn to the west', styled the Magonsæte from the early ninth century (a name used hereafter for the sake of clarity).[11] In the second section, one of the two lists for the 'province of the Mercians' can be understood to represent the Middle Angles of the first section (although this is not explicit in the rubric), resonating with the idea expressed in the first section that the three peoples listed there were members of one province. However, in the second section one of those three peoples, that of Lindsey, is now represented as a separate province. Alternatively, if the use of the singular form *prouincia* in the first section was an error, and the three peoples listed there were all intended as separate provinces (which might be implied by the listing of their three separate names), we would have to explain why the province of the Middle Angles is apparently subsumed within the singular 'province of the Mercians' in the second section.[12] Additionally, the peoples or provinces of the Hwicce and the Magonsæte are not mentioned at all in the first section, but are presented as the product of diocesan division in the second section.

Such a discrepancy in terminology suggests a stratigraphic break between the two sections, and the probability that they derive from different sources produced at different times. This is supported by a close similarity between the first section and a passage in Bede's *Historia Ecclesiastica* concerning the episcopal succession in Mercia, here quoted in translation with the corresponding elements in bold:

> The first bishop in the province of the Mercians, and also of the people of Lindsey and the Middle Angles was Diuma, as we said above, who died and was buried

---

10 BM Cott. Vesp. B VI, f. 108v, col. 2 (Page, 'Episcopal lists', p. 5).
11 *HE*, v.23; see Sims-Williams, *Religion and literature*, pp. 40–3, for further discussion. The name 'Magonsæte', first recorded in a charter of 811 (S 1264), is probably anachronistic for the seventh and eighth centuries.
12 The scribe of the exemplar of BM Cott. Vesp. B VI and Corpus Christi College Cambridge MS 140, copying α, apparently assumed the singular form was an error, as the two uses of the word *prouincia* were altered to *prouinciæ* (Page, 'Episcopal lists', pp. 74 and 78). The original singular form in α is suggested by comparison with Bede's use of the same material, discussed below, and forms in other early versions of the ELT.

among the Middle Angles; the second was Ceollach, who resigned his bishopric before his death and returned to Ireland, for both were Irish; the third was Trumhere, of the nation of the English, but who was taught and ordained by the Irish, and who was abbot of the minster called Gilling.13

The same chapter in Bede's work also enumerates three bishops after Trumhere, although they are numbered according to a sequence starting in Wulfhere's reign:

King Wulfhere ruled over the Mercians for seventeen years and had as his first bishop Trumhere, whom we have already mentioned, his second, Jaruman, his third, Chad, and his fourth, Winfrith. All these in succession held the bishopric of the Mercians under King Wulfhere.14

The list form is again notable. Seaxwulf, the last bishop listed in the first section in the ELT, does not appear in Bede's list, although he does appear three times elsewhere in the *Historia Ecclesiastica*, in parts that were probably derived from information Bede received from the monastery at Lastingham, from Canterbury, and from Bishop Cyneberht of Lindsey.15 Excepting a mention for Bishop Ealdwine in his contemporary summary at the very end of his work, Bede has nothing to say about Seaxwulf's successors.

It might be argued that the first section of the Mercian episcopal lists was derived from Bede, but, given Bede's explicit enumeration of the bishops, it seems more plausible to suggest, as does Page, that 'both they and Bede derive from a common source, presumably a primitive series of bishop's lists'.16 Assuming this to be the case, Bede's apparent ignorance of Headda and of a formal division of the see allows us to hypothesise that he possessed a version of a memorandum from which the first section of the Mercian lists also derived, but that he knew nothing of the content of the second section concerning the bishopric after Seaxwulf; indeed, he may have known of Seaxwulf only from his appearance in other elements of his source material, as Seaxwulf is not explicitly listed in Bede's enumeration of the Mercian bishops. Bede's ignorance of the second part of the ELT is supported by his prefatory discussion of his sources: 'as to the province of Lindsey, I learned of the growth of their faith in Christ and of the succession of bishops, both through a letter from the reverend Bishop Cyneberht and from the lips of other trustworthy men';17 if Bede was able to

---

13 *HE*, iii.24.
14 *HE*, iii.24.
15 *HE*, iv.6: Seaxwulf's consecration is described in the context of his predecessor Winfrith's deposition, a narrative that probably formed part of an account from the monastery at Lastingham, for which see Chapter 2. *HE*, iv.12: Seaxwulf is mentioned as the grantor of a church to Putta, formerly bishop of Rochester, in the context of the latter's dispossession of his see through Mercian violence. *HE*, iv.12: Seaxwulf is mentioned as the bishop of Lindsey in the context of the creation of a separate see there in 678.
16 Page, 'Episcopal lists', p. 84.
17 *HE*, preface.

Lichfield and the Lands of St Chad

copy from a memorandum concerning the earliest Mercian bishops, but received his information concerning the bishops of Lindsey from their bishop, then he cannot have had anything like the second section of the ELT before him, as this also includes the bishops of Lindsey.

It is therefore proposed here that a 'Mercian episcopal memorandum', containing the succession of the Mercian bishops from Diuma to Winfrith and probably arranged very similarly to the first section of the Mercian lists in the ELT, existed by the third decade of the eighth century when a version of it was used by Bede in the writing of his *Historia Ecclesiastica*.[18] The date of composition of this memorandum can be plausibly narrowed. The list in the first part of the ELT ends with Seaxwulf, and thus it is possible that it was composed during his episcopate (673×674 to 691×692), but if Bede's list ended with Winfrith, as proposed here, then it was probably produced during his episcopate (672 to 673×674), the version lying behind the ELT having been subsequently updated.[19] In any case, it is significant here that the diocese of Lindsey was created by King Ecgfrith of Northumbria in 678, who, according to Bede, had wrested the province from the Mercian king Wulfhere in a battle fought before the Mercian king's death in 674. Bede explains that Seaxwulf had been bishop in Lindsey before this event, but was expelled on Ecgfrith's conquest.[20] Bede's information in this passage, which also includes the episcopal succession in Lindsey, probably came from Bishop Cyneberht. The Mercian episcopal memorandum presents Lindsey as part of the province of the early Mercian bishops, and must therefore have been produced before the conquest of 674, which it does not mention. Thus, even if Seaxwulf was included in the memorandum, it cannot date any later than 674, the very earliest stage of his episcopate. When added to the likelihood that Winfrith was in fact the latest bishop recorded in the memorandum, the most plausible dating bracket is 672×674.

The second section of the Mercian lists in the ELT was probably written as part of the compilation of all the English episcopal lists into one set. If, as seems likely, this occurred as part of the creation of α, when the episcopal lists were set beside the genealogies and regnal lists, then the second section can be dated with the compilation of α to 796×814; it is possible that specific elements within the episcopal lists for other dioceses were created earlier and combined in α later, but, excepting the first section of the Mercian lists, this cannot be demonstrated textually. As mentioned earlier, this context of compilation is likely to have occurred in Southumbria, as at least one of the lists of Northumbrian bishops might have been out of date at the inception of α, and the metropolitan status of York is not explicitly recognised. A Canterbury context is likely, as all the extant early manuscripts derived from α consistently begin with the archbishops of Canterbury, and, although the subsequent ordering varies in some manuscripts, the southern (Saxon) bishoprics always precede the northern (Anglian) ones, which we might expect from a Canterbury perspective. Moreover, it will be argued below that the Mercian episcopal memorandum was itself a product of

---

18 *HE*, v.23.
19 Seaxwulf's episcopate cannot be dated precisely. The date ranges given here derive from integrating information contained in *HE*, iv.6, iv.12, iv.23 and iv.26, and *VW*, 43 and 44.
20 *HE*, iv.12.

the ecclesiastical community at Canterbury; if this is accepted then its later reuse in 796×814 would also support a Canterbury context for the compilation of α.

Theodore's church

If, as argued above, the Mercian episcopal memorandum was created in 672×674, then it was contemporary with the early years of the tenure of Theodore as archbishop of Canterbury (669–90). Theodore was born in Greek-speaking Tarsus in the province of Cilicia, now in Turkey, and probably studied at Antioch and Edessa before moving to Constantinople, perhaps as a refugee from Persian or Arab invasions.[21] At some point he became a monk, and after a subsequent move to a monastery in Rome he drew the attention of Hadrian, abbot of another monastery near Naples; when the archbishop elect of Canterbury died in Rome in 667 the pope asked Hadrian to take his place, but Hadrian refused and nominated Theodore in his stead, though he subsequently travelled with Theodore to Britain. On his arrival in Britain (at the age of 67), Theodore found only three or four of the existing seven sees occupied: those at York (Chad), Dunwich (Berhtgisl) and London (Wine) were certainly in post, while Jaruman of Mercia may have been alive when Theodore arrived, but if so he was certainly dead shortly afterwards. Theodore devoted his archiepiscopate to increasing the number of dioceses and to the religious instruction of a new generation of clergy; to this end, with Hadrian's help he established a school at Canterbury and took an energetic interest in the appointment of new bishops (some of them to newly created sees) and, on several occasions, the deposition of those who displeased him (including Chad, an event discussed further in Chapter 2).[22] Theodore's exertions appear to have had a profound effect, not least on how he was remembered: Bede eulogised him as 'the first of the archbishops whom the whole English church consented to obey', and, indeed, Patrick Wormald has traced to Theodore's archiepiscopate the promotion of the discourse of a unitary Church (in the sense of a hierarchically ordered community of Christians) associated by contemporaries with both 'Britain' and the 'English people', two identities that probably implied each other in Theodore's understanding.[23]

Wormald takes the institutional idiom of Theodore's Church very much to heart, arguing that a council he convened at Hertford in September 672 should be understood as the 'founding charter' of the English Church.[24] We need not follow him this far; nevertheless, the council at Hertford appears to have been important in

---

21 M. Lapidge, 'The career of Archbishop Theodore', in M. Lapidge (ed.), *Archbishop Theodore: commemorative studies on his life and influence* (Cambridge, 1995), pp. 1–29.
22 Brooks, *Canterbury*, pp. 71–6.
23 *HE*, iv.2. P. Wormald, 'Bede, the *Bretwaldas*, and the origins of the *gens Anglorum*', in P. Wormald, D. Bullough and R. Collins (eds), *Ideal and reality in Frankish and Anglo-Saxon society: studies presented to J.M. Wallace-Hadrill* (Oxford, 1983), pp. 99–129; especially at p. 125, where Wormald notes Theodore's styles at the Council of Hatfield in 679 ('archbishop of Britain') and in the epilogue to his Penitential ('archbishop of the English').
24 P. Wormald, 'The Venerable Bede and the "Church of the English"', in G. Rowell (ed.), *The English religious tradition and the genius of Anglicanism* (Wantage, 1992), pp. 13–32.

laying down rules to be followed by members of this community, which, in Catherine Cubitt's words, were rooted in 'adequate episcopal provision ... governed by the deliberations of its bishops in accordance with canon law'.[25] One particular decree was of utmost importance: that a synod should be held 'once a year on 1 August at the place known as *Clofesho*'.[26] The regular gathering of bishops in synods was crucial to building the kind of super-regnal solidarity required if Theodore's Church was to acquire concrete form. The first synod at *Clofesho* for which a reliable record exists occurred in 747, and evidence for regular English synods does not emerge until after 780 (in the charters that record business undertaken there), but Cubitt has assembled a corpus of evidence to make the plausible case that synods continued to be convened on a regular basis both during and after Theodore's episcopate.[27] In the words of Simon Keynes, these councils 'would have done much to nurture a sense of collective identity among the leaders of the Church, and to sustain their sense of collective purpose'.[28] Here we see the initiation and development of an ecclesiastical community defined by regular assembly that is crucial to understanding the actions and authority of the bishops of Lichfield from Chad's episcopate onwards.

A sense of collective identity not only emerged through repeated collaborative activity but was actively promoted through the discourse of the 'English Church', a set of normative ideas concerning institutional identity. Patrick Wormald ascribes the origin of the idea of the English 'as a single people before God' who 'were known in Heaven as the *gens Anglorum*' to the vision of Pope Gregory the Great, 'apostle of the English', whose correspondence with his first convert, Æthelberht of Kent, styled him *rex Anglorum* and implied his rulership of Britain.[29] However, such an imagined community might have stayed within Gregory's head had it not been promoted later by members of the integrating, solidary community that Theodore created during his archiepiscopate. Crucially, this ecclesiastical community must not be seen as an institution in itself, but as the associative context within which such a normative institutional identity was formulated and promoted. This is highlighted by the creation of a second archbishopric at York in 735, encompassing the Northumbrian kingdom.[30] The two metropolitan provinces appear thereafter to have assembled in separate councils; nevertheless, the discourse of the 'Church of the English' remained significant, was given high-profile press by Bede and arguably later informed the style used of Æthelstan, 'king of the English', when he convened councils attended (among others) by both Northumbrian and Southumbrian bishops from the late 920s.

The English ecclesiastical community might have depended heavily on regular face-to-face meetings, but it was also a distinctively textual community. The acts of the Council of Hertford, which survive as a result of their reproduction in Bede's *Historia*

---

25 C. Cubitt, *Anglo-Saxon church councils c.650–c.850* (Leicester, 1995), p. 9.
26 Cap. 7 of the canons of the Council of Hertford, reproduced in *HE*, iv.5.
27 Cubitt, *Church councils*, pp. 18–23.
28 S. Keynes, *The councils of* Clofesho, Vaughan Paper 38 (Leicester, 1993), p. 22.
29 Wormald, 'Bede, the *Bretwaldas*, and the origins of the *gens Anglorum*', pp. 123–6.
30 Recorded in the 'Continuation of Bede': *EHD* 1, p. 259; and in the northern chronicle in the *Historia Regum*: *EHD* 1, p. 239.

Ecclesiastica, describe a synod assembled under the auspices of Theodore 'after venerable canonical custom'.[31] The ten canons promulgated there were extracted by Theodore from a 'book of canons' (*librum canonum*) in his possession.[32] Theodore convened another council in 679, at Hatfield, in order to ensure the orthodoxy and unity of the English Church in the face of the Monophysite heresy, and according to Bede he 'took care to have this recorded in a synodal book to serve as a guide and a record to their successors'.[33] More broadly, penitentials and biblical commentaries produced within Theodore's ambit, emerging from the context of the school he and Hadrian established at Canterbury, have also survived.[34] Theodore appears as a locus of textual activity, employing the written word for many purposes, but in particular to authorise conciliar action and to preserve its results for future reference in the tradition of canonically inspired behaviour in which he had been educated.

It thus appears less surprising that, if the above arguments concerning the existence and date of the Mercian episcopal memorandum are accepted, it was produced early in Theodore's episcopate, when a more integrated textual community encompassing all the English bishoprics first began to develop. Bede states that, soon after his arrival, Theodore 'visited every part of the island where the English peoples lived', perhaps beating the bounds of his new domain;[35] we might plausibly imagine that at that time, or at least during the earlier years of his archiepiscopate, he drew up various memoranda to create a schematic history-to-date of this Church as he found it, 'to serve as a guide and a record'. This possibility can be demonstrated textually only for the diocese of Lichfield, but it is at least plausible that earlier versions of the lists for other dioceses were also produced. In the hands of Theodore and the community that he fostered the written word became a hegemonic tool, a medium for the political negotiation of narratives and goals, used by bishops and their clergy, alongside monks, nuns and their monastic rulers, to steer attitudes and mark positions in emerging hierarchies and to scope out possibilities for future activity. The personal histories of members of this community no doubt connected it in the understandings of contemporaries with the earlier history of formal Christian community in England, which Bede later sought to narrate, but there is an important sense in which Theodore not only unified or standardised the English ecclesiastical community but actually *created* it.

Church and kingdom

There is a danger, however, in viewing this English ecclesiastical community in isolation: it can only be properly understood alongside contemporary lay communities,

---

31 The acts were copied by Bede into his *Historia Ecclesiastica*: *HE*, iv.5.
32 M. Brett, 'Theodore and the Latin canon law', in M. Lapidge (ed.), *Archbishop Theodore: commemorative studies on his life and influence* (Cambridge, 1995), pp. 120–40.
33 *HE*, iv.17.
34 See M. Lapidge (ed.), *Archbishop Theodore: commemorative studies on his life and influence* (Cambridge, 1995), and B. Bischoff and M. Lapidge (eds), *Biblical commentaries from the Canterbury school of Theodore and Hadrian* (Cambridge, 1994), for further examples.
35 *HE*, iv.2.

and in particular regnal communities. Kings and their lords are constant features of Bede's narrative, and their hierarchical communities emerged before the coming of Christianity to the English: it was a king of Kent, Æthelberht, who welcomed the papal missionary Augustine in 597 and gave him resources to support his mission. Æthelberht was in fact an overking, with power over rulers outside Kent, and overkingships such as his continued to dominate the seventh-century world conjured in Bede's *Historia Ecclesiastica*.[36] In this regard there is a striking similarity of form between the Mercian episcopal memorandum and what might be called the 'imperial list', located in Bede's chapter on Æthelberht's death, a much-studied list of seven kings who wielded overkingship (*imperium* in Bede's Latin) in much of Britain from the later sixth century onwards.[37] Both texts are presented as a series of names, explicitly enumerated, with additional brief commentaries given after the names of some individuals. In particular, each king is connected with the name of the 'people' from which he derived: (1) Ælle of the South Saxons; (2) Cælin (or Ceawlin) of the West Saxons; (3) Æthelberht of the Kentish people; (4) Rædwald of the East Angles; and (5) Edwin (6) Oswald and (7) Oswiu, all of the Northumbrians.

We do not possess an independent 'imperial list tradition' against which to set Bede's imperial list, but if the form of Bede's Mercian episcopal list was so readily derived from its source in the proposed memorandum then it is quite plausible that the imperial list was also derived from an equivalent source. It is noteworthy that the seventh and last king in the list, Oswiu, died in February 670, during the first year of Theodore's episcopate; this termination, which has aroused some debate, might be explained rather simply if the list is considered to represent another memorandum drawn up by or for the archbishop at or not long after the end of Oswiu's reign, being intended to provide a history of the royal powers that then framed the contemporary political situation in England.[38] It was, after all, such overkingships that defined the organising frames for the proliferation of missionaries across England, whether those of the Roman mission under the patronage of Æthelberht of Kent, whose overkingship allowed them introductions to the courts of the East Saxon and East Anglian kings, or those Irish missionaries working within the later *imperia* of the Northumbrian kings, which at their widest reached to the borders of Kent.[39]

However, it may be that the imperial list did more than simply describe a self-evident political situation. Certainly, there is no denying the importance in Theodore's

---

36   D.N. Dumville, 'The terminology of overkingship in Anglo-Saxon England', in J. Hines (ed.), *The Anglo-Saxons from the Migration Period to the eighth century: an ethnographic perspective* (Woodbridge, 1997), pp. 345–73.

37   *HE*, ii.5; see, for example, S. Fanning, 'Bede, imperium, and the Bretwaldas', *Speculum*, 66/1 (1991), pp. 1–26.

38   However Nicholas Higham has argued that this list was constructed by Bede himself, and denies the possibility that it derives from a lost source: N.J. Higham, *An English empire: Bede and the early Anglo-Saxon kings* (Manchester, 1995), pp. 47–73 (chapter 2), especially at p. 49.

39   Alex Woolf has recently argued that the legend of Hengest, the legendary founder of Kent, was also created in a Theodoran context: A. Woolf, 'Imagining English origins', *Quaestio Insularis*, 18 (2017), pp. 1–20, at pp. 5–9.

time of the royal dynasties represented by these overkings: of the seven bishoprics that existed when he arrived in 669, one (York) represented the Northumbrian kingdom ruled by the last of them, and four more (Canterbury, Rochester, Winchester and Dunwich) were equated with the Kentish, West Saxon and East Anglian kingdoms ruled by descendants of the earlier overkings. Only one 'imperial' dynasty, that of the South Saxons, was without episcopal representation at that time, while the dynasties of only two kingdoms represented by the seven bishoprics, those of the East Saxons and Mercians, do not appear on the imperial list. In subsequent years Theodore worked closely with the bishops of all these sees, the presence of many being recorded in the acts of the church councils convened at Hertford (672) and Hatfield (679).[40] Thus, while not exact, the overlap between the imperial dynasties and the dioceses of Theodore's time is notable.

In this context it is worth pursuing an observation made by David Kirby that the names of the major English kingdoms comprising ethnic groups with directional qualifiers (the West Saxons, the East Angles, etc.) were coined from a perspective situated in the London region, quite possibly in the context of the ecclesiastical councils that began to meet there at the behest of Theodore.[41] It may be relevant that two of the kingdoms without such names, Kent and Northumbria, were pre-eminent at this time: the imperial list excludes Kent from the wide overkingship enjoyed by the Northumbrian kings, and the rulers of these two kingdoms consulted about the future of the church in England before Theodore's arrival. This may indicate that the kingdoms named after ethnic groups, each the result of a past *imperium*, were subkingdoms within the hegemonies of others when they were named. The practice of naming such *imperia*, whether past or present, had perhaps tended to be quite fluid (much like their internal composition): the name of the Northumbrian kingdom itself – known as both that of the 'Humbrians' and as the dual kingdom of Deira and Bernicia into the early eighth century – appears to have been unstable at this time, and Nicholas Higham has suggested that Bede's use of the style 'Northumbrian' was an innovation inspired by the initial coinage of this term in the acts of the council at Hertford.[42] It is therefore possible to propose that Theodore's early church councils were responsible for actively conceiving an influential understanding of the contemporary geographies of royal power, one that endured and came to define elite conceptions of their statuses and allegiances more generally.

This is significant, because we are aware of a host of smaller polities in seventh-century England, often ruled by 'subkings' (*subregules*) or 'princes' (*principes*) – a

---

40 *HE*, iv.5: Bishops Bisi of the East Angles, Wilfrid (via proctors) of the Northumbrians, Putta of the Kentish city of Rochester, Leuthere of the West Saxons and Winfrith of the Mercians were present at Hertford. *HE*, iv.17: Kings Ecgfrith of the 'Humbrians' (*Hymbronenses*), Æthelred of the Mercians, Ealdwulf of the East Angles and Hlothhere of Kent were present at Hatfield.

41 D.P. Kirby, *The earliest English kings*, rev. edn (London, 2000), pp. 20–2. The acts of the councils at Hertford and Hatfield provide our earliest record (assuming Bede transcribed them without altering them) of the names of the East Angles and West Saxons.

42 N. Higham, 'Northumbria's southern frontier: a review', *Early Medieval Europe*, 14/4 (2006), pp. 391–418.

terminology that informed James Campbell's characterisation of 'a world in which there were hierarchies of kings and relativities of kingliness' – from sources such as the Tribal Hidage or from their appearance in Bede's work.[43] Theodore's interest lay only in the largest and most powerful of the English kingdoms, those that already possessed bishoprics when he arrived and/or were ruled by a dynasty marked by 'imperial' status, even if such authority lay in the past. Barbara Yorke has argued that

> the primary unit for Bede was the individual kingdom, for which his normal term was *prouincia*, whose inhabitants could also be designated as a *gens* ['people'] ... and the equation of *gens*, *prouincia* and bishopric was ... central to Bede's conception of the natural order of things.[44]

Yet this taxonomic neatness was anything but natural; it had to be imposed, and, as the same equation is visible in Theodore's concerns, it is plausible to suggest that it subsequently colonised the shared understanding of the nascent English ecclesiastical community and provided the source of Bede's perception.

The spiritual authority of the English bishops, their power and influence as shepherds of the souls of their dioceses, must have been enhanced by the solidification of an organised English ecclesiastical community under Theodore; but its effects were more profound because the members of this community were drawn from (and continued to exist within) a broader social elite. The emerging fora of ecclesiastical politics, especially church councils, actively enabled the process by which particular kingdoms and their dynasties were stabilised or naturalised within elite discourse as the primary units of political action, inseparable from the dioceses that were mapped onto their boundaries; by extension, this process also hastened the demotion of other polities to various states of dependency. Michael Moore has demonstrated that the bishops of fifth- and sixth-century Gaul increasingly understood themselves as a distinct 'order' (*ordo*) whose purpose was 'the creation of a new people: the People of God (*populus Dei*)', to be brought into being through spiritual labour among the worldly 'peoples' (*gentes*).[45] In practice, bishoprics became the 'building blocks of Merovingian kingdoms': they 'served to organise the space of the kingdoms and to stabilise the integration of Gallo-Roman bishops with the Frankish nobility'.[46] In England, if we accept the connection suggested above between early ecclesiastical councils and the names of the major kingdoms, then it is also possible that the nascent episcopal order was influential in actively constituting the three-fold division of the English between 'Angles', 'Saxons' and 'Jutes' as the *gentes* at

---

43 J. Campbell, 'Bede's *reges* and *principes*', in J. Campbell (ed.), *Essays in Anglo-Saxon history* (London, 1986), pp. 85–98, at p. 91.
44 B. Yorke, 'Political and ethnic identity: a case study of Anglo-Saxon practice', in W.O. Frazer and A. Tyrrell (eds), *Social identity in early medieval Britain* (Leicester, 2000), pp. 69–90, at p. 75.
45 M.E. Moore, *A sacred kingdom: bishops and the rise of Frankish kingship, 300–850* (Washington, DC, 2011), p. 36.
46 Moore, *Sacred kingdom*, p. 105.

the heart of their own activities.[47] More broadly, the development of an integrated English ecclesiastical community was a fundamental part of the development of a more self-confident elite within the English kingdoms, and indeed of those kingdoms themselves, in which lay and religious roles were thoroughly interdependent.

We must return now to the place of the Mercian diocese in this picture. The Mercian dynasty is not represented in the imperial list, although a Mercian see had existed for about fifteen years by the time of Theodore's arrival in Britain in 669. The Mercian bishopric was nevertheless the most recently founded of those in existence when Theodore arrived, having been established within the context of Northumbrian overkingship when Oswiu had conquered the Mercians by killing the Mercian king Penda in battle in 654. Bede makes clear that the Mercians had become an independent kingdom in 657 when

> three years after King Penda's death the ealdormen of the Mercian people, Immin, Eafa, and Eadberht rebelled against King Oswiu and set up as their king Wulfhere, Penda's young son, whom they had kept concealed; and having driven out the ealdormen of the foreign king, they boldly recovered their lands and their liberty at the same time.[48]

Wulfhere appears to have gained considerable power and influence over the course of his reign.[49] The Mercian episcopal memorandum indicates that, by the time it was produced in 672×674, Wulfhere ruled directly over the Mercians, Middle Angles and Lindsey. Occasional references in Bede's work also demonstrate that Wulfhere managed to impose his overkingship on the East Saxons and the South Saxons, and that he conquered the Isle of Wight and adjacent parts of the mainland.[50] Towards the end of his reign Wulfhere led 'all the southern peoples' into battle against the Northumbrians, although he was defeated by the Northumbrian king Ecgfrith.[51] Clearly, Wulfhere was a power to be reckoned with during the early years of Theodore's episcopate.

However, this power does not appear to have translated into any great influence within the nascent English ecclesiastical community. After the death of Deusdedit, archbishop of Canterbury, in 664, it was the Northumbrian king Oswiu and the Kentish king Ecgberht who 'consulted together as to what ought to be done about the state of the English Church', and who sent Wigheard to Rome for the pallium,

---

47 It would also be plausible to suggest that Bede's famous passage concerning the origins of the English among the Angles, Saxons and Jutes was derived from a Canterbury memorandum of Theodore's archiepiscopate, especially given its combination with the Kentish origin legend involving Hengist and Horsa (*HE*, i.15) and the way it integrates with the names of most of the kingdoms represented in the acts of the councils.
48 *HE*, iii.24.
49 For a biographical summary see S. Keynes, 'Wulfhere', in M. Lapidge, J. Blair, S. Keynes and D. Scragg (eds), *The Blackwell encyclopaedia of Anglo-Saxon England* (Oxford, 1999), pp. 490–1.
50 *HE*, iii.7, iii.39, iv.13.
51 *VW*, c.20.

initiating a sequence of events that would result in Theodore's arrival.[52] Wulfhere must have made several of his conquests by 664, and yet he apparently had no claim on the direction of the English Church. The early Mercian bishops all emerged from Northumbrian contexts: the first two were Irish and the third, although English, had been taught by Irish ecclesiastics and had earlier ruled a Northumbrian monastery; lack of information prohibits us from assigning Jaruman to any particular background or context, but Chad had been bishop of York and was abbot of Lastingham in Northumbria before becoming the fifth Mercian bishop; Winfrith was one of Chad's clergy. The events surrounding Chad's appointment in 669 may also be instructive: Wulfhere, in need of a new bishop for his people, asked Theodore to provide him with one, but the newly arrived archbishop 'did not wish to consecrate a new bishop for them', and instead requested of Oswiu that Chad, recently deposed from York, might be given to them.[53] Theodore's reasoning is unclear here, but Wulfhere appears to have been in no position to force his own candidate on Theodore, while the latter relied on the resources of the Northumbrian diocese. It seems plausible to suggest that Wulfhere's power was new-won in the 660s, and perhaps insecure; the Mercians could not be ignored, and the name of their kingdom was not of the ethnic variety suggested above to have been applied to subkingdoms – theirs was an independent kingdom worthy of separate episcopal provision. However, the imperial list, if it has been correctly assigned to this period, makes clear that there was as yet no role for Mercian kings in contemporary understandings of significant overkingship, except perhaps as a destructive footnote. The 'English Church' was viewed as a product of the established history of Kentish and Northumbrian greatness, a view that Theodore may have actively promoted.[54]

The division of the Mercian see

According to the Mercian episcopal memorandum, the territory of the Mercians formed only part of the initial Mercian see, which also included the territories of the Middle Angles and Lindsey. It seems plausible to claim that this diocese represented the area directly ruled by Penda at his death in 654, which Oswiu subsequently gave into Diuma's hands to administer as a bishopric. It is possible that Wulfhere had to work to reacquire the entirety of this territory after he took the Mercian kingdom from Oswiu, but there can be no doubt that he did so. Indeed, the presence of the sees of the Hwicce and Magonsæte among the 'Mercian' sees in the second section of the Mercian lists in the ELT implies an expansion rooted in the growing self-confidence of Wulfhere's reign. The death of Oswiu in 670 removed a powerful and influential king from the British stage, and it is possible that Wulfhere became bolder when freed from the Northumbrian monarch's shadow. The raid in which he led 'all the southern peoples' against Oswiu's son and successor, Ecgfrith, speaks starkly of his ambition, which perhaps emulated his father's. The early 670s also witnessed the appointment of the first Mercian bishop to come from a Mercian

---

52 *HE*, iii.29 and iv.1.
53 *HE*, iv.3; see also *VW*, c.15.
54 See Higham, *English empire*, pp. 66–8, for stimulating commentary on some of these issues.

context: Seaxwulf. According to Bede, in a passage that probably drew on information received from the monastery at Lastingham, Seaxwulf was the 'founder and abbot of the monastery of *Medeshamstede* [now Peterborough] in the territory of the Gyrwe'.[55] The Gyrwe formed one of the Middle Anglian polities that appear to have been securely under Wulfhere's rule by the 670s. As we have seen, the end of Seaxwulf's episcopate (691/2) forms an important point in the vision of the 'Mercian' bishoprics presented by the archetype of the ELT, specifically the division of an initial see into five dioceses (*parrochiae*) in a single event, recorded in the second section of the Mercian lists. There are, however, problems with this narrative. The following discussion will explore the various divisions of the initial Mercian see undertaken in the later seventh and earlier eighth centuries and will demonstrate that the compiler of the episcopal lists, writing in 796×814, was rationalising a more complex history.

Patrick Sims-Williams has drawn attention to a Canterbury document purporting to report a session of a papal council of 679, at least a decade before the end of Seaxwulf's episcopate, which supported the maintenance of twelve bishops under one archbishop.[56] Taking into account the other dioceses that had been founded by that date, there is room for three additional Mercian bishoprics.[57] One of these was the diocese of Lindsey, which had been founded in 678 when Lindsey was in Northumbrian hands, and was taken back soon afterwards by Wulfhere's brother and successor, King Æthelred of the Mercians, probably at the battle of the river Trent, which Bede dates to 679.[58] The other two dioceses must have been those of the Hwicce and the Magonsæte: their first bishops, Bosel and Putta, attested a charter together in 680.[59] Sims-Williams has conducted a thorough study of these dioceses, and they need detain us no longer here.[60] Suffice it to note that there is no reason to assume that either territory was initially within the Mercian diocese to which Seaxwulf and his predecessors were appointed; the evidence for the earliest history of these provinces, such as it is, hints at the intrusion of Wulfhere's overkingship in the 660s and 670s, providing a broad context for the creation of new dioceses by their ruling

---

55 *HE*, iv.6; see Chapter 2 for the Lastingham provenance of this passage.
56 Sims-Williams, *Religion and literature*, p. 88; the Canterbury document can be found in A.W. Haddan and W. Stubbs, *Councils and ecclesiastical documents relating to Great Britain and Ireland: volume III, the English Church 595–1066* (Oxford, 1871), pp. 131–6, and the relevant charter is S 1167.
57 From Bede's *Historia Ecclesiastica*, it is possible to establish that, by 679, the sees of Canterbury, Rochester, London, Winchester, Dunwich, Elmham, Lichfield, York, Lindisfarne, Ripon and Lindsey were in existence, leaving two to account for.
58 *HE*, iv.12, iv.21 and v.24.
59 S 1167; Sims-Williams has noted that a foundation charter for the minster at Bath in the territory of the Hwicce, dated 675, 'indicates that the foundation of the see had recently been accomplished by [the Hwiccian] King Osric', although it was not attested by a bishop of Worcester, and the charter may not be entirely trustworthy in the form that we have it (Sims-Williams, *Religion and literature*, p. 88; the relevant charter is S 51).
60 Sims-Williams, *Religion and literature*, passim.

subkings early in Æthelred's reign.[61] Thus the dioceses of Lindsey, the Hwicce and the Magonsæte were all created at a time early in Seaxwulf's episcopate, and of these only the territory of Lindsey had initially lain within his diocese, before it was removed from his control by force of Northumbrian conquest.

The diocese of the Middle Angles (based at Leicester) is worth more attention here, as its territory was denied a separately named identity in the second section of the Mercian episcopal lists of 796×814, instead being subsumed within a 'Mercian' province alongside the bishops of Lichfield; the date of its foundation as a separate bishopric is less clear than the other Mercian dioceses. The fact that the episcopal memorandum distinguishes three peoples – the Mercians, Middle Angles and the people of Lindsey – within the initial Mercian diocese is notable, as none of the other English bishoprics were named in any surviving textual sources with reference to more than one people. If Theodore's nascent ecclesiastical community provided the context for the naming of many of the larger English kingdoms, as argued above, then the territories of their earliest bishoprics plausibly represent the extent of the direct rule of their kings at this time, and it would presumably have been simple enough to name the entire region (and its population) governed by the Mercian bishop 'Mercian'. That three peoples were distinguished in the episcopal memorandum may thus indicate (if its creation in 672×674 is accepted) that Theodore wished at that time to divide the Mercian diocese into three, given the importance that he appears to have given to the equation between bishopric, people and kingdom. Theodore's desire to increase the number of dioceses in the English Church is well known:[62] it was formalised as the ninth chapter of the canons of the Council of Hertford in 672;[63] it resulted in the division of the East Anglian see shortly after the council;[64] it probably accounts for the creation of the sees of Lindsey, the Hwicce and the Magonsæte in the mid- to late 670s (discussed above); and it prompted discord between Theodore and the Northumbrian bishop Wilfrid in the later 670s.[65] If Theodore had considered dividing the Mercian diocese in 672×674, it is possible, as Sims-Williams has suggested, that the Mercian bishop Winfrith, who was deposed by Theodore for 'some act of disobedience' at about this time, had disagreed about whether or how this should be carried out.[66]

The possibility that the Middle Anglian diocese was first conceived within Theodore's circle is also supported by its name, which is of the form comprising an ethnic group with directional qualifier, and thus belongs with the other major English polities whose names plausibly emerged within the context of church councils in the early 670s. Against this it might be argued that the name appears to relate to an earlier context. It occurs twelve times in the *Historia Ecclesiastica*, of which nine appear to

---

61 Sims-Williams, *Religion and literature*, pp. 25–53 and 87–91.
62 Brooks, *Early history of the church of Canterbury*, pp. 73–6.
63 *HE*, iv.5.
64 *HE*, iv.5.
65 A good summary of the conflict is given by Brooks, *Early history of the church of Canterbury*, pp. 73–6.
66 *HE*, iv.6; Sims-Williams, *Religion and literature*, p. 88.

derive from just two sources.[67] The first of these is the episcopal memorandum, which clearly lies behind sections in which the Mercian bishops are enumerated and the territory administered by them is labelled with reference to 'the Mercians, the people of Lindsey and the Middle Angles'.[68] The second is an account of the conversion of the Middle Angles that was almost certainly part of a larger narrative that Bede received from the community at Lastingham, to be discussed in Chapter 2.[69] That account describes how Peada, son of King Penda of the Mercians, having been created 'prince' (*princeps*) of the Middle Angles by his father in 652, subsequently desired to marry Alhflæd, daughter of King Oswiu of Northumbria; the king agreed on the condition that Peada accept the Christian faith for himself and for his people. Peada was duly baptised in Northumbria and returned to the Middle Angles with a mission of four priests, one of whom, Diuma, was subsequently consecrated bishop of both the Mercians and the Middle Angles after Oswiu had conquered Mercia by killing Penda in 654. The name thus labels a polity created about fifteen years earlier than Theodore's arrival. However, the writing of the narrative must have occurred after 672 (see Chapter 2), and the use of the label may well represent a back-projection of the writer's contemporary terminology, applied to distinguish the political sphere of Penda's son. In this context it is worth noting that the Tribal Hidage does not use the name, but instead lists several smaller peoples who were later subsumed within the Middle Angles; the coherence and dating of the Tribal Hidage is still debated, but David Dumville's argument, dating its initial composition to the period between *c.*635 and *c.*680, remains the most plausible.[70]

If Theodore did intend to create a Middle Anglian diocese in the early 670s, it is notable that Seaxwulf appears to have succeeded to a unitary diocese in 673/4. Perhaps there was a staffing problem: in the passage describing Diuma's consecration as first bishop over the Mercians and Middle Angles in 655 Bede's Lastingham source explained that 'a shortage of bishops made it necessary for one bishop to be set over both peoples'.[71] It is again possible here that more recent issues were being back-projected

---

67 The remaining three uses of the label are as follows: that at *HE*, i.15 concerns Bede's explanation of the coming of the English 'from three very powerful German peoples, the Saxons, Angles and Jutes', of whom the Middle Angles are said unsurprisingly to derive from the Angles; that at *HE*, iv.12 concerns the bishops of Lindsey, and defines the remainder of Seaxwulf's jurisdiction as the 'Mercians and the Middle Angles' (plausibly, though not necessarily, a Bedan gloss based on the Mercian episcopal memorandum); and that at *HE*, iv.23 concerns Wilfrid's episcopal role in Mercia, on which see further below.

68 *HE*, iii.24, iv.3.

69 *HE*, iii.21 (four times), iii.22, iii.24 and v.24.

70 D.N. Dumville, 'Essex, Middle Anglia and the expansion of Mercia', in D.N. Dumville (ed.), *Britons and Anglo-Saxons in the early Middle Ages* (Aldershot, 1993), Essay IX, pp. 16–17.

71 *HE*, iii.21. The people of Lindsey do not appear in this passage, perhaps because it was not informed directly by the memorandum, and because the people of Lindsey, unlike the Mercians and the Middle Angles, were not the subject of this narrative, as they had been converted years before by Paulinus: see Sims-Williams, *Religion and literature,* p. 58. Bede had earlier written of Paulinus' success in converting the people of Lindsey around 630 (*HE*, iii.21).

to explain a situation in the mid-650s that looked anomalous only in hindsight. There is no other evidence for a separate bishop of the Middle Angles during Seaxwulf's episcopate, but there are several sources for the period after his death, although they cannot be interpreted in a straightforward manner. Bede states that the exiled Northumbrian bishop Wilfrid, when asked by King Æthelred of the Mercians to consecrate a bishop for the Hwicce, 'at that time ruled the bishopric of the Middle Angles'.[72] This, of course, matches the narrative given by the second section of the Mercian episcopal lists, although the latter might well have drawn on Bede's work. Frustratingly, it is not possible simply to take Bede at his word here, because it is not explicitly supported by the work of Wilfrid's biographer, Stephen of Ripon. Stephen states that, after being welcomed by Æthelred, king of the Mercians, Wilfrid 'remained amid the great reverence of his [Æthelred's] bishopric, which the most reverend bishop Seaxwulf earlier ruled up to his death, continuing under God's and his [Æthelred's] protection'.[73] He therefore implies that there was only one Mercian diocese at issue, referring to the bishopric (*episcopatus*) in the singular.

Headda, apparently Seaxwulf's successor at Lichfield (according to the ELT), appears alongside Wilfrid in the witness lists of three charters dated to the 690s, two concerning land in Essex and one land in Worcestershire, supporting the idea that Wilfrid was one of two bishops in Mercia at this time.[74] Bede's passage concerns Oftfor, bishop of the Hwicce and a graduate of Hild's monastery at Whitby, and comes within a chapter dedicated to Hild's life and achievements. David Kirby has suggested that all of Bede's knowledge of the see of Worcester 'came through Whitby and Wilfridian sources', and, as Wilfrid's Middle Anglian diocese is not mentioned by that name in Stephen's *Life*, the detail is best ascribed to a Whitby source.[75] We also know that one of Wilfrid's principal minsters in Mercia was at Oundle (Northamptonshire), in the Middle Anglian region.[76] All this might indicate that the Middle Anglian bishopric, first planned just before Seaxwulf's episcopate, had finally been established at the end of it, if Stephen's comments did not appear to contradict this. However, it is possible that Stephen's passage should not be taken quite so literally: after all, Seaxwulf did indeed rule the Middle Anglian region as Æthelred's bishop, even if he also ruled other regions as well, and Stephen might not have known or cared about the finer points of episcopal arrangements in Mercia. The balance of probabilities does perhaps allow us to accept Bede's statement, if not quite so resolutely as we would like. The ELT suggests that Wilfrid was banished at some point; this must refer to his suspension from episcopal duties enacted at a synod at Austerfield in 702/3, after which he was excommunicated and decided to travel to Rome to appeal the judgement, an episode described by Stephen in his *Life*.[77]

---

72 *HE*, iv.23.
73 *VW*, 45.
74 S 53, S 1171 and S 1246. The bishop of this name who attests these charters is sometimes equated with Hædde of Winchester, but the lands concerned were within the broader Mercian overkingship at this time.
75 D.P. Kirby, 'Bede's native sources for the *Historia Ecclesiastica*', *Bulletin of the John Rylands Library*, 48 (1966), pp. 341–71, at p. 368.
76 *HE*, v.19; *VW*, c.65.
77 *VW*, cc. 49 and 50.

The remainder of the narrative in the second section of the Mercian lists in the ELT is supported by charter evidence, as far as it goes. Headda's eventual successor Ealdwine *alias* Wor may have attested a charter with him as 'Elwine' in 705, and the two more certainly appear together in the witness list of a charter dated 716;[78] however, Headda appears in several other charters after 702/3 by himself, and also in Felix's *Life of St Guthlac*, in which he consecrates the hermit's church at Crowland in the Middle Anglian region.[79] It therefore seems unlikely that Ealdwine filled Wilfrid's position before succeeding Headda; perhaps he was a suffragan in Headda's see without a formal seat of his own. No bishops of the Middle Angles can be certainly identified until 737, when, in the words of an entry from the northern annals in the *Historia Regum*, 'Bishop Ealdwine, also called Wor, died, and in his place Hwitta and Totta were consecrated bishops for the Mercians and the Middle Angles'.[80] From this date the two sees remained in separate hands, but it is notable that the Middle Anglian see also began to be labelled as 'Mercian' instead. In the acts of the synod at *Clofesho* in 747 the bishops of Lichfield, Leicester and Hereford were all labelled 'Mercian', while bishops of the Hwicce and Lindsey were given their own names.[81] The second part of the Mercian episcopal lists in α ascribed the bishops of Lichfield and Leicester to the 'Mercian' province in 796×814, as we have seen, and the acts of the synod at *Clofesho* in 816 employed the same terminology a little later.[82] Nevertheless, a charter of 803 subscribed by Werenberht 'bishop of the Middle Angles' demonstrates that the earlier terminology continued to be used occasionally.[83]

The apparent absence of a Middle Anglian bishop for over three decades following Wilfrid's expulsion in 702/3 is notable, and needs to be set beside the fact that 'Middle Anglian' and 'Mercian' terminology became somewhat interchangeable. Both phenomena may be explained by the fact that the Middle Anglian territory was often ruled directly by the Mercian king. Wendy Davies has suggested that the concentration of references to the 'Middle Angles' in the Peada narrative might indicate that his brief tenure as *princeps* was the only time at which the term gained a political valence.[84] In fact, this concentration is more likely to be a product of Bede's source material, but Davies is probably correct to argue that a Middle Anglian territory first achieved political expression under Peada as a conglomeration of various smaller polities in the region, even if it was not then so called. However, it is quite possible that such a province continued to exist as an important political entity within the Mercian kingdom for some time thereafter, or at the very least was periodically revived as an 'intermediate overkingship' or 'mesne kingdom', to use David Dumville's terminology,

---

78 S 248 and S 22.
79 *VG*, caps 46 and 47.
80 *EHD* 1, p. 240; see also P. Hunter-Blair, 'Some observations on the *Historia Regum* attributed to Symeon of Durham', in N. Chadwick (ed.), *Celt and Saxon, studies in the early British border* (Cambridge, 1963), pp. 63–118.
81 Haddan and Stubbs, *Councils*, p. 362.
82 Haddan and Stubbs, *Councils*, p. 579.
83 S 1431.
84 W. Davies, 'Middle Anglia and the Middle Angles', *Midland History*, 2/1 (1973), pp. 18–20.

appropriate for the rule of a powerful ealdorman or junior member of the royal dynasty.[85] Arguably, only some kind of continuing political role will explain why the territory appeared suitable for the creation of a bishopric in the early 670s and later.

Nevertheless, that role had perhaps diminished by the eighth century, when the 'Mercian' label appears, and it is probably significant that the province of the Hwicce, whose bishop continued to be identified by 'Hwiccian' terminology, was still ruled by subkings at this time. This is partially borne out by the characterisation of the Hereford diocese as 'Mercian' in 747, as we have no evidence that the sub-royal dynasty of the Magonsæte continued in power beyond the early eighth century;[86] however, this diocese was styled that of 'Hereford' in the early ninth century, so the pattern is not neat enough to provide definitive proof.[87] Perhaps, like the province of the Hwicce, that of the Magonsæte became associated with important ealdormen, whose roles maintained its secular importance.[88] It is at least plausible to suggest that the Middle Anglian polity had ceased to have any sub-regnal significance by the mid-eighth century at the latest, and that the territories of the dioceses of Lichfield and Leicester appeared more 'Mercian' than the other provinces under Mercian rulership because Mercian monarchs continued to hold a more direct dominion over these areas. Perhaps the early decline of the Middle Angles as a separate sub-regnal polity enabled Mercian bishops to keep the two episcopal provinces under one rule until 737. The history of the Middle Anglian polity also illustrates nicely how the establishment of bishoprics could act to define and stabilise the frame of politics more generally during this period, here fossilising a short-lived secular territory in ecclesiastical guise.[89]

Returning finally to the collection α, and the view of its compiler on earlier Mercian episcopal history, of the four additional Mercian bishoprics supposedly established 'after Seaxwulf' only the diocese of the Middle Angles was created in an area that had been firmly within the power of the Mercian kings since well before Theodore's arrival, and its creation, though perhaps mooted in the early 670s, did indeed have to wait until Seaxwulf's death, when it appears to have been established for Wilfrid. The other three dioceses were created during Seaxwulf's episcopate towards the end of the 670s, but in territories that he did not then rule, and all at times of political upheaval: Northumbrian conquest in the case of Lindsey and the extension of Mercian overkingship into new territory in the case of the Hwicce and Magonsæte. The narrative enshrined in the episcopal lists of α is thus partially erroneous, and simplifies a more complex set of historical moments, illustrating how the discourse of episcopal

---

85 Dumville, 'Terminology of overkingship', p. 358. See also Dumville, 'Essex, Middle Anglia, and the expansion of Mercia', pp. 13–18.
86 Sims-Williams, *Religion and literature*, pp. 34–9 and 47–51.
87 There is no evidence at all for subkings in Lindsey; only a genealogy of the kings of the province in the Anglian collection attests to its once-royal status (Dumville, 'Anglian collection', pp. 31, 33, 37, and 45–7).
88 Sims-Williams, *Religion and literature*, pp. 38–9.
89 For a similar idea regarding the persistent identity of the province of the Hwicce, see P. Featherstone, 'The Tribal Hidage and the ealdormen of Mercia', in M.P. Brown and C.A. Farr (eds), *Mercia: an Anglo-Saxon kingdom in Europe* (London, 2000), pp. 23–34, at p. 31.

power might be reimagined at times. Instead the ELT promotes a particular view of the territories that were claimed as 'Mercian' in the late eighth or early ninth centuries, essentially claiming that all had been unproblematically Mercian since the end of Seaxwulf's episcopate.

In contrast, it is apparent that none of the Mercian dioceses represent natural divisions of an older 'Mercian' polity; all express the contours of power, both secular and spiritual, their borders fixed at particular moments in the emergence and development of different hierarchies. It was only with the establishment of the English ecclesiastical community as a distinct power bloc during Theodore's archiepiscopate, promoted and reinforced by the ritualising influence of regular synods, that episcopal authority began to affect the framing of power within the English kingdoms, crystallising the 'provincial' discourse in which both kingdoms and bishoprics were suspended. The diocese of Lichfield was perhaps often seen as the most 'Mercian' of the Mercian dioceses, and it appears to have contained some of the most important Mercian royal estates, as later chapters will explore, but its bounds were set by a series of political developments in the later seventh and early eighth centuries that were by no means territorially inevitable.

The English Church and the Mercian kingdom

The entanglement of the English ecclesiastical community and the Mercian regnal community can be further explored during the period of Mercian dominion during the late seventh, eighth and early ninth centuries by considering the assemblies that embodied, maintained and enabled both regnal and ecclesiastical communities during this period. Bishops were members of regnal elites, often associated with the closest circle of advisors and office-holders around the thrones of the English kingdoms, and their attendance at Mercian royal councils can be investigated through the witness-lists of charters, although the survival of such evidence, and its reliability, do not offer a complete picture. During the late seventh and eighth centuries bishops of Lichfield were recorded in attendance at a significant proportion (although not all) of the royal councils represented by surviving charters, which were held at a number of different places within the Mercian dominion over the English Midlands. Even accepting the partial nature of this corpus of evidence, some patterns can be identified regarding the Mercian sees. Of thirty-one charters apparently attested by bishops of Lichfield between 672 and 781, twenty-one were also attested by bishops of Worcester, ten by bishops of Hereford, fifteen by bishops of Leicester and nine by bishops of Lindsey.[90] The predominance of the bishops of Worcester among the other attesters may be

---

90 This survey is based on S.D. Keynes, *An atlas of attestations in Anglo-Saxon charters, c.670–1066* (Cambridge, 2002). The charters, in chronological order of probable production date, are as follows: S 51, S 71, S 73, S 1246, S 1171, S 76, S 77, S 53, S 1175, S 79, S 65, S 81, S 85, S 89, S 93, S 94, S 95, S 99, S 92, S 55, S 106, S 110, S 109, S 145, S 113, S 141, S 147, S 57, S 114, S 120 and S 121. The corpus omits certain or probable church councils during this period represented by S 248, S 22, S 1429, S 90 and the acts of the Council of *Clofesho* in 747 (Haddan and Stubbs, *Councils*, pp. 362–76).

partly explained by the fact that sixteen of the thirty-one charters came from the Worcester archive; the remainder were more evenly distributed among seven other archives.[91] Nevertheless, the temporal distribution of these attestations is also notable: before 716 bishops of Worcester had attested with bishops of Lichfield eight times (only three of them from the Worcester archive), but the bishop of Hereford only once and the bishop of Lindsey not at all; from 716 onwards the attestations of the bishops of these three sees are more evenly distributed among the remaining charters. Finally, Wilfrid, probably acting as the bishop of Leicester, attested three charters before 716; thereafter bishops of Leicester attested only in and after 737, as would be expected, and crucially they attested every charter witnessed by bishops of Lichfield from this date until 781.

Interpreting these patterns is not simple, but some general points might be made. First, it is possible that absence from a witness-list does not necessarily imply absence from a royal council, although if this was generally the case we would expect the attestations of bishops to be distributed rather more randomly than in fact they are. Assuming, then, that the witness-lists largely give us a real impression of episcopal attendance, albeit not particularly focused, we might infer that the bishops of the Mercian dominion did not attend the king at every royal council, but only those deemed for some reason more significant, and those within or near their bishoprics. Unfortunately information on the place of issue is largely absent from these charters, but where it is present it supports this assumption as far as it goes: a council at Gumley (Leics., in the diocese of Leicester) in 749 was attended only by the bishops of Lichfield and Leicester, as was a council at Tamworth (Staffs., in the diocese of Lichfield) in 780; both places were located near the mutual boundary of the two dioceses.[92] Other Mercian charters outside this corpus add a little to the picture: a council at London in 748 was attended by the bishop of Worcester and a council at Brentford (Middlesex) was attended by the bishops of Leicester, Lindsey and Worcester; excluding only the presence of the bishop of Lindsey (who may have been based at Lincoln), in both these cases the absent Mercian bishops were otherwise further away.

There is no sense here that the five Mercian bishops acted collectively to create a specifically 'Mercian' Church. Only the constant attestation of the bishops of Lichfield and Leicester together after 737 stands out and, when viewed alongside the use of the 'Mercian' style for these provinces discussed earlier, it is convincing evidence that the territories of these two sees was largely treated as a core political unity by this time. In this context it is worth noting that a royal council at Gumley in 749, at which the king granted various immunities, appears to have been convened specifically to address problems with Æthelbald's relationship with the churches in this core region.[93] Hwita, the bishop of Lichfield, attests as 'bishop of the church of the

---

91 The distribution is as follows: Evesham, 5; Christ Church, Canterbury, 3; Malmesbury, 2; Barking, 2; Abingdon, 1; Bath, 1. The remaining document is the privilege granted by Æthelbald at Gumley in 749 (S 92).
92 S 92, S 120 and S 121.
93 S 92.

Mercians', but this style would appear to label his own diocese (on which see Chapter 2), rather than any larger entity;[94] nevertheless, the bishop of Leicester, Torhthelm, is given no title, and it is possible that Hwita held some kind of superiority over him, and that a 'Mercian Church' constituting the Christian population of both dioceses was intended by his style. However, there is no other evidence for the dependency of Leicester on Lichfield, and given the well-attested 'Middle Anglian' label for the former, it is more plausible to connect the Mercian Church solely with Hwita's diocese. This characterisation of territory must be kept separate from Æthelbald's concern at the council, which appears to have lain with the minsters and churches located in his core 'Mercian' province. More broadly, there is no evidence that bishops conceived of Churches – imagined communities of Christians – at any level intermediate between the Churches of their dioceses and the entire English Church, excepting only the latter's Northumbrian and Southumbrian halves.

The charters indicate that Mercian kings occasionally convened larger councils, at which all five Mercian bishops were present: one such council was held at *Bearuwe* ('Barrow') in 737×740, and between three and five were held between 775 and 779, of which one was again at Gumley and another at Hartleford (Glos.).[95] Such councils are a minority among the corpus examined here, although it is impossible to claim that the corpus is representative. Nevertheless, beyond the united provinces of Lichfield and Leicester, there is no sense that the Mercian kings held councils representative of their overkingship as a whole before 781, and this picture is reinforced by the occasional and irregular attestation of bishops from the outlying, less dependent parts of that overkingship, notably the archbishop of Canterbury and the bishops of Rochester and London, representing the kingdoms of Kent and the East Saxons;[96] their attendance was perhaps governed by the same principle of proximity suggested above. This also applies to Mercian royal councils that were not apparently attested by bishops of Lichfield, reinforcing the sense that Mercian kings perambulated around their dominion holding assemblies at which attendance was mostly dependent on location and perhaps political contingency.[97] The more inclusive councils of the second half of the 770s may mark a step-change, as in 781 a church council at Brentford was attended by King Offa and his court, inaugurating about half a century (up to a council at *Clofesho* in 825) during which Mercian kings, in particular Offa and Cœnwulf, regularly attended Southumbrian church councils, making land grants and adjudicating disputes while there that dominate the surviving charter record for this period.

Catherine Cubitt's study has revealed much about these regular ecclesiastical assemblies, often held in late summer or autumn at one of a small number of places close to London evidently judged suitable for the purpose.[98] Bishops had a duty to

---

94 'Huita Mercensis æcclesiæ … episcopus'.
95 S 99, S 109, S 145, S 113, S 147 and S 114.
96 Canterbury: S 51, S 71, S 73, S 53, S 1175, S 79, S 81, S 106 and S 110; Rochester: S 53, S 1175, S 79, S 81, S 109 and S 145; London: S 51, S 1246, S 1171, S 79 and S 65.
97 Keynes, *Atlas*, Tables 3, 6 and 8; see also Cubitt, *Church councils*, pp. 213–15.
98 For much of what follows in this paragraph see Cubitt, *Church councils*, pp. 15–76 (Chapters 1 and 2).

attend these councils, and the evidence suggests that they fulfilled this obligation, probably accompanied by some proportion of the abbots and more important clergy of their dioceses. Even when kings also attended, Cubitt argues that 'a distinction seems to have been recognised between purely ecclesiastical questions, and disputes where the king, as the ultimate guarantor of property rights, was involved';[99] this testifies to the fact that the archbishop was recognised as the president of these councils, responsible for convening them by virtue of his authority over all other ecclesiastics in his metropolitan territory. A variety of different kinds of business might take place at these councils. Five surviving sets of canons promulgated at councils in the period between 672 and 816 may stand for many more that have been lost. However, although other councils may well have debated the kinds of issue that appear in these canons, Cubitt has suggested that their formalisation in written form actually reflects a real distinctiveness, and that each of these five 'reforming' councils took place at 'crucial' conjunctions in negotiating the idea of the English Church.[100] More generally, councils might discuss doctrinal questions and debate elements of the administration of the Church, before authorising judgements on these matters. Many of the disputes that appear in surviving records concerned land with ecclesiastical connections, and it is possible that an archbishop's paramount authority over 'bookland', land granted by charter often for the purpose of founding a minster, was promoted and widely recognised during this period. Crucially, while the consent of kings might be mentioned, the judgements of these councils were given force and meaning through the agency of the archbishop and his assembled bishops.

As noted earlier, such councils had probably been convened on a regular basis since the episcopate of Archbishop Theodore, although our evidence largely concerns councils of the late eighth and early ninth centuries at which a Mercian king was present. Offa's decision to attend in 781 was not entirely novel, however; kings from several different kingdoms had attended church councils sporadically before 781, usually accompanied by their more significant followers and companions, those who also attended the royal councils.[101] Nevertheless, the Mercian king's persistent attendance after this date, and that of his successor Cœnwulf, marked a definite alteration in practice. Cubitt has argued that this development was in part pragmatic: 'synods of the whole Southumbrian church, held on Mercian-controlled territory, may have proved a particularly important forum for the transaction of business concerning the subkingdoms of the Mercian hegemony.'[102] Crucially, despite the undoubted significance of the presence of Offa and Cœnwulf at these councils, 'there is nothing to suggest that their power could operate directly over the Southumbrian bishops, displacing that of the archbishop'; rather, 'it was the metropolitan who was the pivotal figure, acting almost as a go-between for the Mercians and the church'.[103]

---

99 Cubitt, *Church councils*, p. 55.
100 Cubitt, *Church councils*, pp. 62–3.
101 Cubitt, *Church councils*, pp. 44–9.
102 Cubitt, *Church councils*, p. 210.
103 Cubitt, *Church councils*, p. 217.

One particularly fruitful context for exploring this relationship between the English ecclesiastical community and the Mercian kings is provided by the elevation of Lichfield to the status of an archbishopric in 787 and the consequences of this act immediately after Offa's death in 796. These events have been studied by Nicholas Brooks and can be quickly summarised.[104] According to the *Anglo-Saxon Chronicle*, 'a contentious synod at Chelsea' in 787 resulted in the creation of a new archbishopric at King Offa's behest, carved out of the metropolitan see of Canterbury and ruled by Bishop Hygeberht of Lichfield, now raised to the dignity of archbishop, after which Offa's son Ecgfrith was consecrated king to rule alongside his father.[105] The juxtaposition of these two events is probably no accident, and it has been suggested that Offa's actions resulted from an irreparable animosity between himself and Archbishop Jænberht (together with a significant proportion of the Kentish aristocracy) on the one hand, and his desire to have Ecgfrith consecrated as his heir in the Frankish manner on the other.[106] Offa's ability to engineer the creation of a new metropolitan testifies to his dominance of Southumbrian politics, and Catherine Cubitt has suggested that he was considered to be 'the secular head of the Southumbrian church' at this time, a status apparently mirrored by treatment of the Northumbrian king as secular head of the Northumbrian church.[107] Interestingly, all the Southumbrian bishops continued to meet together at joint synods of the two archbishoprics.[108] In 796 Charlemagne sent the Mercian king two silk pallia, which Cubitt suggests were intended for his two archbishops, demonstrating that recognition of the second Southumbrian archbishopric extended to the highest elite circles in western Europe.[109] However, after Offa's death the existence of the archbishopric of Lichfield was challenged, ultimately successfully.

Letters preserved in a collection associated with the contemporary Northumbrian scholar Alcuin and in the twelfth-century works of William of Malmesbury illustrate something of the process of dissolution. In 797 Alcuin wrote to Archbishop Æthelheard of Canterbury on the matter, suggesting 'that the unity of the Church ... may, if it can be done, be peacefully united and the rent repaired', although he was concerned that it be done 'in such a way, however, that the pious father [Hygeberht] be not deprived of the pallium in his lifetime, although the ordination of bishops is to revert to the holy and original see [Canterbury]'.[110] Although Alcuin was Northumbrian by birth, and had been raised at the church of York, he had subsequently entered the court of Charlemagne, where he became an influential churchman with a central role in Frankish politics. Retaining and cultivating connections with many of the kings and bishops in England, Alcuin was well placed to give advice, although Æthelheard was at that time less well placed to receive it, as he had fled from his see in the face

---

104 Brooks, *Early history of the church of Canterbury*, pp. 111–27.
105 *ASC* s.a. 785 (*recte* 787).
106 Brooks, *Early history of the church of Canterbury*, pp. 111–18.
107 Cubitt, *Church councils*, p. 213.
108 Cubitt, *Church councils*, p. 218.
109 *Alcuin ep.*, No. 101; Cubitt, *Church councils*, p. 213.
110 *Alcuin ep.*, No. 128; for translation see *EHD* 1, pp. 789–90.

Lichfield and the Lands of St Chad

of Kentish revolt after Offa's death in 796.[111] To what extent Alcuin's interventions helped to form opinions, rather than simply reflecting them, is a moot point, but he is unlikely to have been alone in his dissatisfaction with the Southumbrian metropolitan arrangement. In 798 the new Mercian king Cœnwulf invaded Kent and removed a rival Kentish claimant, Eadberht Præn, from power, enabling Æthelheard to return to his see. The archbishop set about drawing the allegiance of Hygeberht's bishops back to Canterbury; professions of faith and loyalty to the archbishop dating between the years 798 and 801 survive from bishops of Lindsey, Dunwich, Hereford and Worcester, all likely to have been within Lichfield's metropolitan province.[112] In 801 Æthelheard travelled to Rome and gained formal papal approval for the restoration of Canterbury's metropolitan see in a document issued on 18 January 802; the metropolitan of Lichfield was finally abolished in October 803 at a council at *Clofesho*.

One important impression that emerges from the letters written about these events is the crucial significance of texts to the creation and exertion of ecclesiastical authority. In a letter of 798 to Pope Leo III King Cœnwulf explained that 'our bishops and certain most learned men' had objected to the division of Canterbury's metropolitan see because it was 'against the canons and apostolic decrees which were established for us by the direction of the most blessed Father Gregory ... though twelve bishops ought by that same father's command to be subject to its rule'.[113] The connection of these texts with Rome was significant, and indeed Cœnwulf had sought the pope's advice 'lest the traditions of the holy fathers, and the rules handed down by them to us, be corrupted in anything among us, as if unknown'.[114] For his part, Pope Leo accepted that his predecessor Pope Hadrian's actions were 'contrary to custom';[115] Leo's confirmation of 802 addressed to Æthelheard, concerning the 'dioceses' restored to Canterbury, 'that is, of the bishops and monasteries, whether of monks, canons, or nuns', justified his actions by the fact that 'your church held them in ancient times, as we have learnt from investigations in our sacred archives'.[116] Finally, by this act the earlier text enacting Hadrian's division of the metropolitan province became dangerous, and at the council of *Clofesho* in 803, at which the archbishopric of Lichfield was formally abolished, Æthelheard pronounced 'with the consent and permission of the lord apostolic, Pope Leo, that the charter sent from the Roman see by Pope Hadrian about the pallium and the archiepiscopal see in the church of Lichfield is invalid'.[117]

We see here a textual community, encompassing the bishops and 'learned men' of the English Church and extending to Rome, acting through its texts to reverse the

---

111 Brooks, *Early history of the church of Canterbury*, p. 121.
112 Brooks, *Early history of the church of Canterbury*, p. 125.
113 Preserved in William of Malmesbury's *Gesta Regum*, cap. 88 (Haddan and Stubbs, *Councils*, pp. 521–3, and *EHD* 1, pp. 791–3, at p. 792).
114 *EHD* 1, pp. 791–3, at p. 792.
115 *Alcuin ep.*, No. 127 (*EHD* 1, pp. 793–4).
116 Preserved in William of Malmesbury's *Gesta Pontificum*, cap. 38 (Haddan and Stubbs, *Councils*, pp. 536–7); Æthelheard appears travelling across Francia to Rome in a letter written by Alcuin to Charlemagne in 801: *Alcuin ep.*, No. 231 (*EHD* 1, pp. 794–5).
117 S 1431a.

actions of Offa; the texts became powerful when mobilised by the community. The letters also reveal other elements of the strategy by which this was accomplished. For example, a discourse emerges by which, in Alcuin's words, the Church was divided 'not, as it seems, by reasonable consideration but by a certain desire for power'.[118] This, a reference to Offa, added to criticism that Alcuin expressed to a Mercian ealdorman, to the effect that Ecgfrith had died as a divine judgement on his father, 'for you know very well how much blood his father shed to secure the kingdom on his son'.[119] King Cœnwulf apparently acceded to this narrative, as he was happy to explain to the pope that Offa had divided the Southumbrian metropolitan 'on account of the enmity he had formed against the venerable Jænberht and the people of Kent'.[120] Finally, Æthelheard explained at *Clofesho* in 803 that the archbishopric of Lichfield had been created 'by deception and misleading suggestion', and that the pope, 'as he heard and understood that it had been done wrongfully, immediately made a decree by the privilege of his authority'.[121] This notion of 'wrongful' division could apparently be set beside circumstances in which such division would be appropriate, as Pope Leo initially claimed that 'it was the united wish and unanimous petition of you all, both on account of the vast size of your lands and the extension of your kingdom, and also for many more reasons and advantages'.[122] Canonical custom could be overridden by unanimous decision (as it apparently was in 787), and the restoration of Canterbury's primacy was not inevitable; Hadrian's earlier charter could have been added to the stock of English canons as a seal on the third archdiocese. Thus texts were not enough on their own to undo what had been done, but they could be selectively activated in contemporary negotiations, in this case combined with an attack on the memory of Offa's character and motivation.

Cœnwulf appears to have resisted the loss of Mercian control over the southern metropolitan by appealing to the pope to authorise its transfer from Canterbury to London.[123] He justified this on the basis of a letter to Augustine 'read throughout our churches' in which Pope Gregory envisioned 'two metropolitan bishops of London and York'.[124] However, by fighting on the terrain of papally authorised texts Cœnwulf had ceded the battlefield to his bishops and their ally in Rome, and he was easily outflanked by Pope Leo, who appealed to 'the canons' and to 'the order that was arranged by our predecessors' in order to justify leaving the metropolitan at Canterbury.[125] There is no indication that the king had support from any of his bishops on this matter, even from Æthelheard, who is otherwise considered by Cubitt to have been a 'Mercian ecclesiastical stooge'.[126] In their reverence for the canons,

---

[118] *Alcuin ep.*, No. 128 (*EHD* 1, 789–90).
[119] *Alcuin ep.*, No. 122 (*EHD* 1, 786–8).
[120] Haddan and Stubbs, *Councils*, pp. 521–3 (*EHD* 1, pp. 791–3, at p. 792).
[121] S 1431a.
[122] *Alcuin ep.*, No. 127.
[123] Brooks, *Early history of the church of Canterbury*, pp. 123–5.
[124] *Alcuin ep.*, No. 127.
[125] *Alcuin ep.*, No. 127.
[126] Cubitt, *Church councils*, p. 216.

the bishops may have formed a united textual community against the Mercian king. Unfortunately we have no record of Hygeberht's voice in all this, but he may well have found it hard to deny the strength of feeling displayed by his fellow bishops on this issue, and perhaps even helped the process along. Hygeberht last attested a charter as archbishop in 799;[127] he witnessed a charter of 801 as a simple bishop, although he is listed before the archbishop of Canterbury, indicating some form of primacy.[128] In a charter of 803, the last surviving document to include his attestation, he is styled as abbot, indicating that he had resigned his episcopal rank;[129] indeed, his successor at Lichfield, Ealdwulf, attested the charter of 801 alongside Hygeberht, perhaps suggesting that the latter had already resigned his see (probably soon after Æthelheard was restored to Canterbury in 798) and was now *episcopus emeritus*.[130] This sequence of titles indicates that Hygeberht's personal dignity continued to be respected throughout the process.

The texts surrounding the abolishment of the archdiocese of Lichfield thus illustrate the workings of this extensive textual community, encompassing the sees of the English Church but stretching to a crucial anchor in Rome. The members of this community informed and justified their actions with regard to an ever-increasing body of texts authorised by the approval of the popes. The identities and authority of the bishops were partly suspended in these texts, so that their lives were bound up with maintaining the appearance of textual integrity. This no doubt aroused emotive responses, and Cubitt has suggested that, while the division of sees had in fact occurred peacefully in the past after the death of one bishop and before the consecration of successors, Offa's division of Canterbury's province while its incumbent, Jænberht, still lived would have been found deeply insulting, and that it was only 'Hygeberht's retirement [that] enabled the new province of Lichfield to be demoted'.[131] Offa, at the height of his power, successfully repressed any episcopal outcry in 787, but Cœnwulf, in the first tender years of his reign, not yet securely established and perhaps more in need of the support of the English Church, was unable to do the same. Thus, in the early ninth century, the English ecclesiastical community was able to face down the ruler of the leading English kingdom.

The English Church from the late ninth century

Cubitt has noted that the evidence for church councils after Ecgberht's conquest of the south in 825 declines rapidly (and none were held at *Clofesho* after this year);[132] three further synods are known from the years before the Viking ravaging of London in 851, an event which inaugurated a period during which the extent of raiding in the region may have severely limited the ability of bishops from across the English

---

127 S 155.
128 S 158.
129 S 1431b.
130 S 158.
131 Cubitt, *Church councils*, p. 233.
132 Cubitt, *Church councils*, pp. 235–6.

kingdoms to assemble in council together.[133] The decline before 851 may be more apparent than real, as after 836 neither of the two remaining known synods was attended by a king; Cubitt suggests that the more pertinent issue here is the inability or unwillingness of Mercian kings to attend or make use of synods soon after 836, and she connects this with the expanding power of the kingdom of Wessex.[134] Cubitt also points to the fact that archbishops appear to have lost the right to adjudicate cases related to ecclesiastical property, which henceforth occurred at royal assemblies, and speculates that an agreement between the West Saxon kings Ecgberht and Æthelwulf and Archbishop Ceolnoth of Canterbury in 838, which allowed the kings to exercise lay lordship over monasteries while the archbishop retained spiritual lordship, might have excluded the archbishop's right to intervene in such cases.[135] It is thus clear that the regular convocation of synods may have continued up to the middle of the century, but that their nature changed in important respects during this time, whether one chooses to assign the causes of that change to the agreement of 838 or to a more gradual shift in attitudes.

It is difficult to say much at all of synodal activity in the late ninth, tenth and eleventh centuries. Cubitt highlights the role of an expanded royal government, such as the shire courts, in adjudicating cases concerning ecclesiastical property from the later tenth century, but also points to the importance of large assemblies convened by English kings during the tenth century, noting that two (in 941×946 and 989×990) held at London were explicitly called 'synods'.[136] Beginning, perhaps, in the reign of Edward the Elder (899–924), for which the evidence is patchy, more certainly established by the reign of his successor Æthelstan (924–39) and extending through to the reign of the last king of this dynasty, Edward the Confessor (942–1066), bishops from across England attended royally convened councils, their attendance largely correlated with the territories then within the direct power of these kings.[137] Levi Roach, in his study of this English assembly politics in the late ninth and tenth centuries, has suggested that 'the national synod was taken under the aegis of the *witan*, which might be both [royal] assembly and church council', during this period.[138] His broader point, that the nature of assemblies during this period might not be served by too rigid a distinction between royal council and church synod (hence an inclusive sense of the latter term in contemporary documents), is important, but it is surely worth emphasising also the difference between this situation and that prevailing during the late seventh, eighth and early ninth centuries: in the earlier context councils attended by all Southumbrian bishops were convened by the archbishop of Canterbury and held at a small number of places in the London region; in the later context, councils attended by many English bishops were convened by the king and held at a greater number of places within the region south of the Thames (so-called 'Greater Wessex'), and only occasionally north of it.

---

133 The three synods were: *In cræft*, 836 (S 190); *Æt astran*, 839 (S 1438); and London, 845 (S 1194).
134 Cubitt, *Church councils*, pp. 236–8.
135 Cubitt, *Church councils*, pp. 237–8; the agreement is referenced in S 1438 and S 281.
136 Cubitt, *Church councils*, pp. 238–9.
137 Keynes, *Atlas*, Tables 33, 37, 41, 44, 54, 60, 60a, 60b, 66, and 72.
138 Roach, *Kingship and consent*, p. 23.

Lichfield and the Lands of St Chad

From the reign of Æthelstan a 'diplomatic mainstream' has been identified in many of the surviving charters, established by the draftsman–scribe Æthelstan A and continuing to the Norman Conquest, in which the witness-lists 'show remarkable consistency in the ordering of attestations across draftsmen and archives'.[139] It is surely significant that, of the 'Mercian' bishops of Lichfield, Worcester, Hereford, Dorchester (successor to Leicester) and Lindsey, only the see of Worcester is represented in the attestations of charters from 936 (immediately after the end of the floruit of 'Æthelstan A') until about 960, or perhaps a little later, when the bishop of Lichfield started to attest more regularly. The bishopric of Dorchester was by this time in the hands of Oscytel, who was also archbishop of York and thus attested regularly;[140] however, after the death of Oscytel in 971 the bishop of Dorchester did not attest regularly until the beginning of the reign of Æthelred II, and the bishop of Lindsey attested only very sporadically through that king's reign.[141] Nevertheless, two sets of charters outside the mainstream, those known as the 'Alliterative' group and those ascribed to the draftsman–scribe 'Dunstan B', indicate that the bishops of the Mercian sees did attend royal councils for the most part during much of this period. Both sets of charters feature more inclusive witness-lists, and regularly record bishops of Lichfield at councils alongside their peers from the early 940s into the mid-970s.[142] Charters witnessed at councils convened by Edgar between the years 957 and 959, when he was king of Mercia and Northumbria, but not of Wessex, also reveal the bishop of Lichfield alongside the bishops of Dorchester (who also held York), Worcester, Hereford and Lindsey, as well as those of Chester-le-Street and Elmham, who were also absent from the mainstream diplomatic of charters during much the same period as the Mercian bishops.[143]

---

139 Roach, *Kingship and consent*, p. 34, who also uses the term 'diplomatic mainstream'. Much of the work of identifying this mainstream has been undertaken by Simon Keynes in *The diplomas of King Æthelred 'the Unready' 978–1016* (Cambridge, 1980), pp. 1–153 and 'Regenbald the Chancellor (sic)', *Anglo-Norman Studies*, 10 (1988), pp. 185–222.

140 Keynes, *Atlas*, Tables 37, 41, 44 and 54. Note that Keynes assigns a bishop named Ælfric to the see of Hereford between the years 939/40 and 951, but it is more likely that he should be assigned to the sees of Sherborne and Ramsbury in succession: a charter of 939 concerning land in Dorset (S 445) may be addressed to him; there are no attestations certainly assignable to a bishop of Sherborne between 936 and 943, when Bishop Wulfsige begins to attest; there are no attestations assignable to a bishop of Ramsbury between late in 941 and 951 (the year of Ælfric's latest surviving attestation), when Bishop Osulf begins to attest; and Bishop Wulfhelm of Hereford, who had featured in the witness-lists of the charters of 'Æthelstan A' between 931 and 935, probably also appears in the witness-list of an undated charter alongside Ælfric (S 1497).

141 The sees of Lindsey and Dorchester may have been held in plurality by Bishops Leofwine, Ælfnoth and Æscwig during the late tenth century. One final bishop of Lindsey, Sigeferth, attests a set of charters between 996 and 1004 (Keynes, *Atlas*, Tables 60a and 60b).

142 Keynes, *Atlas*, Tables 41, 44 and 54.

143 S 674, S 679, S 677, S 675 and S 681. Three charters of the 'Dunstan B' group also belong to this period (S 678, S 676 and S 676a).

Lichfield and the English Church

There is no obvious interpretation of this pattern. It is possible that four of the Mercian bishops were considered to be somehow dependent on the fifth, the bishop of Worcester, from late in Æthelstan's reign to the reign of Edgar, when significant administrative reforms, including the establishment of shires and hundreds across much of England, may have altered the way the Midland regions were perceived.[144] The phenomenon certainly emphasises a peripheral aspect to the Midlands during this period, outside the southern focus of the royal dynasty of England; indeed, the territory covered by the sees of those bishops who did attest the mainstream charters regularly between 936 and c.960 overlaps very closely with the territory within which the vast majority of royal councils were held in the late ninth and tenth centuries.[145] The nature of the evidence for these councils indicates a hierarchy that applied during royal conventions, and we have no way of knowing whether a similar hierarchy was at play among the bishops of the kingdom at any associated church council sessions, although the close entanglement of secular and religious politics during this period implies the possibility that it was.

It may be significant that we know next to nothing of the bishops of the four Mercian sees absent from the mainstream diplomatic before Edgar's reign, although the patchy nature of the evidence is such that this may not be surprising. Nevertheless, it is notable that there is enough evidence to highlight the importance of Bishop Cœnwald of Worcester (928×929–958), who may have started his career as priest in Æthelstan's household, as a bishop was entrusted with a diplomatic mission to Germany, and was probably responsible in some way for the 'Alliterative' group of charters.[146] It is possible that Bishop Ælfwine of Lichfield (903×915–935×941) played an important role in Æthelstan's government, as he is nearly always listed immediately following the two archbishops in the witness-lists of the 'Æthelstan A' charters, and may indeed have had some connection with that draftsman–scribe.[147] However, following Ælfwine's tenure we can say nothing of bishops of Lichfield until much later

---

144 G. Molyneaux, *The formation of the English kingdom in the tenth century* (Oxford, 2015), pp. 116–230.
145 The relevant sees are: Canterbury, Rochester, Selsey, London, Winchester, Ramsbury, Sherborne, Crediton, Wells and, from 942, the archbishop of York. Bishops of Rochester and Wells disappear from the mainstream in the reign of Eadred (946–55), although probable candidates, Bishops Beorhtsige and Wulfhelm, are recorded in 'Alliterative' and 'Dunstan B' charters. During Edgar's reign a Bishop Ælfstan could be assigned to the sees of London or Rochester, and a Bishop Ælfwold could be assigned to Sherborne or Crediton; the lack of a second bishop to fill the other see in each case may indicate that both these bishops held two sees in plurality. See Roach, *Kinship and Consent*, pp. 53–64, for the locations of royal councils between 871 and 978.
146 Lapidge et al., *Encyclopaedia*, pp. 273–5 ('Koenwald').
147 S.E. Kelly, *Charters of Abingdon abbey, Part I*, Anglo-Saxon Charters 7 (Oxford, 2000), pp. 102–3; S. Foot, *Athelstan: the first king of England* (New Haven, 2011), p. 98; Foot's suggestion that the bishop and draftsman-scribe were one and the same does not necessarily follow, as the mainstream diplomatic that follows the retirement or death of 'Æthelstan A' does not include the bishop of Lichfield in witness-lists, and so it is not possible to state exactly when Ælfwine retired or died.

in the tenth century. Incidental notices inform us that Ælfheah, 'bishop of the church of the people of Lichfield' (975–1002×1004), had been a monk in Æthelwold's Old Minster in Winchester;[148] and Bishop Cynesige (946×949–963×964) was a kinsman of Dunstan, the abbot of Glastonbury who replaced Cœnwald as bishop of Worcester (957–59) and later became archbishop of Canterbury (959–88).[149] These connections with privileged southern churches and the men that ruled them should probably be set beside the emergence of the Mercian bishoprics into the mainstream diplomatic of Edgar's reign, both probably symptoms of the closer integration of the Midlands into the English kingdom (and perhaps the English Church) at this time.

Conclusions

This chapter has sought to demonstrate the importance of the English ecclesiastical community during the early medieval period, and it remains only to make a few final points. First, it is crucial to re-emphasise the distinction between the English ecclesiastical community and the English Church. In line with the principles outlined in the Introduction, this community is here defined by the creation, maintenance and development of ritualised practices in specific environments, which acted to normalise certain experiences of personhood. In this case, the regular assembly of English bishops and other ecclesiastics (divided between two assemblies, Northumbrian and Southumbrian, after 735) is key, as is the regular and repeated use of specific textual instruments to enshrine the self-understanding of this group and to define roles within it. In contrast, the English Church was an imagined community of contemporary discourse, often denoting the corporate body of all English Christians, and/or the hierarchical structure in which they were organised. The English ecclesiastical community, as a tool of historical interpretation, cannot necessarily be equated with the meanings intended by those who used the term 'English Church' during the period. The English ecclesiastical community comprised an elite, whose core members were the bishops, abbots, abbesses and select monks, nuns and priests of the dioceses; they assembled regularly, and their roles were embodied in engagements with texts, especially those conferring canonical authority of various kinds. We might also define a broader 'associative field', a larger social entity constituted by the repeated use of conglomerations of associated norms, but with a more fluid, less structured form. This field was populated not only by members of the English ecclesiastical community, which essentially crystallised out of it, but also by people whose engagement with this community was less regular but nonetheless important; this included ecclesiastics from other church communities, both within and without England, and in particular the pope and members of the Roman church, whose ultimate spiritual authority was

---

148 Recorded in the *Liber Vitae* of the New Minster: W. de G. Birch, *Liber Vitae: register and martyrology of New Minster and Hyde Abbey Winchester* (London and Winchester, 1888), pp. 22–3.

149 Stated in the tenth-century *Life* of St Dunstan written by 'B': 'Vita Sancti Dunstani, auctore B' in W. Stubbs (ed.), *Memorials of St Dunstan, archbishop of Canterbury* (London, 1874), pp. 3–52, at p. 32; *Cynesius*, Dunstan's *consanguineus*, is called a bishop but not given a see, although only one Cynesige appears in charters of the time, and he was the bishop of Lichfield.

appealed to on several occasions. This field, characterised by the spiritual form of the norms that it enabled, thus stretched from the British Isles via parts of Francia to northern Italy and Rome, defined by the networks of movement, interaction and encounter that maintained it in a dynamic relationship with the tighter knots of communities within it.

This chapter has focused on relations and activities *within* this elite ecclesiastical community, but it is also important to emphasise the extent to which this activity was grounded in a hierarchical relationship with members of the wider society that supported it. Crucial here is the idea that the acceptance of Christian baptism created an understanding of personhood centred on the soul. Bede's tale of a thegn at the Northumbrian king Edwin's court is instructive: the thegn argues in favour of the adoption of Christianity by likening his present understanding of life to a sparrow flying into a fire-lit hall in winter and then out the other side, the fleeting brightness of a human life contrasted with the darkness of his ignorance about what lay beyond; Christianity, the thegn suggests, provides knowledge of what came before an individual's life and what follows it.[150] Engaging with the normative ideas of Christianity inevitably meant discovering one had a soul with a destiny; and, moreover, that its ultimate destination remained uncertain until the End Times, but could be affected by efforts made for its health during life. That such efforts might be proposed, guided and judged by bishops and their priests was as much an element of such discovery as the soul itself, reinforced by the ritualised sacramental roles of the clergy. The introduction and acceptance of Christianity thus constructed a new set of affective norms, spiritual norms, through which subjects sought to define themselves. The self-fashioning of members of the clergy involved a dialectical act that also personified other people, asserting a hierarchal relationship through which these clerics apprehended members of their broader society as flocks of souls and themselves as shepherds set over them. To this extent we might speak of a normative 'spiritual lordship' that the bishops and their clergy sought to impose and exercise as spiritual lords in their relations with lay people, but which also acted as the basis for ideas of hierarchy within their own ecclesiastical communities.

This chapter has also drawn attention to the emergence of a broader hybrid elite, rooted in both spiritual and worldly hierarchies, of which the English ecclesiastical community formed one distinctive part. The diocese of Lichfield can be understood on the one hand as an imagined community within the broader English Church, ruled by bishops whose authority stemmed from their roles in the maintenance and reproduction of the English ecclesiastical community. On the other hand, these bishops were members of an aristocracy focused on the royal dynasties of kings, and therefore bound by concerns that cut across the ecclesiastical community, often following the more fluid boundaries of hegemonies; we can usefully here speak in terms of regnal communities, whose members assembled regularly at the courts of their kings, their roles grounded in their exercise of worldly forms of lordship over people in the wider society. The extent to which the ecclesiastical and regnal elements of this broader, if decentred, ecclesio-regnal community were experienced as distinct

---

150 *HE,* ii.14.

from one another varied over time. Indeed, it might be argued that identifying a distinct English ecclesiastical community implies a degree of continuity in form that is in fact illusory. The identification will be maintained here because bishops continued to assemble and to collectively maintain their spiritual lordship within an imagined English Church throughout the period, even if the church councils of the eighth and early ninth centuries and the assemblies of the *witan* in the tenth and eleventh centuries were distinctly different affairs. Developments across the period are better understood not as the linear progressions of institutions but as a series of unique conjunctions, each born out of conditions inherited from the past but created and directed by contemporary concerns and motivations. At each conjunction the English ecclesiastical community can be identified, but the apprehensions and actions of its members might be understood quite differently in each case.

Several such conjunctions have been explored in this chapter. The stabilisation of English regnal communities around their respective royal dynasties appears to have occurred during the episcopate of Archbishop Theodore, whose creation of a far more coherent English ecclesiastical community may well have driven this process. Here, worldly and spiritual elements of this developing hybrid elite interacted in a mutually beneficial fashion, its members establishing authoritative roles for themselves that their successors were able to maintain for a considerable amount of time; however, it should not be imagined that this was achieved without tension and conflict, as the case of Bishop Chad will demonstrate in Chapter 2. Another important conjunction played out over the last two decades of the eighth century, when Offa brought his own expanding Mercian regnal community into closer relationship with the English ecclesiastical community. His creation of the archbishopric of Lichfield illustrates the extent to which authority generated in one community implied some degree of authority in the other, and might be used to affect the conditions of both; tension and resistance to such alterations appear to have been sublimated into an allegiance to the Mercian king's overbearing power during his reign, but the establishment of a greater degree of independence for spiritual lords emerged as an urgent project after Offa's death. Indeed, the heightened sense of self-identity visible in the compilation α may well have formed an active response to the threat represented by the kind of power wielded by Offa.

The compilation α appears from its initial inception to have included a list of popes, a list of the seventy-two disciples of Christ, the English episcopal lists, royal genealogies and regnal lists (the latter for Mercia and Northumbria only); essentially, it established a framework for the passage of time defined by the spread of Christianity into the world, but with a special focus on Rome and England, where bishoprics were established with the support of the kings.[151] The pegs of this construct comprise the names of popes, disciples, bishops and kings, whose authority stemmed from their ultimate relationship with Christ, and whose sequential listing expressed a definitive vision of the establishment and propagation of these authorities up to the end of the eighth century; the compilation of α was thus designed to express a particular vision of the past. Within this vision, it is the episcopal participation that impresses: the royal

---

151 Dumville, 'Anglian collection', p. 24.

genealogies were out of date for Kent, East Anglia and Wessex as much in 765 as in 796×814, but all the episcopal lists, at least in Southumbria, were up to date in α. A triumphant vision of the English Church as an institution emerges, presented as such to solidify the affective presence of the ecclesiastical element within the broader elite community. The precise context of its compilation will remain a mystery, but might easily be conceived as part of the campaign of Archbishop Æthelheard and his peers to tame King Cœnwulf's ambitions, or perhaps to set the seal on their victory at some point in the early years of Archbishop Wulfred, whose own battles with the impact of lay power on spiritual concerns brought him into renewed conflict with the Mercian king.[152]

The importance of the explicitly ecclesiastical discourse emphasised here continued through the first half of the ninth century; this is perhaps attested by the fact that thirteen of the seventeen bishoprics listed in the recension of α contained in the manuscript Cotton Vespasian B VI were brought up to date in c.833, indicating a continued interest in the shape of the broader ecclesiastical community at the place where this manuscript was kept, thought to be somewhere in Mercia.[153] Nevertheless, the events of subsequent decades appear to have disrupted existing structures to a considerable extent, and the next conjunction highlighted by this chapter, plausibly centred on the reign of Æthelstan, 'king of the English', represents a notably distinct rearrangement of familiar elements. From the early tenth century the English ecclesiastical community was integrated with the English regnal community to a far greater degree, most obviously manifested in the fact that they shared the same geographical extent and assembled regularly together. The situation in these centuries, including a distinct coalescence of spiritual and regnal elements of this hybrid community, will be further explored in later chapters. First, however, the scale of analysis needs to be reduced to the diocese of Lichfield itself. The roles of the bishops and significant clergy of the diocese might have been suspended in the English ecclesiastical community, but their day-to-day existence as bishops of the 'Church of Lichfield' relied on their places within regional and local communities; the next chapter explores some of these.

---

152 Brooks, *Early history of the church of Canterbury*, pp. 175–206.
153 Page, 'Episcopal lists', pp. 75–6: curiously, for a Mercian manuscript, this operation omitted Lindsey and Hereford, as well as Rochester and Hexham.

Chapter 2

The Church of Lichfield

The life of Chad, fifth bishop of the Mercians, occupies an interesting conjunction in the history of ecclesiastical communities in England. In the decades before his appointment to the Mercian see in 669 the activities of ecclesiastical men and women had been shaped by the politics of overkingships. First, the mission sent by Pope Gregory I to the English, led by St Augustine, had arrived in 597 and managed to convert the Kentish king Æthelberht, and then other kings within his overkingship. Later, in 634, a second mission from the Irish monastery on Iona had been invited to convert the people of Northumbria by its newly established king Oswald, and proceeded to spread its efforts into territories taken into his overkingship and those of his northern successors. Such endeavours involved people such as Chad's brother Cedd, who was sent by Oswald's brother Oswiu to convert the people of his subking in the East Saxon kingdom. Greatly extended ecclesiastical communities thus spanned the length and breadth of the large territories under the sway of these overkings, and so straddled the boundaries of the provincial kingdoms that gained greater coherence from the 670s. After Chad's death in 672 ecclesiastical communities were increasingly shaped through the developing structures of the English ecclesiastical community, explored in the previous chapter, and in particular by the diocesan communities of the bishops, whose bounds were staked out within the borders of the provincial kingdoms. This chapter explores the development of these different forms of ecclesiastical community, and Chad's place in them, within the diocese of Lichfield. The first half of the chapter explores Chad's life, and the extended community that he and his brother Cedd created, based at the various minsters they founded, including Lichfield. Chad's subsequent importance to this community as one of its founding saints informed the activities of bishops of Lichfield in later centuries, who worked to create a coherent diocesan community across the north-west Midlands; this process is explored in the second half of the chapter.

The Lastingham narrative

The known details of Chad's life are found in two eighth-century texts: Stephen of Ripon's *Life of Bishop Wilfrid*, probably written at Ripon soon after the death of its subject in 710, and Bede's *Ecclesiastical History of the English People*, completed at Jarrow in 731.[1]

---

[1] B. Colgrave, *The life of Bishop Wilfrid by Eddius Stephanus. Text, translation, and notes* (Cambridge, 1927); C. Plummer, *Venerabilis Bedae opera historica* (Oxford, 1896); B. Colgrave and R.A.B. Mynors (eds), *Bede's Ecclesiastical History of the English People* (Oxford, 1969). Bede appears to have been involved in slight editorial alterations to his work up to his death in 735, probably resulting in the two recensions now recognised by scholars, c-type and m-type, from which all extant manuscript witnesses derive: see J. Story, 'After Bede: continuing the Ecclesiastical History', in Stephen Baxter, C.E. Karkov and J. Nelson (eds), *Early medieval studies in memory of Patrick Wormald* (Farnham, 2009), pp. 165–84, at pp. 166–8.

These works enable us, with a little inference, to construct an approximate chronology of Chad's life. He was probably born in the mid-630s, and was a disciple of Aidan, bishop of Lindisfarne;[2] he might have been fostered with the bishop alongside his brother Cedd (who was certainly brought up at Lindisfarne) and perhaps also their brothers Cælin and Cynebil, as all four grew up to become clerics.[3] Aidan died in 651, when Chad was perhaps in his early or mid-teens.[4] Chad spent a period of time studying in Ireland with a man named Ecgberht when they were both 'youths' (*adolescentes*); as Ecgberht was born in 638/9, their time together must date to the mid- to late 650s or early 660s, although we do not know whether Chad went to Ireland with Ecgberht or met him when already there.[5] According to Bede, many of the English went to Ireland to study or to live an ascetic life during the episcopates of Aidan's successors, Finan and Colman (651–64).[6] In 664 Cedd died in a plague, having bequeathed to Chad the abbacy of a monastery he had founded at Lastingham (*Laestingaeu*), located in the foothills of the North York Moors in the Northumbrian subkingdom of Deira; this event probably acted to recall Chad from Ireland.[7] Later that year Chad was consecrated bishop of the Northumbrians, an office he carried out for five years before being deposed in 669 by Archbishop Theodore, a crucial event in his life that is discussed further below.[8] Soon afterwards he was appointed to the bishopric of the Mercians, and settled the see at Lichfield, ruling it until he died of plague on 2 March 672; he was probably only in his mid- to late thirties.[9]

Much of this narrative is gleaned from Bede's work, although Bede was born in the year of Chad's death, 672, or perhaps the year after, so cannot have had any personal recollection of him; Bede's sources of information about Chad must be sought elsewhere.[10] It was suggested in Chapter 1 that Bede made use of a Mercian episcopal memorandum, probably received from Canterbury, concerning the succession of the Mercian bishops up to Bishop Winfrith. This putative source would account for one

---

2   *HE*, iii.28. Chad was consecrated bishop of the Northumbrians in 664, by which time we might expect him to be about thirty, so he was probably born during a period centred on 635.
3   For Cedd's upbringing at Lindisfarne see *HE*, iii.23. The passage introduces some small confusion, as it is ambiguous concerning whether Cedd or his brother Cynebil (who had completed the consecration of the site at Lastingham when Cedd was summoned by the king) built the minster at Lastingham 'and established in it the Rule of Lindisfarne, where he had been brought up'; however, the general sense of the text emphasises Cedd's role as the founder and first abbot of Lastingham, implying that the sentence should be read in reference to Cedd.
4   Aidan died on 31 August 651 (see *HE*, iii.14 and v.24).
5   *HE*, iv.3. Ecgberht died on 24 April 729 at the age of ninety, so must have been born between 25 April 638 and 24 April 639 (*HE*, iii.27 and v.22).
6   *HE*, iii.27.
7   Chad had apparently come from Ireland when he was consecrated to the bishopric of Northumbria in 664 (*VW*, c.14).
8   *HE*, iii.28 and iv.2.
9   *HE*, iv.3.
10 *HE*, v.24.

purely nominal reference to Chad in the *Ecclesiastical History*.[11] The source of all the other references appears to be revealed by a statement in Bede's preface:

> I learned from the brethren of the minster known as Lastingham which was founded by Cedd and Chad, how through the ministry of these devoted priests of Christ, the kingdom of Mercia achieved the faith of Christ which it had never known, and how the kingdom of Essex recovered the faith, which it had formerly neglected. I also learned from the monks of Lastingham about the life and death of these two fathers.[12]

Sure enough, if the references to Cedd and Chad are extracted from Bede's text and laid together, they form a coherent narrative that begins with Cedd's assignment to evangelise the Middle Angles in 652, followed by his career as bishop of the East Saxons, his foundation of the monastery at Lastingham and his death there in 664.[13] The narrative continues with Chad's succession to the abbacy of Lastingham in the same year and his successive appointment to the bishoprics of the Northumbrians and the Mercians, and ends with his death at Lichfield in 672.[14] We are thus presented with a history of the first two abbots of Lastingham. The 'original' version of this text, composed at some point in the period 672–731, presumably at Lastingham, does not survive; we only have it refracted through Bede's *Ecclesiastical History*, but this does at least offer a representation of it. The text as extracted from Bede's work will hereafter be labelled the Lastingham Narrative (LN).

In fact, there are two reasons to suppose that Bede made a fairly faithful copy of the exemplar of the LN into his *Ecclesiastical History*, the first textual, the second thematic. The former involves an extended section of the LN concerning Chad's death at Lichfield, constructed around two perspectives: the first apparently derived from the account of one of Chad's monks, a man named Owine;[15] the second concerning the holy man Ecgberht in Ireland. The first part explains that Chad had built a 'more retired dwelling-place not far from the church [at Lichfield], in which he could read and pray privately with a few of his brothers, that is to say, seven or eight of them; this he did as often as he was free from his labours and from the ministration of the Word'.[16] It was in this structure, when he was alone one day, that Chad was visited by a company of angel spirits, come to summon him to heaven, who promised they would

---

11 *HE*, iii.24.
12 *HE*, preface.
13 *HE*, iii.21, iii.22, iii.23, iii.25, iii.26 and iv.3. The evangelisation of the Middle Angles is said to have begun two years before Penda's death (*HE*, iii.21), and thus in 652; Bede gives 653 (*HE*, v.24), but appears to have misdated Penda's death to 655.
14 *HE*, iii.21, iii.22, iii.23, iii.28, iv.2, iv.3 and v.19; in addition, some of the details of the narrative are repeated in iii.24. Cedd's appearance as an interpreter at the synod of Whitby (*HE*, iii.25 and iii.26) is probably derived from Bede's source for the council rather than the LN.
15 Owine is prominent in the tale, and at one point Owine's actions are followed by the words 'as he afterwards related'.
16 *HE*, iv.3.

return for him in seven days.[17] Chad reported this solely to Owine (as the disciple had heard the angels singing), and told him to tell no one until after Chad's death. Subsequently Chad explained to his assembled brethren that his death was close, '"for", he said, "the beloved guest who has been in the habit of visiting our brothers has deigned to come today to me also, to summon me from this world."'[18] The identity of the 'beloved guest' at this point in the narrative remains mysterious; sure enough, Chad sickened of a plague that struck the minster, dying seven days later, and 'in the company of angels, as one may rightly believe, sought the joys of heaven'.[19]

At this point the narrative changes direction to include an anecdote explicitly in Bede's voice concerning his tutor in the scriptures at Jarrow, a man named Trumberht, who had earlier been educated in one of Chad's minsters (perhaps Lastingham) under his Rule, and remembered how Chad considered thunderstorms to be teachers of both a fear of and love for God.[20] After this the section concerning Ecgberht begins as follows: 'This brother's account of the bishop's death also agrees with the story of a vision related by the most reverend father Ecgberht ... .'[21] As Trumberht's anecdote does not concern Chad's death, this can only refer to Owine's account, which must originally have immediately preceded it; this indicates that Bede had inserted his own account into a pre-existing text, and at this point had copied from that text directly, neglecting to modify the phrasing to account for his own interpolation. Such close copying is also supported by Andrew Breeze, who has suggested that Bede copied another part of the LN from a pre-existing text, specifically a closely structured list of locations in which Chad preached when travelling throughout Northumbria, which is not common in Bede's style.[22]

The second reason to argue for Bede's faithful representation of the LN is prompted by its narrative coherence and thematic unity. One obvious example of this is Ecgberht's vision, just referred to, which draws on Ecgberht's shared history with Chad, both having lived the monastic life together as youths in Ireland, 'diligently engaged in prayer and fasting and meditating on the divine Scriptures'.[23] When Chad later returned to Britain, Ecgberht remained in Ireland, gaining much renown as a holy man, and many years later was visited by Hygebald, an abbot from Lindsey. The two men got to talking about the lives of earlier church fathers and Chad was mentioned, 'whereupon Ecgberht said, "I know a man in this island, still in the flesh, who saw the soul of Chad's brother Cedd descend from the sky with a host of angels and return to the heavenly kingdom, taking Chad's soul with him."'[24] The tale thus reveals the identity of the 'beloved guest' of Owine's story, a narrative consummation that is

---

17 *HE*, iv.3.
18 *HE*, iv.3.
19 *HE*, iv.3.
20 *HE*, iv.3.
21 *HE*, iv.3.
22 A. Breeze, 'Bede's *castella* and the journeys of St Chad', *Northern History*, 46/1 (2009), pp. 137–9, at p. 137.
23 *HE*, iv.3.
24 *HE*, iv.3.

marred by Bede's interruption. More broadly, different elements of the LN connect with each other despite their separation in different chapters of Bede's *Ecclesiastical History*. For example, when he is sent by King Oswiu to Kent for ordination, Chad is described as 'modest in his ways, learned in the scriptures, and zealous in carrying out their teachings';[25] later in the same section, as bishop of the Northumbrians, Chad 'immediately devoted himself to the task of keeping the Church in truth and purity, to the practice of humility and temperance, and to study'; and, when visiting the different parts of his diocese to preach the gospel, he travelled 'not on horse-back but on foot after the apostolic example'.[26] Such praiseworthy qualities might be reckoned typical of hagiography such as this, but the particular and repeated emphasis on Chad's humility sets up important elements of the account of his deposition from the Northumbrian see (discussed further below) and his time as bishop of the Mercians, which again greatly emphasise Chad's humility, but were placed by Bede not only in a different chapter but also a different book within his work.[27] Other connections, more casual in nature, might also be invoked to support the unity of the LN. For example, as bishop of the Northumbrians Chad is said to have behaved as 'one of Aidan's disciples and sought to instruct his hearers in the ways and customs of his master and of his brother Cedd', a neat reference back to the first section of the LN concerning Cedd.[28]

The LN belongs to a recognisable genre of texts describing the founders and early rulers of English minsters: the two versions of the *Historia Abbatum* of Wearmouth-Jarrow (the earlier anonymous, the later by Bede) form a notable example, but we can also invoke the house chronicle that informed Bede's knowledge of the minster at Barking, or even the narrative concerning the foundation of Minster-in-Thanet represented by the so-called Kentish Royal Legend.[29] As a product of the collective knowledge of the community at Lastingham, or at least certain members of it, the Lastingham narrative appears to have relied in several instances on the reminiscences of individuals who are explicitly identified, such as Owine and Ecgberht (or perhaps his interlocutor, Hygebald) who feature in the account of Chad's death discussed above. In other instances the relation of events and their import probably relied on knowledge more widely known, a product of the sharing and negotiation of memories among members of the Lastingham community. The horizon of this group memory, as far as it is represented in the narrative, concerns events of the year 652, when Cedd was sent as part of a mission to the Mercian kingdom with Peada and his Northumbrian wife. The end of the LN is less easy to identify, as it is unclear what information in Bede's *Ecclesiastical History* should be ascribed to it beyond that which directly bears on Cedd and Chad. Bede may well have derived short passages about Winfrith and Seaxwulf, Chad's successors as bishops of Lichfield, from the LN's exemplar, if only

---

25   *HE*, iii.28.
26   *HE*, iii.28.
27   *HE*, iv.2 and iv.3.
28   *HE*, iii.28.
29   Bede's *Historia Abbatum*: Plummer, *Venerabilis Bedae opera historica*, vol. 1, pp. 364–404; The Barking house chronicle: *HE*, iv.6 to iv.10; Kentish Royal Legend: S. Hollis, 'The Minster-in-Thanet foundation story', *Anglo-Saxon England*, 27 (1998), pp. 41–64, at p. 57.

because he appears otherwise uninformed about Mercian history.[30] Details about the treatment of Chad's relics (to be discussed in Chapter 3) must also be included in the LN. It is interesting to note that the LN does not include any mention of Seaxwulf's successor, Bishop Headda, as a notice in the Lichfield Chronicle appended to his entry in the episcopal list explains that 'through this Bishop Headda the church of the people of Lichfield was constructed, 31st December 700; and the bones of St Chad, bishop, were translated inside it'.[31] Taken as a whole, this derives from no known source; it is possible that Alan of Ashbourne combined the fact of Chad's translation into a newly built church of St Peter, taken from the LN, with details concerning the construction of an early church at Lichfield derived from a calendar or perhaps even a surviving dedication inscription.[32] Headda's church can be plausibly connected with the church described in the LN into which Chad's relics were translated.

We must now consider the forms of community that might lie behind the production of the LN's exemplar, and those that we might identify within its narrative. It might seem logical to focus on the individual minster communities invoked by the writers of the narrative: the text was certainly produced within the context of the community at Lastingham, while much of its material on Chad must have come from people at Lichfield who knew Owine's story and could explain the later movements of Chad's relics. We might also point to a minster at Barrow (*Adbaruae*) in Lindsey, which Chad founded on a fifty-hide estate given to him by Wulfhere;[33] Chad's episcopal successor Winfrith (formerly his deacon) later retired there, and is described warmly as 'a good and discreet man' who lived a 'very holy life until his death' at the minster, demonstrating that people at Lastingham were aware of his character and his fate.[34] In contrast, there is nothing in the text to suggest that contact with any of Cedd's East Saxon minsters had been maintained beyond the time of his death.[35] We might thus satisfy ourselves with an impression of the network of contacts discernable behind the LN, but this would be to underestimate the form of community represented here.

The LN places regular emphasis on Rules of monastic life established at each of these minsters: after the founding of Lastingham Cedd 'established in it the religious observances according to the custom of Lindisfarne, where he had been brought up';[36] Chad 'sought to instruct his hearers in the ways and customs of his master [Bishop Aidan] and of his brother Cedd', and when close to death urged his brethren at Lichfield to follow 'the Rule of life which he had taught them and which they had seen him carry out';[37] when commenting on Chad's foundation at Barrow, the LN

---

30 *HE*, iv.3 and iv.6.
31 BL Cott. Cleo. D IX, ff.74v–75r.
32 For other examples of the latter see J. Higgitt, 'The dedication inscription at Jarrow and its context', *Antiquaries Journal*, 59 (1979), pp. 346–74.
33 *HE*, iv.3.
34 *HE*, iv.3 and iv.6.
35 Indeed, the LN includes an account of about thirty monks who came from one of these minsters after Cedd's death to live at Lastingham, close to the body of their founder: *HE*, iii.23.
36 *HE*, iii.23.
37 *HE*, iii.28 and iv.3.

states that 'up to the present day traces of the monastic Rule which he established still survive';[38] and even those in the minsters founded by Cedd among the East Saxons were taught 'to observe the discipline of a Rule, so far as these rough people were capable of receiving it'.[39] Such monastic Rules get to the heart of the communities living at these minsters, defined through the repetition of everyday collective activity, but they are also in a very important sense one Rule, the Rule of Cedd and Chad (and ultimately of Aidan at Lindisfarne). We must conceive of one community that was defined not simply by its location at a minster but by its attachment to specific people and their legacies, a community that needs to be considered as a single unit even though its members might have been dispersed across several different locations. Such communities were somewhat fluid, morphing over time according to the personal histories of their members: in the case of the community of the abbots of Lastingham, the East Saxon minsters appear to have fallen away by the time the LN was written (their members viewed as ultimately incapable of receiving the Rule), and only 'traces' of the Rule remained at Barrow, perhaps drifting from the core community after the death of Winfrith. This community remained centred on the graves of its founders, St Cedd and St Chad.

Bishop Chad and Bishop Wilfrid

Our understanding of this extended form of ecclesiastical community and its importance to episcopal life in the seventh century can be improved by analysing the relationship between Bishop Chad and Bishop Wilfrid. This not only illustrates how such communities might be mobilised, but how events in the lives of their central figures might be enrolled into subsequent structures of remembrance that enabled their persistence. In comparison to Bede's *Ecclesiastical History*, informed by the LN, references to Chad in Stephen of Ripon's *Life of Bishop Wilfrid* are few.[40] They concern the consecration of Chad to the see of York, which previously had apparently been given to Wilfrid, and Wilfrid's recovery of this see after Chad's deposition by Archbishop Theodore. Chad is therefore not much more than an extra, one of many whose lives briefly intersected with Wilfrid's. Stephen is nevertheless a useful source here, for he tells this incident differently to the LN and comments on Chad's character. Stephen may also have remembered the incident personally. He is universally accepted to be identical with 'Aeddi cognomento Stephanus', a master of ecclesiastical chant who Bede states was brought by Wilfrid to Northumbria from Kent. Stephen himself describes this incident, talking of himself in the third person and relating its occurrence at some time between 666 and 669, at the end of which period Chad was deposed and Wilfrid reinstated. Stephen would thus have been a new arrival in Wilfrid's following at the time and, whether he was present at the events surrounding Chad's deposition or heard of them indirectly while teaching at Wilfrid's minsters, the source of his narration must derive from his proximity to the *dramatis personae*.

---

38 *HE*, iv.3.
39 *HE*, iii.22.
40 *VW*, cc. 11, 12, 14 and 15.

The accounts of the events surrounding Chad's tenure of the bishopric of the Northumbrians given by the LN and the *Life of St Wilfrid* are distinctive in many ways.[41] In particular, while Wilfrid is unsurprisingly central to the events related by Stephen, the LN hardly mentions his involvement at all. In what follows the specific differences between the accounts are discussed in relation to four discrete issues, taken chronologically: first, the context of the appointment of Wilfrid and then Chad to, apparently, the same see; second, the nature of the irregularity for which Chad was deposed; third, the context of Chad's subsequent reconsecration; and, fourth, his appointment to the see of Lichfield. We are completely reliant on these two accounts for our knowledge of these episodes, so it is impossible to hold up one as more 'truthful' or 'reliable' than the other. Nevertheless, the very fact of the differences between the accounts points to different ideas about how past events should be remembered, and enables us to 'read between the lines' to speculate on the motives driving each author. This analysis is concluded by a more general consideration of the nature of extended ecclesiastical communities, like those inhabited by both Chad and Wilfrid, and of their relation to diocesan communities.

According to the LN, in 664 King Alhfrith sent the abbot Wilfrid to Gaul for consecration as bishop of his people, but Wilfrid lingered there, and King Oswiu, imitating his son, sent Chad, now abbot of Lastingham, to Kent to be consecrated bishop of York. In Stephen's version no distinction is made between Oswiu and Alhfrith; Wilfrid was elected to the bishopric by both kings and all their counsellors. Instead, Oswiu's later decision to forestall Wilfrid in his see was motivated by envy and the devil, and by the counsel of those who followed liturgical customs prevalent in many Irish churches (and therefore many in Northumbria as well), derogatively referred to as 'those who adhered to the Quartodeciman party in opposition to the rule of the Apostolic See'.[42] There are two cruxes at the heart of the differences between the accounts here. The first is Alhfrith, whom both accounts style 'king' (*rex*) alongside his father; Charles Plummer suggested plausibly that Oswiu had made Alhfrith king of Deira under his own overkingship, as Oswiu's nephew had certainly earlier filled this position, and it is possible that his sons Ecgfrith and Ælfwine did so later.[43] The second crux is the bishopric of York, which appears here in both sources as the see of the Northumbrians, a role previously occupied by Lindisfarne in Bede's work.

There are several possibilities here, of which two are particularly worth considering. First, Alhfrith might have prevailed upon his father to divide the Northumbrian see into two halves so that he could have a bishop of his own (at York in Deira);[44] second, father and son might have agreed on the removal of the Northumbrian see from Lindisfarne to York as part of a restructuring of episcopal arrangements after the departure of the Irish bishop Colman following the synod of Whitby earlier that year.[45]

---

41 *HE*, iii.28, iv.2; *VW*, cc. 11, 12, 14 and 15.
42 *VW*, c.14.
43 Plummer, *Venerabilis Bedae opera historica*, vol. 2, pp. 119–20.
44 This might be supported by the LN's reference to Alhfrith's actions on behalf of 'his' people, indicating only the people of Deira.
45 *HE*, iii.26.

Either possibility might be placed immediately after Colman's departure, or after the death of Colman's successor, a man named Tuda, who died in an outbreak of plague shortly afterwards (whom Stephen does not mention).[46] The LN and Stephen agree that Chad was appointed to a bishopric at some point after Wilfrid's appointment, so we can at least be confident that these two men were not appointed simultaneously.[47] The lack of clarity here is almost certainly due to the fact that Alhfrith's involvement in Wilfrid's consecration marks his last appearance in the historical record, excepting Bede's cryptic statement that Oswiu was attacked by Alhfrith at some point during his reign.[48] This attack, which evidently failed, must have occurred after Wilfrid left for Gaul, and possibly fairly soon afterwards. Chad's consecration to the see of York should be viewed as part of the contest between the two kings, whether in its full fury or its aftermath. The precise sequence of events can never be known, but the episode certainly reverberated subsequently. Wilfrid returned from Gaul a bishop without a see, perhaps being viewed by Oswiu as too closely associated with Alhfrith. However, as a result of the events of 664 he appears to have viewed the Northumbrian see as his by right. Stephen's work supports this belief and obscures all past complexity in Northumbrian episcopal arrangements by omitting any suggestion of a bishopric based at Lindisfarne, suggesting instead that Colman had been bishop of York. There was only one Northumbrian see, it was based at York, and it was Wilfrid's.

For five years Chad served as bishop of the Northumbrians, but when Archbishop Theodore arrived Chad was promptly deposed. According to the LN, which does not mention Wilfrid at all here, this was because Theodore thought Chad had been consecrated irregularly: on reaching Kent, Chad had found the archbishop of Canterbury recently deceased, and had continued to the kingdom of the West Saxons, where he was consecrated by Bishop Wine with the assistance of two British bishops; in what is possibly a Bedan gloss, the narrative explains that, although the Britons kept Easter from the fourteenth to the twentieth day of the moon, 'there was not a single bishop in the whole of Britain except Wine who had been canonically

---

46 *HE*, iii.26. Bede calls Tuda's see the bishopric of the Northumbrians (*pontificatum Nordanhymbrorum*), which would indicate that Tuda did not only hold one half of a newly divided see, although the terminology might be indicative of a view of the situation in hindsight, rather than of arrangements actually made in 664.

47 Following the possibilities outlined above, Wilfrid was either appointed to a newly created see of York alongside Tuda (appointed only to Lindisfarne, although see the previous note), or to the undivided bishopric of the Northumbrians (after Tuda's death) located at York (where it had been established either during or immediately after Tuda's episcopate). The account contained in the earliest versions of the Episcopal List Tradition suggests that the diocese was divided in two after Tuda's episcopate and that Wilfrid was appointed to Hexham and Chad to York (Page, 'Anglo-Saxon episcopal lists', p. 6). It also suggests that Chad was succeeded at York by Bosa, making no mention of Chad's deposition or Wilfrid's claim to York; Bosa was appointed to the see in 678 on Wilfrid's deposition according to Bede (*HE*, iv.12), and we can confidently assume that the ELT account represents a later simplification of earlier events.

48 *HE*, iii.14.

ordained'.[49] However, according to Stephen, the primary wrong for which Chad was deposed was an 'offence against the canon law, that one bishop had dared, like a thief, to snatch another bishop's see';[50] he also mentions the 'ignorance' of the people who consecrated Chad, grouping them in the 'Quartodeciman party', and later explains that Chad was reconsecrated, thus adding the fault described in the LN as a secondary consideration.[51] Again, we cannot know the whole truth of Chad's predicament, but, given that Theodore subsequently reconsecrated Chad, the LN certainly omits something of the situation, as no reason is given for Chad's loss of the Northumbrian see; indeed, the loss is not explicitly stated at all.[52] Stephen's account provides more detail, and we must suspect it reveals more plainly the nature of the accusations levelled at Chad. Wilfrid had perhaps delayed his challenge, considering it unlikely to succeed while Oswiu continued to view him as a relic of Alhfrith's bloc; however, a new archbishop, especially one appointed by Rome, offered new possibilities, and the 'irregularity' of Chad's consecration and his 'uncanonical' possession of the Northumbrian see were both doubtless useful arguments in securing Theodore's support.

The two accounts also differ when describing Chad's response to these accusations. The LN explains that, having been accused of irregularity,

> [Chad] humbly replied, 'If you believe that my consecration was irregular, I gladly resign from the office; indeed I never believed myself to be worthy of it. But I consented to receive it, however unworthy, in obedience to the commands I received.' When Theodore heard his humble reply, he said that he ought not to give up his office; but he completed his consecration a second time after the catholic manner.[53]

Though humble and submissive, Chad stubbornly refused to countenance the accusation; his tactful willingness to resign on the basis of Theodore's opinion admits no agreement with it. In contrast, Stephen relates that

> Chad, being a true and meek servant of God and fully understanding then the wrongdoing implied in his ordination to another's see by the Quartodecimans, with humble penances confessed his fault in accordance with the decision of the bishops: whereupon Theodore, with Chad's consent, installed St Wilfrid as bishop in his own see of York.[54]

---

49 *HE*, iii.28. The passage begins with the comment that the Britons' fault had already repeatedly been stated (referring to earlier parts of the *Ecclesiastical History*), and the topic was of particular interest to Bede.
50 *VW*, c. 15.
51 *VW*, c. 14.
52 The loss is implicit, as later in the narrative Chad is depicted in retirement at Lastingham, while Wilfrid ruled the see of York (*HE*, iv.3).
53 *HE*, iv.2.
54 *VW*, c.15.

Chad's full confession presents a very different version of the episode, but the two accounts are notably united by an emphasis on Chad's expressions of humility and obedience to Theodore.

Indeed, the hostile tone of Stephen's account gives way to an urgent reconciliation after Chad's confession. According to Stephen, Chad was made bishop of the Mercians immediately after his deposition: Wilfrid gave him the place (*locus*) at Lichfield (*Onlicitfelda*) which he himself had earlier received from Wulfhere, a gesture on Wilfrid's part by which 'he returned good for evil, not evil for evil', and

> a friendly arrangement was made with that true servant of God, Chad, who in all things obeyed the bishops: they thereupon consecrated him fully to the said see through all the ecclesiastical degrees.[55]

In contrast, the LN separates Chad's reconsecration from his appointment to the Mercian see, explaining that Chad was recalled from retirement at Lastingham by Oswiu at Theodore's request after the previous incumbent of the Mercian see had died.[56] Again, the LN omits Wilfrid: it does not explain how Chad acquired Lichfield (*Licidfelth*), only stating that he had his 'episcopal seat' (*sedes episcolpalem*) there; given that it does describe Wulfhere's gift of Barrow in the immediately preceding lines, this silence is noteworthy.[57] Indeed, Wilfrid's absence from almost the whole series of episodes discussed here suggests that the author of the LN was anxious to omit any mention of Wilfrid's accusations concerning the see of York, and to disguise the resulting conflict and its reconciliation.

In place of Wilfrid, the LN emphasises Theodore's agency, whether in judging Chad's consecration irregular, reconsecrating him or appointing him to the bishopric of the Mercians, and describes Chad's continual obedience to his archbishop. Although never explicitly criticised, Theodore is presented in a notably ambiguous light by the LN: Chad certainly offered him unfailing obedience, but his opinion of Chad's irregularity is never explicitly endorsed, and perhaps even implicitly denied. There is an important similarity here with the LN's presentation of Chad's successor Winfrith. As noted earlier, Winfrith was remembered warmly by the community of St Cedd and St Chad; even so, the LN informs us that he was deposed by Theodore, 'displeased by some act of disobedience', and replaced by Seaxwulf, and that Winfrith subsequently retired to his monastery at Barrow.[58] We might assume that Winfrith was given or bequeathed Barrow by Chad, who had earlier received the estate from Wulfhere; it was evidently not part of the episcopal estate given to Seaxwulf on his appointment. Chad's goodwill here might have informed Winfrith's continued membership of the saint's wider community, his reputation within it evidently undimmed by Theodore's disapproval. We might also speculate, somewhat more tenuously, that Winfrith's decision to disobey Theodore was at least partly informed by a cool disposition

---

55 *VW*, c.15.
56 *HE*, iv.3.
57 *HE*, iv.3.
58 *HE*, iv.6.

The Church of Lichfield

towards the archbishop prompted by Chad's earlier troubles. Both Chad and Winfrith retained their dignity when faced with Theodore's impositions, according to the LN, which otherwise gives the impression of a distinctly prickly archbishop.

At issue here is the impossibility of separating events from how and why they were remembered. It is certainly possible to make suggestions about what 'actually' happened based on the differences between the two accounts, but even these have to be placed within some kind of broader framework: there is no such thing as a 'true' list of events. In this case it is the fact of negotiation between the parties that impresses, despite the partisan force of some of the rhetoric. Neither Wilfrid nor Theodore was able to destroy Chad, and perhaps neither wanted to, especially at a time when there were so few bishops in the English kingdoms.[59] We must remember that all these men possessed spiritual authority because of their positions in wider networks and extended ecclesiastical communities. Chad's has been discussed above; Wilfrid's is better known to historians, owing in no small part to its large size and geographical extent. Characterising Wilfrid's community has proved difficult; Stephen himself might have called it a *parochia*, and historians have tried labels such as 'monastic empire', 'monastic confederation' and, most recently, 'affinity'.[60] In her analysis, Sarah Foot has suggested that, 'although geographically dispersed, the saint's community was spiritually and emotionally close and that the bond they felt was to their bishop (and perhaps hence to other houses in his affinity, although this is less clear)'.[61] This has great resonance with the form of the community of Cedd and Chad discussed here; Chad and Wilfrid shared a general approach to the creation of extended ecclesiastical communities, despite the obvious differences between their lives. There was certainly conflict between them, but ultimately their reconciliation might have been prompted by their shared interest in maintaining a kind of ecclesiastical solidarity, the spiritual basis of which supported the influence and authority of both in a world otherwise dominated by lay interests.

The similarities extend to the development of the two men's communities after their departures from the world. 'Beyond Wilfrid's death his houses apparently continued at least for a time to see themselves as part of a wider connection, albeit one now linked by their commemoration of Wilfrid's memory as a saint.'[62] Such commemoration often drew on standard perspectives of sanctity, which, as Catherine Cubitt has demonstrated, often informed the memory of hagiographers, even those who had known their subject personally.[63] It also drew on more singular elements, and in Chad's case, commemoration was focused on his personal qualities of humility and obedience. At the heart of this was his conflict with Wilfrid and/or Theodore: its resolution within a

---

59   Other than Chad and Wilfrid, there remained alive only Wine, probably bishop of London at this date, and the bishop of the East Angles, either Berhtgisl or Bisi. On Wine, see *HE*, iii.7 and iii.28; on the East Anglian bishops see ii.15, iii.18, iii.20 and iv.5.
60   See Foot, *Monastic life*, pp. 258–68, for the most recent review.
61   Foot, *Monastic life*, p. 261.
62   Foot, *Monastic life*, p. 263.
63   C. Cubitt, 'Memory and narrative in the cult of early Anglo-Saxon saints', in Y. Hen and M. Innes, *The uses of the past in the early Middle Ages* (Cambridge, 2000), pp. 29–66.

ritualised context of episcopal collegiality demanded explicit expressions of humility and obedience from Chad, which thereafter threw these qualities into sharp relief; they became his defining characteristics and were remembered as such by those who later spoke or wrote about him. When memories of Chad were synthesised at the Lastingham community in the later seventh or earlier eighth centuries, tales that emphasised these qualities (whatever their ultimate 'truth') cried out for inclusion, such as the anecdote in which Theodore himself lifted Chad onto a horse, forcing him to ride around his diocese where Chad would have preferred to walk. The author of the LN's exemplar, Stephen of Ripon, and Bede's tutor Trumberht each stressed Chad's association with humility and obedience, these qualities achieving proverbial status within the communities that remembered him. Even Stephen, appreciating the important example that men such as Chad offered to the integrity of his ecclesiastical world, overlooked the theft by which Chad had wronged his hero Wilfrid and offered him a eulogy, stating that Chad 'performed many good and pious deeds during his life, and at the fitting time he passed to his fathers, awaiting the day when the Lord shall come in judgement, a day which we believe will rightly have no terrors for him'.[64] Such memories were not simply the products of extended ecclesiastical communities, but their very substance; their repetition and commemoration gave these communities focus and tied their members together.

The diocesan community

An important conclusion to be drawn from the analysis in the first half of this chapter concerns Theodore's agency in the creation of the English ecclesiastical community. The archbishop's role was emphasised in Chapter 1, and his central place as a focus for episcopal assembly and solidarity should not be underestimated. However, the focus on extended ecclesiastical communities in this chapter emphasises the degree to which Theodore had to work with pre-existing connections and loyalties, and indeed relied on harnessing them to his own project rather than destroying them and building something new in their place. He was able in some contexts to exert the spiritual authority that his position in the textual community of canonically informed Christianity afforded him, but the negotiations highlighted above between Theodore, Chad and Wilfrid, for all that their subtleties now elude us, clearly demonstrate that the orchestration of power could be complex. Extended ecclesiastical communities continued to form an important phenomenon within early medieval society in England, often overlapping with what might be called the domestic communities that articulated experiences of household and family during this period; some good examples of monastic groupings within the dynasties of royal and aristocratic founders have been studied within the evidence afforded by the archive of the bishopric of Worcester.[65] Nevertheless, the importance of such communities among bishops, especially those

---

64 *VW*, c.15. It is interesting to note that Wilfrid's prior at Ripon in the early eighth century was a man named Caelin, who need not, but just might, if aged in his sixties or seventies, have been Chad's clerical brother of the same name (*VW*, c.64).

65 Sims-Williams, *Religion and literature*, pp. 115–76.

such as Wilfrid's or Chad's, which spanned the boundaries of kingdoms, appears to have waned after the late seventh century in favour of what are here called diocesan communities: families of minsters, churches and estates centred on a cathedral church located within the bounds of the bishop's diocese. The Worcester archive demonstrates this development clearly, but the lack of textual evidence in the diocese of Lichfield hampers our understanding. The following section therefore seeks to reconstruct something of this phenomenon by analysing a source at the other end of this study's chronological range: the bishop's estate recorded in Domesday Book.

It should be stated at the outset that the early medieval bounds of the diocese of Lichfield after 737, when all other Mercian bishoprics in the Midlands had been established, are nowhere given in any detail.[66] The earliest source that allows a fairly precise boundary to be delineated around the diocese is the *Taxatio Ecclesiastica* imposed across England and Wales in 1291 on the authority of Pope Nicholas IV. By that time the diocese contained the counties of Staffordshire, Derbyshire, Cheshire, the southern part of Lancashire between the rivers Mersey and Ribble, the northern half of Shropshire and the north-eastern two thirds of Warwickshire. The estates of the bishop of Lichfield in 1066, revealed by the Domesday survey, were confined within this region, which also excluded the estates of any other bishops, so it is reasonable to suppose that the thirteenth-century boundaries give a good indication of the mid eleventh-century arrangement. The diocesan bounds largely correlate with shire boundaries, but two significant stretches that cut across Warwickshire and Shropshire are usually understood to indicate that the diocesan bounds predate those of the Midland shires, which were established in the tenth century.[67]

Patrick Sims-Williams has demonstrated the probable correlation of the bounds of the Worcester diocese with the seventh- and eighth-century kingdom of the Hwicce, in part through an analysis of place-names referencing that people;[68] the presence of two place-names names referencing the 'Mercians' at places on the south-east boundary of the diocese of Lichfield is similarly suggestive.[69] Nevertheless, by the same logic, the presence of Markfield (*Mercna-feld*, 'the open country or common pasture of or towards the Mercians') in the midst of western Leicestershire, to the

---

66 See Chapter 1 for the creation of these other dioceses.
67 M. Gelling, *The West Midlands in the early Middle Ages* (Leicester, 1992), pp. 97–100. For the creation of the shires see Molyneaux, *The formation of the English kingdom*, pp. 157–64.
68 Sims-Williams, *Religion and literature*, pp. 383–94. Some place-names related to the Hwicce are also pertinent to the diocese of Lichfield: for example, Wychbury, meaning 'fortified enclosure of the Hwicce', is now in northern Worcestershire but close to the diocesan boundary along the southern edge of Staffordshire, and was probably named due to this proximity (Sims-Williams, *Religion and literature*, p. 390).
69 The field-name 'Martimow' in Radway (Warks.), situated on the south-eastern diocesan boundary, is derived from *Mercna-mere*, 'boundary of the Mercians', and an unlocated *mercne mere* (with the same derivation) is given in a charter boundary relating to nearby Kineton (S 773), dated AD 969 (Sims-Williams, *Religion and literature*, p. 388; W.J. Ford, 'Some settlement patterns in the central region of the Warwickshire Avon', in P.H. Sawyer (ed.), *English medieval settlement* (London, 1979), pp. 143–63, at p. 146).

Lichfield and the Lands of St Chad

east of the diocese, would indicate that the boundary there has shifted.[70] The precise relationship between place-names, polities and dioceses is no doubt a complex issue, which cannot be tackled in detail here. Suffice it to state that unstable political boundaries of the ninth and tenth centuries, or even later, such as those between the Mercian (later English) kingdom and Danish polities to the east or Welsh kingdoms to the west, may well have prompted or forced some movement of diocesan boundaries. Boundaries on the southern side of the diocese between the Mercians and the Hwicce and Magonsæte perhaps remained more stable, and Nick Higham has recently argued for the long-term stability of the boundary between the kingdoms of Northumbria with Mercia, from the Humber to the Mersey, which defined the diocese to the north; the section between the rivers Ribble and Mersey is not considered here, as it was probably a tenth-century addition.[71]

In the following section, an initial review of the information provided by Domesday Book on the locations and structure of the bishop's holdings enables the production of a complete list of his estates in 1086, when the Domesday survey was compiled (see Figure 3). Thereafter, a detailed analysis results in three main conclusions. Firstly, a study of the terminology used to describe the holders of the bishop's estates demonstrates an important distinction between a set of large estates distributed across much of the diocese associated with the cathedral church at Lichfield and sets of smaller estates on the western edge of the diocese associated with three further episcopal churches at Shrewsbury, Farndon and Chester. Secondly, analysis of a sub-set of the bishop's estates that shared vills with the estates of other landholders adds depth to this distinction, identifying a larger 'integrated' type of estate with a complex internal structure and contrasting it with complexes of 'less integrated' smaller estates. Finally, the implications of these distinctions and structures are discussed in relation to the history and development of the episcopal holdings across the diocese; it is concluded that an initial set of 'integrated' estates acquired across the seventh, eighth and ninth centuries was augmented by 'less integrated' complexes of estates provided to support the three more recently acquired western churches in the tenth and eleventh centuries. It should be noted that the term 'estate' is used in the following discussions to encompass both the post-Conquest 'manor' and the pre-Conquest entity that preceded it, deliberately implying a considerable similarity between them

---

70   Barry Cox has suggested that the name was 'evidently given by Anglo-Saxon peoples to the east who were not Mercians themselves' (B. Cox, 'The place-names of Leicestershire and Rutland', PhD thesis (University of Nottingham, 1971), pp. 41–2, and see also etymology given at pp. 516–17); for *feld* denoting common pasture, see M. Gelling, *Signposts to the past: place-names and the history of England* (London, 1978), pp. 126–8. The inclusion of parts of western Leicestershire in the Mercian province represented by the diocese of Lichfield may be supported by the apparent location of the minster at Breedon-on-the-Hill (now in north-west Leicestershire) within the territory of the Tomsæte, a Mercian territory that otherwise included Tamworth and the eastern part of the Birmingham plateau, both within the diocese of Lichfield (S 197; see also D. Hooke, *The landscape of Anglo-Saxon Staffordshire: the charter evidence* (Keele, 1983), pp. 10–12).

71   Higham, 'Northumbria's Southern Frontier'.

The Church of Lichfield

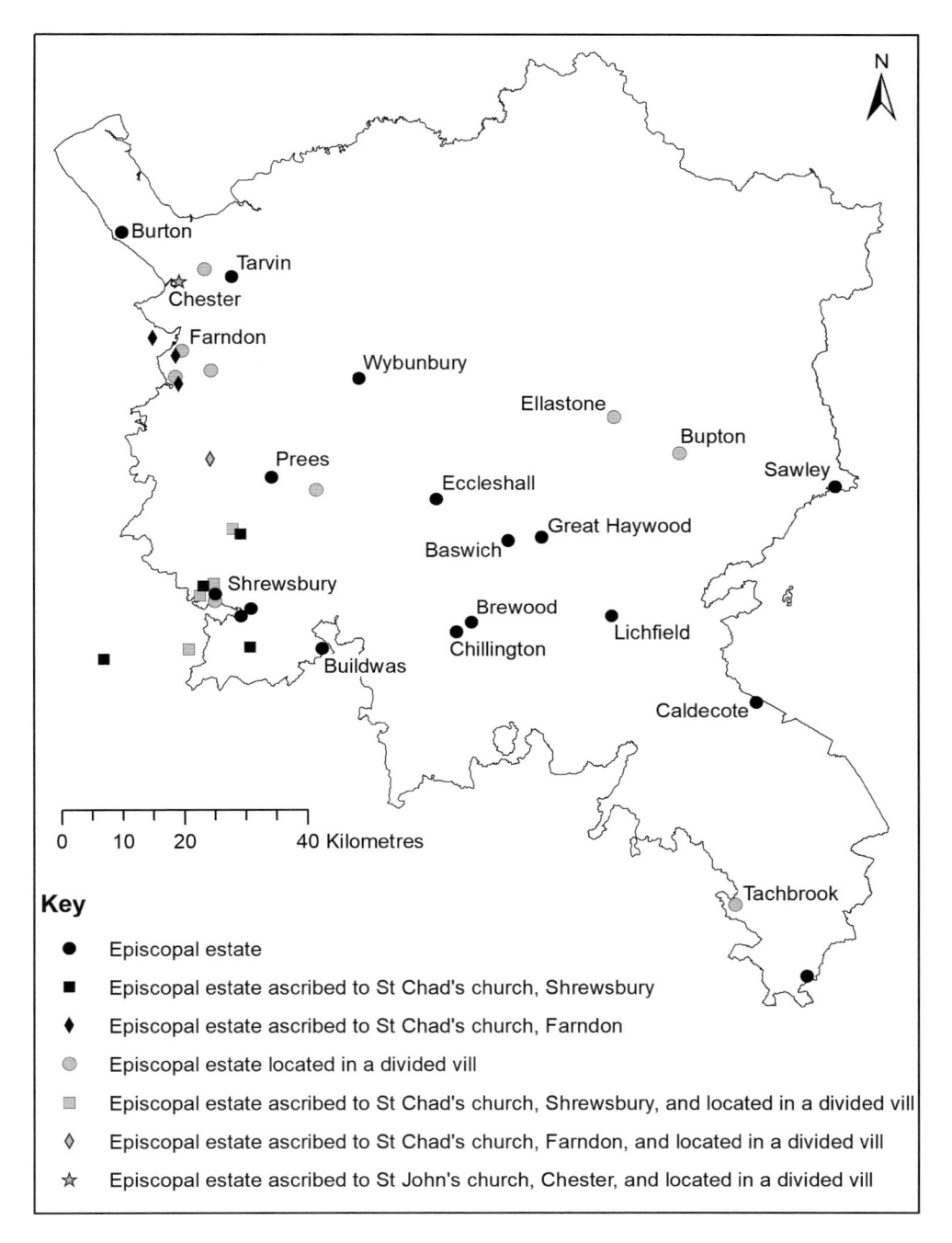

Figure 3 Distribution of estates of the bishop of Lichfield in 1066 represented in Domesday Book.

but acknowledging the specifically post-Conquest application of the term *manerium*;[72] more is said of this in Chapter 5.

Domesday Book is arranged by shire, and within each shire by sections listing the lands of the tenants-in-chief, those landowners holding directly of the king. Landholdings are described in a variety of ways, but a common denominator is assessment to the king's geld or tax, which is enumerated for each landholding in terms of a certain number of 'hides' or 'carucates'. It should be noted that the names of landholdings were usually taken from the name of the 'vill' in which they were located; the vill was the smallest territorial unit recognised by royal administrators, and was used to organise collection of the geld. Further details given in Domesday Book usually include an assessment of the productive potential of each landholding (enumerated in 'ploughlands') and various items concerning the tenements, material appurtenances and resources within it, among which is sometimes found information on priests and/or a church. Certain information, in particular the cash render of each landholding, is given for both the time of the survey (*tempus regis Willelmi*, or TRW) and the time of King Edward, 1066 (*tempus regis Edwardi*, or TRE). Finally, it should be noted that the bishop of Lichfield moved his see to Chester in 1075, and he is therefore styled the 'bishop of Chester' in Domesday Book.

The Domesday shires are conventionally categorised by historians according to the 'circuit' in which they lay, referring to the groups of shires that individual bodies of commissioners were assigned, each of which tends to share various similarities in the nature of the records they produced that distinguishes them from the other circuits. Of the shires relevant to this analysis, Derbyshire was in Circuit VI, Staffordshire and Warwickshire were in Circuit IV and Shropshire and Cheshire were in Circuit V. Beginning in Derbyshire, the only shire in Circuit VI in which the bishop held land, we find that the record of episcopal landholdings shares a concern with the details of estate structure that is visible in some of the other shires of this circuit, but is largely absent from the shires of other circuits represented in Domesday Book. Thus, the entry for an estate at Sawley is flanked by a marginal 'M' and 'B', indicating the estate centre (*manerium* or *caput*) at Sawley and two 'berewicks' at Draycott and Hopwell, which are also mentioned in the entry.[73] This is followed by an entry for land at Long Eaton flanked by a marginal 'S', indicating 'sokeland'.[74] While no one definition is likely to be entirely satisfactory, current scholarly consensus would distinguish sokeland as lands held by people who rendered fixed rents and various light services to the lord of the estate, as against the estate's 'inland', located either at the estate centre or in its detached 'berewicks', which was held directly by the estate's lord and whose inhabitants owed various payments and labour services.[75] Thus, in Circuit VI, the entry for any given landholding does not necessarily represent a complete estate;

---

72 C.P. Lewis, 'The invention of the manor in Norman England', *Anglo-Norman Studies*, 34 (2012), pp. 123–50.
73 *DB Derbys.*, 2,1.
74 *DB Derbys.*, 2,2.
75 D. Roffe, *Decoding Domesday* (Woodbridge, 2007), pp. 176–82. Inland and sokeland are discussed further in Chapter 5.

often it comprises a discrete component of an estate, whether estate centre, berewick or sokeland. Unfortunately the entry for the second episcopal estate in Derbyshire, at Bupton, is not as detailed, referring only to associated *appendicia*, which might conceivably have been berewicks or sokelands.

The Derbyshire entries also use other diplomatic features to indicate the varied status of different portions of an estate; for example, the names of berewicks and sokelands are also distinguished by use of miniscule lettering with initial capitals, contrasting with the rubricated rustic capitals used for the entire name of the estate centre. This is also the case in Staffordshire, an important detail as the shire lies in Circuit IV and is therefore bereft of the marginal notation used in some of Circuit VI. Six estates are identified in Staffordshire, at Lichfield, Eccleshall, Baswich, Great Haywood, Brewood and Ellastone, and in all but the last two details of associated lands are also given.[76] At Lichfield and Eccleshall place-names in miniscule with initial rubricated capitals are used to describe what are called 'members' (*membra*); considered in relation to the structure revealed in Derbyshire these might have been berewicks or sokelands, but it is not possible to distinguish between these two options.[77] The same diplomatic is used to describe several members pertaining to lands at Sugnall and Seighford, which themselves provide two examples of a distinct kind of landholding found more widely in the bishop's Staffordshire entries.[78] The names of these holdings are given entirely in rubricated rustic capitals, and are thus indistinguishable from the estate centres, but they appear nevertheless to have been dependent on the latter, and so are best labelled sub-estates; crucially, all but one are assessed only in ploughlands or lack assessment in any form, their hidage assessments presumably being part of that of their parent estates.[79] Sometimes their dependency is made explicit in the text, and often they are positioned after the entries for their parent estates, but there is a series of five such holdings that, together with a second entry for Lichfield, appear at the end of the bishop's section, apparently detached from earlier entries by scribal confusion, and which can only be assigned to their respective estate centres by geographical logic.[80]

Unfortunately none of the sections detailing the bishop's lands in other shires are as revealing of estate structure as those in Derbyshire and Staffordshire; even in Warwickshire, which was in the same circuit as Staffordshire, the bishop's section features only simple entries for his three estates there.[81] The bishop's sections in Shropshire and Cheshire both derive from another circuit (Circuit V), although the

---

76 *DB Staffs.*, 2,1, 2,2, 2,5 (with 2,9), 2,10, 2,15, 2,16 (with 2,22).
77 This can be done in one case only: the members attached to the sub-estate at Sugnall in Eccleshall are also called berewicks.
78 *DB Staffs.*, 2,2, 2,3, 2,4, 2,6, 2,7, 2,8, 2,11, 2,13, 2,14, 2,17, 2,18, 2,19, 2,20, 2,21.
79 The exception is Great Haywood, where half a hide is recorded at the dependency of Wolseley (*DB Staffs.*, 2,7).
80 Later sources can also be used to confirm these attributions: for example, Sugnall was part of Eccleshall in the 1298 survey of the episcopal estates, and even there it retained the attributes of an estate, with its own court, and was described as a fee.
81 *DB Warks.*, 2,1, 2,2, 2,3.

Lichfield and the Lands of St Chad

Table 1
The estates of the bishop of Lichfield in 1066 represented in Domesday Book.

Estate (d = in divided vill)	Hidage (carucatage)	Church or priest	Holder TRE	Church dedication
Lichfield	25.75	5 canons	The Church	St Mary & St Chad
Sawley	(24)	1 priest + 2 churches	Not given	St Chad (Wilne)
Prees	8	1 priest	Bishop	St Chad
Eccleshall	7	1 priest	St Chad	St Chad[1]
Tachbrook (d)	7	1 priest	St Chad (TRW)	St Chad
Tarvin	6		Bishop	St Andrew
Bupton (d)	(5.25)		Not given	St Chad (Longford)
Brewood	5	1 priest	The Church	St Mary and St Chad[2]
Baswich	5	1 priest	The Church	Holy Trinity
Farndon (d)	4	2 priests + 1 priest	Bishop	St Chad
Burton in Wirral	3	1 priest	Bishop	St Nicholas
Chillington	3		Bishop	n/a
Farnborough	3		Stori	St Botolph
Betton	2		Bishop	n/a
Marton	2		St Chad's, Shrewsbury	n/a
Bicton	2		St Chad's, Shrewsbury	n/a
Yorton	2	1 priest	St Chad's, Shrewsbury	n/a
Broughton (d)	2		St Chad's, Shrewsbury	n/a
Bettisfield (d)	2		St Chad's, Farndon	St Chad (Hanmer)
Caldecote	2	1 priest	Tonna	St Theobald and St Chad
Shelton	1.5		Bishop	n/a
Wrentnall (d)	1.5		St Chad's, Shrewsbury	n/a
'Chatsall' (d)	1.25		Bishop	n/a
Great Haywood	1	1 priest	St Chad	All Saints/St Michael and all Angels (Colwich)
Longner	1		Bishop	n/a
Buildwas	1		Bishop	n/a
Rossall (d)	1		St Chad's, Shrewsbury	n/a
Onslow (d)	1		St Chad's, Shrewsbury	n/a
Guilden Sutton (d)	1		Bishop	St John the Baptist
Eyton	1		St Chad's, Farndon	n/a
Sutton	1		St Chad's, Farndon	n/a
'Chespuic'/'Radenoure'	1		St Chad's, Farndon	n/a
'Burwardestone' (d)	1		Bishop	n/a
'Redcliff' (d)	⅔		St John's, Chester	St John the Baptist
Little Eton	0.5		St Chad's, Shrewsbury	n/a
Wybunbury	0.5	1 priest	Bishop	St Chad
Tilston (d)	0.5		Bishop	St Mary
Ellastone (d)	0.25		St Chad	St Peter
Meole (d)	Not given		Bishop	n/a

Notes:
1 The current dedication is to Holy Trinity, but there is earlier evidence for a dedication to St Chad: *SHC* 3rd Series 20 (1926).
2 *SHC* 3rd Series 240 (no. 498) (1924).

diplomatic is very similar to that of Staffordshire and Warwickshire.[82] The entries describe the estates in these shires, seven in each, in brief terms, usually with only the typical sets of Domesday statistics. There are some extra details in the Cheshire section about the church of St John at Chester, the bishop's new cathedral church, appended to the entry for the estate held by that church from the bishop at 'Redcliff'. In Shropshire an entirely separate section is provided for the church of St Chad in Shrewsbury, constituting it a separate tenant-in-chief, which lists seven estates, and a note in the bishop's section mentions sixteen canons that he used to have in Shrewsbury, who presumably belonged to this church.[83] The bishop's sections in both shires also include details of his burghal properties, eight houses (*domus*) in Chester and sixteen houses (*mansurae*) in Shrewsbury;[84] those in Chester are explicitly linked with the dean and seven canons at St John's and it seems very likely that those in Shrewsbury were once occupied by the canons he used to have there. The section of the Cheshire Domesday on the borough of Chester includes notice of fifty-six houses held by the bishop, presumably additional to those held by St John's.[85] Similar details are found in the burghal sections of Staffordshire and Warwickshire;[86] the bishop had fourteen *mansurae* in Stafford and seven in Warwick.[87] There is no record of any burghal properties held by the bishop in Derby. Finally, seven additional estates (distributed across three shires) were claimed but not held by the bishop in 1086.[88]

This information allows us to produce a list of thirty-nine estates (excluding

---

82   *DB Salop.*, 1,3, 1,4, 1,5, 1,6, 1,7, 1,8, 1,9; *DB Chesh.* B3, B4, B5, B6 (with B7), B8, B9, B10 (with B11).
83   *DB Salop.*, 1,2, 3f,1, 3f,2, 3f,3, 3f,4, 3f,5, 3f,6, 3f,7.
84   *DB Salop.*, 1,1; *DB Chesh.*, B12.
85   *DB Chesh.*, C2.
86   *DB Staffs.*, B2; *DB Warks.*, B2.
87   The bishop still held seven tenements in Warwick in 1298, when they were administered through the estate at Bishops Tachbrook. The same survey records ten burgages in Stafford administered through Baswich; the church of St Chad in Stafford was appropriated to the prebend of Pipa Minor or Prees, which may account for the other four (see H. Baylis, 'Prebends in the cathedral church of Saints Mary and Chad in Lichfield', *Transactions of the Lichfield Archaeological and Historical Society*, 2 (1960/61), pp. 38–52, at p. 48, and M.W. Greenslade and D.A. Johnson (eds), *VCH Staffordshire*, vol. 6 (London, 1979), pp. 245–8).
88   Warwickshire: William son of Corbucion's section notes that the bishop claimed land in Staffordshire at Chillington (*DB Warks.*, 28,19). Shropshire: St Chad's claimed land in Wrentnall, but it had been held by two thegns in 1066 (*DB Salop.*, 4,26,3). Cheshire: the bishop's breve finishes with a note about an estate at Bettisfield claimed by the bishop against Robert fitz Hugh, and this is also noted in Robert's breve, where it is explained that St Chad had held it in the time of Cnut but lost it since; in 1066 St Chad held lands west of the Dee in Eyton and Sutton, although had lost them since; land previously held by the church of St Chad (*ecclesia S. Cedde*) in the estate at Gresford (at 'Chespuic' and 'Radenoure') was claimed by the bishop; and the bishop also claimed lands that he had previously held in the estates at 'Burwardestone' and Tilston (*DB Chesh.*, 16,2, 27,3, 2,2). This has been reckoned as seven additional estates, not eight, because the bishop held an estate at Eyton TRW, from which it is here assumed the land in the claim was subtracted.

members, berewicks and sokelands) held by the bishop of Chester in 1086. Table 1 displays this list, ranking the estates in order of hidage, highest first, and providing some additional information. Estates that shared vills with additional estates held by other landholders are indicated by a (d) after the name, and those belonging to 'less integrated' complexes are shaded grey. These are discussed below, but first the distinction between estates focused on Lichfield and on the three western churches mentioned earlier is elucidated; this requires a focus on information about who actually held the episcopal estates, beyond 'the bishop of Chester' (written at the top of his section in each shire), which is provided in some individual estate entries in all shires except Derbyshire. All six estates in Staffordshire are said to have been held TRE by either 'the church [*ecclesia*]' or 'St Chad', which probably amount to the same thing: namely the religious community centred on St Chad's shrine at Lichfield. In Warwickshire a note at the end of the entry for the estate at Bishop's Tachbrook states that it is land of 'the church of St Chad', which presumably applies to 1086 but may well have applied to 1066 as well. Information about ownership TRE is also given in Shropshire and Cheshire: in Shropshire four of the bishop's seven estates are said to have been held by 'the bishop', along with the houses in Shrewsbury, while the information is not given for the other three estates; in Cheshire all the estates were held by 'the bishop', except for 'Redcliff', which was held by St John's church at Chester, and for a group clustering on the river Dee at Eyton, Sutton, Bettisfield and 'Chespuic'/'Radenoure', all of which (except one of two holdings at Eyton) were not held by the bishop in 1086 but had been held by 'St Chad' in 1066. There is thus a division between the six estates in Staffordshire and one in Warwickshire on the one hand, which were held by 'the church of St Chad' (whether TRE or TRW), and most of the estates in Shropshire and Cheshire on the other, which were held by 'the bishop' in 1066, with a minority held by St John's church in Chester and St Chad's in Shrewsbury, the latter described in a separate section, and a cluster near the Dee ascribed to 'St Chad'.[89] It is unknown how the remaining estates in Shropshire and those in Derbyshire fitted into this pattern, although we might suspect that the unattributed Shropshire estates would also have been described as held by 'the bishop' TRE.

The possibility that this pattern describes a real division in tenure of the estates between bishop and the community at the cathedral church must be examined. There is certainly contemporary precedent for this: evidence for the so-called 'division of the *mensa* [Latin for 'table', referring to provision]' between ruler and community has been noted in charters from the beginning of the ninth century onwards, largely relating to various cathedrals but also including the minster at *Medeshamstede* (Peterborough).[90]

---

89   The distinction between tenure TRE and TRW is probably not important. Elsewhere in Domesday Circuit IV, in which Staffordshire and Warwickshire were located, lands are said to have belonged *and belong* to cathedral churches (e.g. *DB Oxon*, 6,5, where the cathedral church of St Mary in Lincoln held and holds land in Cropredy); the situation may not have been quite so clear-cut in Staffordshire because of the move of the bishopric to Chester in 1075, which could have raised uncomfortable questions about the competing identities of old and new cathedral churches.

90   E. John, 'The division of the *mensa* in early English monasteries', *Journal of Ecclesiastical History*, 6/2 (1955), pp. 143–55.

It is, moreover, readily observable later in the period in the copious records and Domesday Book sections of the monastic cathedral church at Worcester.[91] However, in this case, as in the others where it is apparent, the division took the form of an intermixed allocation of estates to bishop and community, which, in the Domesday Book sections for the diocese of Lichfield, is better represented by the explicit division of estates between the bishop and his churches at St Chad's, Shrewsbury and St John's, Chester. The near-complete dominance of tenure by St Chad in Staffordshire and Warwickshire does not fit this pattern. In fact, it seems more likely that the distinction is more apparent than real, and that the Domesday agents in Circuit IV (Staffordshire and Warwickshire) used a different format and terminology to those in Circuit V (Shropshire and Cheshire) when describing episcopal landholdings. The commissioners of Circuit IV may simply have desired to distinguish the tenure of the episcopate as an institution, represented by the cathedral church, from lands that might have been held personally by the bishop.[92]

The Domesday Book sections for other bishops represented in Circuit IV also include entries in which lands are ascribed to their cathedral churches rather than 'the bishop', and these tend to reinforce the suggestion that such terminology was not intended to distinguish between the possessions of the bishop and the cathedral community. Instead, in some cases the distinction appears to indicate where land is held directly rather than let to tenants, as is probably the case in the bishop of Chester's Warwickshire section.[93] Conversely, in the counties of Circuit V there is a dominant tendency for the entire episcopal section to be ascribed to the cathedral church; for example, the Worcestershire section is styled 'land of the church of Worcester'.[94] Within this section the 'division of the *mensa*' between bishop and monastic community is indicated by attributing some estates 'for the provision of the monks', or similar.[95] Shropshire and Cheshire are thus distinctive within the context of Circuit V because the bishop's sections are entitled with reference to the bishop rather than his cathedral church;[96] this may relate to the fact that the episcopal churches of St Chad's, Shrewsbury and St John's, Chester, held lands in their own right, the former with its own section in Domesday Book, and reference to the church of St Chad at Lichfield might have confused matters. Indeed, given

---

91 F. Tinti, *Sustaining belief: the church of Worcester from c.870 to c.1100* (Farnham, 2010), particularly Chapter 4.
92 For example, lands held by the bishop of Chester in Hertfordshire are explicitly said not to belong to the bishopric (*non est de episcopatu*): DB Herts., 7,1.
93 E.g. *DB Leics.*, 3, where the first three entries are ascribed to St Mary's Lincoln, and the remainder are held by tenants.
94 *Terra Ecclesiae de Wirecestre*: DB Worcs., 2; tellingly, the sections in Worcestershire and Gloucestershire in Circuit V are styled in this way, while that in Warwickshire in Circuit IV is styled 'land of the bishop of Worcester' (*Terra Episcopi de Wirecestre*) and does not mention the church in any of its entries.
95 *ad victum monachorum*.
96 Sally Harvey has suggested that Shropshire and Cheshire formed a separate circuit, which she labels VIII: S. Harvey, *Domesday: book of judgement* (Oxford, 2014), pp. 87–90.

that landholdings in Cheshire and Shropshire not explicitly linked to these local churches are usually described as belonging to 'the bishop' TRE, the distinct group of estates clustering near the Dee said to have been held by 'St Chad' should almost certainly be ascribed to the episcopal church at nearby Farndon, giving us a third church in the west of the diocese holding land distinct from the bishopric in 1066.[97] The recording of landholdings in Domesday Book thus reveals an important division between the lands of the episcopate, scattered across the diocese but associated with the cathedral church of St Chad at Lichfield, and lands associated with the three distinct episcopal churches at Chester, Shrewsbury and Farndon. The distinction appears to have persisted, as cathedral prebends were formed between the eleventh and thirteenth centuries in many estates belonging to the former group but in none belonging to the latter.[98]

It is possible to deepen our understanding of this distinction by focusing on the form and distribution of the episcopal estates. As mentioned earlier, the estates can generally be classified as either 'integrated' estates, with more complex internal structures, or as members of 'less integrated' estate complexes, within which the estates are generally smaller. Integrated estates are easiest to identify as those for which a sense of internal structure is provided in Domesday Book – namely Sawley in Derbyshire and all those in Staffordshire except Ellastone – comprising estate centres with dependencies of various kinds, often encompassing large areas. In other cases the Domesday format obscures similar kinds of estate structure that can nevertheless be discerned in other sources; for example, in the late thirteenth century Prees had members at Darliston, 'Leeton', 'Wotenhull', Mickley, Willaston and Millenheath, which together (where now locatable) take in a large area south and east of Prees itself, many lying within the parish of its church.[99] This is important because record of members or berewicks is rare in the Shropshire and Cheshire folios, but, as they clearly existed, as indicated by examples such as this, it is possible that the Domesday commissioners did not tend to record such dependencies in these shires. In contrast to these estates, less integrated concentrations of estates can also be identified in the bishop's Domesday folios, in which individual estates were in close geographical proximity but were otherwise not apparently structurally integrated. Three distinct concentrations of less integrated estates in the vicinity of the three episcopal churches in the western part of the diocese are analysed in what follows.

The less integrated concentrations correlate notably with a distinctive phenomenon observable in the relationship between some estate centres and the vills in which they were located. Many vills across the diocese contained only one estate centre, but a significant minority contained two or more that belonged to different landholders TRE. These 'divided vills' are found at fifteen of the episcopal estates, if the estates held by St Chad's, Shrewsbury, and those merely claimed rather than actually held

---

97 Farndon church continued to possess interests across the Severn in the later medieval period: N.J. Higham, *The origins of Cheshire* (Manchester, 1993), p. 134.
98 M.W. Greenslade (ed.), *VCH Staffordshire*, vol. 3 (London, 1970), pp. 140–1.
99 *DB Salop.*, 1,8 note.

in 1086 are also included in the count.[100] Seven were explicitly held by one of the three western churches, just over half of the total of thirteen estates ascribed to them; the remaining eight estate centres in divided vills accounted for less than a third of the other twenty-six episcopal estates, and were also primarily located in the western part of the diocese among the less integrated estate concentrations, with a minority elsewhere. The episcopal share of the hidage in all but one of the divided vills can be calculated, and appears to have varied considerably:[101] in three cases the bishop held the majority of the vill;[102] in six cases the episcopal portion was about half of the whole vill;[103] and in five cases it was less than half, often considerably so.[104] If we consider the identity of the other landholder in each of the divided vills, we find that Earl Edwin of Mercia held in a fairly coherent group of four to the east and south-east of the Dee, including Farndon, in close proximity to others of his estates at Malpas and Worthenbury in Cheshire, and Ellesmere and Dodington in Shropshire. Another high-status holder is probably represented by the Edith who held an estate at Meole near Shrewsbury, who was probably King Edward's queen. The remainder were held by various named thegns.

It should be noted that the presence of divided vills may be more apparent than real among a specific sub-set of the corpus. It was noted above that Domesday commissioners in Cheshire and Shropshire do not appear to have noted the presence of berewicks and sokelands within integrated estates, limiting their information to the relevant estate centres. The episcopal sections of the survey in these two shires include a small number of claims made by the bishop to parts of estates that were

---

100 Ellastone in Staffordshire, Tachbrook in Warwickshire, Meole, 'Chatsall', Broughton, Rossall, Onslow and Wrentnall in Shropshire, Bupton in Derbyshire and Farndon, 'Redcliff', Guilden Sutton, Bettisfield, Burwardestone' and Tilston in Cheshire. In Cheshire, Eyton was divided between the church and Hugh Fitz Osbern TRW, but both holdings belonged to St Chad's church, Farndon, TRE (and are therefore counted as one estate here); the estate at Gresford TRW included one hide held by St Chad's, Farndon, TRE, but this was distributed across vills at 'Chespuic' and 'Radenoure' (which may have been independent of Gresford at the time), so Gresford is not treated as a divided vill here.

101 At Meole, the bishop's assessment is not given, but Edith held three hides and the canons of St Mary's (Shrewsbury) one virgate.

102 Bupton, bishop five carucates two bovates, Ulfkil six bovates; Wrentnall, St Chad's (Shrewsbury) one and a half hides (claim), Ernwy and Ketel half a hide (if claim accepted); 'Redcliff', bishop two-thirds of a hide, Gunnor one-third of a hide.

103 Ellastone, bishop one virgate, six thegns one virgate; Tachbrook, bishop seven hides, Baldwin seven hides three virgates; Farndon, bishop four hides, Earl Edwin four hides; Rossall, St Chad's (Shrewsbury) one hide, Hunning one hide; Onslow, St Chad's (Shrewsbury) one hide, Ernwy one hide; Guilden Sutton, bishop one hide, Toki one hide.

104 'Chatsall', bishop one hide one virgate, Ledwi one hide three virgates; Broughton: St Chad's (Shrewsbury) two hides, St Mary's (Shrewsbury) five hides; Bettisfield, St Chad's (Farndon) two hides (claim), Earl Edwin five hides (if claim accepted); 'Burwardestone', bishop one hide (claim), Earl Edwin four hides (if claim accepted); Tilston, bishop half a hide (claim), Earl Edwin three and a half hides (if claim accepted).

held TRW by others, each identified by the name of a single vill (namely Wrentnall, Bettisfield, 'Burwardestone' and Tilston); superficially these can be classified as divided vills if the bishop's claim is given credence. However, it is possible that the two holdings recorded in each case – the main estate and the part claimed by the bishop – were actually located in different vills, but that the bishop's part, earlier a separate estate, had been made into a dependency of the other estate at some point between 1066 and 1086; as the locations of such dependencies were not recorded in these shires, they would appear TRW under the name of the estate centre. An explicit example is provided by the large estate of Gresford (Cheshire), in which the bishop claimed a one-hide share TRW, but in this case his claim is explicitly stated to apply to vills at 'Chespuic' and 'Radenoure'; the estate in these vills was presumably subsumed as a dependency within the estate at Gresford at some point after 1066, but had formerly been independent of it, and thus Gresford should clearly not be treated as a vill divided between two estates TRE. Such certainty is not possible in the four cases listed above, for which no further information on the locations of the bishop's claims is given, although Bettisfield and 'Burwardestone' will be revisited below.

The most distinct of the less integrated concentrations of episcopal estates is that around Shrewsbury, comprising Meole, Shelton, Longner and Betton recorded in the bishop's section, and Bicton, Rossall and Onslow in St Chad's section, all clustered around the southern and western reaches of the borough, with Little Eton a little further to the south and Broughton and Yorton a little further still to the north. Each was recorded as a separate estate in Domesday Book, and indeed several were granted away as separate estates shortly after 1086, yet despite this lack of integration they must have been recognised as possessing a certain unity, as all were in St Chad's parish, which featured several detached portions in order to contain them all.[105] It has been suggested that the college of St Chad at Shrewsbury had ceased to exist shortly before 1086, as an entry in the bishop's section refers to sixteen canons that he 'had' but does not appear to 'have', and also sixteen houses in the city, then occupied by burgesses, but perhaps earlier occupied by the canons.[106] Likewise, the church had apparently lost land in Wrentnall before King Edward's time, and estates at Welbatch and Woodcote, which were held by freemen in 1066, lay in St Chad's parish, so might have been held by the church at some point. Indeed, the estates listed in the bishop's section but located in the vicinity of Shrewsbury might also have belonged to St Chad's at one point, although the reverse has been suggested, that St Chad's estates had earlier belonged to the bishop.[107] Either way, we could assume that they all formed part of a unitary holding at some earlier time, but the passing of various elements from one to the other, whether to St Chad's or to the bishop, would not explain why the remaining elements of the holding also fragmented into independent estates rather than persisting as a rump of dependencies and members attached to a central estate centre. Moreover, while there is a certain geographical coherence to the estates closest to Shrewsbury, even here they were intermixed with other estates

---

105 A.T. Gaydon (ed.), *VCH Shropshire*, vol. 2 (London, 1973), p. 114.
106 Gaydon, *VCH Shropshire*, pp. 114–15.
107 Gaydon, *VCH Shropshire*, pp. 114–15.

held by other churches and laymen. It therefore seems more plausible to suggest that these estates were never integrated into a larger unitary structure, but comprised from the outset an assemblage of individual estates, probably brought together to support the bishop's church in Shrewsbury.

Of the two less integrated complexes in Cheshire, that around St John's church in Chester is perhaps the least coherent. According to the bishop's section in Domesday Book, St John's held only one estate in the divided vill of 'Redcliff'. Nevertheless, it also held eight geld-free houses in the city for its dean (*matricularius*) and seven canons, and there is reference to a monastery dedicated to St Mary next to the church: St John's thus sat at the nexus of a variety of individual elements in and around Chester, and it is worth noting that the church of the bishop's nearby estate of Guilden Sutton (in a divided vill) was also dedicated to St John, possibly indicating the past patronage or ownership of the church in Chester. Several of the bishop's other Cheshire estates clustered around Chester, and by 1298, according to a survey conducted that year, they were in part administered together, as all the free tenants of the estates at Farndon, Tarvin and Burton in Wirral owed suit at Chester along with the bishop's tenants in the city.[108] This can be compared with the complex of estates around Shrewsbury, although while none of the latter estates were particularly large, and none were larger than two hides, several of the estates around Chester were considerably larger. Burton in Wirral at three hides, Farndon at four hides and Tarvin at six hides were the three largest of the bishop's estates in the shire. Moreover, while the Shrewsbury estates were all located in St Chad's parish, the Chester estates possessed significant parishes of their own. Thus, for the purposes of this classification, it seems sensible to consider Tarvin and Burton in Wirral as integrated estates in their own right rather than parts of a less integrated complex around St John's, although they appear to have joined the latter group at a later date.

Farndon, of course, was the third of the western land-holding churches, and was the centre of a less integrated complex of estates in its own right. There is no mention of a college of canons in Domesday book, but two hides of the estate were held by two priests, and a third (the 'priest of the vill') is also noted. Farndon was itself a divided vill, also hosting one of Earl Edwin's estates, and the bishop's estates in the remainder of the distinct group of vills in this area shared with the earl, 'Burwardestone', Tilston and Bettisfield, probably formed part of this complex, although only Bettisfield was explicitly ascribed to St Chad's in the Domesday text. Bettisfield was in the medieval parish of St Chad's church at Hanmer, and Alan Thacker has suggested that the land with its church at Hanmer formed the bishop's share of Bettisfield claimed TRW, having been absorbed within it at some point subsequent to 1066; if so, we could remove Bettisfield from the list of divided vills, because (as discussed in relation to Gresford earlier) the bishop's estate would presumably have been recorded under

---

108 My thanks to Nigel Tringham for sharing his transcript of the survey with me.

the vill at Hanmer had it survived.[109] Across the Dee the estates at Eyton and Sutton, which belonged TRE to St Chad's, Farndon, were in the parish of St Chad's church at Holt, later a chapelry of Gresford; it is distinctly possible that the dedication of Holt church relates to an earlier parochial connection with Farndon, but that the acquisition of Eyton and Sutton by the lord of Gresford resulted in their transfer to the church of the latter. Indeed, it seems very likely that the dedications to St Chad at both Holt and Hanmer derive from an early parochial dependency on the church at Farndon, articulated through its landholdings. The various estates around Farndon are scattered across a region of similar size to that defined by the penumbra of estates surrounding St Chad's church in Shrewsbury, and the similarity would be more striking if they were all originally within the parish of Farndon. St Chad's had lost all its outlying holdings other than a hide in Eyton by 1086, and it seems fair to suggest that its importance had declined by this time, perhaps suffering neglect as the bishop's focus shifted to the college of St John's in Chester.

To summarise this analysis of the bishop's Domesday holdings thus far, it is possible to conceive a division in the diocese between the more integrated estates that dominate in Staffordshire, Warwickshire and Derbyshire, with some in Shropshire and Cheshire, and the less integrated concentrations of estates either explicitly associated with or at least within close geographical proximity to the three churches of St Chad's, Shrewsbury, St Chad's, Farndon, and St John's, Chester. The majority of the divided vills hosting the bishop's estates (eleven out of fifteen) appear to group with these less integrated estate complexes, either being explicitly connected with the western churches or, if not, then in close geographical proximity to them. In three of the four remaining divided vills (Ellastone, Bishops Tachbrook and Bupton) the bishop held almost half or more of the hidage of the vill, and two of these were the largest episcopal estates within the entire set of divided vills, Tachbrook at seven hides and Bupton at five carucates and two bovates. Of the divided vills among the three less integrated complexes, only Farndon (four hides) was assessed at more than two hides, and this almost certainly reflects its status at the centre of one of these complexes.

It is now necessary to consider the implications that the structures and distributions of the episcopal landholdings have for our understanding of the mechanisms that formed them. For none of the episcopal estates, apart from Lichfield, can it be positively demonstrated that the bishop acquired them and established their churches during the seventh, eighth or ninth centuries. Neither can we simply project the estate structures described in Domesday Book back into the seventh, eighth and ninth centuries. Nevertheless, comparison with other English bishoprics (notably Worcester) suggests that a significant proportion had been acquired by the tenth century.[110] The data given in Table 1 demonstrates that nine of the integrated holdings

---

109 B.E. Harris with A.T. Thacker (eds), *VCH Cheshire*, vol. 1 (Oxford, 1987), p. 271. Thacker likewise suggests that the bishop's share of 'Burwardestone' (if the latter of the two can be identified with Iscoyd in the parish of Malpas) might be represented by the chapelry of St Chad in Tushingham, in which case, again, 'Burwadestone' could be removed from the list of divided vills.

110 M.F. Giandrea, *Episcopal culture in late Anglo-Saxon England* (Woodbridge, 2007), pp. 131–45, especially at p. 135.

formed a solid core, none of which were assessed at less than five hides; four of these were located in Staffordshire, two in Derbyshire and one each in Warwickshire, Shropshire and Cheshire. This core also dominates the record of priests or churches among the statistics given in Domesday Book, and the extent of dedications to St Chad among their parochial churches is impressive (seven of the nine). It is certainly plausible that this core represents the major part of the episcopal estate across the diocese, which had probably been acquired by the end of the ninth century and had witnessed sustained episcopal investment in its various churches. This possibility is explored further in the final section of the chapter.

Beyond this easily identifiable core there are nine estates that did not belong to less integrated assemblages, but were assessed at less than five hides, only two of which hosted parochial churches with St Chad dedications. The latter, Caldecote in Warwickshire and Wybunbury in Cheshire, were both also recorded with priests in Domesday Book.[111] Caldecote was held by a layman, Tonna, who may have been an episcopal tenant as he is said to have been unable to go where he would with his land, a sure sign of dependent tenure. At Burton in Wirral and Great Haywood the ploughland assessments (seven and ten respectively) are significantly larger than the hidages, indicating larger holdings for which beneficial hidage assessments had somehow been obtained.[112] Chillington lay in the parish of Brewood church, and was probably a dependency of that estate before being lost to the see. These five holdings can thus be fairly easily reconciled with elements of the core group; the same cannot be said of the remaining four estates. 'Chatsall' and Ellastone represent two of four estates that were located in divided vills but were not obviously associated with any of the less integrated holdings centred on the three western churches.[113] In 1066 Farnborough had been held by a layman, Stori, described as a freeman, and therefore unlikely to have been an episcopal tenant; perhaps the estate had been given to the see by a lay donor after the Conquest.[114] Finally, Buildwas may have belonged to the assemblage of estates supporting St Chad's church, Shrewsbury, but an alternative possibility will be discussed below. Aside from these four estates all episcopal holdings not associated with the western churches represent coherent integrated estates, relatively large for the most part, which might have been acquired by the see through a variety of means as distinct packages of land, either already possessing a central *caput* with subsidiary dependencies and associated church or thereafter acquiring these elements through processes of targeted investment.

It has been argued above that the less integrated complexes of estates centred on Shrewsbury, Farndon and Chester appear to indicate the assemblage of smaller holdings intended to support the bishop's churches at these centres. It is important

---

111 Caldecote was held for quarter of a knight's fee administered through Lichfield in the 1298 survey; Wybunbury remained a distinct episcopal estate.
112 Both remained distinct episcopal estates in the 1298 survey.
113 By 1298 Ellastone had been combined with Bupton in Derbyshire and other lands to support two knight's fees administered through Lichfield. Interestingly, Bupton was also one of the estates located in a divided vill but not associated with the western churches, alongside Bishops Tachbrook.
114 Neither estate was among the possessions of the see in the 1298 survey.

to reiterate that these complexes were fundamentally less territorially coherent than integrated holdings: even if their component estates are considered similar in kind to the dependencies within integrated holdings, they were often intermixed with the estates of other landholders. In the cases of St Chad's churches at Farndon and Shrewsbury, Nick Higham and Steven Bassett have proposed that this pattern of scattered lands and associated multi-part parishes emerged as a result of the fragmentation of earlier unitary landholdings through the loss of substantial parts to lay landholders.[115] Such fragmentation is essentially the opposite of the mechanism of assemblage proposed here to explain the formation of these complexes, but cannot be entirely ruled out. These two mechanisms also have different implications for explaining the divided vills: a model of fragmentation would imply that the bishop granted away or otherwise lost parts of vills within larger integrated holdings, while a model of assemblage would instead focus on the granting of parts of vills to the bishop by the king or other landholder. An example of one way in which the bishop might lose a holding can be found in the folios of Domesday Book: an episcopal estate at Selly Oak in Worcestershire (a divided vill TRE) was leased by the bishop for three lives to a certain Wulfwin before the Conquest, but it did not return to the see at the end of the term, instead remaining in lay hands.[116] Nevertheless, this evidence is essentially anecdotal, and the mechanism of fragmentation does not explain why less integrated estates should be found predominantly along the western edge of the diocese; in contrast, a model employing the mechanism of assemblage can be connected directly to the distinctive status of the three western churches among the diocesan holdings.

The possible roles of episcopal tenants in the structuring of episcopal holdings can be investigated further, as it has been suggested that one particularly important tenant can be identified in the western heartland of the less integrated holdings. In 1066 a thegn named Thored, whom we met earlier as lord of Gresford, held a scattering of estates, some of them of considerable size, in the vicinities of Shrewsbury, Farndon and Chester, and almost nowhere else; indeed, the rarity of his name provides a plausible reason to identify him as one man rather than several landholders of the same name in these rather specific areas.[117] On the basis of the territorial overlap between Thored and the bishop, Alan Thacker has suggested that Thored was an episcopal tenant (despite the epithet 'free man' applied to him on several occasions in the Domesday folios); Thacker also points to the fact that Thored's holdings at Barrow and Ashton were located not only near the bishop's holding at Tarvin but within the parish of Tarvin church.[118] We might add to this the fact that a member of Thored's

---

115 Higham, *Origins*, pp. 133–40; S. Bassett, 'Anglo-Saxon Shrewsbury and its churches', *Midland History*, 16 (1991), pp. 1–23.
116 *DB Worcs.*, 23,1.
117 *DB Salop.*, 4,3,14, 4,3,20, 4,3,26, 4,3, 30, 4,3,31, 4,3,69; *DB Chesh.*, 5,1, 9,5, 16,1, 20,1, 22,1, 27,3, FD 7,1.
118 Harris with Thacker, *VCH Cheshire*, pp. 271–3; Thacker's reasoning also includes the summation of hidage assessments for various contiguous estates held by Thored and the bishop to give multiples of the 'five-hide unit'. Barrow was described as a 'free chapel' in the prebend of Tarvin (Higham, *Origins*, pp. 149–50).

holding at Wroxeter, called Little Buildwas (unrecorded in Domesday Book, but found in later texts), lay adjacent to the episcopal holding at Buildwas: given the use of the same place-name, we would appear to have here another divided vill.[119] Thored's dominance of land in *Exestan* hundred west of the Dee (through his large estate at Gresford and another at nearby Allington) can be made to support or undermine Thacker's theory when viewed in the light of a statement appended to the entry for the bishop's estate at Eyton in that hundred: at some point King Edward had given 'all the land that lay beyond the water which is called Dee' to Gruffydd ap Llywelyn, king of Wales (1055–63), but, after Gruffydd wronged him, Edward took back the land 'and restored it to the bishop of Chester and to all his men who had formerly held it'.[120] The correct reading of this statement is elusive: if the 'men' who formerly held land were the bishop's, then we would almost certainly be correct to count Thored among them, but if the men were the king's, then there is no support here for seeing Thored as an episcopal tenant, as he would more plausibly be viewed as an important king's thegn.

If Thored was an episcopal tenant, the distribution of his holdings would support the model of fragmentation to explain some of the less integrated episcopal estates; viewing him as a king's thegn offers support to the assemblage model. Unfortunately neither position can be proven definitively, but there is some reason to treat the latter more seriously. Thored's holding at Barrow, in the parish of the bishop's church at Tarvin, had been given to the church of St Werburgh in Chester by King Edgar in 958.[121] There is no evidence to illuminate how St Werburgh's subsequently lost it, but the fact of former royal possession should be noted. Thored's holdings in Cheshire passed to several different lords after the Conquest, indicating that he was not a formal 'antecessor' of the kind identifiable elsewhere in the survey, whose lands passed *en bloc* to a post-Conquest successor.[122] Likewise, while Thored's Shropshire holdings all passed to the sheriff of Shropshire, the latter's holdings appear to have derived from a larger pool of thegns like Thored.[123] Thored thus appears to have had much in common with the other middle-ranking thegns of these shires. His only real distinction was the confinement of his Cheshire holdings to the western edge of that shire, which may relate to the role the king or earl expected him to fulfil, perhaps in relation to the Welsh border; Higham has suggested similar targeted roles for other Cheshire thegns associated with circumscribed groupings of estates.[124] In fact, all the less integrated episcopal holdings can also be viewed productively in relation to royal interests. Chester and Shrewsbury were royal boroughs, and Farndon was a divided vill shared with Earl

---

119 *DB Salop.*, 4.3.26 note. S. Bassett, 'Medieval ecclesiastical organisation in the vicinity of Wroxeter and its British antecedents', *Journal of the British Archaeological Association*, 145 (1992), pp. 1–28, at p. 3.
120 *DB Chesh.*, B7.
121 J. Tait, *The chartulary of Chester Abbey*, Chetham Society New Series 79 (Manchester, 1920), pp. xviii and 9.
122 D. Roffe, 'From thegnage to barony: sake and soke, title, and tenants-in-chief', *Anglo-Norman Studies*, 12 (1990), pp. 157–76.
123 *DB Salop.*, 4,3 *passim*.
124 Higham, *Origins*, pp. 126–81.

Edwin TRE, but formerly perhaps a royal possession, as King Edward the Elder had died there in 924.[125] Royal patronage may thus be the common denominator behind both the holdings of the bishop and of Thored, and indeed behind the number of divided vills in the western reaches of the bishop's estate, the patterns having been formed by successive royal grants to bishops, earls and thegns in a region already populated by a considerable number of landholders and thus not amenable to the provision of large integrated holdings at the time the grants were made.[126] Indeed, the post-Conquest poaching of episcopal holdings in *Exestan* hundred and the incorporation of them into the large estate at Gresford may represent the creation of a more integrated holding there from formerly independent elements.

If the deliberate granting of components out of royal holdings explains the three distinctive assemblages focused on churches at the western edge of the bishop's Domesday estate, it might also explain other holdings in the diocese that do not fit comfortably within the core distribution, in particular those of notably small size, some in divided vills. The small holding at Wybunbury (Cheshire) might plausibly be considered part of an earlier royal holding centred on the important salt-producing site at nearby Nantwich, which was administered in 1066 from a *caput* at Acton held by Earl Morcar, who divided the profits and renders of eight salthouses with the king (King Edward held no land in Cheshire in 1066).[127] As such, Wybunbury was perhaps granted to an earlier bishop as a means of providing the diocesan community with a stake in salt production, but at some point received additional investment from the see in the form of a church. Likewise, the small holding in the divided vill at Ellastone was located in the midst of a complex of royal estates at Rocester, Crakemarsh, Uttoxeter and Mayfield, ascribed to Earl Ælfgar TRE; it might have given successive bishops access to the lush cattle pastures of the Dove valley. Great Haywood, although not as small as its hidage assessment might indicate, interlocked territorially with a royal holding at Chartley, again ascribed to Ælfgar TRE, and was perhaps granted to an earlier bishop to provide a hunting ground on Cannock Chase at the southern edge of the holding, and perhaps charcoal from its woods (the place-name Haywood means a 'fenced' or 'enclosed' part of a 'wood', perhaps implying hunting, while the church of the holding was at nearby Colwich, meaning a 'specialised settlement associated with charcoal').[128] Finally, Statfold, a distant member of the estate at Lichfield, not recorded in Domesday Book but present in later texts, was located in close proximity to the royal borough at Tamworth and has a place-name meaning 'stud-fold', associating it with the breeding of horses.[129] In all cases, these holdings were potentially granted out of royal estates in order to provide the diocesan community with access to some specific kind of resource.

Association with royal holdings is also notable at some of the larger integrated episcopal holdings that form the main part of the core diocesan estate. Geographical

---

125 *ASC* (C and D), 924.
126 This is pursued in Chapters 5 and 6.
127 *DB Chesh.*, S1; see Higham, *Origins*, pp. 143–5.
128 D. Horovitz, *The place-names of Staffordshire* (Brewood, 2005), pp. 204 and 306–7.
129 Horovitz, *Place-names*, p. 510.

proximity might be expected in areas where elite establishments clustered in the more productive parts of the landscape, a phenomenon explored in Chapters 5 and 6, but in some cases the association may indicate something closer still. The large holding at Bupton (Derbyshire) was centred on a vill that it shared in 1086 with another estate there and the member of a further estate at Thurvaston; these two estates were held by a man named Elfin under Henry de Ferrers.[130] Elfin held a coherent cluster of estates in this area, including one at Brailsford that had been held by Earl Waltheof TRE; the others had been held by various thegns in 1066, and it is unclear whether Elfin's assemblage was based on some kind of pre-Conquest predecessor.[131] Support for the existence of such an entity is offered by the dedication of the church at Brailsford to St Chad in the sixteenth century (it was later All Saints), which may indicate association with the bishop's church on his Bupton holding (which was located in neighbouring Longford).[132] The possibility here, tenuous though it must remain, is that a larger unitary holding was shared at some point between earl (perhaps ultimately king) and bishop, its components never entirely disentangled.[133] A similar, although less complex, possibility is offered by the large episcopal holding at Tarvin (Cheshire), which did not share any vills with other estates but included the holdings of Barrow and Ashton in the parish of its church; these were held by Thored TRE, but Barrow was certainly in royal hands in the mid-tenth century, and it was suggested above that Thored had benefited from royal patronage. In both cases, these connections need not represent features that had existed since the initial acquisition of the holdings by the see; indeed, the parochial association at Tarvin can date only to the tenth century at the earliest, when the tithes that formed the essence of parochial territories were introduced.[134] Nevertheless, whenever they emerged, they point to distinct links in the organisation of episcopal and royal holdings in these cases, in place by the mid-eleventh century at the latest.

One final case is worth exploring. As noted above, the small episcopal holding at Buildwas (Shropshire) appears to have shared a vill with a member of the estate at Wroxeter, held TRE by Thored.[135] Thored's other holdings in the vicinity of Wroxeter were distributed within the two hundreds of Wrockwardine and Condover, a territory from which the twelfth-century bishop of Chester Roger de Clinton received a customary due called 'church-amber'; he granted this due to a Savignac abbey that he founded

---

130 *DB Derbys.*, 6,52, 6,60.

131 *DB Derbys.*, 6,40, 6,52, 6,58, 6,60.

132 R. Clark, 'The dedications of medieval churches in Derbyshire: their survival and change from the Reformation to the present day', *Derbyshire Archaeological Journal*, 112 (1992), pp. 48–61, at p. 57. Note that in the sixteenth century the dedication of Longford church was recorded as St Mary, but thereafter St Chad; the long-standing association of the estate with the bishop suggests that St Chad's was the older dedication (Clark, 'Dedications', p. 58).

133 Further evidence in support may be offered by the fact that the bishop's Bupton estate was later recorded with a member at Thurvaston: *SHC* 1st Series, vol. 1, p. 152.

134 See further discussion in Chapters 4 and 6.

135 *DB Salop.*, 4,3,26.

at Buildwas in 1135.[136] There is no record of a church at Buildwas before 1135, but there was an earlier church at Wroxeter, for which four priests were recorded in its Domesday entry. Royal interest in the vicinity was focused in holdings at Wrockwardine and Condover.[137] These various elements would permit several possibilities, but it seems plausible that the church at Wroxeter once lay at the centre of a royal holding (later granted to Thored) and that the bishop also had some interest in it (hence the 'church-amber', which is discussed in more detail in Chapter 4). The episcopal holding at Buildwas is resonant of the 'small estate' (*agellus*) that Bishop Aidan possessed in association with a church at the royal vill where he died in mid seventh-century Northumbria.[138] It is also worth noting that the church at Wroxeter was dedicated to St Andrew, as was the church on the bishop's holding at Tarvin; this was a suitable apostolic dedication for an early church, but Higham has noted that Bishop Wilfrid, who undertook episcopal work in Mercia for Kings Wulfhere and Æthelred, particularly favoured it.[139] The apparent connection of episcopal and royal interests in the church at Wroxeter, and perhaps also those at Tarvin and Longford, indicates that both parties continued to play a part in the organisation of the combined holding, which itself hints at the possible complexity of relationships between the diocesan community and the king.

The Church of Lichfield and the diocesan community

In 749, at a royal assembly at Gumley (Leicestershire), the Mercian king Æthelblad granted a series of privileges to all the minsters and churches of his core Mercian province.[140] It was attested by two representatives of the ecclesiastical order: Torhthelm, the bishop of Leicester, and the bishop of Lichfield, Hwita, who was styled 'bishop of the church of the Mercians'.[141] As argued in Chapter 1, the word 'church' here was probably intended as a 'community of believers', and such a concept was not normally assigned to a population intermediate between the individual diocese

---

136 The dues are recorded in a confirmation charter of Richard I dated 1189 (M.J. Franklin, *Coventry and Lichfield 1072–1159*, English episcopal *acta* 14 (Oxford, 1997), pp. 10–11). Bishop Hugh de Nonant's confirmation of 1192 states that the render was appurtenant to the singular estate at Buildwas and Meole, which had been assembled in 1135 from the bishop's separate holdings at these places; to which estate they pertained before this date is ambiguous, and Steven Bassett favours Meole (Bassett, 'Anglo-Saxon Shrewsbury', p. 6). The recorded population of Buildwas included a reeve in 1086, which may or may not be pertinent.

137 *DB Salop.*, 4,1,1, 4,1,2.

138 *HE*, iii.17. He apparently had similar arrangements at other royal vills. Steven Bassett has suggested that Wroxeter was once the mother church for the territory represented by the hundreds of Wrockwardine and Condover (S. Bassett, 'Church and diocese in the West Midlands: the transition from British to Anglo-Saxon control', in J. Blair and R. Sharpe (eds), *Pastoral care before the parish* (Leicester, 1992), pp. 13–40, at pp. 35–9), although see Chapter 5 for criticism of the methodology by which he derives this conclusion.

139 Higham, *Origins*, p. 149.

140 S 92.

141 *Mercensis ecclesiae episcopus*. Torhthelm was styled only *episcopus*.

and the Church of the English. The fact that Torhthelm also attested as a bishop in the Mercian realm represented by Æthelbald's assembly would seem to rule out the possibility that the 'Mercians' of Hwita's style represented the inhabitants of the entire province.[142] Hwita's 'Mercian Church' therefore plausibly represented only the inhabitants of the diocese of Lichfield, although in what follows the 'Church of Lichfield' will be used as a synonym in order to avoid confusion with the broader political hegemony of the Mercian kings. Moreover, just as Chapter 1 explored the ways in which the English Church as an imagined community was supported within the discourse of the English ecclesiastical community, so here the Church of Lichfield must be understood similarly as an imagined community that emerged through the discourse of a Lichfield-centred diocesan community.

The above analysis of the bishop's Domesday estate identified a core of large integrated holdings scattered across the diocesan territory alongside three less integrated complexes centred on churches on the western side of the diocese; very few elements of the estate fail to fit within these two elements. The broader implications of this structure for the nature, origins and development of the diocesan community can now be explored. The better-documented episcopal estate at Worcester was assembled over the course of the late seventh, eighth and earlier ninth centuries by the acquisition and accumulation of previously independent minsters, although it also included some holdings that had never been minsters.[143] Within the group of appropriated minsters, Patrick Sims-Williams has pointed to a distinction between 'a monastic community under an abbot, who might or might not also be a priest ordained by the bishop' and 'a pastoral "minster" under a priest, with or without a community'.[144] The Worcester evidence indicates a general transformation of the former into the latter that was largely complete by the late ninth century, and John Blair has traced a similar pattern more widely both in England and elsewhere.[145] Thus, by the time of the Domesday survey, it is often impossible to distinguish a church more recently established on a holding, with a priest or two serving the local inhabitants, from an older minster church no longer hosting a community and served instead by one or two priests. Unfortunately we do not have any textual evidence from the diocese of Lichfield that can be compared with that from Worcester, making it difficult to see beyond the mid-eleventh-century horizon offered by Domesday Book. However, structural similarities between the episcopal estates of Worcester and Lichfield offer some promising possibilities.

At the centre of the Worcester estate was a unitary block of land representing the original grant establishing the see for the direct support of the cathedral;[146] this

---

142 Assuming that no other bishops were present at the assembly, Æthelbald's *regnum* appears to have occupied the territories encompassed by the dioceses of Lichfield and Leicester, probably indicating that other Southumbrian provinces within the Mercian kingdom at this time were considered part of the king's *imperium* rather than his own kingdom.
143 Sims-Williams, *Religion and literature*, particularly Chapter 6; Tinti, *Sustaining belief*, Chapter 4.
144 Sims-Williams, *Religion and literature*, p. 170.
145 Blair, *Church*, pp. 323–9 and 341–6.
146 Tinti, *Sustaining belief*, pp. 165–8; in 1086 the major components of this block were estates at Wick Episcopi, Northwick and Cropthorne, with smaller estates interspersed.

compares well with the holding at Lichfield, originally given to Chad in 669, which was of a similar geographical extent. Outside this central portion the majority, though not all, of the diocesan estate of Worcester comprised formerly independent minsters appropriated at various different times, and we might therefore assume much the same to be true of the core group of the bishop of Lichfield's holdings identified above, although it was suggested that some episcopal holdings originated as direct grants for specific purposes, and therefore had non-monastic origins. The less integrated complexes of holdings on the western side of the diocese of Lichfield are less easily compared with the Worcester evidence. However, the focus of two of these complexes on Chester and Shrewsbury may point to the context of their origins: Roman Chester was renovated as a fortified 'burh' by Æthelred and Æthelflæd, Lord and Lady of the Mercians, in 907, and Shrewsbury appears to have been established as another of their bases by 901;[147] it is therefore likely that the bishop's interest in establishing churches within these burhs dates only from this period at the earliest. Indeed, Paul Everson and David Stocker have recently suggested that St John's originated as a church serving a tenth-century trading community, and if this is accepted it is possible to suggest that the third less integrated complex around Farndon represents the bishop's initial establishment in the vicinity of a revived Chester, located a little further down the navigable river Dee. The Farndon complex perhaps began to decline in importance once the bishop had managed to acquire St John's, perhaps in the later tenth or earlier eleventh century.[148] Conceiving the origin of the less integrated complexes in this way supports a view of their distinctiveness as the product of active assemblage (as argued above) rather than fragmentation from some earlier unity, their form owed to the specific circumstances of their establishment in the tenth or earlier eleventh centuries through royal patronage in the vicinity of royal burhs, in a context dominated largely by dispersed landholdings and few integrated estates.

Both St John's, Chester, and St Chad's, Shrewsbury, hosted large clerical communities in 1066, but in this they were exceptional in the diocese outside Lichfield itself, where five canons were recorded. Excluding Farndon, none of the other churches recorded on episcopal holdings appears to have been in any sense independent of the bishop, nor were any of them credited with independent landholdings; at best these churches might have held some small portions of their host estates, as indicated by the holdings ascribed to the priests listed in the Domesday statistics. This resonates with the fate of many of the appropriated minsters noted above in the well-documented diocese of Worcester: namely, conversion into pastoral churches served by priests, and with no necessary control of the former minster holdings, in whole or in part. It also prompts us to consider the intentions lying behind this process. The ex-minsters of the Worcester diocese were

---

147 S. Bassett, 'Anglo-Saxon fortifications in western Mercia', *Midland History*, 36 (2011), pp. 11–12; M. Blake and A. Sargent, '"For the protection of all the people": Æthelflæd and her burhs in northwest Mercia', *Midland History*, 43 (2018), pp. 120–54.

148 I intend to argue elsewhere that Whitchurch in Shropshire represents another of the burhs established by Æthelred and Æthelflæd, in which case it should be noted that Farndon lies approximately halfway between Chester and Whitchurch.

explicitly listed as part of the 'Church of Worcester' in 1086, implying a unitary sense of community that encompassed them, and indeed all of the episcopal churches and landholdings, whether formerly monastic or not. To explore this kind of community we need to look outside the minster-dominated narratives of John Blair and Sarah Foot, which, in Catherine Cubitt's words, have 'a tendency to view all Anglo-Saxon religious establishments as minsters regardless of size or purpose and to suggest that this was the primary category of Anglo-Saxon classification'.[149]

In an important article Cubitt has demonstrated that eighth-century writers such as Bede, Boniface and Aldhelm, as well as the canons of Church councils, were careful to distinguish between clergy and monks, who were held to be subject to different authorities – the former to bishops and the latter to abbots and abbesses. They also made a second distinction, which cut across the first, between 'minsters' (*monasteria*), which possessed a community living under a Rule (members of which may or may not have also been priests), and 'churches' (*ecclesiae*), also called 'oratories' (*oratoria*), buildings which appear to have been consecrated by bishops on royal or other lay estates, or were situated on small estates of their own, and which did not support regular communities but perhaps only a small group of clergy; these churches, Cubitt suggests, are unlikely to have been called minsters by eighth-century authors.[150] The significance of this terminology is debated. Blair argues that the rarity of references to small community-less churches, when coupled with their apparent absence from the archaeological record, indicates that, in contrast to Francia, they were the exception rather than the rule.[151] Cubitt, however, while accepting the rarity of these references, emphasises that 'they are, on the other hand, routine and commonplace', and therefore that the monastic focus of writers such as Bede and Aldhelm obscures an important facet of the English ecclesiastical scene.[152] If this is the case, then by accepting Blair's inclusive definition of a minster as a catch-all for seventh-, eighth- and ninth-century religious institutions we are glossing over some important contemporary distinctions.

The word *ecclesia* was, of course, also used to describe an episcopal see such as the Church of Lichfield, and, although this was intended imaginatively, to describe an entire Christian community of believers, its application could not be separated from the hierarchical community within which the term was regularly used, with the bishop at its head. The practice of the Circuit V commissioners preserved in Domesday Book demonstrates that such terminology was used to ascribe the ownership of episcopal landholdings, which were also understood to be ruled by the bishop as an element of his office. The authors discussed by Cubitt indicate that churches and communities on these lands were used by bishops from at least the eighth century to administer the religious life of their dioceses. We therefore need to acknowledge two kinds of organised religious community during the seventh, eighth and ninth centuries: the

---

149 C. Cubitt, 'The clergy in early Anglo-Saxon England', *Historical Research*, 78/201 (2005), pp. 273–87, at pp. 277–8.
150 Cubitt, 'The clergy', p. 279.
151 Blair, *Church*, pp. 118–21.
152 Cubitt, 'The clergy', p. 280.

independent ecclesiastical community living according to a Rule of religious life in a minster; and the diocesan community centred on a bishop, but encompassing a clerical membership distributed in minsters and smaller churches throughout the diocese with whom the bishop had regular contact and over whom he wielded an administrative authority. The independence of the former was essentially defined by its relation to the latter, although the two forms had always overlapped: independent communities included both ordained and non-ordained members, of which the former were also members of the bishop's diocesan community. The scope of episcopal authority within these independent communities, and its relationship to the authority of their rulers, the abbots and abbesses, is explored in more depth in Chapter 4.

The Lichfield diocesan community was centred on the minster at Lichfield, but by 1066 it encompassed all the integrated holdings forming the core estate identified above. The dedication of churches on most of these holdings to St Chad emphasises the extent to which those who lived and served there belonged just as much to the community of Lichfield, where Chad's cult was focused, as did those who actually lived at the cathedral. The emergence and development of the diocesan community was in part rooted in the kind of extended ecclesiastical community discussed at the beginning of this chapter, in which the several minsters were united by veneration of a founding saint, but it retained a greater distinctiveness. Extended communities tended to dissolve over time, as parts of their memberships located at different minsters died off or pursued their own independent courses; the creation of a multi-centred diocesan community thus required active strategies of integration, including the acquisition of independent minster-based communities subsequently made dependent on the see, often eventually to become churches served by one or two priests. Elsewhere some episcopal holdings probably never hosted formerly independent minster-based communities in the first place, but comprised elements of the diocesan community from the outset, perhaps granted by kings or other landholders. Only the communities based at the three western churches at Shrewsbury, Farndon and Chester exhibit distinct independence from the community based at Lichfield; as argued above, they are likely to have been established at a later date, in the tenth or eleventh centuries.

The discussion in this chapter has sought to demonstrate that it is possible to gain a coherent appreciation of the Lichfield diocesan community, even if the precise chronology of its formation will forever remain uncertain. The outline, at least, of the development of the episcopal estate is clear: the minster at Lichfield, initially acquired by St Chad as part of his extended ecclesiastical community (encompassing Lastingham and Barrow in Lindsey), subsequently became the nucleus of a diocesan community that expanded primarily through the acquisition of formerly independent ecclesiastical communities based at minsters, but also as the recipient of various direct grants. Crucially, this estate formed the basis for support of a diocesan community, but was not coterminous with it, as the community itself comprised the full complement of clerics under the bishop's authority. Outside the dependent minsters and churches of the episcopal estate, these included clerics living in independent minster-based communities, and perhaps those serving churches on lay holdings, if such are assumed to have existed in any number. The close relationship of some episcopal holdings with royal holdings revealed in Domesday Book opens an insight into the means by which episcopal oversight of clerics not directly supported by the episcopal estate might have been managed in some cases.

Such conclusions disturb the primacy accorded by John Blair to minster-based communities as institutions, which, he suggests, provided English bishops with both their sole source of organisational resource and, in the form of independent communities, their greatest difficulty in attempting to rule their dioceses.[153] In this book, minsters are acknowledged as an important structuring frame, but their significance is promoted in terms of the distinctly varied forms of communities that they enabled; notably, the diocesan community was not coterminous with any specific minster, or even a set of minsters. Of greater importance in understanding this community is an awareness of the regular practices that connected the bishop with the clerics of his diocese, which essentially formed the substance of the diocesan community. The cult of St Chad stands out, even if we are ignorant of the details of the annual liturgical rituals that must have united much of the community. It also provides the connection between that community and Chad's earlier extended community, which persisted after his death precisely because its members invested so much in the memory of their founders; this memorialisation subsequently became central to the Lichfield diocesan community, and is explored further in Chapter 3.

Other forms of collective activity must also have contributed to the maintenance of the diocesan community, but unfortunately we begin to run up against the limits of the evidence. Nothing can be said for certain on the probable existence of diocesan synods, as there is no evidence for them in this region, although such assemblies are known to have taken place elsewhere; for example, Willibald's *Life of St Boniface* describes such synods in the West Saxon diocese in the late seventh and early eighth centuries.[154] Likewise, the annual procession of a bishop around his diocese, advocated by a canon issued at the Council of *Clofesho* in 747, might be invoked to add depth to the relationships that bishops of Lichfield must have cultivated with their diocesan communities.[155] Such perambulations were intended to enable bishops to visit the entire community of Christians within their dioceses, and remind us that, in participating in the diocesan community, its members inhabited a vision of the Church of Lichfield, the 'Church of the Mercians'. We clearly need to think about this Church in terms of the several different communities, religious and lay, that were invested in it or touched by it. The next chapter begins this exploration by focusing on the ecclesiastical communities of the diocese that emerged during the seventh, eighth and ninth centuries, based primarily at minsters.

---

153 Blair, *Church*, pp. 108–17.
154 *EHD* 1, pp. 715–16 (no. 158).
155 Canon 3: see Haddan and Stubbs, *Councils*, pp. 360–76, at pp. 363–4.

Chapter 3

The cathedral and the minsters

John Blair's definition of a minster, quoted in the introduction, is broad enough to encompass different proportions of clerics, monks and nuns among the inhabitants, and a variety of material forms and sizes, reminding us that not all minsters were the same, and thus the communities they supported are bound to have differed as well. Nevertheless, his rather institutional view recognises the primacy of minster-centred communities, entities largely confined within the bounds of the places they inhabited. In contrast, this book has proposed that it is not enough to talk of minster communities as if they were self-evident phenomena, simply because people living at minsters probably encountered each other on a regular day-to-day basis. We might easily accept the existence of minster-based (rather than minster-centred) communities, whose members lived much of their lives at minsters, but the nature and form of such communities has to be understood in terms outside the purely geographical: this book seeks communities in the regular, ritualising activities that their members performed collectively, whether or not they lived their everyday lives in close proximity to one another. Nevertheless, having considered some forms of community that often extended across several minsters and other ecclesiastical sites, we now need to consider the kinds of community that can in fact be understood largely within the confines of single minsters. An important barrier to revealing the nature and variety of these communities is the partial nature of the evidence available. Studies such as Blair's have revealed that many earlier minsters were later refashioned as parish churches, but it is by no means simple to identify former minsters behind the dense distribution of parish churches across the landscape, many more of which owe their origins to the tenth century or later. An important task of this chapter is thus identifying those minsters in the diocese likely to have been founded before the early tenth century. Beyond this, however, the chapter explores how the material elements of these minsters enabled specifically place-centred communities to develop and outlines the significance of regularly repeated liturgical ritual, particularly as focused on the cults of saints, in creating 'liturgical communities'.

In the first part of the chapter the evidence available to enable the identification of minsters is discussed. There is very little textual evidence to illuminate the precise nature of the minster-based communities of the diocese. This dearth is particularly pronounced in the diocese of Lichfield, but a similar problem is encountered across much of England outside privileged islands of textual survival, such as the diocese of Worcester. This has encouraged scholars to innovate other methods of finding minsters; one particularly influential idea promotes the role of minsters as centres of pastoral care and connects them to the earliest identifiable structures through which such care was implemented, the mother parishes of the tenth or eleventh centuries and later, developing a methodology that projects back from later parochial geographies to identify mother churches, which are then assumed to represent earlier minsters. This methodology is criticised in Chapter 4, and judged far more reliable for identifying mother parishes than anything earlier; it is thus unsuited to the hunt for earlier minsters, which forms the main purpose of this chapter. Likewise, Domesday Book is a wonderful source for the later eleventh century, and records several superior churches across the region, but none of them can necessarily be assumed to have histories before the eleventh, or perhaps the tenth century, unless documentary and/or archaeological evidence indicates otherwise. We therefore require alternative methods of identifying earlier minsters in the diocese.

In what follows, the evidence provided by documentary sources (primarily hagiography), archaeological excavations and surveys of early medieval stone sculpture are reviewed across the diocese to reveal the distribution of probable minsters. Thereafter, the evidence for the cathedral and a corpus of thirty-eight probable minster sites is presented and discussed on a site-by-site basis, making clear the nature and limitations of the evidence used in each case. The detail provided here not only acts to ground analysis throughout the rest of the book for the period before the tenth century but also enables the development of a fine-grained understanding of the materiality of these early minster sites, and thus of their contribution to the creation and maintenance of liturgical communities in particular. One further result of the analysis is the development of a chronological framework for interpretation, which emphasises the importance of the period between the late seventh and earlier tenth centuries for the foundation of minsters as important bases for ecclesiastical communities; this is a slightly longer period than is often envisioned for the 'heyday' of the minsters, which many scholars would close with the Viking invasions of the mid-ninth century. The final part of the chapter attempts to draw some initial conclusions about the forms of community that were established and maintained at these minsters. This involves a restatement of the importance of liturgical communities as those most often commensurate with the physical bounds of individual minsters. But these must not be viewed in isolation, and the relations between these communities and larger associations revealed by the evidence are also explored.

Hunting for minsters

Hagiography

John Blair has argued that the cults of local saints in England were overwhelmingly supported at minsters of the seventh, eighth and ninth centuries, going so far as to suggest that every minster probably once had its saint, or saints.[1] Chapter 2 demonstrated various ways in which appeals to St Chad acted to create communities. In the later seventh and earlier eighth centuries Chad was a common point of reference for many who had been brought up within or later served within his extended ecclesiastical community, people who remembered him personally or at one remove. By 1086 the 'Church of St Chad' was one way in which the Domesday surveyors envisioned the community served from the episcopal estate across the diocese. There is no doubt that devotion to a saint such as Chad was not simply a religious

---

1   Blair, 'A saint for every minster?', pp. 455–94.

duty but often a meaningful social act whose relevance changed with circumstance. If we follow Blair's lead here, by identifying saints' cults in the diocese we also identify the minsters that supported them and, in some cases, can say something about the way these cults created and mediated relationships. Our knowledge of such cults comes in a variety of forms, which need to be considered in their own right so that the information they contain can be treated in a suitably critical manner. Much of the textual material is hagiographical: it relates to the lives of holy men and women venerated in a variety of ways in church-based communities, and was produced over a long period from the early eighth century to the fourteenth or even fifteenth centuries; for our purposes it can be understood in terms of four broad phases of production.

The first of these phases, from the early eighth to the early tenth centuries, includes the context discussed in the previous chapter from which emerged Lastingham's work of abbatial history. Works such as this were usually written by people with their own memories of their living subjects, or at least in direct contact with people possessing such memories. The demands of the genre required that their subjects were presented as paragons, but the fact of direct and shared remembrance meant in practice that such works also derived in part from the real concerns of their subjects and feature facts and events that we might consider 'reliable'. For example, we can deduce from the Lastingham Narrative (LN) that Chad was a much-admired abbot who then dwelt in the memories of those who knew him personally in the 660s and early 670s, or who had at least heard stories from those who had; the LN's concern with Chad's humility and canonical obedience represents the effects on those who knew him of Chad's experiences during that period, even if these effects were then channelled into a more hagiographical reverence for the learning of the church fathers and the fervent expression of his own humility before God. 'House histories' such as the LN were also focused on the death and burial of their subjects, and thus on a continuing focus of veneration in the form of special graves and shrines, often the locus of miracles. Two other probable examples of the genre exist from the diocese of Lichfield: one concerning St Wærburh and produced by her community at Hanbury in the early eighth century, which described the divinely inspired theft of her body for her community there and the subsequent elevation of her relics;[2] and another focused on St Wigstan of Repton, a royal martyr whose death was described in a narrative, or *Passio*, perhaps close to the beginning of his cult in the second half of the ninth century.[3]

Outside these narratives the only textual activity before the tenth century concerning saints in the diocese of Lichfield comprised elaboration of the existing hagiography of St Chad. A Latin narrative or *Life* derived from Bede's account of St Chad was produced probably in the eighth or ninth century, and an Old English

---

2   This narrative has no independent existence, but forms part of the *Vita Sanctae Werburgae* composed by Goscelin of St Bertin, perhaps while he was at Ely in 1087 or 1088: R.C. Love, *Goscelin of Saint-Bertin: the hagiography of the female saints of Ely* (Oxford, 2004).

3   See D. Rollason, *The search for St Wigstan, prince-martyr of the kingdom of Mercia*, Vaughan Paper 27 (Leicester, 1981), and D.W. Rollason, 'The cults of murdered royal saints in Anglo-Saxon England', *Anglo-Saxon England*, 11 (1983), pp. 1–22, at pp. 5–9, and sources cited therein.

Life was translated from this, possibly in the later ninth century but not necessarily earlier than the first quarter of the tenth century.[4] The compiler of the Old English Martyrology (c.850–900) included an epitome of St Chad's life, also deriving his material from Bede's work.[5] Liturgical evidence for this period is sparse, and none of it was produced at places within the diocese of Lichfield; the only known reference to a saint of the diocese concerns Chad, who appears as an eighth-century addition on the calendar of the Northumbrian missionary St Willibrord.[6] Catherine Cubitt has noted 'that all the native saints in the Martyrology are known to us from literary sources', concluding that the composition of the document was very much a literary endeavour.[7] We might extend this conclusion to the elaborated hagiography of St Chad during this period, all of which probably testifies to the spreading of his fame through Bede's *Ecclesiastical History*.

Our second phase of hagiographic activity spans a period from the early tenth to the mid-eleventh centuries, and is characterised by interest in a broader range of local saints by those producing hagiographical texts. One particularly important product of this period (and extending beyond it) is a genre of lists describing saints' resting-places.[8] David Rollason connects the form of these lists to lists of the apostles and their resting-places produced in the Mediterranean world at an early date, and in particular to the association of such lists with an interest in relic cults expressed by Pope Gregory the Great, whom inhabitants of the English kingdoms came to regard as the father of their own Christianity, the apostle of the English Church.[9] Only one list survives in pre-Conquest manuscripts, in a text entitled *Secgan be þam Godes sanctum þe on Engla lande ærost reston* ('Account of God's saints who earliest rested in England', hereafter *Secgan*), although Rollason has demonstrated that several post-Conquest resting-place lists, dating from the twelfth to the fifteenth centuries, and including a particularly expansive example in Hugh Candidus' Peterborough Chronicle, must also have owed their contents to pre-Conquest sources with varying degrees of relation to the *Secgan*.[10]

The earliest manuscript witnesses to the *Secgan* list date from the eleventh century, but the first part of the list displays a distinctive format, in which a nearby topographical feature is given to aid in locating each saint, and this may represent

---

4   R. Vleeskruyer, *The life of St Chad. An Old English homily* (Amsterdam, 1953), pp. 12–18, for the possibility of a Latin *Life* underlying the Old English version; see also J.M. Bately, 'Old English prose before and during the reign of Alfred', *Anglo-Saxon England*, 17 (1988), pp. 93–138, at p. 118 for the date of composition of the Old English *Life*.

5   G. George (ed.), *An Old English Martyrology*, Early English Text Society 116 (London, 1900), pp. 32–3: 'ond þæs wundor ond líf Beda se leornere wrát on Angelcynnes bocum'.

6   C. Cubitt, 'Universal and local saints in Anglo-Saxon England', in A. Thacker and R. Sharpe (eds), *Local saints and local churches in the early medieval West* (Oxford, 2002), pp. 423–53, at p. 439, n. 70.

7   Cubitt, 'Universal and local saints', p. 441.

8   D.W. Rollason, 'Lists of saints' resting-places in Anglo-Saxon England', in *Anglo-Saxon England*, 7 (1978), pp. 61–93.

9   Rollason, 'Lists of saints' resting places', pp. 74–82.

10   Rollason, 'Lists of saints' resting places', pp. 61–72.

Lichfield and the Lands of St Chad

a textual stratum with earlier origins. All saints listed in this part, where known, lived during the seventh, eighth and ninth centuries, the latest probably being St Edmund, king and martyr of East Anglia (d. 869);[11] moreover, the associated resting-places generally attest to the locations at which saints could be found before the many translations of the tenth century, and again Edmund's location at Bury, to which he was translated in the early tenth century, represents the latest dateable event.[12] Thus the first part of the *Secgan* probably represents a compilation of the earlier tenth century. It includes St Chad at Lichfield on the river Tame, together with two other saints, *Cedde*, perhaps his brother, and an obscure *Ceatta*.[13] Also included are St Wigstan at Repton on the river Trent, St Ealhmund at Northworthy (Derby) on the river Derwent and St Eadgyth at Polesworth on the river Anker. Eadgyth's presence is interesting in so far as St Modwynn of Burton-upon-Trent is absent; the two saints are otherwise closely connected in a miracle story set at Polesworth and written down by the Irish writer Conchubran, which also belongs to this second hagiographical phase. Cults with no previous textual expressions were therefore coming to the attention of those who were perhaps now interested in seeking them out.

Liturgical evidence paints a slightly more conservative picture. Rebecca Rushforth's study of pre-1100 calendars shows that the only saints in the diocese to appear with any great frequency are St Chad and St Wærburh. Of twenty-two calendars produced between the mid-tenth century and 1100, St Chad's feast on 2 March appears in sixteen, testifying to a widespread awareness of him in the southern English centres at which most of the surviving calendars were created.[14] St Wærburh's appearance in seven of these calendars is also a respectable showing,

---

11 Rollason, 'Lists of saints' resting places', p. 63, suggests that St Eadgyth of Polesworth was a tenth-century saint, but this is disputed later in this chapter.

12 Rollason suggests that the notice of St Cuthberht at Durham with St Oswald's head, and the latter's body at Gloucester, are later interpolations made to the original tenth-century compilation (see Rollason, 'Lists of saints' resting-places', pp. 63–4, 68 and 81). Rollason's dating of St Eadburh's enshrinement at Southwell to the late tenth century is based on a charter testifying to the gift of the place to the archbishop of York in 956, where he apparently established a collegiate church (Rollason, 'Lists of saints' resting places', p. 63, n. 12); however, this takes no account of the possibility that the archbishop simply refounded an older minster already possessing the saint's relics, which, judging by the floruit of all the other saints in the first part of the *Secgan*, seems very likely.

13 This distinctive triad is also included in the post-Conquest resting-place lists discussed by Rollason, suggesting that its formulation predated all the various pre-Conquest sources used by these lists compilers, some of which appear to have predated the list used by the compiler of the *Secgan* (Rollason, 'Lists of saints' resting-places', pp. 70 and 72). See also J. Blair, 'A handlist of Anglo-Saxon saints', in A. Thacker and R. Sharpe, *Local saints and local churches in the early medieval West* (Oxford, 2002), pp. 495–565, at p. 520.

14 R. Rushforth, *Saints in English calendars before AD 1100*, Henry Bradshaw Society 117 (London, 2008), Nos 6, 7, 9, 12, 13, 14, 15, 17, 18, 19, 21, 22, 23, 24, 25, 27 (all 2 March).

most marking her feast on 3 February.[15] The emphasis in the calendars on two of the three saints in the diocese for which earlier *Lives* existed is suggestive, again indicating a reliance on written sources on the part of the calendar compilers. This inference is supported by the fact that St Wigstan, the only other saint with a pre-tenth century *Life*, is also the only other saint to appear in the pre-1100 calendars; his inclusion in only two, both eleventh century, one with Evesham connections, may express the obscurity of his cult at Repton before his translation to Evesham during the reign of Cnut.[16] In contrast, Chad's appearance in Bede's work, and the association of Wærburh with the reformed tenth-century community at Ely, imply the importance of networks associated with the Benedictine reform of the later tenth century to their more frequent appearances in these calendars. This picture is supported by pre-Conquest litanies, forty-six of which have been studied by Michael Lapidge: of the diocese's local saints, St Chad and St Wærburh again appear most frequently, although a mere four and two times respectively.[17] Three of Chad's appearances and one of Wærburh's belong to calendars that Lapidge concludes to be 'acts of scholarly compilation rather than of local devotion' at centres such as New Minster, Winchester, Christ Church, Canterbury and Worcester, part of the network of reformed centres responsible for most of the calendars.[18]

Taking these first two phases together, it is possible to argue that, while all of the diocese's local saints very probably lived and died during the seventh, eighth and ninth centuries (as with most other such saints across the English kingdoms), most of them did not inspire written texts soon after their deaths. It might perhaps be objected that other houses probably wrote *Lives* like those of St Wærburh and St Wigstan, which were not popularised by works such as Bede's *Ecclesiastical History* and therefore remained obscure, but, unlike the *Lives* of those two saints, they have since been lost. However, it is surely telling that the only such *Lives* we know of concern the only two saints to appear alongside St Chad in pre-1100 calendars; if any other such *Lives* once existed, we might expect their saints to appear in calendars of the tenth and eleventh centuries. Instead, the cults of local saints other than Chad, Wærburh and Wigstan began to appear in texts only when their writers, such as the author of the *Secgan*, looked not for *Lives* but for the cult sites themselves. It is therefore proposed here that the lack of textual expressions associated with most of the other saints in the diocese during this period is a real phenomenon, not simply a product of lost source material. That said, it is unwise to rule anything out completely, including the possibility of a lost *Life* or two. The lack of tenth- or eleventh-century reformed houses in the diocese of Lichfield outside Burton-upon-Trent and Coventry is an important

---

15 Rushforth, *Saints in English kalendars*, Nos 9, 13, 16, 17, 19, 21, 22, 27 (all 3 February, except No. 19, 4 February, and No. 27, 1 May); while 4 February is probably a simple error, 1 May perhaps misidentifies the feast of St Wærburh with the feast of the translation of St Walburh (G. Jones, *Saints in the landscape* (Stroud, 2007), p. 86).

16 Rushforth, *Saints in English kalendars*, Nos 22 (1 June) and 25 (1 January, perhaps an error).

17 M. Lapidge, *Anglo-Saxon litanies of the saints*, Henry Bradshaw Society 106 (London, 1991), XVI. ii.256, XXIII.258, XXIV.174 and XXXIV.46 (St Chad), and XII.162 and XXXII.129 (St Wærburh).

18 Lapidge, *Anglo-Saxon litanies*, p. 74.

consideration here, as this movement was responsible for so many of the surviving corpus of Old English texts during this period.[19]

A third phase of hagiographical activity belongs to the later eleventh and early twelfth centuries, during which several saints in the diocese found their way into Latin *Lives* and chronicles. St Wærburh received a new *Life* at the hands of Goscelin, written for the community at Ely rather than any of the churches in the diocese. Nevertheless, this *Life* was apparently quickly taken up by the saint's newly reformed Benedictine community at Chester, where it formed part of their legendary by the early twelfth century, to which a set of local miracle stories was appended.[20] The only new *Life* written within the diocese was that for St Modwynn, significantly composed at another one of the diocese's few Benedictine abbeys, Burton, by its abbot, Geoffrey.[21] In addition, the chronicler John of Worcester, working outside the diocese, included an epitome of St Wigstan's *Life* in his work.[22] All these writers were using pre-existing texts as the bases for their efforts, even if, especially in Geoffrey's case, they were able to add some local knowledge to them, and indeed it is at this point that a general lack of detailed local knowledge begins to become apparent. Goscelin probably added to his exemplar only a legend from Weedon (Northamptonshire), which may not itself have been that old, although he transformed much of what he had with reference to pious intentions and Christian humility.[23] He perhaps had excuse for a lack of further detail, as he was not, as far as can be determined, in contact with the saint's own community at Chester. However, Geoffrey, as ruler of her community, had personal responsibility for Modwynn's relics, and yet was unable to add anything to the saint's life-story except a refashioned version of Conchubran's miracle story, alongside a set of much more recent miracles performed at the saint's church and in the surrounding area.[24]

The fourth and final hagiographical phase in the diocese stretches from the second half of the twelfth century to the end of the medieval period. St Beorhthelm of Stafford and St Osburh of Coventry appeared for the first time in the resting-place list in Hugh Candidus' Peterborough Chronicle, in which they accompany St Chad, St Wærburh, St Ealhmund, St Wigstan, St Eadgyth and St Modwynn.[25] Hugh's information may have

---

19   See Blair, 'A handlist'.
20   Love, *Goscelin of Saint-Bertin*, p. lviii.
21   R. Bartlett (ed.), *Geoffrey of Burton: Life and miracles of St Modwenna* (Oxford, 2002).
22   John of Worcester's *Chronica Chronicarum*, s.a. 849 (R.R. Darlington and P. McGurk, *The chronicle of John of Worcester, volume II, the annals from 450 to 1066* (Oxford, 1995), pp. 262–3).
23   Weedon miracles: *VSW*, cc. 5–7; the first of the miracles, a tale in which Wærburh miraculously rounds up a flock of geese eating the seed in her fields, sending them away never to return, 'is told from generation to generation by all the people there', the present tense suggesting a recent report from Weedon. The second miracle concerns a local hermit, Alnoth, apparently one of Wærburh's herdsmen, and is laden with details concerning Weedon and its locality, again indicating that report of the miracle had come from Weedon.
24   A. Sargent, 'A misplaced miracle: the origins of St Modwynn of Burton and St Eadgyth of Polesworth', *Midland History*, 41 (2016), pp. 1–19.
25   W.T. Mellows, *The chronicle of Hugh Candidus, a monk of Peterborough* (London, 1949), pp. 56–64.

come from lost Old English resting-place lists, conceivably dating to the ninth, tenth or eleventh centuries, but this is conjecture, and it may equally be more recent, testifying to a continuing interest in the compilation (as opposed to the mere copying) of such lists. Wulfhad and Ruffin of Stone first appear together in a fourteenth-century resting-place list. *Lives* for St Ealhmund, St Beorhthelm and St Wulfhad and St Ruffin were first composed during this phase, and were all in existence by the end of the fourteenth century.[26] None of these *Lives* appear to have been based on pre-Conquest texts, and all demonstrate the prolific and creative use of contemporary folklore and biblical themes to construct legends around sparse chronicle notices or the silent presence of relics. Such a methodology is first glimpsed in our third phase, in particular in Geoffrey's incorporation of local miracle stories into his *Life* of St Modwenna and in the addition of miracle stories to Goscelin's *Life* of St Wærburh at Chester, but the difference here is that all compositions of the third phase were building on more expansive written material; the authors of these fourth-phase *Lives* had very little, if any, textual material relating to their own saints to work with.

The four phases of hagiographical activity identified above illustrate the nature of much of our evidence for saints' cults, and therefore early minsters, in the diocese. Crucial here is the fact that only three of the diocese's local saints are the subjects of *Lives* written within one or two generations of their deaths. Indeed, the limited textual evidence suggests that it was generally unusual for a minster-based community to produce a written celebration of their saint in this way. We cannot therefore rely on some kind of hagiographical impulse to provide us with information. However, if, after two or three generations, the detailed memories of contemporaries had faded or fallen away, the saints remained at the hearts of their communities. The idealisation and veneration of these people, visible in the virtues expressed in the written *Lives*, was probably more consistently displayed in social and ritual practices at the communities concerned, leaving no textual remains.

This is probably also true of those few communities that did initially produce texts. The kinds of personal remembrance of specific events that we find in the LN and the *vitae* of St Wærburh and St Wigstan appear to have been limited to (near) contemporaries of the saints concerned, while later generations were far more interested in the saints as liturgical, ritualised objects, in their roles as bridges between

---

26 St Ealhmund: the *vita* exists in only one manuscript, an early fourteenth-century hagiographical collection now held at the Gotha Library (Gotha, Forschungsbibliothek, Memb. I.81, ff. 29–30; a discussion of this manuscript and edition of the *Life* can be found in P. Grosjean, 'De codice hagiographico Gothano' and 'Codices Gothani appendix' in *Analecta Bollandiana*, 58 (1940), respectively pp. 90–103 and pp. 177–204). St Beorhthelm: the *vita* first appears in a sixteenth-century hagiographical collection, although an internal date suggests it was composed in the fourteenth century (C. Horstmann, *The Life of Saint Werburge of Chester by Henry Bradshaw*, Early English Text Society 88, vol. 1 (London, 1887), pp. 162–7). St Wulfhad and St Ruffin: The *vita* exists in several manuscripts, none earlier than the fourteenth century (for references see A.R. Rumble, '*Ad Lapidem* in Bede and a Mercian martyrdom', in A.R. Rumble and A.D. Mills (eds), *Names, places and people. An onomastic miscellany in memory of John McNeal Dodgson* (Stamford, 1997), pp. 307–19.

earth and heaven. Consequently, when they first appeared in the textual record, from the tenth century onwards, in most cases very little was actually known of the details of their existence beyond the fact of their relics' powerful presence at the churches whose communities maintained their shrines. The recent miracles performed by these relics formed the majority of the information available to members of the reformed Benedictine communities at Burton and Chester when they became interested in providing new textual expressions of their saints' lives in the late eleventh and early twelfth centuries. It should therefore be little surprise to us that we know so little of the details of the lives of many of the saints and the early history of their minsters in the diocese; it is likely that the same was true in many communities for much of the early medieval period. If details did happen to be captured in an early textual composition, so much the better for us, but we should be more impressed by the consistency maintained by all such centres as curators of shrines and their cults, and thus by the roles of the saints in creating liturgical communities.

Stone sculpture

Beyond the saints' cults, the only contemporary source of evidence that survives in any quantity from earlier minster sites in the diocese is stone sculpture, although this brings with it a number of issues, of which two are particularly acute. First, it is not necessarily self-evident that such sculpture was always associated with ecclesiastical sites, although its forms and iconography suggest that this is not an unreasonable assumption;[27] Blair's inclusive definition of a minster also allows some interpretive flexibility as to the precise nature of the sites that hosted these monuments. Second, as Rosemary Cramp warns in her definitive paper on schools of Mercian sculpture, 'there is no sculpture datable by absolute or external means', and, indeed, the whole edifice of research relies primarily on stylistic dating sequences.[28] Nevertheless, research has constructed a dense web of decorative and iconographic affinities between different objects and groups of objects that spans not just the British Isles but the Frankish realms and Italy to the eastern Mediterranean; some confidence can therefore be placed in relative chronologies that follow the creation and diffusion of particular styles and motifs. Absolute dating can be trickier and may rely on a judgement concerning whether changes in style, or in technical ability of execution, are considered to be broadly synchronic or diachronic phenomena. The territory within the diocese of Lichfield has been completely surveyed by scholars working on the *Corpus of Anglo-Saxon Stone Sculpture* project, and thus a dense

---

27 R. Cramp, 'New directions in the study of Anglo-Saxon sculpture', *Transactions of the Leicestershire Archaeological and Historical Society*, 84 (2010), pp. 1–25, at p. 11.

28 R. Cramp, 'Schools of Mercian sculpture', in A. Dornier (ed.), *Mercian studies* (Leicester, 1977), pp. 191–233. For important landmarks at the beginning of the modern stylistic approach to Anglo-Saxon stone sculpture see W.G. Collingwood, *Northumbrian crosses of the pre-Norman age* (London, 1927) and T.D. Kendrick, *Anglo-Saxon art to AD 900* (London, 1938). More recently, Richard Bailey has produced several influential studies on the sculpture of the Viking period; see R.N. Bailey, *Viking-Age sculpture* (London, 1980).

The cathedral and the minsters

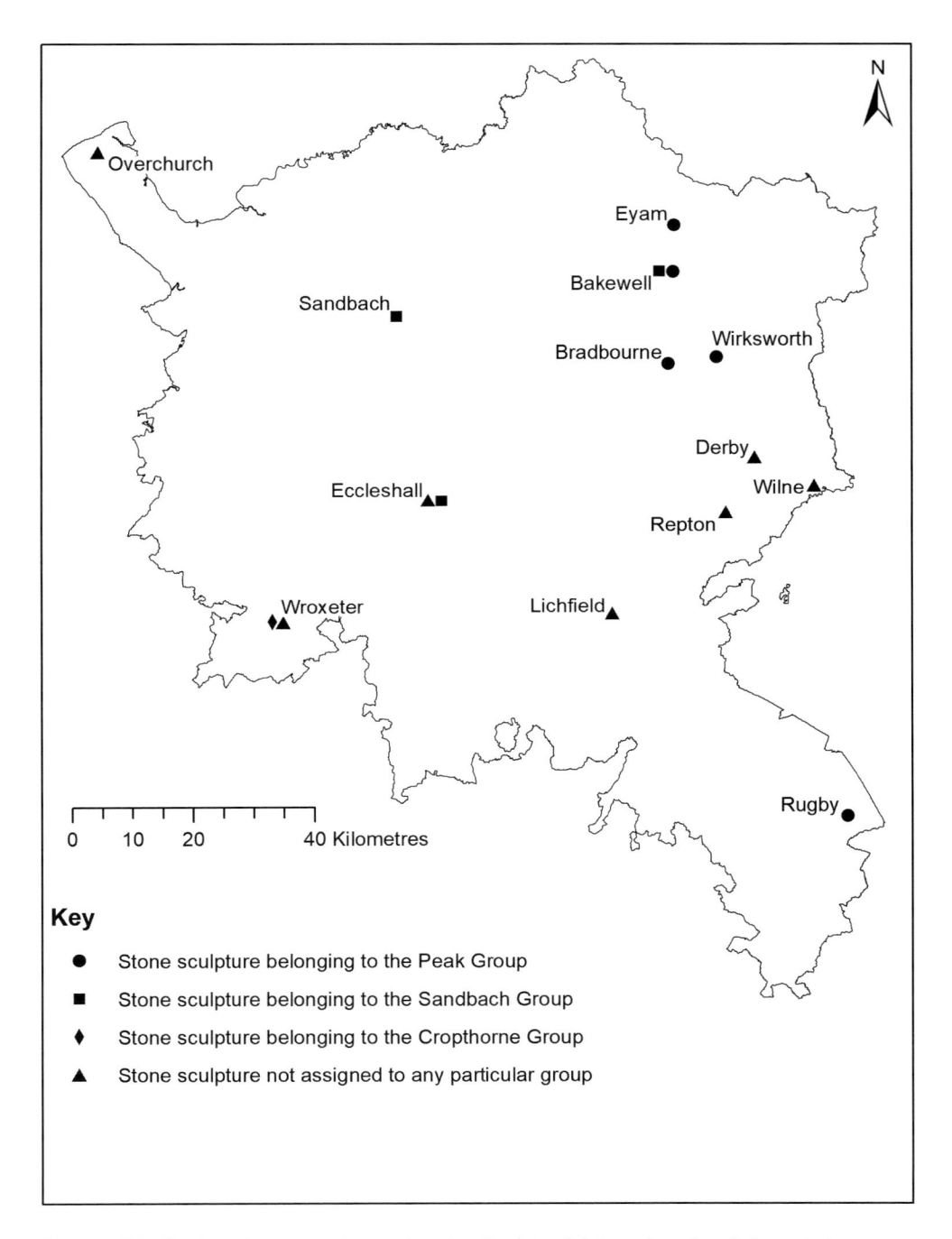

Figure 4 Distribution of stone sculpture dated to the late eighth and earlier ninth centuries.

body of information and analysis exists on which to build arguments concerning the distributions, both chronological and geographical, and significance of the stone sculpture within the diocese.[29]

The authors of the *Corpus* volumes customarily discuss the early medieval stone sculpture of the region within two chronological categories: the eighth and ninth centuries, and the tenth and eleventh centuries; the former is often referred to as the Anglian Period, and the latter as the Viking or Scandinavian Period. This can be unhelpful, because it lays undue emphasis on *c*.900 as a transformative point in the production of stone sculpture, and implies the influence of Viking activity or Scandinavian immigration in the mode of that transformation, although it must be said that the commentary within the volumes is often far more nuanced. Nevertheless, it is here considered more productive to focus on what Philip Sidebottom calls 'regional groups' in the *Corpus* volume for Derbyshire and Staffordshire, comprising 'monuments which share a common repertoire of design elements: repeated and distinctive motifs and patterns, figural types, carving techniques, and any other attributes that, together, define similarity within the group of monuments'.[30] Not every monument possesses sufficient diagnostic similarities to be assigned to a larger group; conversely, some items share a larger number of similarities than others, and general similarities shared by many sometimes coexist with more specific sets of similarities shared by a few, allowing the definition of sub-groups within groups. The flexibility of such analysis is welcome, providing an adaptive tool for thinking about these distinctive monuments. In what follows, the earliest phase of monumental production in the diocese during the later eighth and earlier ninth centuries is introduced, followed by an attempt to shift the dating of associated monuments usually regarded as products solely of the tenth century to a period encompassing the ninth and earlier tenth centuries. This has the effect of detaching them from the purely 'Scandinavian' context of interpretation used by the *Corpus*, and enables them to contribute to an exploration of the earlier minsters in the diocese.

Several regional groups have been identified by the *Corpus* authors within the diocese of Lichfield, including three representing some of the earliest sculpture in the region (Figure 4). The first of these is largely located within the Derbyshire Peak District, and comprises several large free-standing crosses (or fragments thereof) at Wirksworth, Bradbourne, Eyam and Bakewell, and a coped slab, perhaps part of a shrine, at Wirksworth; these are connected by several decorative similarities, including a heavy plant-scroll motif and the arrangement within arcades of figures with deeply drilled eyes (see Figure 5a).[31] A member of this 'Peak Group' at Rugby in Warwickshire should be considered a genuine outlier, as it is made from local

---

29 R. Bryant (ed.), *Corpus of Anglo-Saxon stone sculpture, volume X, the western Midlands* (Oxford, 2012); R.N. Bailey, *Corpus of Anglo-Saxon stone sculpture, volume IX: Cheshire and Lancashire* (Oxford, 2010); J. Hawkes and P. Sidebottom, *Corpus of Anglo-Saxon stone sculpture, volume XIII: Derbyshire and Staffordshire* (Oxford, 2018). Items of stone sculpture are hereafter identified by the reference labels assigned them in these Corpus volumes.
30 Hawkes and Sidebottom, *Corpus*, p. 22.
31 Hawkes and Sidebottom, *Corpus*, pp. 22–5.

Sherwood sandstone, while the sculptors of the Peak District monuments used local millstone grit.[32] A second group, usually labelled the 'Cropthorne Group', comprises monuments located largely outside the diocese, in Gloucestershire, Herefordshire and Worcestershire, but an outlying member, a free-standing cross, is located at Wroxeter in Shropshire, notably sculpted from oolitic limestone sourced from the Cotswold heartland of the rest of the group; the Cropthorne Group is characterised by skilfully rendered animals and birds accompanied by plant- and tree-scrolls.[33] A third group, again comprising free-standing crosses, is located at Sandbach in Cheshire, Bakewell in Derbyshire and perhaps Eccleshall in Staffordshire, and is here labelled the 'Sandbach Group', after its two earliest members, which stand in the market place at Sandbach (see Figure 5b).[34] The group's distinguishing features include scroll motifs with beast-headed terminals, fantastical animals (or zoomorphs) whose bodies dissolve into interlace patterns, and figures, often arranged in arched niches, whose heads are nimbed with a distinctive double outline. The members of all three of these groups have been dated to a period between *c.*750 and *c.*850, with a focus on the late eighth and early ninth centuries.

Several other monuments in the diocese have been dated to the same period, but are not so easily placed within distinctive groups. A set of fragments at Repton, relating to free-standing crosses, a grave cover and perhaps a shrine chest, were recovered during archaeological excavations, and their destruction and burial has been connected with disturbances caused by the Viking Great Army's occupation of the site in 873/4; the fragments are adorned with figural scenes and decorative motifs of various kinds, such as interlace and key patterning.[35] At Lichfield the so-called 'Lichfield Angel', a sculpted shrine panel, has been compared with clusters of sculpture located further east, encompassing sets of architectural strip friezes (decorated with inhabited plant-scrolls) and relief-carved figural panels at Breedon-on-the-Hill in Leicestershire, Castor in Northamptonshire and Fletton in Huntingdonshire,

---

32 For Rugby see Bryant, *Corpus*, Rugby 1; the Peak District monuments are discussed in Cramp, 'Schools', pp. 218–24, and are analysed in Hawkes and Sidebottom, *Corpus*, Bakewell 1, Bakewell 9, Bakewell 11, Bakewell 26, Bakewell 31, Bakewell 34, Bakewell 37, Bradbourne 1, Bradbourne 2, Bradbourne 3, Bradbourne 4, Bradbourne 5, Eyam 1, Wirksworth 2, Wirksworth 3, Wirksworth 5. Another member of the group was found in Sheffield, where it had been used as a grinder's trough: E. Coatsworth (ed.), *Corpus of Anglo-Saxon stone sculpture, volume VIII, western Yorkshire* (Oxford, 2008), Sheffield 1.

33 For Wroxeter see Bryant, *Corpus*, Wroxeter, 1, Wroxeter 2 and Wroxeter 3; for the Cropthorne Group see Bryant, *Corpus*, Cropthorne 1, and at 25–6 and 67–71.

34 For Sandbach see Hawkes, 'Constructing iconographies'; J. Hawkes, *The Sandbach crosses: sign and significance in Anglo-Saxon sculpture* (Dublin, 2002); and Bailey, *Corpus*, Sandbach Market Place 1, Sandbach Market Place 2, Sandbach Market Place 3, Sandbach Market Place 4, Sandbach Market Place 5; for Bakewell see Hawkes and Sidebottom, *Corpus*, Bakewell 12, Bakewell 15, Bakewell 16; for Eccleshall see Hawkes and Sidebottom, *Corpus*, Eccleshall 3. The connection between Sandbach and Bakewell is also explored in Hawkes, *Sandbach*, pp. 138–9.

35 Hawkes and Sidebottom, *Corpus*, Repton 1, Repton 2, Repton 3, Repton 4, Repton 5, Repton 9, Repton 10, Repton 15.

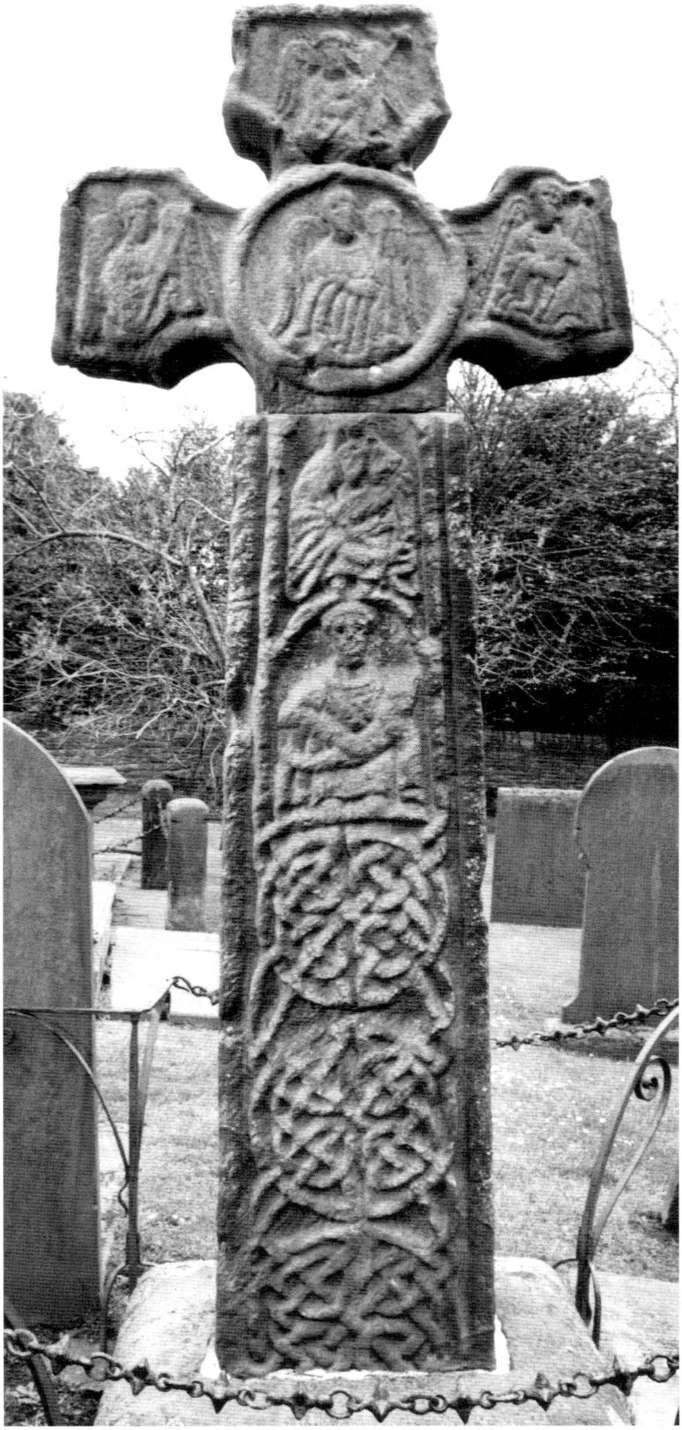
a

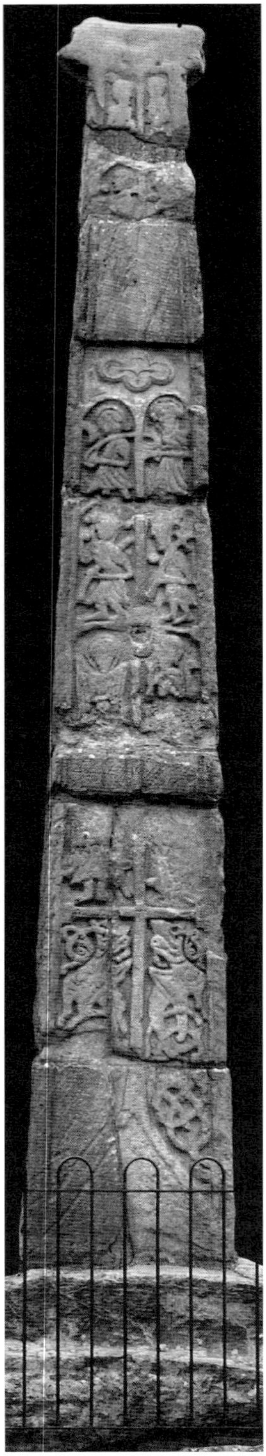
b

The cathedral and the minsters

Figure 5 Examples of stone sculpture dated to the late eighth and early ninth centuries (left to right):

a) cross at Eyam, a well-preserved member of the Peak Group © Jane Hawkes and Philip Sidebottom;

b) one of two crosses in the Market Place at Sandbach, earliest representatives of the Sandbach Group © Ken Jukes;

c) base of a columnar moment at Wilne, altar inverted and hollowed out to make a font © Jane Hawkes and Philip Sidebottom;

d) fragments of a cross at Derby, St Alkmund, featuring zoomorphic ornament © Jane Hawkes and Philip Sidebottom.

all of which have been dated to the late eighth and early ninth centuries.[36] The Angel's eastern associations extend to the stone from which it was carved, an oolitic limestone from Lincolnshire.[37] The decorative scheme of an architectural panel at Wroxeter has also been compared with the friezes at Breedon, although the quality of the carving is not so technically sophisticated.[38] At Eccleshall, the surviving part of a cross shaft decorated with a figural scene is thought to date to the ninth century, as is the fragment of a slab or shrine cover from Overchurch in Cheshire, which features a runic inscription and a decorative scheme in which a zoomorph dissolves into interlace, comparable to a pattern on one of the Sandbach crosses.[39] At Wilne in Derbyshire a fragment represents part of a distinctive tapering columnar monument decorated with a series of arched frames containing animal, bird and foliate motifs, which has been dated to the early ninth century (see Figure 5c).[40] The zoomorphs have been compared to contemporary animal art found elsewhere in the western Midlands, on one of the Sandbach crosses and on several of the monuments in the Cropthorne Group. Such imagery, in which the animals are 'fettered by their extended appendages', is also found on two cross-shaft fragments, perhaps slightly later in date, at Derby (see Figure 5d).[41]

These monuments, along with the more discrete Peak, Cropthorne and Sandbach Groups outlined above, represent a distinctive phase in the production of stone sculpture within southern England. Many of the figural scenes display a reliance on early Christian models from the eastern Mediterranean, which were circulating in Italy and the Frankish realm by the eighth century, or on intermediary Carolingian models produced in the latter regions; these appear to have been acquired by sculptors working across southern England. Likewise, many of the decorative motifs, the plant-scrolls and zoomorphic imagery, can be paralleled in illuminated manuscripts of the period, both in England and on the continent. In particular, the so-called 'Tiberius Group' of English manuscripts dating to the late eighth and first half of the ninth centuries offers a useful set of comparisons to decorative elements on many of the monuments introduced above, such as the beast-headed tendrils of the Sandbach crosses or the distinctive zoomorphs, sometimes called 'Mercian Beasts', of the fragments at Wilne, Derby and elsewhere.[42] Indeed, the overlap in chronology, regional extent and decorative motifs strongly suggests a sculptural analogue to

---

36 Cramp, 'Schools', pp. 194–218 (the fragment from Ingleby, mentioned at 207, is no longer associated with these items); W. Rodwell, J. Hawkes, E. Howe and R. Cramp, 'The Lichfield Angel: a spectacular Anglo-Saxon painted sculpture', *The Antiquaries Journal*, 88 (2008), pp. 48–108; Hawkes and Sidebottom, *Corpus*, Lichfield 1.

37 Hawkes and Sidebottom, *Corpus*, pp. 10–11 and 303; only two stones from Derby and one from Spondon also come from this formation.

38 Bryant, *Corpus*, Wroxeter 4.

39 For Eccleshall see Hawkes and Sidebottom, *Corpus*, Eccleshall 2; for Overchurch see Bailey, *Corpus*, Overchurch 1.

40 Hawkes and Sidebottom, *Corpus*, Wilne 1.

41 Hawkes and Sidebottom, *Corpus*, Derby 1, Derby 2, Derby 5.

42 Brown, 'Mercian manuscripts?', pp. 276–90; Hawkes and Sidebottom, *Corpus*, pp. 73–4.

the 'Mercian *Schriftprovinz*', promoted by Michelle Brown as a useful framework through which to understand the cultural milieu in which members of the Tiberius Group were produced, encompassing Mercian, West Saxon and Kentish spheres in a period dominated by Mercian political hegemony.[43] Emphasis is needed here on the innovation displayed by both textual and sculptural creations; in the latter case sculptors used their models creatively, in many cases adapting them to represent a considerable range of biblical themes depicted in the figural scenes, adorning them with a developing set of various decorative motifs.

Three further groups of stone sculpture within the diocese that are considered stylistically later than the monuments introduced above have been defined by the *Corpus* authors. Of these, the 'Pennine Fringes Group' is predominantly confined to upland locations in northern Staffordshire, northern Derbyshire and eastern Cheshire, and what is here called the 'Wirral Group' is focused on the eponymous peninsula in north-west Cheshire; both have been confidently dated to the tenth and eleventh centuries by comparison with other monuments in the north and west of England, and are not considered further here.[44] The third, the 'Trent Valley Group', comprises crosses and some funerary monuments, and 'is broadly concentrated in the Trent Valley and along its tributaries, especially the rivers Sow, Tean and Dove', and also extends into Leicestershire, Nottinghamshire and Lincolnshire (see Figure 6).[45] Its characteristic features 'are largely pattern types, using specific variations of knot-work and interlace ... described as "A-bend" and "E-bend" interlaces, ... which appear to be specific to the monuments of this group', although many members also share other similarities, such as the so-called 'ribbon beast' or 'Mercian Beast' common to several in south Derbyshire.[46] Most members of this group have been dated by Sidebottom and Jane Hawkes, the two authors of the relevant *Corpus* volume, to the tenth century,

---

43 Brown, 'Mercian manuscripts?', p. 287; see also M.P. Brown, *The Book of Cerne. Prayer, patronage and power in ninth-century England* (London, 1996), pp. 164–72.
44 Hawkes and Sidebottom, *Corpus*, pp. 27–9, and Bailey, *Corpus*, pp. 31–6.
45 Hawkes and Sidebottom, *Corpus*, pp. 25–7; the group is based on the 'South West School' identified by Sidebottom in his doctoral thesis: P.C. Sidebottom, 'Schools of Mercian stone sculpture in the north Midlands', PhD thesis (University of Sheffield, 1994), pp. 100–11. The membership of the group is not given explicitly in the *Corpus* volume, but can be extracted from the gazetteer in Sidebottom's thesis, with additions suggested by individual entries in the relevant *Corpus* volumes, and is given here with reference to the volume in which it has been described. Hawkes and Sidebottom, *Corpus*: Ashbourne 1, Aston-on-Trent 1, Blackwell East 1, Clipshead 1, Derby 6, Derby 7, Derby 8, Derby 11, Hope 1, Ingleby 1, Norbury 1, Norbury 2, Repton 8, Repton 16, Repton 17, Spondon 1, Alstonefield 1, Alstonefield 2, Alstonefield 5, Alstonefield 11, Checkley 1, Checkley 2, Chesterton 1, Ecceshall 1, Ilam 1, Ilam Estate 1, Leek 1, Leek 3, Tatenhill 1; P. Everson and D. Stocker (eds), *Corpus of Anglo-Saxon stone sculpture, volume XII, Nottinghamshire* (Oxford, 2016): Hickling, Shelford, Shelton 1; P. Everson and D. Stocker (eds), *Corpus of Anglo-Saxon of stone sculpture, volume V, Lincolnshire* (Oxford, 1999): Cranwell 2; Sidebottom, 'Schools of Anglo-Saxon stone sculpture': Asfordby 1, Asfordby 2, Asfordby 3, Birstall, Breedon-on-the-Hill 8, Breedon-on-the-Hill 10, Rothley.
46 Hawkes and Sidebottom, *Corpus*, p. 25.

Lichfield and the Lands of St Chad

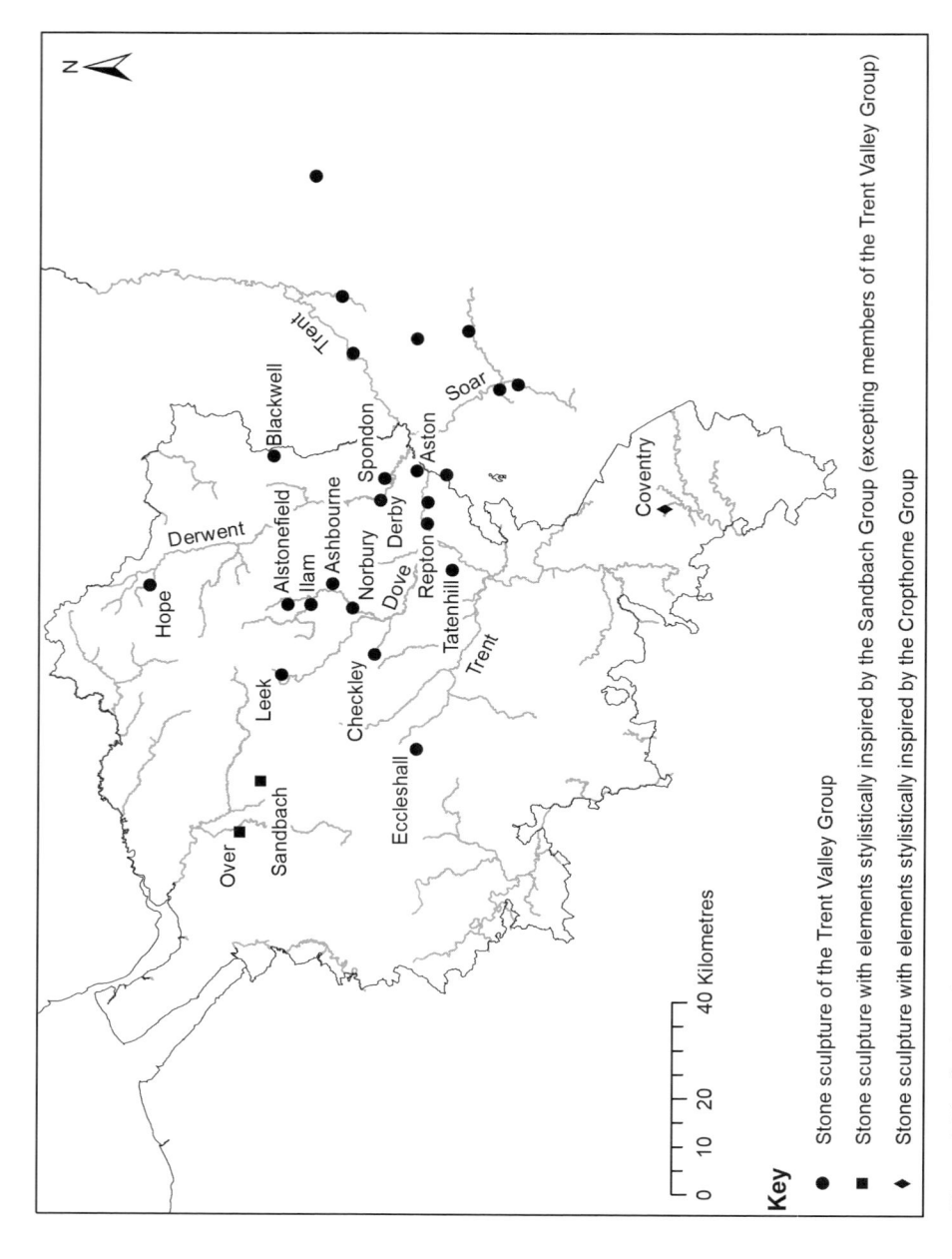

Figure 6 Distribution of sculpture dated to the mid- to late ninth and earlier tenth centuries, showing the entire distribution of the Trent Valley Group and its relation to the river Trent and its tributaries.

occasionally the late ninth century, and Sidebottom has suggested that most have 'Anglo-Scandinavian overtones'.[47] However, elsewhere Sidebottom admits that 'the ability to discriminate between what is or is not characterised as Anglo-Scandinavian influence is difficult and, at times, practically impossible', largely because 'some motifs are long-lived and ambiguous in date'.[48] Elsewhere Hawkes notes that some members of the Trent Valley Group 'at Checkley, Chesterton, Ilam and Leek may be dated to a transitional period where Anglian traditions were carried over into Scandinavian phases of activity at the turn of the tenth century, making it difficult to distinguish the two'.[49] At issue here is the straitjacket imposed by the *Corpus* format on the adjudication of date, in which monuments have to be assigned to one of two periods, defined by the possibility of appeal to a stylistic 'Scandinavian-ness' that often has very little to do with any decorative schemes that may or may not have been imported by settlers in the late ninth or tenth centuries. Indeed, stylistic analysis of much 'Anglo-Scandinavian' sculpture north of the Humber has emphasised its direct derivation from earlier monuments and the lack in many cases of identifiable stylistic 'imports' from Scandinavia.[50]

A more productive approach employs the detailed and nuanced commentary provided by the *Corpus* authors for each piece of sculpture, enabling an analysis of the group based on its members' affinities to other monuments. Many of the monuments in the Trent Valley Group are repeatedly said to owe elements of their decorative or figural styles to the Sandbach Group. Monuments at Alstonefield, Chesterton, Checkley, Eccleshall, Hope, Ilam and Leek make use of one or more of a variety of distinctive motifs associated with patterns and iconography on the crosses at Sandbach, including: a figure depicted in profile, often carrying a cross (see Figure 7a); figures conjoined by haloes; figures arranged in groups of three of which the central, probably representing Christ, is taller than the others; a figure whose body is represented by interlace (the 'interlace man'; see Figure 7b); a figure holding a small book; knots of interlace interspersed with pellets; and zoomorphs dissolving into interlace.[51] These motifs stand at varying distances from the 'originals', often stylised and adapted, implying inspiration rather than attempts at reproduction. A specific example of this is provided by the figural imagery on these monuments. The imagery is itself a notable presence because figural schemes are a widespread feature among the earlier monuments of this region, but are largely absent from sculpture ascribed

---

47   Hawkes and Sidebottom, *Corpus*, p. 25.
48   Hawkes and Sidebottom, *Corpus*, p. 83.
49   Hawkes and Sidebottom, *Corpus*, p. 69. Hawkes presumably refers to the monuments labelled Checkley 1, Checkley 2, Chesterton 1, Ilam Estate 1 and Leek 3, all of which are dated to the late ninth century, although in most cases the suggested bracket also includes the tenth century; only at Leek is the date range confined to the ninth, starting mid-century.
50   For example, see J. Lang (ed.), *Corpus of Anglo-Saxon stone sculpture, volume III, York and eastern Yorkshire* (Oxford, 1991), Chapter 9.
51   Hawkes and Sidebottom, *Corpus*, Alstonefield 2, Alstonefield 5, Checkley 1, Checkley 2, Chesterton 1, Eccleshall 1, Hope 1, Ilam 1, Ilam Estate 1, Leek 3. See also Hawkes, *Sandbach*, pp. 139–41, and Bailey, *Corpus*, p. 24.

Lichfield and the Lands of St Chad

a

Figure 7 Examples of stone sculpture dated to the mid- to late ninth and earlier tenth centuries: a) fragment of a cross at Leek, showing a man in profile carrying a cross, stylistically derived from the Sandbach Market Place crosses © Jane Hawkes and Philip Sidebottom; b) cross at Checkley, showing an 'interlace man', stylistically derived from Sandbach, with mirrored type E interlace below © Jane Hawkes and Philip Sidebottom; c) fragment of a cross at Ilam, showing man in *orans* position, with a group of three figures above © Ken Jukes; d) fragment of a grave cover Repton, showing two 'Mercian Beasts' separated by a panel of interlace © Ken Jukes.

The cathedral and the minsters

to the tenth and eleventh centuries, in particular the Pennine Fringes Group, which occupies part of the same territory as the Trent Valley Group.[52] It is not, however, simply a function of the derivation of decorative schemes from the Sandbach crosses, because as well as stylisation it features a clear case of innovation: a so-called 'Dove Valley Subgroup' within the Trent Valley Group, encompassing monuments at Alstonefield, Checkley, Ilam and Norbury, is distinguished by a figure with raised arms, perhaps signifying the *orans* position of prayer, which does not appear in any form on the Sandbach crosses (see Figure 7c).[53] Hawkes suggests that the stylised figural imagery on the Trent Valley Group crosses reflects 'a transition from earlier interests into the Scandinavian period', but in conforming to the usual *Corpus* dating brackets this conclusion may exaggerate the degree of chronological separation between the Trent Valley Group and earlier monuments in the region.[54]

The influence of Sandbach motifs does not extend to all members of the Trent Valley Group, and inspiration from other earlier monuments in the region has also been detected. The variety of so-called 'Mercian Beasts' that feature on part of a grave cover at Repton and parts of cross shafts at Ashbourne, Aston-on-Trent and Spondon, all in southern Derbyshire, comprise a distinctively localised phenomenon and can be compared with the animal ornament on the earlier monuments at Derby and Wilne (see Figure 7d).[55] The *Corpus* authors date the Repton monument to the ninth or tenth centuries, but the others are placed securely in the latter century. Nevertheless, Sidebottom admits that this animal imagery is 'the most problematic type of motif invoked to distinguish between Anglo-Scandinavian and other Anglo-Saxon carvings', emphasising that 'the differences between the zoomorphs of the two phases of activity are not obvious, if they exist at all', and concluding that 'there is no animal form in this region that can be easily identified as having been produced under clear Scandinavian influence'.[56] Given these problems, it seems far simpler to emphasise simply that the zoomorphs on the monuments of the Trent Valley Group be understood as developments of the animal forms on the earlier monuments at Derby and Wilne, especially given the fact that they all cluster in the same region.

Finally, it is worth noting the use of interlace on many of the Trent Valley Group monuments, as this is not a dominant element on the earlier sculpture of the region, and is often associated in the *Corpus* volumes with monuments of 'Scandinavian' date.[57] Nevertheless, it does appear on some of the earlier monuments, and in some cases the specific forms are instructive. Type A interlace, which forms one of the diagnostic elements of the Trent Valley Group, is found on one of the earlier crosses at

---

52 Hawkes and Sidebottom, *Corpus*, pp. 74 and 91.
53 Hawkes and Sidebottom, *Corpus*, p. 27; the 'Dove Valley Subgroup' should probably be equated with Sidebottom's 'Dove Valley School' (Sidebottom, 'Schools of Mercian stone sculpture', pp. 108–11) and contains Alstonefield 2, Alstonefield 5, Checkley 1, Checkley 2, Ilam 1, Ilam Estate 1 and Norbury 2.
54 Hawkes and Sidebottom, *Corpus*, p. 74.
55 Hawkes and Sidebottom, *Corpus*, Ashbourne 1, Aston-on-Trent 1, Repton 16, Spondon 1.
56 Hawkes and Sidebottom, *Corpus*, p. 90.
57 Hawkes and Sidebottom, *Corpus*, p. 72.

Derby as well as a cross and grave cover of similar date at Repton.[58] Likewise, type E interlace, another diagnostic element of the Trent Valley Group, is found on one of the crosses at Sandbach, albeit in a mirrored form.[59] Just outside the diocese the cross shaft at Stapleford, Nottinghamshire, dated to the ninth century, possibly earlier, by Paul Everson and David Stocker, features both type A interlace and a doubled form of type E interlace that is also a diagnostic element of the Dove Valley Subgroup.[60] Thus, despite its relative rarity on earlier monuments, it is again possible to view the use of interlace on the monuments of the Trent Valley Group as a stylistic development from the former, either directly or via the evolution of a broader creative milieu, rather than invoking the supposed 'Scandinavian' character of the tenth century and later. Ultimately, as has been repeatedly emphasised above, the many similarities between the Trent Valley Group and earlier monuments in the region should prompt us to interpret it in relation to those earlier monuments rather than other 'Viking Age' groups, such as the Pennine Fringes Group, with which it shares far less.

When considered in this way, the Trent Valley Group has more in common with three further cross shafts at St Mary's, Sandbach, and a cross at Over, west of Sandbach, which were all clearly inspired by the two earlier crosses in the market place and have been dated to the ninth century.[61] Likewise, outside the area occupied by the Trent Valley Group, a carved door jamb at Coventry appears to have been inspired by the decorative motifs of the Cropthorne Group to the south, and has also been dated to the ninth century.[62] Further afield, in Gloucestershire and Worcestershire, the animal forms of the Cropthorne Group, which 'combine liveliness of movement with dramatic light-and-shade effects of body texturing or more naturalistic body treatment to create impressively dynamic compositions', appear to have inspired forms on monuments dated to the mid-ninth century in which these elements become more abstract, and towards the end of the century the carving of such forms 'becomes harsher, and twisted, elongated ribbon-animal forms begin to dominate'.[63] In all these cases we have an initial phase of monument production in the later eighth and earlier ninth centuries during which skilled sculptors worked innovatively with early Christian and Carolingian models, followed by a phase of stylisation during which sculptors continued to innovate, but did so now largely focused on stone sculpture from the earlier phase, and sometimes with less precision or subtlety. The subsequent processes of inspiration and stylisation have all been dated to the ninth and early tenth centuries, and on the basis of these parallels it is possible at least to suggest that the Trent Valley Group, which appears to represent a similar process, should be dated to the same broad period, earlier than the predominantly tenth-century bracket offered by the *Corpus* authors.

---

58 Hawkes and Sidebottom, *Corpus*, p. 72, Derby 1, Repton 2, Repton 15.
59 Bailey, *Corpus*, Sandbach 2.
60 Everson and Stocker, *Corpus*, Stapleford 1; for the diagnostic elements of the Dove Valley Subgroup see Sidebottom, 'Schools of Anglo-Saxon stone sculpture', pp. 108–11.
61 Bailey, *Corpus*, Sandbach St Mary 1, Sandbach St Mary 2, Sandbach St Mary 3, Over 1.
62 Bryant, *Corpus*, Coventry 1.
63 Bryant, *Corpus*, pp. 67–9.

One further support can be offered for this shift in the dating of the Trent Valley Group. It has been suggested that the later part of the ninth century was largely a period of regional stylisation, but this need not imply that sculptors ceased to refer to models sourced from further afield, and there is evidence that some continued to use them; for example, the details of figural scenes on cross shafts at Eccleshall and Leek have been explained by direct access to early Christian models.[64] A particularly impressive example of the use of other models from outside the diocese is provided by a finely carved round-shafted pillar at Wolverhampton, which echoes the columnar form of the monument at Wilne but features a decorative scheme including fleshy plant-scrolls and a stiff-leaf motif that have been compared to the artistic elements of ninth-century Carolingian metalwork, and which appear on various media including sculpture, manuscript, ivory and textile associated with the West Saxon royal court and the political heartland of Mercia centred on Gloucester in the early tenth century.[65] The Wolverhampton column has thus been dated to this period, but it is not the only example of such influences on the sculptural art of the diocese. Fragments of a grave cover at Repton and a cross shaft at Ingleby, both members of the Trent Valley Group, feature fleshy plant motifs that have again been compared to ninth-century Carolingian art and its florescence in early tenth-century southern English contexts.[66] Nevertheless, such influences are limited within the Trent Valley Group, which perhaps indicates that its productive period was waning by the early tenth century; a possible reason for this will be considered in Chapter 6. In summary, there are several reasons to suppose that the Trent Valley Group represents monuments that were created for minsters between the mid-ninth century and the earlier tenth century, and that its coherence resulted from the stylisation of several motifs associated with sculpture of the late eighth and early ninth centuries in the region.

The foregoing discussion has demonstrated the extent to which much of the stone sculpture in the diocese can be categorised in terms of coherent groups and associated with a chronology running from the later eighth century to the early tenth. The implications of this sculpture and its distribution must now be considered. The great majority of the items within the entire corpus of stone sculpture were located on the sites of medieval churches. Some clearly formed architectural elements of church buildings or funerary monuments associated with them, the latter sometimes associated with saints' cults. The standing crosses may well have played important

---

64 Hawkes and Sidebottom, *Corpus*, Eccleshall 2, Leek 3.
65 Hawkes and Sidebottom, *Corpus*, Wolverhampton 1. The column has aroused a considerable amount of comment, especially regarding its date: see also Kendrick, *Anglo-Saxon art*, p. 192 (mid-ninth century); R. Cramp, 'Anglo-Saxon sculpture of the Reform period', in D. Parsons (ed.), *Tenth-century studies, essays in commemoration of the millennium of the Council of Winchester and Regularis Concordia* (London, 1975), pp. 184–99, at p. 189 (tenth century, perhaps ninth century); D.M. Wilson, *Anglo-Saxon art, from the seventh century to the Norman Conquest* (London, 1984), p. 105 (late ninth or early tenth century); R. Jewell, 'Classicism of Southumbrian sculpture', in M.P. Brown and C.A. Farr (eds), *Mercia: an Anglo-Saxon kingdom in Europe* (London, 2001), pp. 246–62, at p. 262 (tenth century).
66 Hawkes and Sidebottom, *Corpus*, Ingleby 1, Repton 17.

parts in the liturgy, and we can envisage a variety of roles, such as memorial and, again, involvement in the reverence of saints: Helen Gittos has pointed to the importance of procession in particular, noting the example of the monks of Hexham who processed to the cross that St Oswald had set up at Heavenfield on his feast day.[67] It can therefore be plausibly suggested that most of these items were located at minsters, where they formed parts of the liturgical architecture used regularly by the communities that lived there, communities that can themselves best be defined by these practices. However, these are not the only relationships implied by the sculpture. Gwendoline Bergius has recently suggested that 'through the movement of people, gifts and correspondence, Mercia was linked into an intricate network of communication that reached across Francia and northern Italy to Rome, and which was able to develop during the long reigns of both Offa and Charlemagne to encompass key secular and ecclesiastical centres' such as Pavia and Brescia.[68] Through such connections members of the Mercian elite embraced the sculptural practices of Rome and Lombard Italy, and gained access to the Late Antique models that inspired them.

The more specific similarities shared by monuments within the groups outlined above might be considered in a number of ways: masons and sculptors might have circulated within certain regions, moving from minster to minster; those commissioning these monuments might have been aware of work at nearby minsters, or might have shared models with their neighbours. Significantly, all plausible explanations must involve people communicating and moving between minsters, sometimes across regnal, diocesan and even metropolitan boundaries. For example, the coherence of the Trent Valley Group implies dispersed yet interconnected groups of sculptors, perhaps familiar with each other's work, reproducing established forms but also innovating new compositions. The Dove Valley Subgroup implies a more concentrated nexus of cooperation and interaction. The coexistence within the group of technically well-executed monuments, informed by direct access to appropriate models, and more stylised monuments often created with less precision, further implies the varying extent of intersection between different communities who benefited from the work of the sculptors. Particularly prestigious members of the elite might have drawn on their widespread networks, involving contacts with people on the continent in the Frankish realm, northern Italy and Rome, to supply the models and expert craftsmen for grandiose monumental productions that resonated within the large-scale communities in which they were invested. All sorts of connections between their minsters and other minsters at regional and local levels might then enable the proliferation of stone monuments through the labour of a broader base of sculptors working for those more solely invested in their own local communities. This model is far removed from that implied by the ethno-cultural straitjacket imposed by the format of the *Corpus* volumes.

The stone sculpture thus hints at a range of communities and relationships, from the minster-centred liturgical communities at which they were created to the broader networks and associations through which their exemplars and sculptors circulated.

---

67 H. Gittos, *Liturgy, archtecture, and sacred places in Anglo-Saxon England* (Oxford, 2013), p. 140.
68 G.C.C. Bergius, 'The Anglo-Saxon stone sculpture of Mercia as evidence for continental influence and cultural exchange', PhD thesis (Durham, 2012), p. 48.

Such associations have also been recognised in the development of ecclesiastical architecture during this period, which Richard Gem suggests was driven by ideas about Christian reform of both church and society shared by many across the broad Carolingian realm during a coherent period between the late eighth and early tenth centuries.[69] This is the same period advocated here for the development of stone sculpture in the diocese of Lichfield; crucially, Gem criticises the fact that the Viking invasions of the second half of the ninth century have often been employed to mark the beginning or ending of interpretive periods, thus obscuring the extent to which many ecclesiastical practices continued in recognisable form across the period of these events and beyond; the disruptive effects of the Great Army's activities between 865 and 879 can be acknowledged without having to accept 'a complete hiatus in church life and culture'.[70] Indeed, the brief reinvention of a Mercian political identity under Æthelred and Æthelflæd in the early tenth century might be viewed as an important stimulus to cultural activity that also marked, in its decline after Æthelflæd's death in 918, the end of over a century of sculptural production across much of the diocese. Of prime importance in this chapter is the implication of this sculpture's distribution for the locations of minsters in the diocese that were active during this period, and it is to the cathedral and the minsters that we now turn.

Lichfield cathedral

We begin our analysis of the diocese's religious centres with Lichfield cathedral, which was not only the centre of the diocesan community but also represents the site most abundantly provided with evidence of various kinds for its pre-Conquest existence. Analysis of the cathedral is thus not only important in its own right but raises a number of themes that can be pursued when exploring the other early religious centres of the diocese, in particular the shrine of the saint at the heart of the site and the community that maintained it. The detailed hagiography of the LN, including Chad's acquisition of Lichfield in 669 and his setting there of the episcopal see, has already been discussed in Chapter 2, as has the central importance of the cathedral there four centuries later in 1086. This will be revisited below, along with other textual evidence, but the cathedral has also been blessed by considerable archaeological investigation in recent decades. The cathedral itself sits dramatically atop a sandstone bluff on the north-west side of the Curborough Brook, which was dammed in the mid-twelfth century to form three large pools, two of which survive to the present.[71] The

---

69   R. Gem, 'A B C: How should we periodise Anglo-Saxon architecture?', in L.A.S. Butler and R.K. Morris (eds), *The Anglo-Saxon church: papers on history, architecture, and archaeology in honour of Dr H M Taylor*, CBA Research Report 60 (London, 1986), pp. 146–55, at pp. 152–3.
70   Gem, 'A B C', p. 151. Blair, *Church*, makes the same point at pp. 291–5, but retains c.850 as a chronological hinge, and bizarrely suggests that Staffordshire and Cheshire belonged to a 'Norse-settled zone' in the late ninth century (at p. 308).
71   For this and much of what follows, see A. Sargent, 'Early medieval Lichfield: a reassessment', *Transactions of the Staffordshire Archaeological and Historical Society*, 46 (2013), pp. 1–32, and references therein.

cathedral church and surrounding canons' houses are set within a ditched close that probably had an early medieval antecedent, but the minster also extends into the surrounding landscape, a horseshoe of low hills that encloses the Curborough Brook and its headstreams to the south-west and opens out along the course of the brook to the north-east. A second church, dedicated to St Chad, called the 'monastery' or 'House of St Chad' in the thirteenth century, is sited about 700m north-east of the cathedral compound on the opposite bank of the Curborough Brook at a place called Stowe. This site was associated in later medieval tradition with a well or spring, again dedicated to St Chad, beside which he was said to have lived a hermit's life, and is almost certainly the site of the oratory that features in the LN as the place of his periodic retreat where he received divine foreknowledge of his death. Greenhill, one of the hills to the south-east of the Curborough Brook, opposite the cathedral close, is crowned by a third church, dedicated to St Michael, which is surrounded by a large cemetery, perhaps with early medieval origins.[72] If so this would complement evidence for early medieval burial within the close.[73]

Much of this topography places Lichfield firmly within the stable of large poly-focal minster sites founded in the seventh century across the English kingdoms. Chad's oratory mirrors other 'satellite hermitages' attested textually and archaeologically at places such as Lindisfarne, Hexham and Glastonbury.[74] The cemetery on Greenhill might parallel that on Ailcy Hill, east of Ripon minster, which served as one of several sites of burial across and in the vicinity of the minster complex from perhaps the sixth century, before the minster was founded.[75] Indeed, the parallel may be quite a close one, as recent excavation at Lichfield has revealed a stone-founded building of probable sixth-century date on the bank of the Curborough Brook opposite the cathedral close.[76] The building is of uncertain function, but it does not appear to be a church; its construction across a pit and the presence of archaeobotanical evidence indicative of crop storage may imply a utilitarian role, perhaps on the periphery of domestic settlement nearby. A reassessment of the textual evidence for Lichfield's pre-minster history has emphasised that it provides

---

72 J. Gould and D. Gould, 'St Michael's Churchyard, Lichfield', *Transactions of the South Staffordshire Archaeological and Historical Society*, 16 (1975), pp. 58–61.
73 Burials were found in excavations in the nave and choir aisles, for which see more below; to this might be added an eighteenth-century description of a possible early medieval gypsum burial in a lead coffin found below the nave of the cathedral (J. Gould, *Lichfield: archaeology and development* (Birmingham, 1976), p. 10). A small excavation outside the cathedral, at the southern edge of the close, has revealed evidence for a phase of timber building followed by an inhumation cemetery (M.O.H. Carver, 'Excavations south of Lichfield cathedral', *Transactions of the South Staffordshire Archaeological and Historical Society*, 22 (1981), pp. 35–69, at pp. 37–8); a later excavation a short distance north-east of this location failed to identify any early medieval features (A. Jones, 'Lichfield cathedral close: archaeological evaluation (stages 1–4) 1989–1990', Birmingham University Field Archaeology Unit unpublished report (Birmingham, 1990), p. 9).
74 Blair, *Church*, pp. 217–18.
75 R.A. Hall and M. Whyman, 'Settlement and monasticism at Ripon, north Yorkshire, from the 7th to 11th Centuries AD', *Medieval Archaeology*, 40 (1996), pp. 62–150, at pp. 117–24.
76 Sargent, 'Early medieval Lichfield', pp. 7–12.

no warrant for placing an earlier Christian site there, as previous commentators have done;[77] but future archaeological discoveries may reinstate that interpretation, or propose an alternative character for the sixth-century settlement at Lichfield. The sixth-century building was replaced by two successive sunken-featured buildings of more assured utilitarian character, primarily involving the storage of harvested crops, which spanned the period from the seventh to early tenth centuries, perhaps as part of an outlying processing area associated with the cathedral close.[78]

Excavations undertaken by Warwick Rodwell within the cathedral church over the last three decades have revealed evidence for early churches at Lichfield and for one of St Chad's shrines, and deserve close attention, especially as some of the interpretation offered below differs in significant respects from that offered by Rodwell.[79] Early medieval archaeology has been located in three separate areas within the present Gothic building – the north choir aisle, the south choir aisle, and the eastern end of the nave – and in the first two locations it had been truncated at various points by the footings of the apsidal east end of the Romanesque cathedral.[80] These features are shown on a composite plan, Figure 8, which also shows the centrelines of the thirteenth-century nave and transept arcades for reference.[81] In the north and south choir aisles the remains comprised mortared rubble foundations of the same or a similar phase of construction, in some areas partially robbed out.[82] In the north aisle the north, east and west sides of a square or rectangular structure were truncated by the Romanesque arcade to the south.[83] In the south aisle the foundations formed the east and west sides of a similar structure, and had been truncated to both north and south by the Romanesque east end.[84] Burials were located immediately west of the

---

77   Sargent, 'Early medieval Lichfield', pp. 1–4.
78   Sargent, 'Early medieval Lichfield', pp. 12–16.
79   The relevant reports, both published and unpublished, are: W. Rodwell, 'Archaeology and the standing fabric: recent studies at Lichfield cathedral', *Antiquity*, 63 (1989), pp. 281–94; idem, 'Lichfield cathedral: interim report on archaeological excavations in the south quire aisle and the consistory court', unpublished report, Lichfield Cathedral Library (Lichfield, 1992); idem, 'The development of the choir of Lichfield cathedral: Romanesque and Early English', in J. Maddison (ed.), *Medieval archaeology and architecture at Lichfield*, Conference Transactions of the British Archaeological Association 13 (Oxford, 1993), pp. 17–35; idem, 'Lichfield cathedral: interim report on archaeological excavations in the north quire aisle', unpublished report, Lichfield Cathedral Library (Lichfield, 1994); idem, 'An interim report on archaeological investigations in the nave of Lichfield cathedral', unpublished report, Lichfield Cathedral Library (Lichfield, 2000); idem, 'Archaeological excavation in the nave of Lichfield cathedral; an interim report', Unpublished report (Lichfield Cathedral Library, 2003); Rodwell et al., 'The Lichfield Angel'.
80   Rodwell, 'South quire aisle', idem, 'North quire aisle' and idem, 'Nave'.
81   Rodwell et al., 'The Lichfield Angel', p. 51, Figure 2 shows a similar plan, although the structural features in the nave excavation appear to be too small when compared to the larger excavation plan shown at p. 54, Figure 4.
82   Rodwell, 'South quire aisle' and idem, 'North quire aisle'.
83   Rodwell, 'North quire aisle'.
84   Rodwell, 'South quire aisle'.

The cathedral and the minsters

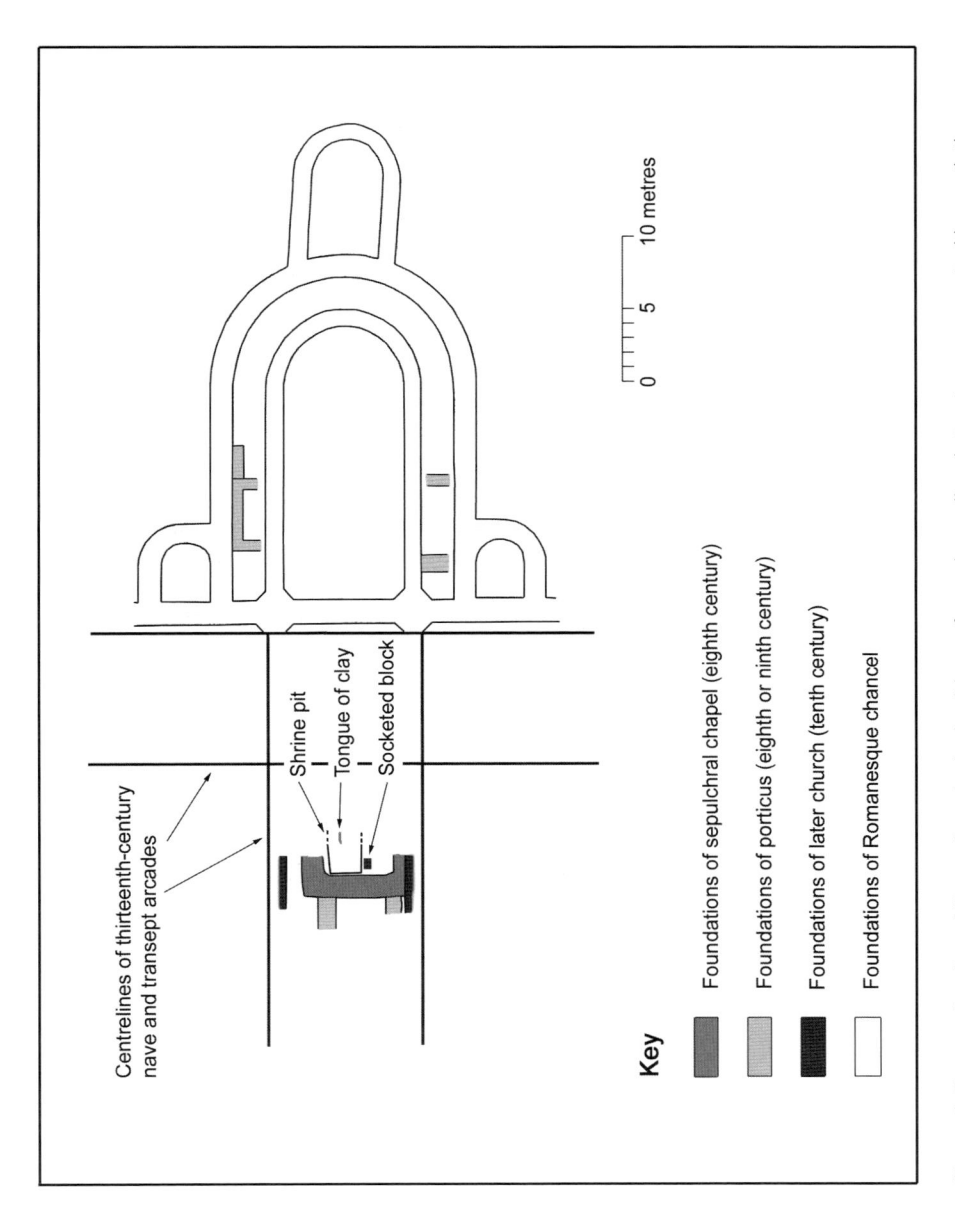

Figure 8 Composite plan of the archaeological evidence for early medieval structures excavated beneath the nave and choir of Lichfield cathedral.

western walls in both aisles, the longer sequence in the south including adults, young children and several babies, with a couple packed with charcoal in the middle of the sequence.[85] Two glass beads in one burial and several radiocarbon dates suggest that the period of interment covered the seventh and eighth centuries, although it should be noted that the charcoal burials would therefore be very early examples of the type, and the sequence perhaps extended a little later.[86] Rodwell proposes reasonably that the structural remains represent a pair of lateral porticus flanking a church, although his implication that these were the easternmost of a series extending westwards is less plausible;[87] the northern wall of the northern chamber does not extend to the west, and the presence of the babies among the dead buried west of the southern chamber probably indicates an exterior burial plot, as groups of infant burials located around the external walls of churches, so-called 'eaves-drip' burials, have been observed at several other cemeteries across the country.[88]

In the nave of the cathedral, the archaeological excavation located three phases of early medieval structural remains.[89] First, clay-and-pebble foundations formed the west, north and south walls of a large structure that extended eastwards beyond the limit of excavation; burials were found within this structure, although none of them were excavated.[90] At a later date the rubble foundations of a second structure (including a sculptured fragment displaying interlace design) were laid to abut the western end of the first, and although its western end was beyond the limit of excavation its dimensions bear comparison with the porticus in the choir aisles; however, unlike the porticus these foundations were un-mortared, suggesting that they were not of the same phase as the porticus.[91] The third phase must have occurred after the demolition of the earlier structures, and comprised two east–west mortared-rubble foundations, later robbed, underlying and severely truncated by the foundations of the thirteenth-century nave arcades. While accepting that the foundations must have supported the Romanesque nave walls or arcade, Rodwell suggests that they may have been reused from an earlier building, as they are most unlike the poured concrete and rubble foundations associated with the Romanesque building elsewhere in the cathedral.[92]

The stratigraphy of the archaeology in the nave excavation was confused by the presence of so many later medieval graves.[93] However, a layer of burnt material was found to provide an historical horizon to which other features could be related, and may have been part of a set of levelling layers deposited after the demolition of the first-

---

85   Rodwell, 'South quire aisle'.
86   Rodwell et al., 'The Lichfield Angel', pp. 51–2; V. Thompson, *Dying and death in later Anglo-Saxon England* (Woodbridge, 2004), pp. 118–19.
87   Rodwell et al., 'The Lichfield Angel', p. 51.
88   D.M. Hadley and J. Buckberry, 'Caring for the dead in late Anglo-Saxon England', in F. Tinti (ed.), *Pastoral care in late Anglo-Saxon England* (Woodbridge, 2005), pp. 121–47, at pp. 144–5.
89   Rodwell, 'Nave'; Rodwell et al., 'The Lichfield Angel', pp. 52–5.
90   Rodwell, 'Nave', p. 3.
91   Rodwell, 'Nave'.
92   Rodwell, 'Nave', pp. 7–8.
93   Rodwell, 'Nave', p. 4.

The cathedral and the minsters

and second-phase structures but before the construction of the third-phase building.[94] Sealed beneath this layer in the south-west corner of the earliest structure was a pit containing the fragments of the Lichfield Angel panel.[95] Within the footprint of the earliest building was a large rectangular vertically sided pit that was 2m wide, over 2m long and extended beyond the eastern limit of excavation; its stratigraphical position is ambiguous in Rodwell's reports, but his latest synthesis associates it with the third-phase structure, probably because it is positioned on the centreline of this structure (and its post-Conquest successors), which lies a little north of the centreline of the earlier structures.[96] Moreover, the pit remained open until the fourteenth century, and provided the focus for prestigious burials within the later incarnations of the cathedral, and on this basis Rodwell identifies it as a small burial crypt associated with the shrine of St Chad.[97] There were indications that the pit had once been lined with timber, and a socketed block had been set into the ground at the south-west corner of the pit, cutting through the burnt layer; Rodwell suggests that this held a corner post for a canopy of honour.[98] The block was later sealed by several layers; a nearby pit that cut through these layers contained a near-mint condition silver coin of King Edgar (957/9–75).[99]

The hiatus between first- and second-phase structures and the third-phase structure cannot be precisely dated, although a plausible bracket can be indicated: the Lichfield Angel is thought to date to the late eighth or early ninth centuries, indicating that the spread of burnt material sealing the pit in which it was placed post-dates this time, probably by several decades if the sculpture was above ground for any length of time.[100] Meanwhile, the socketed block is sealed by layers through which the pit containing the coin of King Edgar was cut; although the coin supplies only a *terminus post quem*, its near-mint condition implies a date somewhere within the last third of the tenth century. The shrine pit appears, from its position, to coincide with or post-date the construction of the third-phase structure, and, assuming that the socketed block was associated with the shrine pit, this probably happened before the mid-tenth century. Taken together, this gives a likely bracket of the later ninth and earlier tenth centuries for the demolition of the earlier structures and the construction of the later, an event that may therefore have coincided with the ascendency of Æthelred and Æthelflæd in Mercian regnal politics. The radiocarbon dates of the burials associated with the porticus in the south choir aisle firmly connect it and its opposite number in the north aisle with the first- and second-phase buildings in the nave, and this is also supported by a consideration of the building with which they may have been associated.

---

94 Rodwell, 'Nave', pp. 4–9.
95 Rodwell, 'Nave', p. 6; at p. 7 Rodwell contradicts this statement by suggesting that the pit was dug after the spreading of burnt material across the site, but affirms that the pit was sealed by the burnt material in his later synthesis in Rodwell *et al.*, 'The Lichfield Angel', p. 59.
96 Rodwell, 'Nave', p. 4, simply states that the pit was 'embraced within the earliest part of the Anglo-Saxon stratigraphic sequence'; Rodwell *et al.*, 'The Lichfield Angel', pp. 53–4, is more concise.
97 Rodwell, 'Nave', pp. 8–9.
98 Rodwell, 'Nave', pp. 4–5.
99 Rodwell, 'Nave', p. 7.
100 Rodwell *et al.*, 'The Lichfield Angel'; see also Hawkes and Sidebottom, *Corpus*, Lichfield 1.

Lichfield and the Lands of St Chad

It is unclear whether Rodwell would support the dating proposed here, as he appears to associate the shrine pit, and therefore the third-phase structure to which it belonged, with the eighth- and ninth-century contexts of St Chad's shrine as represented by the LN and the Lichfield Angel. This shrine therefore needs now to be considered. The LN says the following about Chad's burial:

> Chad died on 2nd March and was first of all buried close to the church of St Mary; but when the church of St Peter, the most blessed chief of the apostles, was later built, his bones were translated in there. In each place frequent miracles of healing occur as a sign of his virtue ... . Furthermore, that same place of burial is covered by a wooden tomb made in the manner of a little house, having an aperture in its side, through which those who visit it out of devotion can insert their hands and take out a little of the dust. When it is put in water and given either to cattle or people who are ailing, they get their wish and are at once freed form their ailments and rejoice in health restored.[101]

The crux of this passage concerns the ambiguous connection between, on the one hand, the two places where miracles occurred, namely Chad's original burial place and his new place of entombment in St Peters, and, on the other, the place of burial covered by the wooden tomb. It is commonly assumed that the tomb overlay Chad's new resting place in St Peter's; however, John Blair has argued that the covered grave should be identified with Chad's initial burial place by comparing the description to that of the site of St Oswald's death.[102] Here, people took away soil from where the king fell, and, as with Chad's 'dust', mixed it with water as a cure for the sick; this became so popular that 'a hole was made, as deep as a man's height'.[103] In both narratives the word *pulvis* is used, and it clearly refers to soil in the Oswald narrative. Blair must surely be right in identifying the covered grave of the LN with Chad's initial grave outside St Mary's church, from which soil, after contact with the saint's body, was regarded as a suitable medium for the working of miracles. We therefore have to reckon with two eighth-century shrines, one on the site of St Chad's initial burial and described in the LN, the other in St Peter's church containing his translated body.

Rodwell supports his equation of the shrine pit with the shrine described in the LN by contending that the description of Chad's grave as 'covered' (*coopertus*) was a reference to his hypothesised canopy of honour; however, this translation will not stand, as the participle 'covered' is associated grammatically with an ablative of instrument in Bede's text that describes the wooden house-shaped tomb: that is, the grave was 'covered by' the tomb shrine.[104] Rodwell also appears to associate the shrine pit, and therefore the third-phase structure, with St Peter's, suggesting that the foundations in the nave and those in the choir aisles belonged to two distinct structures

---

101 *HE*, iv.3.
102 Blair, 'A saint for every minster?', p. 491, n. 98.
103 *HE*, iii.9.
104 Rodwell, 'Nave', p. 6; Rodwell et al., 'The Lichfield Angel', p. 55; *HE*, iv.3: *Est autem locus idem sepulchri tumba lignea in modum domunculi facta coopertus.*

'in view of the distance between them', and asserting that the eastern structure was St Mary's church.[105] This is a reasonable point, but it bundles the third-phase structure in the nave into the same eighth-/ninth-century phase as the eastern structure in the choir, an equation argued above to be unlikely. It is proposed here to resolve the various archaeological components differently.

The structure, almost certainly a church, represented by the porticus in the choir was probably largely contemporary with a separate structure represented by the first- and second-phase foundations in the nave; as Rodwell notes, the presence of burials in the latter structure render it unlikely to represent the 'main body' of a church, as such spaces were usually free of burials during this period, suggesting instead that it may have been a smaller building, perhaps a tower.[106] Given its association with burials, the western structure might profitably be compared to the sepulchral chapel excavated at Whithorn and the analogous structure at Hexham, or perhaps to the mausoleum at nearby Repton.[107] However, it must be noted that if the northern porticus in the choir aisle is assumed to have been square, as was not uncommon with such features, then the northern wall of the church it abutted would have aligned with the north wall of the first-phase building in the nave. At 7m, the proposed sepulchral chapel at Lichfield was slightly wider than the examples cited above, which were 5m or 6m wide, but it may have been deliberately matched to the width of the church to the east, perhaps even abutting it. This proposal is supported by the western porticus attached to the western structure, which, when considered with the two porticus to the east, is reminiscent of a pattern commonly observed elsewhere, whereby two lateral porticus were joined by a third projecting from the western end of the church. Figure 9 shows a possible reconstruction, the church having been provided with a nave approximately 20.5m long, another common feature of eighth- and ninth-century churches.[108]

The location of the sepulchral chapel, immediately west of the church, resonates with the position of Chad's initial grave, described as 'close to the church of St Mary', so it is distinctly possible that the sepulchral chapel was constructed around the site of Chad's original grave. The shrine pit itself appears to be contemporary with the third-phase structure in the nave, which can plausibly be interpreted as

---

105 Rodwell *et al.*, 'The Lichfield Angel', 54; see also Rodwell, 'North Quire Aisle', p. 6.
106 Rodwell, 'Nave', p. 3.
107 P.H. Hill, *Whithorn and St Ninian: the excavation of a monastic town 1984–91* (Stroud, 1997); E. Cambridge and A. Williams, 'Hexham Abbey: a review of recent work and its implications', *Archaeologia Aeliana*, Fifth Series, 23 (1995), pp. 51–138, at pp. 79–80, in which the apsidal structure immediately east of St Andrew's church is argued to be a mortuary chapel (compare Blair, *Church*, p. 200, fig. 24, where the chapel is argued to represent St Mary's church, known from twelfth-century documentation); M. Biddle and B. Kjølbye-Biddle, 'Repton and the Vikings', *Antiquity*, 66 (1992), pp. 36–51; Hawkes and Sidebottom, *Corpus*, pp. 57–9.
108 See, for example, the churches shown in R. Gem, 'Architecture of the Anglo-Saxon church, 735 to 870: from Archbishop Ecgberht to Archbishop Ceolnoth', *Journal of the British Archaeological Association*, 146 (1993), pp. 29–66, at p. 42, fig. 4 (Brixworth, Northants and Wareham, Dorset), p. 47, fig. 7 (Edenham, Lincs.), p. 52, fig. 8 (Billingham, Cleveland), and p. 54, fig. 9 (Deerhurst, Glos. and Wing, Bucks.).

Lichfield and the Lands of St Chad

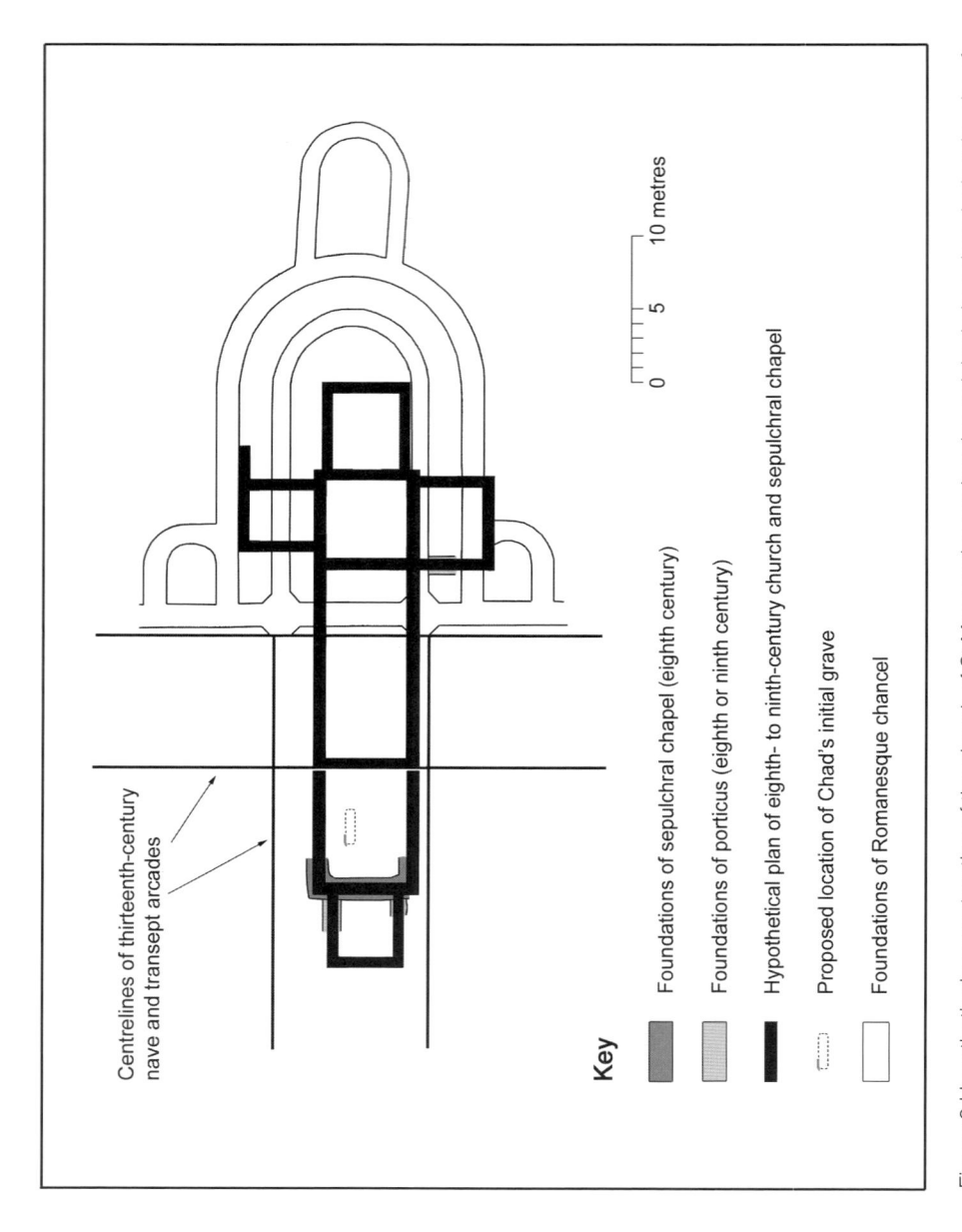

Figure 9 Hypothetical reconstruction of the church of St Mary and associated sepulchral chapel enclosing the site of Chad's original grave at Lichfield.

The cathedral and the minsters

a later church constructed over the remains of the earlier structures. However, it is possible to use an unusual feature within this later shrine pit to advance a hypothesis that links it with the earlier structures as well. Although the sides of the pit were 'cleanly cut and vertical, and the base was near-level', the east-central part of the excavated portion featured 'a tongue of natural clay' upstanding from the base and continuing eastwards with the rest of the pit beyond the limit of excavation.[109] In fact, the site photograph used in publication shows a second tongue a short distance south of the first, the two forming a narrow trough in the bottom of the shrine pit.[110] Nevertheless, even a single tongue allows us to consider the possibility that the later shrine pit was excavated around Chad's original grave, the tongue or tongues representing one or both sides of the grave cut; perhaps it had previously been truncated by ardent pilgrims removing soil over the years, and the pit was excavated to rationalise what was left, or perhaps to show it off to best advantage. Unfortunately, due to the cut of the later shrine pit, there is no existing stratigraphic relationship that would allow this hypothesis to be confirmed, but it does seem to make best use of all the available evidence.

The form of the Lichfield Angel panel might also support this. It has been identified as the left half of an Annunciation scene forming the shallowly gabled end of a shrine chest, which 'preserves the return on the left, but retains no sign of having had a base';[111] as has been recognised, this is a convincing analogue in stone for Bede's description of the wooden tomb shrine, and may have been created to replace the latter.[112] The deposition of the broken sculpture in the pit predates the excavation of the shrine pit and, assuming it did not move very far to its pit, was therefore almost certainly associated with the sepulchral chapel and the putative open grave of St Chad, the latter accessible through the open base of the shrine chest. Moreover, it has been noted that the left side panel of the shrine – part of which survives as the return mentioned above – is undecorated, prompting the suggestion that 'it was designed to stand against a wall or in such a way that the back was inaccessible, only the front and two end panels being on show'.[113] If St Chad's grave has been correctly located above, then it was not centrally positioned within the sepulchral chapel, which was aligned on the church to the east, but lay towards the northern side of the structure, rendering the northern side of the overlying shrine less accessible and perhaps not worth the trouble of carving. Finally, the iconography of the Annunciation, suggested by Jane Hawkes to express 'virginal purity, humility and obedience' and intended to resonate with the memory of Chad's character, was also particularly apt within a sepulchral chapel abutting St Mary's church.[114]

---

109 Rodwell, 'Nave', p. 4.
110 Rodwell, 'Nave', p. 15; Rodwell et al., 'The Lichfield Angel', p. 53.
111 Rodwell et al., 'The Lichfield Angel', p. 60; see also pp. 75–80 for a discussion of the probable involvement of the angel in an Annunciation scene, and also Hawkes and Sidebottom, Corpus, Lichfield 1.
112 Rodwell et al., 'The Lichfield Angel', pp. 64–6.
113 Rodwell et al., 'The Lichfield Angel', p. 64.
114 Rodwell et al., 'The Lichfield Angel', p. 79.

The interpretation argued above supports Rodwell's equation of the structure in the choir with St Mary's church, but it does not support an equation of the sepulchral chapel with St Peter's church, into which Chad's body was translated.[115] Assuming that the sepulchral chapel has been correctly identified here with the location of Chad's original grave, the only valid conclusion is that the church of St Peter is as yet unrepresented in the archaeology of Lichfield cathedral. An argument for locating it beneath the present chapter house has been made elsewhere, but must remain unproven pending further archaeological work.[116] Interestingly, some of the actual relics of St Chad appear to survive in the Roman Catholic cathedral of St Chad in Birmingham. The six surviving bones were removed from the cathedral at Lichfield after Henry VIII's attack on pilgrimage shrines in 1538 and, after a series of adventures with Jesuit priests, were enshrined in Birmingham cathedral in 1841.[117] In 1995 the six bones were submitted for osteological analysis and radiocarbon dating: one was dated to the eighth, less probably the ninth century, while the other five were dated to the seventh, less probably the sixth century. The latter bones represent a minimum of two individuals, owing to the presence of two left femurs.[118] Altogether there are therefore a minimum of three individuals, of which one of the two from the seventh century is surely St Chad. The possibility of two further individuals is strikingly coincident with the two further saints listed at Lichfield in the Secgan: *Cedde* and *Ceatta*. If the former is Chad's brother, then he could be represented by the other seventh-century individual, leaving the eighth-century relic possibly that of St Ceatta. Hugh Candidus, in his resting-place list, states that all three were bishops, which certainly applies to Chad and Cedd, although Ceatta is otherwise unknown. David Farmer equated Ceatta with Bishop Headda of Lichfield, which, while neat, assumes an early corruption of the original text.[119]

Archaeology has enabled the creation of a remarkably detailed impression of the establishment and development of St Chad's cult at the heart of the minster complex at Lichfield. The material form of these churches and shrines enabled the community at the cathedral to maintain the cult through repetitive liturgical rituals. Outside these roles, the nature of the community is more difficult to discern, but at Lichfield there is some evidence, albeit slight, to offer hints. A passage in Alan of Ashbourne's fourteenth-century Lichfield Chronicle, appended to Bishop Æthelwald in his list of bishops of Lichfield, can only be described as tantalising:

---

115 Jane Hawkes (Rodwell *et al.*, 'The Lichfield Angel', p. 66) acknowledges Blair's identification of the holy dust from Chad's tomb with grave-earth, but, unwilling to relinquish the idea that the tomb described in the Lastingham Narrative was that in St Peter's, she suggests that the original grave was incorporated within the latter church when it was built; however, this is contradicted by the Lastingham Narrative, which not only explicitly relates the translation of Chad's bones into St Peter's (*in eandem sunt eius ossa translate*) but also refers to miracles occurring 'in each place' (*in quo utroque loco*), the original grave and the new resting place in St Peter's.
116 A. Sargent, 'Lichfield and the lands of St Chad', PhD thesis (Keele, 2012), pp. 259–61.
117 M.W. Greenslade, *Saint Chad of Lichfield and Birmingham* (Birmingham, 1996), pp. 14–17.
118 Greenslade, *Saint Chad*, pp. 25–6.
119 D.H. Farmer, *The Oxford dictionary of saints* (Oxford, 1978), p. 75.

The cathedral and the minsters

> Through this Bishop Æthelwald canons were first instituted in the cathedral church of Lichfield, in the year 822 under King Ceolwulf of the Mercians, *Huicta* then being provost of the canons. There were then in the Church of Lichfield twenty canons with their provost, of which eleven were priests and nine deacons.[120]

The number of canons was later altered to nineteen, both in the text and in a marginal addition, although the number of priests and deacons was retained, and the correction was probably the response to a concern that twenty canons with their provost might be interpreted to mean twenty-one in total. Some of the details of this entry appear too specific not to have come from an earlier source, although its nature is hard to assess; nevertheless, it is worth entertaining the idea that the information was drawn from a ninth-century charter.

The entire constitutional structure presented in this passage would have been anachronistic in the fourteenth century, and it has been suggested that it instead bears a resemblance to the eighth-century decretum written by Chrodegang of Metz, wherein canons would live a regular life under the jurisdiction of a provost;[121] a similar rule was apparently instituted at Canterbury in 808×813 by Archbishop Wulfred, as attested in a grant of privileges to his community.[122] However, Brigitte Langefeld has cast doubt on this, instead emphasising the lack of any copy of, or reference to, Chrodegang's Rule in England before the mid-tenth century.[123] Instead she suggests that Wulfred's reform was intended to renew the monastic life of the community at Canterbury, and that it harmonises better with the Rule of St Benedict than with the Rule of Chrodegang, there being no evident desire among English communities of this period to separate the lives of monks from the lives of clerics (or canons).[124]

Langefeld's analysis of ninth-century Canterbury charters demonstrates the widespread presence of the offices of priest (*presbiter*) and deacon (*diaconus*) among the signatories of the community, and the comparative infrequency of the offices of provost (*praepositus*) or archdeacon in the same signature lists. Both priests and deacons are envisaged as members of the monastic community in St Benedict's Rule, in which the provost stands at the head of the community under the abbot; in contrast, the archdeacon headed the community of canons in Chrodegang's Rule. In the Lichfield Chronicle fragment the priests, deacons and their provost (presumably one of the priests) bear titles that mirror those at ninth-century Canterbury and resonate with St Benedict's Rule. Indeed, the enumeration of these offices reads very much as if Alan had simply totted up a witness list such as that attached to Wulfred's grant of privileges, in which the names and ranks of the community are given.[125] It is therefore quite plausible that Alan's source for this passage was such a charter, and that,

---

120 BL Cott. Cleo. D IX, f.75r.
121 Greenslade, *VCH Staffordshire*, vol. 3, pp. 140–66.
122 Brooks, *Early history of the church of Canterbury*, pp. 155–60.
123 B. Langefeld, 'Regula canonicorum or Regula monasterialis vitae? The rule of Chrodegang and Archbishop Wulfred's reforms at Canterbury', *Anglo-Saxon England*, 25 (1996), pp. 21–36, at p. 26.
124 Langefeld,'Regula canonicorum or Regula monasterialis vitae?', pp. 27–32.
125 S 1265.

Lichfield and the Lands of St Chad

from the offices given, the structure of the early ninth-century community at Lichfield was similar to that at Canterbury. Alan's use of the word *canonicus* is problematic, as it would be anachronistic in a ninth-century context, given what has been said above. However, his description of the ranks of the community as priests, deacons and provost might suggest that he himself added the idea that these men were also canons, as their existence appears to have served as something of an origin myth in the fourteenth century to explain the initial formation of the contemporary community of canons; certainly, by the sixteenth century, a list of the cathedral prebends was headed by the statement that they had been established by Bishop Æthelwald.[126]

An earlier origin story for the later medieval community of canons is recorded in the early thirteenth-century chronicle of Prior Geoffrey of Coventry, who states that the college was instituted by Bishop Roger de Clinton (1128–48); before this time, he says, 'there were only five priests serving five chapels, each to each'.[127] It has been noted that this corresponds to a reference in Domesday Book that records five canons (*canonici*) holding land in the estate at Lichfield in 1086.[128] Moreover, a division into five appears in a range of later medieval sources concerned with parochial organisation at Lichfield: in a statute dated 1241 five chaplains were given weekly courses of duties in the cathedral and enjoyed special rights and responsibilities in the celebration of mass at the high altar; in the 1330s five parochial chaplains had the duty of licensing a deacon at St Mary's church in Lichfield; and in the mid-fourteenth century five chaplains, appointed by the prebendaries of Freeford, Statfold, Longdon, Handsacre and Weeford, were responsible for serving the three city churches of St Mary's, St Chad's and St Michael's.[129] These five prebends formed the core of the later prebendal system; each was named after one of the townships of the estate at Lichfield, from which it took all the tithes, but they also shared between them most of the tithes of the rest of the core area of that estate, with the remainder held by other prebends, such that in the nineteenth century these five still held between them about 75 per cent of its tithes.[130] Later evidence indicates that the pastoral care of the inhabitants of the estate was initially organised by these five prebendaries, later joined by some of the others, and that

---

126 H. Wharton, *Anglia Sacra*, Part 1 (London, 1691), pp. 444–5.
127 Prior Geoffrey's Chronicle is now lost, but it was available to Dugdale, who extracted parts in his *Monasticon Anglicanum*: W. Dugdale, *Monasticon Anglicanum*, ed. J. Caley, H. Ellis and B. Bandinel, 6 vols in 8 parts (London, 1817–30), vol. 6 (part 3), p. 1242.
128 *DB Staffs.*, 2.16; see Greenslade, *VCH Staffordshire*, vol. 3, p. 140.
129 M.W. Greenslade (ed.), *VCH Staffordshire*, vol. 14 (London, 1990), p. 136.
130 The core part of the estate at Lichfield (and Longdon) is essentially the estate recorded in Domesday Book excepting lands to the north across the Trent (in Yoxall and Pipe Ridware) and detached parts to the south in Harborne, Smethwick and Tipton. A list of places owing 'wax-scot' to the cathedral dated 1191 is largely coterminous with this core, except that it also includes Harborne (Greenslade, *VCH Staffordshire*, vol. 14, p. 135); the core area is represented by the later parishes of St Chad's, St Michael's and St Mary's in Lichfield, Longdon, Armitage, Norton Canes, Weeford, Hints, Whittington and Statfold; the calculation is based on the acreages paying tithe recorded in the nineteenth-century tithe commutation surveys.

although the discrete territories from which each of the prebends was owed tithes were used in aspects of ecclesiastical administration, the prebendaries essentially held the three city churches collectively, as chapels of the cathedral, in which the parochial life of all the parishioners was focused.[131] Only later, perhaps beginning in the twelfth century, did some of the outlying townships gain churches of their own, and only in the sixteenth and seventeenth centuries were the separate parishes of St Chad's, St Michael's and St Mary's distinguished.[132]

We have moved a long way ahead of Æthelwald's ninth-century community, but it is perhaps plausible to suggest that the division of tithes across the estate at Lichfield between five canons responsible for pastoral care predated the institution of the prebendal system, and that these five canons also possessed some land in the estate for the same purpose. The assignment of tithes in this way can date to only the tenth century at the earliest, when tithe payment was first made compulsory in England and enforced through royal legislation (considered in more detail in Chapter 4). It is probably foolish to speculate beyond this, although it is not necessarily unlikely that five of Æthelwald's twenty clerics enjoyed some kind of superiority over the others, even if the elaboration of their parochial roles belongs to a later period. It is possible to offer one straw in the wind here: at the Southumbrian Council of *Clofesho* in 803 Ealdwulf, the bishop of Lichfield, attested the acts alongside Abbot Hygeberht, his retired predecessor, and five priests from his diocese.[133] It is reasonable to assume that these priests were member of the episcopal *familia*, but is it too tenuous to see here a foreshadowing of the later importance of five clerics at Lichfield? The pastoral primacy of their post-Conquest successors might plausibly hint at the liturgical significance of Ealdwulf's five priests and would thus highlight that, whatever the form of the larger community at Lichfield, those members with the greatest significance were also those most closely implicated in the liturgical life of the cathedral, focused on the cult of St Chad.

Minsters attested by pre-*c.*1050 hagiography

None of the other religious centres of the diocese enjoy such a plenitude of evidence as Lichfield, but the presence of saints' cults remains the foremost criterion for identifying them with any degree of certainty, building on the importance of liturgical communities focused on local saints that has been articulated above. In the sections that follow the evidence for the minsters of the diocese is explored in order of the certainty of their identification, from most to least secure. This section begins with those attested by textual evidence produced during the first and second phases of hagiographical activity dating from the early eighth to mid-eleventh centuries, discussed earlier. In each case supporting evidence of various kinds is also elaborated, often including archaeological evidence and the presence of stone sculpture. This evidence

---

131 Greenslade, *VCH Staffordshire*, vol. 14, pp. 135–6.
132 Greenslade, *VCH Staffordshire*, vol. 14, pp. 138–9.
133 Their names were given as Lulla, Monn, Wigferth, Eadhere and Cuthberht: Haddan and Stubbs, *Councils*, p. 546.

Hanbury

Almost all we can claim to know of the earlier minster at Hanbury must be inferred from St Wærburh's hagiography. She does not appear in any pre-Conquest resting-place lists, and her presence in the resting-place list in Hugh Candidus' chronicle, in which she is said to lie at Chester (*Legecestre*), might as easily be a contemporary note as derived from anything earlier;[134] her relics had been translated from Hanbury to Chester by 958 (see below). However, the saint appears in two probable examples of compositions from the first phase of hagiographical activity discussed earlier in this chapter. First, Wærburh and her parents, Wulfhere and Eormenhild, appear in several versions of genealogical material derived from the so-called 'Kentish Royal Legend', a hagiographical composition ultimately perhaps of the eighth century concerning St Mildrith and probably originally produced by her community at Minster-in-Thanet.[135] The genealogical section describes a veritable saintly dynasty of holy men and women, centred on the Kentish royal family but extending into East Anglia and Mercia through various marriages, including Wulfhere's marriage to Eormenhild, who was the daughter of the Kentish king Eorcenberht and his East Anglian queen Seaxburh. Although the material gives little more than Wærburh's name and family connection, and in some versions the fact that she lay at Hanbury (or Chester, in later versions), it testifies to a broad awareness of widespread family connections at Minster-in-Thanet, which must have involved some level of long-distance contact whether direct or indirect, and is crucial early testament to St Wærburh and her cult.[136]

The second source comprises an early narrative concerning St Wærburh that survives as part of the *Vita Sanctae Werburgae* composed by Goscelin of Saint Bertin

---

134 Mellows, *Chronicle of Hugh Candidus*, pp. 58 and 64.
135 David Rollason has studied this material, which he calls the 'Mildrith legend', in some detail: D.A. Rollason, *The Mildrith legend. A study in early medieval hagiography in England* (Leicester, 1982). See also Hollis, 'The Minster-in-Thanet foundation story', pp. 41–64.
136 Christine Fell has argued that the inclusion of both Eormenhild and Wærburh in the Kentish Royal Legend dates to the tenth century as Bede does not mention them, although he does mention the other children of Eorcenberht and Seaxburh, Ecgberht, Hlothhere and Eorcengota (C. Fell, 'Saint Æthelþryð: a historical dichotomy revisited', *Nottingham Medieval Studies*, 38 (1994), pp. 19–34). However, Bede has nothing to say about Mildrith of Thanet, her siblings, or her parents either, and presumably had no direct contact with the community and did not possess a version of the Kentish Royal Legend. Moreover, Bede never explicitly enumerates the children of Eorcenberht and Seaxburh, and, while he does mention Eormenhild's three siblings, these are in specific contexts, in which Eormenhild had no place: Eorcengota is noted only in a narrative concerning English princesses who travelled abroad (*HE*, iii.8) and her brothers appear at several points in Bede's work, always primarily in their roles as kings of Kent. He need not have known about Eormenhild.

for the Benedictine community at Ely, perhaps when he was there in 1087 or 1088.[137] As such, its content must be disentangled from the fruits of Goscelin's creativity and the other sources he drew upon. The body of this narrative relates Wærburh's entry to the minster at Ely as a young woman, the assignment to her care of several Mercian minsters, including Hanbury (*Heanburge*) and Threekingham (*Triccengeham*), by her uncle King Æthelred (675–704), her death at Threekingham, the divinely aided theft of her body by the people of Hanbury and its burial at their minster, the translation into an above-ground shrine of her incorrupt body nine years later at the suggestion of her cousin, King Ceolred (709–16), finishing with the final decay of her body in 'the time of the heathens'.[138] It is possible that Goscelin himself was responsible for much of the earlier part of his *Life*, which articulates around Wærburh's relationship with her mother, both before and after the entry of the former into Ely. He appears to have taken some very bald facts about Eormenhild – essentially the presence of her tomb at Ely and her feast day there, her family relationship to the Kentish kings, her marriage to Wulfhere and her bearing of Wærburh, all probably taken from a version of the Kentish Royal Legend – together with Wulfhere's involvement in the bringing of Christianity to the Mercians described in Bede's work, and mixed them with much holy monastic sentiment to create a well-rounded character for both his Lesson on the feast of St Eormenhild and his *Life* of St Wærburh.[139] Finally, as mentioned earlier, he added two miracle stories from Weedon, apparently based on contemporary reports there.

David Rollason puts forward a convincing case for the ultimate composition of Goscelin's source, the Wærburh narrative, at Hanbury, arguing that this is strongly implied by the emphasis on divine aid given to the people of Hanbury in their successful retrieval of Wærburh's body and by the omission of any explanation as to how her relics came to rest at Chester. However, his suggestion that the dissolution of Wærburh's body in the 'time of the heathens' would not form a good basis for Chester's claim to possess her relics is less convincing, as Goscelin's extended treatment of divine justification for this change in state makes it clear that he at least thought decay, rather than complete dissolution, was intended; he contrasts her formerly incorrupt body (*corpus solidus*) with its present decayed condition (*consumptus*).[140] This is an important point, as Rollason uses this part of the narrative to suggest that it was composed 'before there was any question of a translation to Chester, but after the Danish invasions of the ninth century'.[141] In fact, the details contained in the *Life* would suggest that it was written not long after the translation of Wærburh's incorrupt body, which forms the last substantive event within it; perhaps the narrative was even written at the time of this event, and we might suspect that a justification for the earlier

---

137 Love, *Goscelin of Saint-Bertin*, pp. xix–xxi and lviii–ci, for Goscelin's sojourn at Ely and his prodigious output while there.
138 *VSW*, c. 12.
139 For Goscelin's authorship of the *Lectiones in Natale Sancte Eormenhilde*, a companion piece to his *Lectiones in Festivitate Sancte Sexburge*, see Love, *Goscelin of Saint-Bertin*, pp. lxxviii–lxxx.
140 *VSW*, c. 12.
141 Rollason, *The Mildrith legend*, p. 27.

relic-theft formed part of the context for this. To date the narrative by reference to the 'time of the heathens' is to ask too much of this one phrase, which might have been added to the original text long afterwards, possibly even by Goscelin, appealing to 'the heathens' as a common historiographical *deus ex machina* to explain Wærburh's subsequent decay.

As it stands, the Wærburh narrative illuminates for us the hint of an extended ecclesiastical community spread across several minsters and devoted to their religious head. Competition within this community for control of the saint's relics, and therefore of her tomb and shrine, is an interesting development here, as is the later translation of those relics to Chester. There is no reliable textual record of this latter event. It must have occurred before 958, as the community of St Werburgh in Chester received a grant from King Edgar in that year.[142] Beyond this we have only later guesswork. The *Annales Cestrienses*, or Chronicle of St Werburgh's, compiled at St Werburgh's Abbey in or just after 1255, initially had nothing to say about this, although a later recension recorded the translation *sub anno* 874.[143] This addition probably followed the lead of Ranulph Higden, a monk of St Werburgh's in Chester who composed his *Polychronicon* in the 1320s; he appears to have equated the ambiguous 'time of the heathens' in the *Life* with the coming of the Danes to Repton, recorded in the Anglo-Saxon Chronicle, and assumed that this also marked the time of her translation.[144] More recent commentators have credited Æthelflæd, Lady of the Mercians, whose investment in several Mercian saints during the early tenth century has been emphasised.[145] In the sixteenth century Henry Bradshaw had ascribed to her the establishment of a college of canons at St Wærburh's relic-church, but Ranulph Higden had given this role to Æthelflæd's nephew King Æthelstan (924–39), while a *tabula* hanging in the episcopal church of St John apparently named Æthelstan's half-brother King Edmund (939–46).[146] The variability of the tradition suggests that nobody had access to anything more than their own best guesses.

The community of St Wærburh at Chester retained possession of the site of the church of St Werburgh at Hanbury in 1066 (as part of the estate at nearby Fauld; the estate had fallen into lay hands by the time of the Domesday survey).[147] The

---

142 S 667. See Rollason, *The Mildrith legend*, pp. 26 and 150 n. 66.

143 R.C. Christie, *Annales Cestrienses, or Chronicle of the abbey of St Werburg, at Chester*, The Record Society for Lancashire and Cheshire 14 (n.p., 1887). The surviving manuscript witnesses of the annals both derive from a lost late thirteenth-century text that itself derived, with omissions, from the annals compiled in 1255; see pp. ix–x and xiv. Christie (p. 16, n. 1) notes the probability that the earlier part of the annals were based on a Rouen Chronicle brought from Normandy by the first abbot of St Werburgh's, Richard of Bec; it is thus possible that annals had been kept at Chester, in various degrees of formality, for a significant period of time before the compilation of 1255.

144 J.R. Lumby, *Polychronicon Ranulphi Higden monachi Cestrensis* (London, 1876).

145 A.T. Thacker, 'Early ecclesiastical organization in two Mercian burhs', *Northern History*, 18 (1982), pp. 199–211, at p. 203.

146 Ranulph Higden: Lumby, *Polychronicon*, vol. 6, p. 128; Henry Bradshaw (whose work also contains the reference to the St John's *tabula*): Horstmann, *Life of Saint Werburge*, Book 2, lines 583–638 and 1108–28.

147 *DB Staffs.*, 10,6–7.

community's retention of Hanbury may indicate continuity of a sort: the relocation of the saint included the relocation of her community, which continued to hold on to the old minster site. However, this must remain only one of several plausible reasons for their possession of the estate and, even granting some form of continuity, whether the structure of the later community at Chester can tell us anything about the earlier community at Hanbury is a moot point. The community at Chester was replaced with a Benedictine community in and after 1092, and consequently hardly anything is known of it, other than the presence of twelve canons (*canonices*) and their ruler (*custos ecclesiae*) in 1086, most or all of whom held prebends by the late eleventh century when Earl Hugh of Chester arranged that they should pass into the holdings of his new Benedictine monastery as the canons holding them died.[148] The canons also seem to have been responsible for providing a set of miracles stories appended to the *Life* of St Wærburh in the lost third volume of the new monastery's four-volume legendary, compiled in the early twelfth century.[149] While the two early hagiographical sources provide strong evidence for an important minster at Hanbury ruled initially by a member of the Mercian royal family, perhaps the firmest conclusion to be derived from the later evidence concerns the persistent importance of Wærburh's relics, which formed the nucleus of the community at Chester, just as they had at Hanbury when first acquired through holy theft. It is the focus of specifically liturgical communities on those relics that provides the thread of continuity throughout the period.

Repton

Similar points can be made about St Wigstan, who also appears in a product of the first hagiographical phase, associated with a minster at Repton. The minster was located on a dramatic site atop a river cliff overlooking the river Trent to the north. It appears in a number of textual sources besides St Wigstan's hagiography, including Felix's *Life of St Guthlac*, as St Guthlac spent two years there under Abbess Ælfthryth learning the clerical way of life before seeking out his hermitage in the fens.[150] Guthlac's presence at a monastery ruled by an abbess indicates that Repton was a double house, a 'mixed-sex congregation ruled by an abbess', which was peculiar to the English and Frankish realms.[151] Repton's appearance in charters is disputed in several cases. Of three later

---

148 *DB Chesh.*, A1; B.E. Harris (ed.), *VCH Cheshire*, vol. 3 (London, 1980), pp. 132–46.
149 Our knowledge of the third volume comes from a sixteenth-century contents list, which mentions *Werburg et sic consequenter de Sexburga, Ermenilda, etc.*; Rosalind Love has argued that this refers to a version of Goscelin's *Life* together with *Lectiones* for Sts Seaxburh and Eormenhild (which Goscelin also wrote), largely on the basis of Henry Bradshaw's later use of these texts at Chester in the sixteenth century, and Bradshaw's reference to a Latin Life in 'the thrid Passionarie' (Love, *Goscelin of Saint-Bertin*, p. lviii). The miracle stories are divided between those set in the time of the canons and those in the time of the monks, and now exist only in Bradshaw's English *Life* of St Wærburh; he claimed to have taken them from 'a boke nominate the thrid passionarye' (Horstmann, *Life of Saint Werburge*, pp. xvii–xviii; Love, *Goscelin of Saint-Bertin*, pp. cxviii–cxix).
150 *VG*, cc. 19 and 26.
151 Foot, *Monastic life in Anglo-Saxon England*, p. 174.

texts in the Peterborough archive apparently reproducing seventh-century grants, only one represents a believable charter;[152] this is a grant by the *princeps* Frithuric of thirty-one hides at *Hrepingas* to Hædda, abbot of the minster at Breedon-on-the-Hill that Frithuric had founded in an earlier grant. Ann Dornier suggested that the land at Hrepingas represented the endowment of the minster at Repton, although the charter does not state that the land was intended for such use.[153] Alexander Rumble proposed that the place-name shared the element *Hrype* or *Hreope* with the etymology of Repton (*Hreopa dune*, 'hill of the *Hrype* or *Hreope* people'), but raised the tautological problem of compounding a people name with *-ingas* (which also means 'people').[154] More recently Susan Kelly has proposed that the grant should be considered a simple addition to Breedon's endowment, with no necessary connection to Repton or the region surrounding it, arguing that Repton's status, indicated in particular by several royal burials there (see below), renders it unlikely to be an off-shoot of Breedon and more likely to be a royal foundation *de novo*.[155] If we rule out this charter from those naming Repton, as seems wise, we are left with a grant of 848, again in the Peterborough archive, by the Mercian king Beorhtwulf to Abbot Eanmund and his community at Breedon, which was written in the 'venerable minster' at Repton, indicating a role for the minster in royal administration at this time, though not necessarily an overly formal one.[156] One final charter, a grant of land at Wirksworth by an Abbess Cynewaru to a Mercian *dux* named Humberht in 835, is sometimes assumed to refer to the abbess of Repton, but there is no explicit evidence to this effect.[157]

As mentioned above, the minster became particularly associated with royal burials. Merewalh, seventh-century ruler of the Magonsæte, was apparently buried there according to the *Life* of St Mildburh, an eleventh-century composition by Goscelin drawing on earlier material.[158] In 757 Æthelbald, king of the Mercians, was buried there after his murder at Seckington.[159] Repton is perhaps best known, however, for its association with St Wigstan, member of a ninth-century Mercian royal family, who was buried in an impressive semi-subterranean crypt that has survived to the present. The cult of St Wigstan is attested by his inclusion in the first part of the *Secgan*, so must have been established by the early tenth century.[160] David Rollason, in his analysis

---

152 S 68, S 72 and S 1805 (the last being Frithuric's grant). Frithuric's foundation of Breedon is described in S 1803.
153 A. Dornier, 'The Anglo-Saxon monastery at Breedon-on-the-Hill, Leicestershire', in A. Dornier (ed.), *Mercian studies* (Leicester, 1977), pp. 155–68, at p. 158.
154 A.R. Rumble, '"Hrepingas" reconsidered', in A. Dornier (ed.), *Mercian studies* (Leicester, 1977), pp. 169–71.
155 S.E. Kelly, *Charters of Peterborough Abbey*, Anglo-Saxon Charters 14 (Oxford, 2009), pp. 183–5; 'Hrepingas' may lie somewhere in the Repton region, but the etymological problem remains.
156 S 197; for the date see Kelly, *Charters of Peterborough Abbey*, p. 209.
157 S 1624.
158 H.P.R. Finberg, *The early charters of the West Midlands* (Leicester, 1961), p. 218.
159 *ASC* s.a. 755 (*recte* 757).
160 Rollason, 'Lists of saints' resting-places', p. 89; the resting-place list contained in Hugh Candidus' twelfth-century Peterborough Chronicle places Wigstan at Evesham, reflecting his translation.

of the saint's cult, has suggested that an existing *Passio* probably originated with the establishment of the cult, or soon afterwards, in the mid-ninth century, although the text survives only in several later versions.[161] Illustrating the complexity of relations between various segments of the Mercian royal dynasty by this period, the *Passio* relates that Wigstan, son of an earlier king, Wigmund (840?), refused succession to the kingship, preferring a religious life, leaving the way open for his kinsman Beorhtfrith, son of the king Beorhtwulf (840–52), to claim it; Beorhtfrith attempted to marry Wigstan's widowed mother, Queen Ælfflæd, the daughter of King Ceolwulf (821–3), but Wigstan refused the match because Beorhtfrith was his godfather, making Beorhtfrith Ælfflæd's co-parent (*compater*), and thus legally ineligible to be her husband. Plotting Wigstan's death, Beorhtfrith invited him to a conference on 1 June 849, at a place afterwards called Wistanstow (*Wistanestowe*), and killed him, cutting off the crown of his head as they exchanged the kiss of peace. A column of light subsequently marked the spot for thirty days, and Wigstan's body was taken to the minster of Repton (*Rependune*) and buried in the mausoleum of his grandfather Wiglaf (d. 839), another earlier Mercian king.

The Evesham version of the *Passio* adds that King Cnut, on hearing that St Wigstan was related to the minster's original patron King Cœnred (albeit not closely), advocated that the saint be translated from Repton to Evesham, in order that the martyr's memory be more honourably celebrated. The compiler of the Evesham text, Thomas of Marlborough, explains that the community of the minster at Repton had preserved an account of the life, passion and miracles of St Wigstan, and it is this which his brothers at Evesham had asked him to rewrite.[162] The other two versions of the *Passio* make no mention of the translation of St Wigstan to Evesham, and thus probably derive from a version that antedated that translation, almost certainly originating with the community at Repton mentioned by Thomas.[163] Given the detail contained within it, the *Passio* can almost certainly be set beside the architectural evidence at Repton for the establishment of the cult at some point after Wigstan's death in 849 and its appearance in the early tenth-century part of the *Secgan*.

The chancel of the present church of St Wystan and the crypt beneath it are of early medieval date, as is part of the nave immediately to the west.[164] Archaeological excavation at the church, undertaken by Harold Taylor, Martin Biddle and Birthe Kjølbye-Biddle, has established that the crypt was originally excavated through an area of burials ('Cemetery 1') at some point after *c.*715 (the date of a coin associated

---

161 Rollason, *The search for St Wigstan*; Rollason, 'The cults of murdered royal saints', pp. 5–9.
162 Thomas does not explicitly name the community at Repton as the originators of the *vita*, but his reference to *ipsius ecclesiae habitators quam idem martyr inhabitare dignatus est* must indicate this community.
163 Rollason, 'The cults of murdered royal saints', p. 7.
164 H.M. Taylor and J. Taylor, *Anglo-Saxon architecture* (Cambridge, 1965), vol. 2, pp. 510–16. The latest statement of the archaeological sequence at Repton is given by Martin Biddle in Hawkes and Sidebottom, *Corpus*, pp. 55–6. A useful tabulation of earlier literature on the excavations is given by E. Fernie, 'The eastern parts of the Anglo-Saxon church of St Wystan at Repton: function and chronology', *The Antiquaries Journal*, 98 (2018), pp. 95–114, at p. 96.

Lichfield and the Lands of St Chad

with it).[165] The cemetery was sited in association with a timber structure to the north, the latest in a series of such structures that extend the occupation of the site back into the seventh century.[166] A drain beneath the floor of the sunken structure has prompted the suggestion that it was initially a baptistery, although we might alternatively envisage a more functional role for this feature, ensuring that the subterranean chamber did not flood.[167] The chamber was incorporated into a church structure that presumably succeeded an earlier building elsewhere on the site: an east porticus was constructed over the chamber, and two further porticus were positioned north and south of the main body of the church to the west, a common plan in the English kingdoms since the later seventh century.[168] There is some confusion over the relationship between this church and the crypt: Martin Biddle equates its construction with the insertion of a vaulted ceiling into the sunken chamber, which supported the porticus above and must date after the death of St Wigstan (see below), but before 873/4, as the Viking army occupying Repton in that year incorporated the church, then in existence, into a ditched enclosure, perhaps acting as a 'gatehouse'; the church must therefore have been constructed between 849 and 873. Biddle also argues that the stairways leading diagonally downwards into the chamber from the porticus flanking the main body represent the original access arrangements, contemporary with the construction of the chamber;[169] however, this arrangement appears very odd in plan if it was not initially associated with a structure to the west.

Eric Fernie has recently challenged Biddle's equation of the church's construction with the insertion of a vaulted ceiling in the crypt; instead, he argues convincingly that the vaulting was inserted as part of a process of reconstruction, which also involved the heightening of the church's walls, requiring the thickening of the walls of the eastern porticus and their support by the vaulting beneath.[170] The earlier phase of the church might thus predate 849, its construction having occurred at some point during the eighth century. Indeed, if the diagonal stairways are original features of the sunken chamber, as Biddle argues, it would be reasonable to propose that it had also been surmounted by an eastern porticus *ab initio*, and that the chamber had always been intended to act as a mausoleum or *hypogeum*.[171] Such a *hypogeum* evoked the subterranean burial observed in the Roman catacombs, and John Crook has

---

165 Hawkes and Sidebottom, *Corpus*, p. 223.
166 Hawkes and Sidebottom, *Corpus*, p. 55.
167 Hawkes and Sidebottom, *Corpus*, pp. 55 and 222. A similar drain had been laid through the cemetery, a little north of the site of the later crypt, perhaps indicating that drainage was a pressing issue on this part of the site; Biddle suggests that this earlier drain was built in relation to a church to the west.
168 Hawkes and Sidebottom, *Corpus*, pp. 55–6. For the plan-form see E. Fernie, *The architecture of the Anglo-Saxons* (London, 1982), Chapters 3 and 4, and Gem, 'Architecture of the Anglo-Saxon church', p. 46.
169 Hawkes and Sidebottom, *Corpus*, p. 222.
170 Fernie, 'The eastern parts', pp. 109–12.
171 Fernie, 'The eastern parts', p. 101, suggests that the existing walls of the main body and porticus below the heightened sections might themselves represent the rebuilding of an earlier structure, rather than the extension of a structure to the west over the chamber, as Biddle had argued.

assembled seventh- and eighth-century Gaulish parallels for the association of such a structure with burial rather than, or as well as, the enshrinement of saints.[172] The later insertion of a vaulted ceiling in the crypt has been associated with the cult of St Wigstan because of the twisted or 'barley-sugar' form of the four columns that support it, which Biddle has associated with the columns that originally surrounded the tomb of St Peter in Rome;[173] they thus formed a suitable central focus for the tomb of a Mercian saint. Fernie has suggested that, contrary to preceding interpretations, the insertion of the crypt and accompanying vertical extension of the church walls might be dated after the overwintering of the Great Army in 873/4, as the decorative pilaster strips added to the new walls of the eastern porticus are more likely to belong to the tenth century than the ninth. The architectural elaboration of St Wigstan's cult might thus be dated to a period centring on the early tenth century, notably a similar date to the proposed rebuilding of the cathedral at Lichfield, as discussed earlier.

About 50m to the west of the church a mass grave beneath a mound was excavated and dated to the winter of 873/4; the mound had been erected over an earlier sunken chamber, dating to the later seventh or eighth century, which had been demolished down to ground level.[174] This rectangular structure was entered down a set of steps at its western end, and contained two chambers and evidence for stucco decoration.[175] Fragments of an elaborate grave cover and of a cross that might have surmounted a sarcophagus were found in association with the burial mound, and may represent parts of the tombs that lay within this *hypogeum* before its destruction.[176] The bluff above the river Trent occupied by the minster at Repton thus hosted a church and at least two mausolea, perhaps inspired by Gaulish *hypogea*, all aligned on an east–west axis by the mid-eighth century; such alignment has been observed at several other sites in England, as well as on the continent, and appears to have been a fairly common practice.[177] A fragment of a large decorated cross, dated to the late eighth or early ninth centuries, was found near the chancel of the church, hinting that this linear grouping continued to be augmented by additional monuments.[178] The importance of sepulchral monuments here resonates with the textual evidence for royal burials at Repton in the seventh, eighth and ninth centuries, indicating that the minster remained associated with successive segments of the Mercian royal dynasty and emphasising one of the main roles of the community based there. Again, the importance of the

---

172 J. Crook, *The architectural setting of the cult of saints in the early Christian West c. 300–1200* (Oxford, 2000), pp. 61–3 and 128–30.
173 Hawkes and Sidebottom, *Corpus*, pp. 61–8.
174 Hawkes and Sidebottom, *Corpus*, pp. 57–8; see also Biddle and Kjølbye-Biddle, 'Repton and the Vikings', pp. 36–51.
175 D.M. Hadley, *The Vikings in England. Settlement, society and culture* (Manchester, 2006), pp. 13–15.
176 Hawks and Sidebottom, *Corpus*, Repton 10, Repton 15. The tombs are slightly later in date than the mausoleum, but may represent re-interments or more recent occupants.
177 Blair, *Church*, pp. 199–200; Foot, *Monastic life*, p. 111.
178 Hawks and Sidebottom, Corpus, Repton 1. This cross fragment has been labelled the 'Repton stone', see M. Biddle and B. Kjølbye-Biddle, 'The Repton stone', *Anglo-Saxon England*, 14 (1985), pp. 233–92.

liturgical focus of this community on saints' relics and the remembrance of the dead is particularly apparent.

Andresey/Stapenhill and Polesworth

The potential minsters at Andresey/Stapenhill and Polesworth are considered together because most of what we can say about their early medieval existence derives from the hagiography of their saints, St Modwynn and St Eadgyth respectively, which is thoroughly entangled. They appear together, but under slightly different names, in the *Life of St Monenna*, abbess of Killevy in Ireland, written by Conchubran perhaps in the eleventh century and belonging chronologically to the second phase of hagiographical activity discussed earlier.[179] Conchubran based his work on an earlier *Life* of the Irish abbess, but included several additional episodes set in the area around Andresey and Polesworth, identifiable through the place-names he includes. St Modwynn's cult at Burton-upon-Trent (adjacent to Andresey, which is an island in the river) is revealed by *The Life and Miracles of St Modwenna* by Geoffrey, abbot of the Benedictine monastery at Burton (1114–50), who made use of Conchubran's *Life* as well as information from local sources. Indeed, Geoffrey might have been instrumental in reinvigorating St Modwynn's cult, and subsequently she appears in the resting-place list in Hugh Candidus' Peterborough Chronicle.[180] According to Geoffrey her relics had been moved out of the chapel on Andresey and into the monastic church at Burton at some point in the first half of the eleventh century, after the foundation of the monastery c.1000.[181] St Eadgyth makes her earliest appearance in the early tenth-century part of the *Secgan*, also within the second phase of hagiographical activity.[182] Her relics appear to have remained at Polesworth, and there was certainly a shrine there when the Marmion family established a Benedictine nunnery in the church c.1140.[183] Consequently, we can be sure that when Conchubran described the activities of Monenna and one of her nuns, named variously Ita, Ede or Eda, in this specific region, he was drawing on information concerning St Modwynn of Andresey and St Eadgyth of Polesworth.

Conchubran's material concerning St Modwynn appears to have amounted to little more than the fact that she founded a church on Andresey dedicated to St Andrew (hence the place-name, 'Andrew's island'), in which her body was ultimately buried, and another opposite the first, on the east bank of the river at the foot of *Mons Calvus*, now Scalpcliff Hill, dedicated to St Peter and St Paul, which perfectly matches the location of the existing church of St Peter, Stapenhill. Conchubran also included a

---

179 For a recent study of this hagiography, see Sargent, 'Misplaced miracle', and references therein. Conchubran's *Life* is contained in British Library MS, Cotton Cleopatra A. ii.
180 Mellows, *Chronicle of Hugh Candidus*, p. 62.
181 *VMM*, c. 43; St Modwynn's relics were in the abbey church by the abbacy of Leofric (1051–66), who despoiled her shrine: N. Tringham (ed.), *VCH Staffordshire*, vol. 9 (London, 2003), p. 108.
182 Rollason, 'Lists of saints' resting-places', pp. 61–8.
183 N. Tringham, 'St Edith of Polesworth and her Cult' (forthcoming). Thanks are due to Dr Tringham for allowing me to see a draft of this article.

The cathedral and the minsters

resurrection miracle in the vicinity of Polesworth, in which Modwynn revived a nun who had fallen into a river and drowned while carrying a book between the church Modwynn had founded for Eadgyth at nearby *Streneshalen* and a hermitage that Modwynn had established for herself. The name of Eadgyth's monastery is a problem; Conchubran located it on the edge of the wood of Arden, and it is therefore difficult to connect it with anywhere other than Polesworth, which is on the edge of that forest. Abbot Geoffrey made this assumption, and also turned the unnamed river into the Anker, when he wrote his *Life*; moreover, he was obviously unfamiliar with *Streneshalen*, as he transferred it to the hermitage, which is unnamed in Conchubran's narrative.[184] The name is obviously the same as *Streaneshalh*, St Hild's famous minster at Whitby, and it is possible that Conchubran imported it to Polesworth to add a touch of glamour to his narrative.

However, Nigel Tringham has recently explored the possibility that Conchubran's source, whatever its nature, contained an earlier or alternative name for Polesworth. He builds on the idea that Conchubran's place-name could be interpreted as 'the *halh* of the meeting or discussion', pointing to a location about a kilometre east of Polesworth named Stipershill, which served as the traditional meeting place of the tenants of the honour of Tamworth in the later medieval period.[185] He further suggests that the post indicated by Old English *stipere* in the name of the hill would be a suitable marker for a meeting place, possibly one with even older origins. The broader significance of Polesworth's location is also indicated in Conchubran's narrative, as *Streneshalen* is described as a royal vill, which Modwynn received from the unnamed local king after saving the life of his son, *Alfredus*, when the latter had visited Ireland. Clearly much concerning Polesworth would be resolved if we could identify Eadgyth, characterised by Conchubran as the sister of the above-mentioned king, who was given over to Modwynn with the estate. Geoffrey, identifying *Alfredus* with Alfred the Great, made Eadgyth into a West Saxon princess, and several subsequent writers and chroniclers did likewise, though presenting a variety of different genealogical relationships to the West Saxon dynasty.[186] I have suggested recently that the West Saxon connection is a red herring, and that Eadgyth belongs to the seventh, eighth or ninth centuries, perhaps more specifically the late seventh century, as one of a number of Mercian princesses who achieved fame as holy women during this period, and whose names appear alongside Eadgyth's in an early part of the list of 'queens and abbesses' in the *Liber Vitae* of the community of St Cuthberht.[187] The minster at Polesworth certainly existed by the ninth century, as burials dating to the ninth and tenth centuries have been excavated to the west of the church.[188]

---

184 Sargent, 'Misplaced miracle', pp. 3–4.
185 Tringham, 'St Edith'; Tringham draws on T. Styles, 'Whitby revisited: Bede's explanation of *Streanaeshalch*', *Nomina*, 21 (1998), pp. 133–48, in which Old English *ge-streon* is interpreted to mean not only 'gain' or 'increase' but also 'work' or 'business'.
186 Sargent, 'Misplaced miracle', pp. 11–13.
187 Sargent, 'Misplaced miracle', pp. 13–14.
188 M. Holmes, 'Archaeological excavations at Polesworth abbey, Warwickshire, 2011–2013', unpublished report, MOLA No. 15/31 (Northampton, 2015), pp. 180–1.

Lichfield and the Lands of St Chad

St Modwynn is even harder to place, although there is no reason to connect her with St Monenna as Conchubran did, or to suggest that she was Irish. She, too, is best explained as a holy woman of the seventh, eighth or ninth century. Whether she and Eadgyth were originally connected is a moot point, although there is no obvious reason to think that Conchubran's source was early, or written close to those it describes.[189] Given the late and tenuous nature of the evidence, it is perhaps best to keep them separate. We can thus identify one minster at Polesworth, possibly founded within a royal estate called *Streneshalen* for a late seventh-century Mercian princess who was later enshrined there, and a second minster at Andresey/Stapenhill, in which the cult of St Modwynn was initiated at some point. Interestingly, the evidence for both minsters hints at nearby retreats similar to Stowe at Lichfield. About a mile to the west of Polesworth the site of a chapel built above St Eadgyth's Spring is now known as 'The Hermitage', and may represent a satellite retreat with early medieval origins, perhaps even that which appears in Conchubran's resurrection miracle. The chapel on Andresey would be atypical for the location of a minster church, as it is low-lying and cramped, and would be more suited to another such satellite hermitage; the church at Stapenhill on the river bank appears the more likely candidate for the head church of the minster.

Northworthy (Derby)

St Ealhmund is the final saint to be attested by a product of the second phase of hagiographical activity, appearing in the early tenth-century part of the *Secgan* resting-place list, in which he is said to rest at 'Northworthy' (*Norðworþig/Norðweorðig*) on the river Derwent (*Deorwentan*).[190] Hugh Candidus' twelfth-century Peterborough Chronicle places St Ealhmund at Derby, providing reasonable proof that Northworthy developed into, or was renamed as, Derby in the late ninth or early tenth century.[191] The *Passio* of St Ealhmund exists in an early fourteenth-century manuscript, and must have been composed sometime after the mid-twelfth century, when Lilleshall Abbey, to which it refers at one point, was founded.[192] The *Passio* relates that Ealhmund was a member of the Northumbrian royal family, who journeyed from his kingdom to Wiltshire to protect his possessions there. However, he found himself embroiled in a conflict between Ealdorman Æthelmund of the Mercians and the Wiltshiremen. Having attempted and failed to broker a peace between the two armies he was asked by the Wiltshiremen to stay and strengthen their resolve. The two armies met at Kempsford and the Wiltshiremen were victorious, although Ealhmund and the leaders of both armies were killed. David Rollason has demonstrated that the story was concocted

---

189 Possibilities for the later association of the cults of St Modwynn and St Eadgyth are explored in Sargent, 'Misplaced miracle', pp. 14–18.
190 Rollason, 'Lists of saints' resting-places', pp. 63 and 89.
191 Mellows, *Chronicle of Hugh Candidus*, p. 61.
192 Gotha, Forschungsbibliothek, Memb. I.81, ff. 29–30; for discussion and edition see Grosjean, 'De codice hagiographico Gothano' and 'Codices Gothani appendix', 178–83. For Lilleshall Abbey see A.T. Gaydon (ed.), *VCH Shropshire*, vol. 2 (London, 1973), pp. 70–80.

based on a misreading of John of Worcester's chronicle, where the death of Ealhmund is recorded in 800 immediately after a description of the battle at Kempsford the same year. St Ealhmund thus appears to be a saint about whom almost nothing was known by the later twelfth or thirteenth century, and who had to be reinvented by reference to existing textual sources.

However, Rollason has suggested that Ealhmund should indeed be understood as the Northumbrian royal of that name, and that a more accurate impression of the saint can be gained from the northern chronicle in the *Historia Regum*, in which it is related that Ealhmund, son of King Alhred of Northumbria, was murdered by another Northumbrian king, Eardwulf, in 800.[193] Rollason connects the Mercian promotion of Ealhmund's cult to a war recorded in the same chronicle in 801 between Eardwulf and the Mercian king Cœnwulf over the latter's sheltering of fugitives from the former's kingdom, among whom it is possible that Ealhmund was numbered.[194] Although ingenious, this explanation is unnecessary if we accept that the author of the *Passio* was simply mining texts for information. It is worth noting that a prominent abbot named Ealhmund attested Mercian charters between 780 and 805, often positioned first of his peers in the witness lists.[195] A charter from the church council at *Clofesho* in 803 demonstrates that this abbot ruled a minster in the diocese of Leicester, but this does not preclude significant connections with a minster in another Mercian diocese.[196] An important abbot is perhaps equally, if not more, likely to have been enshrined in a Mercian minster during this period. Whoever he was, we can say more of Ealhmund's cult because the minster church at Derby has been excavated, the finds including a stone sarcophagus with carved decoration of the Trent Valley Group, which can almost certainly be equated with one mentioned in the *Passio* and attributed to the saint (it could be seen 'to this day').[197]

The church of St Alkmund (a later development of Ealhmund's name), at the northern end of what became the historic core of the city of Derby, was demolished in the late 1960s to make way for a new ring road.[198] Although substantially truncated by later activity, the remains of an early church were found, comprising a rectangular main body measuring approximately 15m by 7.5m, with an eastern porticus approximately 5.5m square; fragmentary evidence was also found for

---

193 Rollason, 'The cults of murdered royal saints', pp. 4–5.
194 H.C.G. Matthew and B. Harrison (eds), *Oxford Dictionary of National Biography* (Oxford, 2004), s.n. Ealhmund; *EHD* 1, p. 250.
195 See S.D. Keynes, *Atlas*, Tables IX and XV. The relevant charters are S 118, S 1430, S 131, S 132, S 133, S 138, S 139, S 146, S 151, S 153, S 155, S 1431a, S 1431b and S 40; Ealhmund also subscribes the canons of the legatine synod of 786: *EHD* 1, no. 191.
196 S 1431a and b.
197 Hawkes and Sidebottom, *Corpus*, Derby 7a and b. Note the *Corpus* authors claim it is not possible to connect the sarcophagus to St Ealhmund, but they do not acknowledge the *Passio*, which, although late, testifies to a connection between the sarcophagus and the saint.
198 C.A.R. Radford, 'The church of Saint Alkmund', *Derbyshire Archaeological Journal*, 96 (1976), pp. 26–61.

a southern porticus at the eastern end of the nave.[199] The excavator C.A. Ralegh Radford conjectured another porticus on the northern side to balance the southern, and, whether or not this existed, the plan obviously resembles the common aisleless form displayed at Repton and proposed at Lichfield. The sarcophagus was found in the south-east corner of the main body, buried in a rectangular trench cut for its use; what evidence there is suggests that the altars of earlier English churches of this type were often located at the eastern end of the main body of the church, and thus the position of the sarcophagus may have been immediately south of the altar. Radford compared St Ealhmund's sarcophagus with arrangements made after the death of St Cuthberht, who, according to Bede, was also buried south of the altar, and eleven years later exhumed and placed in a new coffin upon the church floor above his old grave; the elaborate carving along the sides of the Derby sarcophagus suggest that this too once sat above floor level, before its later burial, probably on or near the same spot, dated to the twelfth century, after which only its lid was probably visible at floor level.[200] Interestingly, an empty grave was found alongside the buried sarcophagus, associated by Radford with the later burial of someone *ad sanctos*; however, this might represents Ealhmund's earlier grave, out of which his bones had been translated and above which the sarcophagus initially rested, before being placed in a pit excavated next to it.[201] Other stone sculpture at Derby includes two important crosses of ninth-century date, whose 'Mercian Beasts' may have inspired subsequent sculpture in the region, and several monuments from the Trent Valley Group, including a second decorated tomb cover.[202]

The presence of carved stonework in rebuilt sections of the eastern porticus walls and the destruction of the southern porticus and blocking of the door leading to it from the nave suggested to Radford a period of neglect followed by an episode of renovation, although we should be wary of simplifying what may have been a more lengthy and ongoing process.[203] Likewise, Radford's dating of this period to the Danish occupation of Derbyshire at the end of the ninth century simply grasps one of the few historical events to be ascribed to the area by the textual sources.[204] Nevertheless, the presence of a burial packed with charcoal across the site of the demolished porticus argues for a ninth-century or later date for this event, as such burials tend to appear in ninth- to twelfth-century contexts.[205] Two carved imposts, now lost but drawn in the mid-nineteenth century, were dated by Radford stylistically to the late tenth century, but are now reckoned more likely to be from a Norman context, and indicate a

---

199 Radford, 'The church of Saint Alkmund', pp. 31–2.
200 Radford, 'The church of Saint Alkmund', pp. 35 and 37; the wide appeal of the right-hand side of the altar is also manifest in Bede's description of St Cedd's burial there, in the church of St Mary at Lastingham: *HE*, iii.23.
201 Radford, 'The church of Saint Alkmund', p. 33 (grave no. 53).
202 Hawkes and Sidebottom, *Corpus*, Derby 1, Derby 2, Derby 6, Derby 7, Derby 8, Derby 11; another fragment, Derby 5, may represent another early cross shaft.
203 Radford, 'The church of Saint Alkmund', p. 34.
204 Radford, 'The church of Saint Alkmund', p. 35.
205 Rodwell *et al.*, 'The Lichfield Angel', pp. 51–2; Thompson, *Dying and death*, pp. 118–19.

The cathedral and the minsters

later episode of elaboration.[206] The continued use of the church and its subsequent extension in the twelfth century and later testify to its ongoing significance.[207] Certainly it was of some importance in 871, when Ealdorman Æthelwulf of Berkshire, a Mercian serving a West Saxon king, was killed in battle at Reading and taken to Northworthy for burial.[208] Two centuries later, at the time of the Domesday survey, St Alkmund's was one of two churches in the king's lordship in Derby, probably that held by six clerics (*clerici*).[209] These notices are too sporadic for much to be made of them, but St Alkmund's church at Northworthy/Derby appears to have maintained some importance throughout the period, and the role of the saint's sarcophagus in its later life indicates its continuing liturgical significance.

Minsters attested by post-*c*.1050 hagiography

The previous section has discussed some of the best-attested minsters in the diocese, all of which hosted saints' cults particularly well supported by a variety of forms of evidence. While some have provided evidence for the kinds of community explored in Chapter 2, such as Wærburh's extended ecclesiastical community, most have highlighted the significance of smaller communities based at individual minsters. As has been stressed throughout this chapter, these communities are best defined by reference to liturgical rituals that were regularly repeated, especially those focused on the saints attested by the hagiography; while the fine details of such rituals are not known, the material spaces and objects that enabled them are easily visible in the churches, crosses, chambers and shrines that form the majority of the non-textual evidence. In contrast, the minsters identified in this section feature almost no pre-Conquest evidence for their existence, but they are distinguished by textual evidence resulting from the third and fourth phases of hagiographical activity discussed earlier (dating from the later eleventh century onwards), which usually testifies to the ongoing importance of relic cults dedicated to local saints, often with Old English names, and in some cases can be added to other forms of evidence for those cults. The following discussions thus continue to emphasise the significance of liturgical foci, which can plausibly be understood to have persisted from the earlier medieval period, even if direct evidence is lacking.

Ilam

St Bertram of Ilam has been equated with St Bertelin of Stafford, who is first attested in Hugh Candidus' twelfth-century Peterborough Chronicle, recording him as a martyr resting at Stafford.[210] A *Life* of St Bertelin, which does not describe a martyrdom, first

---

206 Radford, 'The church of Saint Alkmund', pp. 34 and 45; Hawkes and Sidebottom, *Corpus*, Derby 12, Derby 13.
207 Radford, 'The church of Saint Alkmund', pp. 35–42.
208 A. Campbell (ed. and trans.), *Chronicon Æthelweardi* (London, 1962), Book iv, cap. 2.
209 *DB Derbys.*, B1.
210 Mellows, *Chronicle of Hugh Candidus*, p. 61.

appears in a sixteenth-century source, although an internal date suggests it was composed in the fourteenth century;[211] the story is a mix of folklore and an extract from Felix' *Life* of St Guthlac. St Bertram of the church of the Holy Cross at Ilam is associated with a shrine there in the form of a grave cover-slab surmounted by a 'tomb-shrine', a type of monument 'constructed over the graves of saints whose bodies were, for a time at least, left in peace'.[212] This has been identified by John Crook as the only certain example of the type surviving in England, and has been dated to the mid-thirteenth century, although the cover slab is perhaps earlier than this, as it has been cut back to accommodate the tomb-shrine; the whole can plausibly be considered the latest incarnation of some earlier form of grave marker.[213] The tomb itself is located within a small chapel abutting the south side of the chancel, and is reminiscent of the Welsh phenomenon of the *eglwys-y-bedd*, although in this case the building is not independent of, but abuts, the main church, and there is no evidence that it was ever known as St Bertram's chapel. It is possible that the church itself contains early medieval fabric: Harold and Joan Taylor identified the south wall of the nave, pierced by a tall, narrow doorway, as early medieval in date, although they include it with a group of churches for which the evidence is not satisfactorily diagnostic.[214] Two decorated stone cross shafts associated with the church at Ilam belong to the Dove Valley Subgroup of the Trent Valley Group.[215] A cross shaft of the Pennine Fringes Group testifies to a continued significance for the church into the later tenth or eleventh centuries.

The equation of St Bertelin with St Bertram rests on more than the similarity of their names, both of which can be viewed as later developments of Beorhthelm. The *Life* of St Bertelin ends with the saint wandering into the hills to seek solitude, where he eventually died – possibly a reference to the presence of a tomb-shrine at Ilam. Another point of overlap between them concerns the initial part of the *Life*, in which a young Bertelin, described as the son of a local king, visited Ireland and fell in love with a king's daughter. Eloping together to England, they hid in a forest where the woman went into labour, and she and her newborn were killed by a wolf while Bertelin was away seeking help. It is this episode that persuaded Bertelin to take up the life of an ascetic hermit. The tale appears to be depicted on the twelfth-century font in the church at Ilam: six bays depict scenes that can be linked to elements in the tale, notably including two in which a wolf devours human heads.[216] One of the wolf scenes includes two heads, presumably the mother and baby, while a second includes only one, raising the possibility that Bertram was also believed to have been killed by the wolf at a later point in the tale. St Bertelin is believed to have been associated with Stafford thanks to the efforts of Lady Æthelflæd of the Mercians, who appears to have

---

211 C. Horstmann, *Nova Legenda Anglie* (Oxford, 1901), vol. I, pp. 162–7.
212 Crook, *The architectural setting*, p. 253; Blair, 'A saint for every minster?' pp. 491–2.
213 Crook, *The architectural setting*, pp. 262–263; see also Blair, 'A saint for every minster?', pp. 491–3.
214 H.M. Taylor, 'Anglo-Saxon architecture and sculpture in Staffordshire', *North Staffordshire Journal of Field Studies*, 6 (1966), pp. 7–11, at p. 9; Taylor and Taylor, *Anglo-Saxon architecture*, vol. 2, p. 719.
215 Hawkes and Sidebottom, *Corpus*, Ilam 1, Ilam Estate 1.
216 See The Corpus of Romanesque Stone Sculpture in Britain and Ireland: Holy Cross, Ilam, Staffordshire, at http://www.crsbi.ac.uk/site/536/.

The cathedral and the minsters

promoted a number of Mercian cults at her fortified burhs in the early tenth century.[217] Stafford supported an interesting expression of the cult in its own right, but it seems likely that Ilam represents the earlier centre of St Beorhthelm's cult. That said, none of the surviving evidence sheds much, if any, light on the early medieval cult, beyond the persistent importance of the saint's grave at Ilam.

Stone

The church of St Michael at Stone is the successor to that of an Augustinian priory dedicated to St Mary and St Wulfhad, which was founded in the 1130s or 1140s.[218] A Latin *Passio* of St Wulfhad and his brother Ruffin survives in three versions, all of the early fourteenth century.[219] One of these is contained within a Peterborough chartulary known as the Book of Walter of Whittlesey, and might have been derived from an earlier fourteenth-century Peterborough chartulary containing the *Passio* that was destroyed by the Cottonian fire in 1731.[220] The tale describes the two saints as sons of King Wulfhere, whom he murdered because of their conversion to Christianity, later repenting of his act and founding churches throughout Mercia in penance, including the church at Stone where the saints were buried. The *Passio* was used in the Peterborough texts to explain Wulfhere's motivation for the foundation of the minster there, and indeed the text refers to Peterborough as Wulfhere's especial foundation. However, if the *Passio* was created at Peterborough its author was probably working after the later twelfth century, as the story was not part of a forged Peterborough foundation grant of the early twelfth century, nor are the two saints mentioned in Hugh Candidus' later twelfth-century Peterborough Chronicle.[221] The form and structure of the *Passio* might also support a comparatively late date, as it is a mix of folkloric tropes and pre-existing hagiography, similar to that relating to Wærburh and Eormenhild generated by Goscelin and the monks at Ely from the late eleventh century.

It is perhaps more likely that an initial version of the *Passio* was created at or for the Augustinian priory at Stone, as Alexander Rumble has suggested.[222] The earliest extant reference to Wulfhad's murder at the hands of his father occurs in a thirteenth-century rhymed antiphon, indicating that this part of the story predates the existing versions of the *Passio*.[223] Moreover, St Wulfhad first appears in textual sources in the early twelfth century, when charters associated with the priory referred to him as the dedicatee of the church

---

217 A.T. Thacker, 'Kings, saints and monasteries in pre-Viking Mercia', *Midland History*, 10 (1985), pp. 1–25, at pp. 18–19.
218 Greenslade, *VCH Staffordshire*, vol. 3, pp. 240–7.
219 See Rumble, '*Ad Lapidem*', pp. 315–16, for details and references.
220 BL Cotton Otho A XV i. The text of the *Passio* in this manuscript was printed in Dugdale, *Monasticon*, vol. 6 (part 1), pp. 226–30; an edition of the version in the Book of Walter of Whittlesey can be found in Mellows, *Chronicle of Hugh Candidus*, pp. 140–59 (Appendix 2).
221 Kelly, *Charters of Peterborough abbey*, pp. 131–44 (No. 1).
222 Rumble, '*Ad Lapidem*', pp. 314–15.
223 Rumble, '*Ad Lapidem*', pp. 316–17: Bodleian, Bodley MS 343, f. iiiv.

at Stone in which it was founded.[224] Other elements of the story itself might also have earlier origins, if not necessarily early medieval in date. For example, Wulfhere's fortress in the *Passio* is called *Wlferecestria*, a name that was applied locally to a hillfort a mile north-west of Stone, known now as Bury Bank, which is attested in early thirteenth-century entries in the Stone Chartulary.[225] Rumble has suggested that the *Passio* represents a version of a tale told by Bede in the eighth century concerning the execution of two young princes immediately after their baptism at a place called *Ad Lapidem* ('Stone') somewhere in Hampshire after the ravaging of the Isle of Wight in the seventh century by Cædwalla of Wessex. The similarities between the two stories, notably the place-name, are striking, but the earlier tale is perhaps better understood as only one of many possible sources drawn upon by the creator of the later one; certainly Rumble's contention that the earlier event was 'remembered in oral tradition and was later reconstituted as a Mercian royal cult', presumably after the original identities of Wulfhad and Ruffin had been forgotten, pushes the bounds of credibility over so many centuries.[226]

It appears far more likely that St Wulfhad was a Mercian saint like many of those already considered, whose identity was 'reconstituted' in and after the twelfth century around a pre-existing shrine-church; such development probably occurred in several phases and was not necessarily particularly coherent, with myths taking root in the surrounding landscape before being gathered into the later *Passio*. Ruffin, unlike Wulfhad, is not a plausible Old English name;[227] his first textual appearance is the *Passio* itself, and he may well have been intruded into the mythology from the dedication of a chapel at nearby Burston (in Stone parish, perhaps originally St Rufinus), which was destroyed at some time between the late seventeenth and earlier nineteenth centuries.[228] We can therefore plausibly identify only an early medieval cult of St Wulfhad at Stone. Wulfhad himself might well have been Wulfhere's son, as the *Passio* and antiphon suggest, given the similarity of their names, but it is perhaps more likely that this element, too, is part of the saint's later medieval afterlife.

Coventry

St Osburh's cult is attested in the resting-place list contained in Hugh Candidus' chronicle, wherein she is said to rest at Coventry;[229] a fifteenth-century antiquary thought that her nunnery was destroyed by Cnut, although a fifteenth-century insertion into the Lichfield Chronicle states that Cnut was founder of the nunnery there, demonstrating no very stable tradition.[230] In 1043 Earl Leofric of Mercia and his wife

---

224 Rumble,'*Ad Lapidem*', pp. 316–18: Cambridge, Corpus Christi College, MS 470.
225 Horovitz, *Place-names*, p. 165; *SHC* vol. VI, pt I, pp. 9–10.
226 Rumble,'*Ad Lapidem*', p. 314.
227 Rumble,'*Ad Lapidem*', p. 312, n. 25.
228 Rumble,'*Ad Lapidem*', p. 318 and n. 58.
229 Mellows, *Chronicle of Hugh Candidus*, p. 62.
230 S. Baxter, *The earls of Mercia: lordship and power in late Anglo-Saxon England* (Oxford, 2007), p. 158. For the insertion into the Lichfield Chronicle, perhaps from a Coventry source, see Wharton, *Anglia Sacra*, p. 433.

Godgifu founded a Benedictine monastery at Coventry, probably reusing or rebuilding an earlier church. A foundation charter forged in the mid-twelfth century at Westminster Abbey for the prior of Coventry claims that the monastery had been dedicated to 'St Mary, St Peter, St Osburga and All Saints'.[231] Stephen Baxter has suggested that the charter might have been based on an authentic mid-eleventh-century charter or other document issued by Earl Leofric and his wife; if so, its reference to St Osburh would be the earliest attestation of the saint, although such is speculation.[232] St Osburh's feast on 30 March was officially established in 1410 at the request of the clergy and people of Coventry, who emphasised the popularity of the saint's shrine and the miracles performed there.[233] We can therefore plausibly postulate that the relics of St Osburh provided a pre-existing liturgical focus in the church later reused by Leofric and Godgifu. The presence of an earlier church is supported by part of a carved door jamb found close to St Mary's church and dated stylistically to the ninth century.[234]

Minsters securely attested by stone sculpture

The identification of the minsters discussed in this section is considered fairly secure because each is associated with stone sculpture dated by authors of the relevant *Corpus* volumes to the period between the late eighth and early tenth centuries. Some also feature additional evidence that supports the identification. However, none provide very strong evidence for the nature of the communities that lived at these places, apart from the liturgical roles generally assumed for much of the stone sculpture in the diocese.

Wroxeter

St Andrew's church at Wroxeter is one of two in the diocese (the other being Repton) in which pre-Viking fabric certainly survives: in this case, in the north wall of the nave, which the Taylors considered to date to the seventh or eighth century; Cameron Moffett has reconstructed the church as comprising a small nave, about 13m long, perhaps with a porticus at the eastern end.[235] A fragment of a carved architectural panel dated stylistically to the early ninth century was built into the twelfth-century chancel arch, but may well represent 'part of a decorated impost or string-course, similar in subject matter if not in quality to one of the early ninth-century friezes from Breedon-on-the-

---

231 Baxter, *Earls of Mercia*, p. 156 nn. 14 and 18, for references to the body of scholarship in which the nature and details of these forgeries was established.
232 Baxter, *Earls of Mercia*, pp. 159–60.
233 Blair, 'A handlist', pp. 548–9; Farmer, *Dictionary of Saints*, p. 366; S. Foot, *Veiled women: female religious communities in England, 871–1066*, 2 vols (Aldershot, 2000), vol. 2, pp. 71–2.
234 Bryant, *Corpus*, Coventry 1.
235 Taylor and Taylor, *Anglo-Saxon architecture*, vol. 2, pp. 694–5; C. Moffett, 'Archaeological investigations at the Anglo-Saxon church of St Andrew, Wroxeter: 1985–6', *Transactions of the Shropshire Archaeological and Historical Society*, 66 (1989), pp. 1–14.

Hill, Leicestershire', belonging to the minster church.[236] A decorated cross dated stylistically to the early ninth century once stood at Wroxeter, but in 1763 it was broken up and used in the rebuilding of the southern wall of the nave; made of limestone from the Cotswold Hills, it belongs to the Cropthorne Group in Gloucestershire and Worcestershire.[237]

Wirksworth, Bakewell, Bradbourne, Eyam and Rugby

These churches are here considered together because they host members of the Peak Group of stone sculpture, almost the only indication that any of these sites might once have supported minsters before the mid-tenth century.[238] The group is best known for the crosses that stand at each site, dated to the late eighth and early ninth centuries, and sharing some decorative parallels with crosses in Yorkshire and Lancashire, as well as Breedon-on-the-Hill.[239] The group also contains some important sepulchral monuments: a monolithic coped monument at All Saints' church, Bakewell, and a coped lid at the church of St Mary, Wirksworth.[240] Only a fragment of the monument at Bakewell survives, but it has been compared to the complete coped monolithic monument at Peterborough known as the 'Hedda Stone', and has been dated stylistically to the early ninth century. The Wirksworth slab has been given a slightly earlier date, in the late eighth century. Two cross-shaft fragments and the pieces of an unidentified monument, perhaps a shrine chest, all at Bakewell and dated to the late eighth or early ninth centuries, have been associated with the figural style on the Wirksworth lid, and may have been produced by the same agency.[241]

There is scarce textual evidence for these minsters. The churches of All Saints' at Bradbourne, St Helen's at Eyam and St Andrew's at Rugby do not appear in any texts of the period before the mid-tenth century, and can be counted among the corpus of possible early minsters in the diocese only because of their sculpture. Land at Wirksworth was granted by an Abbess Cynewaru in 835 to Humberht, *dux*, on the proviso that he send an annual render of lead to Ceolnoth, archbishop of Canterbury.[242] While hinting at the organised exploitation of natural resources in or close to Wirksworth, this tells us nothing about a minster community there. It has been assumed that Cynewaru was abbess of Repton, perhaps hinting that Wirksworth was a dependency of this important royal minster; however, there is no explicit evidence to support this, and it is possible that she was instead based at Wirksworth or elsewhere.[243] The point must remain moot, but, wherever Cynewaru is placed, an

---

236 Bryant, *Corpus*, p. 318.
237 Bryant, *Corpus*, pp. 314–17.
238 Hawkes and Sidebottom, *Corpus*, pp. 22–5; Cramp, 'Schools', pp. 218–25.
239 Hawkes and Sidebottom, *Corpus*, Bradbourne 1, Bradbourne 2, Bradbourne 3, Bradbourne 4, Bradbourne 5, Eyam 1, Bakewell 1, Bakewell 26, Bakewell 31, and Bryant, *Corpus*, Rugby 1.
240 Hawkes and Sidebottom, Corpus, Bakewell 34, Wirksworth 5.
241 Hawkes and Sidebottom, *Corpus*, Bakewell 9, Bakewell 11, Bakewell 37.
242 S 1624.
243 Biddle and Kjølbye-Biddle, 'The Repton stone', p. 235 n.14.

association of Wirksworth with female religious has been promoted by Jane Hawkes based on a consideration of the decorative scheme of the coped lid.[244]

The only minster to feature in the textual record of this period is that at Bakewell, which appears in a charter originally produced in 949.[245] King Eadred granted land at Bakewell to Uhtred, *miles* and *dux*, for the endowment of a minster (*coenobium*) there, and Peter Sawyer has connected this charter to an earlier one of 926, in which King Æthelstan confirmed Uhtred, his *fidelis*, in an estate of sixty hides (*manentes*) centred on Hope and Ashford, which Uhtred had earlier bought from 'the pagans' at the command of King Edward and Lord Æthelred of the Mercians (so between 899 and 911).[246] Sawyer has suggested that this estate included Bakewell, and that Eadred's grant was intended to enable Uhtred to give that part of it over to the minster.[247] There is no suggestion that Uhtred was establishing a minster *de novo* here, and the presence of monuments belonging to the Peak Group at Bakewell indicates that he was not; the endowment appears to give control of land on which the minster was located into the hands of the minster itself. The charter can be used to illuminate the politics of landholding during this period, and must be viewed in conjunction with Edward's foundation of a *burh* ('stronghold') at Bakewell in 920. However, it provides no information on the community that was presumably based at the minster. There are a number of monuments at Bakewell that have not been assigned to any of the groups defined by Sidebottom: one set features stylised plant-scrolls and/or berry clusters probably inspired by that on the Peak Group Bakewell cross;[248] another set features distinctive figures that may have been inspired by such figures on the two crosses in Sandbach market place;[249] both sets are largely ascribed tenth-century dates by the *Corpus* authors, but can be understood to represent the same process of stylisation based on earlier monuments invoked to explain the Trent Valley Group, and thus might be dated accordingly. If accepted, this would provide evidence for a community based at Bakewell in the later ninth and earlier tenth centuries; a set of monuments belonging to the Pennine Fringes Group demonstrates the continued activity of such a community after Uhtred's endowment.

Sandbach, Over and Overchurch

These three Cheshire churches are identifiable as possible minster sites only because of the stone sculpture they host. The two large crosses at Sandbach, probably dating to the early ninth century, require little further comment.[250] Jane Hawkes has

---

244 Hawkes and Sidebottom, *Corpus*, Wirksworth 5.
245 S 548; see Sawyer, *Charters of Burton Abbey*, Anglo-Saxon Charters 2 (Oxford, 1979), pp. 6–7, for commentary.
246 S 397.
247 Sawyer, *Charters of Burton Abbey*, p. 7.
248 Hawkes and Sidebottom, *Corpus*, Bakewell 2, Bakewell 4, Bakewell 8, Bakewell 20, Bakewell 23.
249 Hawkes and Sidebottom, *Corpus*, Bakewell 10, Bakewell 14, Bakewell 29.
250 Bailey, *Corpus*, Sandbach Market Place 1, Sandbach Market Place 2; Hawkes, 'Constructing iconographies'; Hawkes, *Sandbach crosses*.

suggested that they were probably brought to the market place, where they are now set in a stepped platform of probable sixteenth-century date, from the nearby church of St Mary;[251] the churchyard hosts three further fragmentary cross shafts bearing decorative schemes derived from the earlier crosses at Sandbach, but not executed so expertly, and testament to the same process of stylisation discussed earlier.[252] Another example is provided by two fragments from a coped slab, decorated with figures and motifs that enable its ascription to the Trent Valley Group, and which, unsurprisingly, display strong influences from the market place crosses.[253] These monuments indicate the activity of a community based at Sandbach into perhaps the earlier tenth century. Nearby, the cross-shaft fragment at the church of St Chad, Over, also derived its decorative scheme from that on the Sandbach market place crosses and, like the crosses in the churchyard at Sandbach, probably belongs to the later ninth century.[254] Further west, a fragmentary slab or shrine cover at Overchurch on Wirral has been dated to the early ninth century and, while it is a distinctive monument in its own right, it shares with one of the Sandbach market place crosses the image of a winged beast dissolving into interlace; however, perhaps its most distinctive feature is a runic inscription that can be translated 'The people raised up a monument; pray for Æðelmund'.[255] The presence of an early minster here is also supported by the nearby settlement at West Kirby, to the west of Overchurch; the place-name here probably means 'the western settlement dependent on the church', and belongs within a family of place-names derived from the Scandinavian term *kirkjubý*, considered 'a standard Norse one for an established minster centre'.[256]

Wolverhampton

The church of St Peter (earlier St Mary) at Wolverhampton was of superior status when its lands were recorded by the Domesday survey, its canons holding part of the endowment as tenants-in-chief.[257] The place-name signifies 'Wulfrun's high or chief *tun*', and a twelfth-century copy of an authentic charter dated 985 survives, complete with Old English bounds, in which King Æthelred grants an estate centred at Wolverhampton to a lady named Wulfrun.[258] There is no mention of the existence of a minster on the estate, or of Wulfrun's intention to found one, but another charter exists purporting to be confirmation of Wulfrun's land grants to the minster at Wolverhampton by Archbishop Sigeric, dated 994, and including a set of Old English boundary

---

251 Hawkes, *Sandbach crosses*, pp. 23–7.
252 Bailey, Corpus, Sandbach St Mary 1, Sandbach St Mary 2, Sandbach St Mary 3; Hawkes, *Sandbach crosses*, pp. 121–7.
253 Bailey, *Corpus*, Sandbach St Mary 4, Sandbach St Mary 5.
254 Bailey, *Corpus*, Over 1.
255 Bailey, *Corpus*, Overchurch 1.
256 Blair, *Church*, p. 310; see also n. 104, referring to work by Thomas Pickles supporting the application of the term to a minster's satellite settlements.
257 *DB Staffs.*, 7,1–4, 6–16.
258 S 860.

clauses.[259] Unfortunately this document is a forgery, Simon Keynes suggesting that a witness list dating to 995×996 was used to authenticate a confirmation of freedoms and privileges (probably based on a papal privilege) ostensibly produced by Archbishop Sigeric, who died in 994, with an authentic set of boundary clauses tacked on the end.[260] The text credits Wulfrun with endowing the church 'which now in modern times was constructed', and that it should hold these lands 'as your aforesaid minster of Hampton held them in former times'. This hints that Wulfrun had rebuilt and re-endowed an earlier minster, but, given the nature of the charter, it is only possible to say that she was thought to have done this by the forger, who was perhaps operating in the twelfth century or later.[261]

There is other evidence that lends some support to the presence of a minster on the site before Wulfrun's involvement, whatever form it took. In his will a man named Wulfgeat of Donington left bequests to a series of minsters in the vicinity of Wolverhampton and to a minster named *Heantune*, usually identified as Wolverhampton.[262] Dorothy Whitelock, the will's editor, suggested that this Wulfgeat might be equated with a *minister* of that name who appears in charter witness lists from 964 to 974; if he died *c*.975, Wulfgeat of Donington's bequest would predate Wulfrun's formal acquisition of Wolverhampton a decade later.[263] Of more direct relevance to this chapter, a large decorated round-shafted stone pillar featuring a banded decorative scheme stands outside the church at Wolverhampton. As mentioned earlier, the *Corpus* authors have dated it to the early tenth century based on the presence of fleshy plant-scrolls and stiff-leaf motifs.[264] The monument stands outside the prevailing pattern of stylised decorative schemes that, it has been argued here, otherwise characterise this period; its form and decoration associate it with activity further south in Gloucester and the West Saxon royal heartland, and perhaps hint at the establishment of new connections between a community based at Wolverhampton and these southern regions. As with Uhtred's charters at Bakewell, Wulfrun's later

---

259 S 1380; the charter is now lost, but a transcript is provided in Dugdale, *Monasticon*, vol. 6 (part 3), pp. 1443–46; Hooke, *Landscape of Anglo-Saxon Staffordshire*, pp. 27–8 and 64–85.
260 Keynes, *The diplomas of King Æthelred*, p. 252. A writ of King Edward to the priests of the minster, granting them freedom, with all their land to be held with sake and soke, is also considered a forgery; see F.E. Harmer, *Anglo-Saxon writs* (Manchester, 1952), pp. 403–7 (No. 114), at p. 404.
261 Other commentators have been unhappy with the vagueness of this passage: D. Styles, 'The early history of the king's chapels in Staffordshire', *Transactions of the Birmingham Archaeological Society*, 60 (1936), pp. 56–95, at p. 59; Hooke, *Landscape of Anglo-Saxon Staffordshire*, p. 27; D. Hooke, 'Wolverhampton: the foundation of the minster', in J. Maddison (ed.), *Medieval archaeology and architecture at Lichfield*, Transactions of the British Archaeological Association 13 (1993), pp. 11–16, at p. 11.
262 D. Whitelock, *Anglo-Saxon wills* (Cambridge, 1930), pp. 54–7 and 163–7 (No. 19).
263 This Wulfgeat might also have been the recipient of land at 'Duddestone' and Upper Arley in 963 (S 720), the latter place later forming part of Wolverhampton's endowment; he can also be equated with a kinsman of Wulfrun named in the forged confirmation charter: Sawyer, *Charters of Burton Abbey*, pp. 32–3 (No. 20).
264 Hawkes and Sidebottom, *Corpus*, Wolverhampton 1.

Lichfield and the Lands of St Chad

involvement with the minster tells us very little concerning its community, but does illustrate something of its role in the politics of the landed elite.

Wilne (Sawley), Prees, Eccleshall, Tachbrook, Tarvin, Longford (Bupton), Brewood and Baswich

This group of churches comprises those on episcopal estates that were identified as the 'core' possessions of the see in Chapter 2, probably acquired by *c*.900. They may represent minsters that were founded by members of the elite before coming into the hands of the bishop at a later date, or churches founded directly by the bishop upon land granted to him for the purpose. The inclusion of all eight churches in this section is somewhat dishonest, as six of them feature no further evidence for existence before the tenth century. Two of them, however, do host notable examples of stone sculpture: St Chad's church at Wilne and the church of the Holy Trinity (earlier St Chad's) at Eccleshall. At Wilne part of a circular pillar or shaft featuring a decorative scheme arranged in bands around its circumference was later reused to create the bowl for the church's font.[265] The form of this monument has been compared by Jane Hawkes to other freestanding columns at Wolverhampton (Staffordshire), Masham and Dewsbury (Yorkshire) and Reculver, Wantage and Winchester (all south of the Thames), which she dates to the ninth century and suggests were inspired by Roman triumphal columns.[266] Eccleshall hosts part of an early to mid-ninth-century cross shaft from the Sandbach Group and a second ninth-century cross shaft probably inspired by direct access to an early Christian model;[267] another cross shaft from the later Trent Valley Group displays the strong influence of several Sandbach motifs.[268]

Minsters less securely attested
Berkswell, Norbury and Bangor-is-y-Coed

The existence of these three minsters before the tenth century is advocated based on little more than the names of saints who may have been revered at them, and so must be considered less secure pending the discovery of further evidence. John Blair has noted references to St Barloc at Norbury in Derbyshire and St Milred at Berkswell in Warwickshire. Blair suggests a possible relationship between Barloc's name and the North Welsh name Barrog, anglicised as Barroc;[269] however, it is also conceivable that the name is Old English, with *locc*, 'hair, curl', as its last element, perhaps bearing

---

265 Hawkes and Sidebottom, *Corpus*, Wilne 1.
266 J. Hawkes, 'The legacy of Constantine in Anglo-Saxon England', in E. Hartley, J. Hawkes and M. Henig (eds), *Constantine the Great: York's Roman emperor* (London, 2006), pp. 104–14, at p. 109. The column at Masham has been dated to the late eighth or early ninth centuries: J. Lang (ed.), *Corpus of Anglo-Saxon stone sculpture, volume VI, northern Yorkshire* (Oxford, 2002), pp. 168–71.
267 Hawkes and Sidebottom, *Corpus*, Eccleshall 2, Eccleshall 3.
268 Hawkes and Sidebottom, *Corpus*, Eccleshall 1.
269 Blair, 'A handlist', pp. 513–14.

comparison with the attested names Brunloc and Bægloc.[270] St Barloc's church hosts two stone cross shafts of the Trent Valley Group, one of which has been ascribed to the Dove Valley Subgroup.[271] St Milred of Berkswell shares his name with an eighth-century bishop of Worcester, but need not necessarily be equated with him; Blair points to the elaborate twelfth-century crypt beneath the chancel of the church in support of the cult's historicity.[272] The dedication of the church at Bangor-is-y-Coed to St Dunawd can be associated with Bede's references to a monastery at Bangor ruled by an abbot named Dinooth in the early seventh century, which sent representatives to a synod with Augustine and later sent a contingent of monks to pray for the Britons fighting against the Northumbrian king Æthelfrith at Chester.[273] However, the early medieval history of the monastery thereafter is otherwise unknown, and the specific connection between early monastery and later church is not clear.

Leek, Checkley, Hope, Blackwell, Spondon, Ashbourne, Tatenhill, Alstonefield and Aston-on-Trent

The only evidence for these minsters before the early tenth century is the presence of stone sculpture belonging to the Trent Valley Group, which has here been dated to the later ninth and earlier tenth centuries; this is generally a little earlier than the dates offered by the *Corpus* authors and thus potentially more contentious, although it should be noted that some of the dates offered by those authors fall within this date range. The churches of St Mary and All Saints, Checkley, and St Peter's, Alstonefield, complete the set of four churches hosting cross shafts of the Dove Valley Subgroup, also represented at Ilam and Norbury.[274] More broadly, the Trent Valley Group encompasses two cross shafts at the church of St Edward the Confessor at Leek (earlier Edward the Martyr, but even then necessarily a rededication if the church predates the late tenth century) and a cross shaft at St Peter's church, Hope, a distinct northern outlier associated with one of the two estate centres referenced in Uhtred's charter of 926; like the Dove Valley Subgroup, these monuments were inspired by elements of the decorative schemes on the Sandbach market place crosses.[275] The cross shafts at St Oswald's church in Ashbourne, All Saints' church in Aston-on-Trent (earlier St Peter and St Paul), and St Werburgh in Spondon all feature Mercian Beasts, perhaps inspired by the earlier crosses at nearby Derby.[276]

---

270 See O. von Feilitzen, *The pre-Conquest personal names of Domesday Book* (Uppsala, 1937), p. 210. Brunloc: *DB Essex* B3a; Bægloc: S 96.
271 Hawkes and Sidebottom, *Corpus*, Norbury 1, Norbury 2.
272 Blair, 'A handlist', pp. 545–6.
273 *HE*, ii.2.
274 Hawkes and Sidebottom, *Corpus*, Alstonefield 2, Alstonefield 5, Checkley 1, Checkley 2; Alstonefield 11 belongs to the Trent Valley Group but cannot be assigned to the Dove Valley Subgroup.
275 Hawkes and Sidebottom, *Corpus*, Hope 1, Leek 1, Leek 3.
276 Hawkes and Sidebottom, *Corpus*, Ashbourne 1, Aston-on-Trent 1, Spondon 1; another shaft at Ashbourne, Ashbourne 2, was recorded in the nineteenth century but has since been lost. Aston-on-Trent's earlier dedication is given in Clark, 'Dedications of medieval churches in Derbyshire', p. 57.

Lichfield and the Lands of St Chad

Intriguingly, Spondon shares its dedication to St Werburgh with the nearby church at Blackwell, the only two dedications to the saint in the county outside Derby, where there is a third; the cross shaft at Blackwell also shares with that at Spondon an irregular interlace with 'V-loop' returns, a pattern that both share with earlier monuments at Derby and Repton, as well as the distinctive ring-headed cross of the Trent Valley Group at the church of St Michael in Tatenhill (probably dedicated to St John the Baptist before the Reformation).[277] The interconnections between these sites extend to a probable Roman column, perhaps from the fort at Little Chester north of Derby, reused in the church at Blackwell and similar to those used at Repton in the renovations of the later ninth or earlier tenth century associated with St Wigstan's cult.[278] Taken together, these associations hint at a nexus of interests and contacts within the Derby region, perhaps even representing part of St Wærburh's extended ecclesiastical community, although an interest in the saint might equally have arisen later.

Monuments of the Trent Valley Group are also present at Chesterton, Ingleby and Clipshead, but are not here considered to represent the sites of earlier minsters. The cross shaft at Chesterton displays inspiration from the Sandbach market place crosses;[279] it was discovered in use as a feeding trough at a local farm, and nothing is known of its earlier provenance. There was no medieval church at Chesterton, which lay in the parish of St Margaret's church at Wolstanton; the nearest church associated with surviving stone sculpture is St Peter's in Stoke-on-Trent, about four miles away, which hosts a cross shaft of the later Pennine Fringes Group.[280] The cross-shaft fragment found at Ingleby is one of the few Trent Valley Group monuments influenced by Carolingian styles that first appear in English media in the early tenth century.[281] It was found in a garden close to the site of a chapel, which lay in the medieval parish of Repton; and close also to a second fragment, also found in a garden, which may date slightly later, to the tenth or eleventh centuries.[282] Clearly the Ingleby fragments might initially have been associated with the chapel, but this provenance cannot be unequivocally demonstrated, and the site stands out against the other ecclesiastical sites hosting members of Trent Valley Group, which are almost all parish churches, not dependent chapels. These issues render it unwise to make too much of the Ingleby fragments. Likewise, the cross-head fragment found at Clipshead Farm near Brassington formed part of the wall of an agricultural building; its decorative interlace can be associated with monuments at Derby, but its specific initial provenance remains unknown.[283]

---

277 Hawkes and Sidebottom, *Corpus*, Blackwell East 1, Spondon 1, Tatenhill 1; compare with Derby 1 and Repton 15. For the earlier dedication at Tatenhill see N.J. Tringham (ed.), *VCH Staffordshire*, vol. 10 (Woodbridge, 2007), p. 227.
278 Hawkes and Sidebottom, *Corpus*, Blackwell East 2.
279 Hawkes and Sidebottom, *Corpus*, Chesterton 1.
280 Hawkes and Sidebottom, *Corpus*, Stoke-on-Trent 1.
281 Hawkes and Sidebottom, *Corpus*, Ingleby 1.
282 Hawkes and Sidebottom, *Corpus*, Ingleby 2.
283 Hawkes and Sidebottom, *Corpus*, Clipshead 1.

The cathedral and the minsters

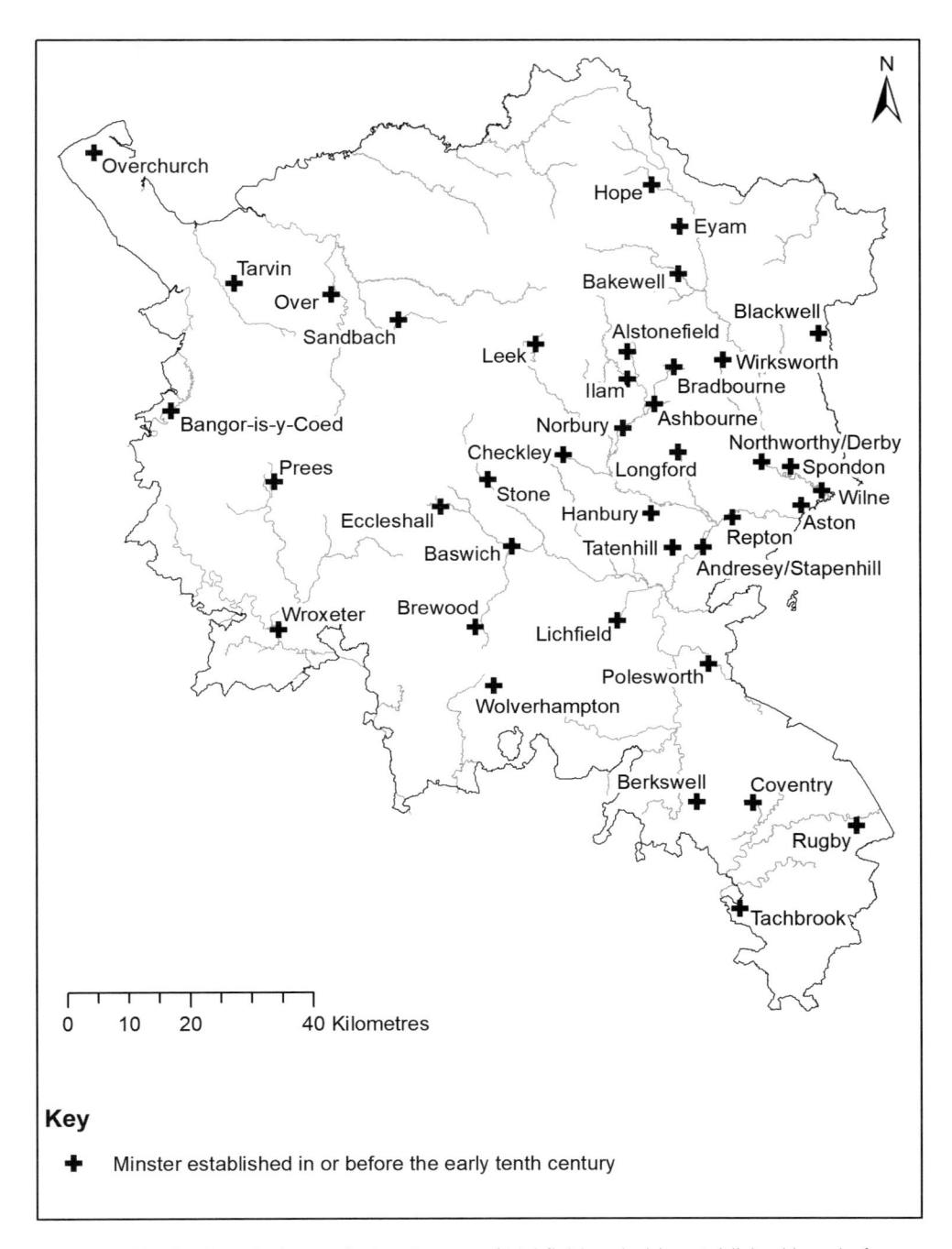

Figure 10 Distribution of minsters in the diocese of Lichfield probably established in or before the early tenth century, overlain on the main rivers of the region.

Minsters and communities

This review of possible minster sites in the diocese of Lichfield has illustrated several points, not least the fragmentary and tenuous nature of the evidence for many of them. There is a limited but perhaps significant overlap between the various categories of evidence invoked here: of the episcopal churches, Lichfield, Eccleshall and Wilne possess sculpture dated before the early tenth century; of the churches associated with saints' cults, Repton, Derby, Coventry, Ilam and Norbury possess such sculpture. We would not, of course, expect to find saints' cults other than that of St Chad at episcopal churches. There remains the question of the representativeness of the distribution of minsters presented by this review. We might, for example, worry that the evidence for decorated sepulchral structures, perhaps shrines, at Bakewell, Wirksworth, Sandbach and Overchurch indicates that we are missing references to saints' cults that were once supported there, and likewise that sites currently lacking stone sculpture might nevertheless once have possessed it. The overall distribution of minsters identified here is notably skewed towards the southern and eastern parts of the diocese (see Figure 10), but we cannot draw any meaningful conclusions from this if reliance can be placed on neither the representativeness of the stone sculpture distribution nor that of the saints' cults.

Indeed, Blair has argued that the notable absence of saints in the north-west of England is more apparent than real, owing to 'the lack of local sources, combined with the remoteness of the region from the centres where lists and calendars were compiled'.[284] However, it is possible to suggest otherwise. When, c.1140, Prior Robert of Shrewsbury Abbey wrote his *Life* of St Winifred, he deplored the initial lack of a local saint at his house and explained that, hearing of the profusion of saints in Wales, the community had decided to acquire one of them, and subsequently translated St Winifred (or Gwenfrewi) from Gwytherin, Denbighshire, to Shrewsbury.[285] In the late eleventh century Shrewsbury Abbey had acquired, among others, the churches at Baschurch, Berrington, Hodnet, Great Ness, Wrockwardine, Condover, Edgmond, Ercall Magna and Wellington; these were all important churches, several on royal estates at the centres of hundreds, and it is difficult to believe that, had one of them contained a relic cult, the Benedictine community would not have latched onto it. Indeed, the community at Lilleshall Abbey did precisely this in the mid-twelfth century, taking over the cult of St Alkmund from the church of St Alkmund in Shrewsbury, which formed the core of their original endowment.[286] The comparative lack of saints in the western parts of the diocese was thus as apparent in the late eleventh and twelfth centuries as it is now. There are no doubt early minsters left unidentified by this review, which might be found by future excavation, but, despite the limitations of the evidence, the relative concentration of both saints' cults and stone sculpture in the south and east of the diocese can be considered representative of something real. This has implications for how we explain the varieties of reasoning behind these minsters' foundation, and is revisited in the conclusion.

---

284 Blair, 'A saint for every minster?', p. 467.
285 Acta Sanctorum (eds), 'Vita secunda Sanctae Wenefredae, et ejusdem translatio', *Acta Sanctorum*, Nov., I (1887), pp. 708–31, cap. 3.
286 Gaydon, *VCH Shropshire*, vol. 2, pp. 70–80.

The cathedral and the minsters

The remainder of this concluding section focuses on commonalities between the minsters identified above and asks to what extent we can define minster-based communities. The wide variety and range in the quality of evidence presented above renders direct comparison difficult, but one exception to this is the topographical locations of the minsters, which, despite the variety of landscapes found in the diocese, reveal distinct patterns. All the minsters can be placed with reference to two important elements of the landscape – elevation and the presence of water – though the degree of association with each varies, and can be categorised into three different types according to their association with these elements, although it would be foolish to insist too rigidly on the distinctions between them. First, a number of the minsters are located next to the more significant rivers of the diocese, often on the edge of the floodplain, elevated on a bluff, river cliff or small hill, and sometimes backed up against rising higher ground in the more topographically dramatic parts of the diocese; in these cases, closeness to the watercourse is the defining feature.[287] Good examples are provided by Repton, Wilne, Aston-on-Trent and Bangor-is-y-Coed, which all perch on the edge of, or even within, broad floodplains associated with the Trent, the Derwent and the Dee, but others, such as Polesworth, Stone and Baswich, occupy similar positions with regards to smaller floodplains. The second category relates to very similar forms of elevation above watercourses in which the latter are not major rivers, but rather small tributary streams or headwaters that become or converge with larger watercourses further downstream.[288] Lichfield is a good example of this, but the category is quite broad, and also includes the churches at Leek, which sits atop a distinctive hill above one of the headstreams of the river Churnet in a moorland region, and Tatenhill, located on a shelf on the side of a hill in the secluded valley of a small stream that emerges onto the Trent floodplain just over half a kilometre to the south. A final category concerns minsters in locations where elevation seems to be the defining feature, and the closest watercourses are often some distance away.[289] A distinctive example here is the church at Hanbury, which overlooks the floodplain of the river Dove, but sits about a kilometre away from its edge in order to take advantage of a dramatic steep-sided plateau. The churches at Rugby and Spondon are also located on high points in the landscape overlooking the floodplains of major rivers some distance away, and Overchurch looks out over the Dee estuary and the Irish Sea, but otherwise the churches in this category tend to be closest to small streams and headwaters, often set upon hills and plateaux that are flanked by such watercourses.

Of course, these categories do not necessarily exclude the locations of later churches (quite the reverse), but the qualities of these locations remain important. The elevation that characterises all these locations to varying degrees is in one sense pragmatic, raising churches above the level of winter floods, but all are most

---

287 Repton, Polesworth, Andresey/Stapenhill, Wroxeter, Wilne, Baswich, Stone, Coventry, Norbury, Northworthy (Derby), Ilam, Bakewell, Aston-on-Trent, Bangor-is-y-Coed.
288 Lichfield, Berkswell, Wirksworth, Sandbach, Over, Tachbrook, Longford, Eccleshall, Tarvin, Brewood, Leek, Hope, Checkley, Ashbourne, Tatenhill.
289 Hanbury, Bradbourne, Eyam, Rugby, Overchurch, Prees, Wolverhampton, Blackwell, Spondon, Alstonefield.

certainly consciously placed: many produce a striking effect when approached from below, and those on hilltops can often be described as dramatic. An association with rising water is particularly notable: the church at Berkswell is set on a gentle slope above a slight fold in the landscape within which rises a small stream (witness the place-name, 'Be(o)rcol's spring'), which eventually finds its way to the river Blythe;[290] the church at Ilam sits above a broad lawn edging the river Manifold, notably close to the point where the river emerges from a long subterranean passage through the limestone rocks of its bed in the drier months of the year. The significance of such locations should probably be understood alongside the propensity displayed by other sites for headwaters and tributary streams. Elevation and association with water are two aspects of minster location across England more generally that have been noted by John Blair, and so the corpus in the diocese of Lichfield can be seen to fit into broader ideas about the attributes of Christian holy places during this period.[291] Moreover, sources of water might easily become associated with spiritual qualities and activities such as purification and baptism (note dedications to St John the Baptist at Berkswell and Tatenhill).[292] Nevertheless, a broader commonality of ideas on these themes should not be allowed to obscure the importance of their local integration into specific landscapes.

Considerations of placement in the landscape represent the end of a spectrum of possibilities regarding the ways in which space was used to enable specific collective activities, and thus to define communities. At the other end of this spectrum, the shrines, churches and other liturgical objects and spaces that form much of the material evidence discussed above emphasise one of the activities that persisted at the heart of such communities: the curation of saints' cults. Early texts give important details here, but while texts were important instruments of memory within minster-based communities when used, to focus only on a textual hagiographic record limits our understanding of other kinds of 'hagiographic' activity, using non-textual instruments, that were evidently important at these places. Indeed, the survival of many saints' relics and shrines into the later medieval period, when all other elements of their early medieval contexts had long been forgotten, highlights the ritualised liturgical form of their veneration through which they persisted. These cults were established within the spaces of buildings specially constructed for the purpose, such as the chapel postulated above for St Chad at Lichfield, or the crypt renovated for St Wigstan at Repton. Standing crosses appear to have accompanied churches and shrines at many minsters across the diocese, and it was suggested earlier that they played important parts in the liturgy, perhaps often serving as processional foci. Such activities were incorporated into the lives of those living at the minsters, creating liturgical communities. Regular patterns of movement and spoken observance created 'memories' of the saints that were not in our sense historical, but cyclical, renewed through each course of the ritual year. We might also invoke a

---

290 J.E.B. Gover, A. Mawr and F.M. Stenton, *The place-names of Warwickshire* (Cambridge, 1936), pp. 56–7.
291 Blair, *Church*, p. 193.
292 Blair, *Church*, pp. 377–8.

The cathedral and the minsters

'subordinate penumbra' at the edges of these liturgical communities, encompassing those groups of people spiritually dependent on the community, who perhaps visited it on a fairly regular basis and submitted their souls to the intercession of the saints. Such groups might have lived close to the minsters, on their estates, but might equally have encompassed a variety of people, both local and far-flung, through a variety of different kinds of connection and association.

The evidence for saints' cults at many of the diocese's minsters, whether in the survival of a saint's name or of the buildings and shrines built around their relics, is therefore very significant, representing one of the strongest forms of place-centred community now identifiable, and the one most commensurate with the minster as a bounded physical place. However, as has been repeatedly emphasised in this book, we need to understand minsters as an important part of the infrastructure that supported a variety of different communities, overlapping, intersecting and formed at a variety of different scales. At the larger end of the scale, Chapters 1 and 2 introduced the English ecclesiastical community, the diocesan community and the extended ecclesiastical community, all of which relied to some degree on the minsters where their various memberships spent much of their time. Chapter 1 also introduced the notion of the 'associative field', a looser, more decentred, concentration of activities articulated around shared norms that were subject to a greater degree of fluidity and alteration. Such fields often formed the grounds for the emergence of more tightly orchestrated communities, as those within them worked collectively to define the basis of their own personhood more stringently. In Chapter 1 this process was briefly explored in relation to the formation and persistence of the English ecclesiastical community within a large spiritually defined field stretching from Britain via Francia to Italy. A different aspect of that field can be discussed here in relation to the sepulchral stone sculpture of the diocese.

Despite the use of different decorative schemes and forms, the sepulchral monuments of the diocese shared a common function, elaborating the resting places of the very special dead. This appears to have been of great concern at many minsters across the diocese, as such monuments form a significant part of the sculptural corpus from its beginnings in the late eighth century to the waning of the Trent Valley Group in the early tenth century. It is possible that this concern was informed by a vision of cosmic community that can also be found in the Book of Cerne, an early ninth-century Mercian prayer book of the Tiberius Group that has been studied by Michelle Brown.[293] The book might have been created at Lichfield, as an acrostic poem features the name of the early ninth-century bishop Æthelwald (although stylistically Worcester is another possibility).[294] The composer of the book drew on 'a strong earlier Insular tradition of private devotions' and arranged their material thematically to produce an original meditation on the Communion of Saints (*communio sanctorum*), a vision of the Church as a body of the faithful, past, present and future, headed by Christ, 'the prayers of the user serving to invoke the intercession of all the faithful on his behalf and

---

[293] Brown, *Book of Cerne*, pp. 164–72; see also Brown, 'Mercian manuscripts?'
[294] Brown, *Book of Cerne*, pp. 181–3.

in turn contributing to the common good of all'.[295] That such was a concern of a bishop at Lichfield during a period when lavish stone sculpture was enveloping the graves of many saints in the diocese indicates a shared sense of spiritual understanding between those commissioning the sculpture that was also experienced by the liturgical communities of each and every minster with a saint's cult.

It is perhaps tempting to view such widely shared ideas and experiences as simply a kind of cultural background, informing the patterns in our evidence through a form of social osmosis. This, however, would create a rather ethereal impression of the relation between culture and society. The relations between associative fields and communities were mediated in a dialectical manner through the activities and encounters of their overlapping memberships. The *communio sanctorum* is a good example: it provided a compelling vision for many, shared within many different kinds and scales of community, manifest through different media and playing out to different rhythms, and its persistent influence relied on all of those communities continuing to organise the day-to-day existence of their members, and on the intersection and interrelation of these communities through individual life experiences. The production of stone sculpture provides a useful illustration of this. Each sculpture is different, but at the same time it was connected to others by the form of its creator's inspiration; for example, the sculptor of the distinctive shrine-chest at Lichfield displayed an attitude to models of religious decorative forms from the Christian East similar to those of the creators of equally distinctive sculpture at Breedon-on-the Hill, Castor and Fletton.[296] Likewise, in studying the Sandbach crosses Jane Hawkes has emphasised the uniqueness of each context of production: the crosses drew upon pre-existing models, such as portable ivories and metalwork, both from overseas and from insular sources, in an original composition.[297] Each context of production provided access to these shared models and reproduced shared normative ideas about the Communion of the Saints, but each was also a unique nexus of connections dedicated to the creation or maintenance of specific communities. Such communities were often the liturgical communities at the hearts of minsters, but not always: for example, Hawkes suggests that the iconography of the two large crosses at Sandbach 'provides an impressive statement that is repeatedly reiterated, of the power and authority of Christ's Church in Mercia in the ninth century', an attitude that must have particularly gripped members of the diocesan and English ecclesiastical communities.[298]

Clearly then, it is useful to envisage associative fields both generating and generated by the activities of the communities suspended within them. The fluid networks supporting such broad fields enabled the sharp thrusts of new encounters, opening possibilities, creating new connections and relinquishing old ones, but also supported the shared imaginings and attitudes that focused the activities of communities on specific goals. This emphasises the point made repeatedly here, that minsters were not simply communities in their own right. This must be fundamental to

---

295 Brown, *Book of Cerne*, pp. 155 and 148 respectively.
296 Rodwell et al., 'The Lichfield Angel'; Cramp, 'Schools'; Jewel, 'Classicism of Southumbrian sculpture'.
297 Hawkes, 'Constructing Iconographies'; Hawkes, *Sandbach Crosses*.
298 Hawkes, *Sandbach Crosses*, pp. 147–8.

our understanding of minsters. As settlements in the landscape they emerged from the intersection of different communities working simultaneously at different scales within broad associative fields enabling encounter and interaction. This perspective decentres the minsters as place-centred communities and instead focuses on the kinds of social investment that enabled their rulers and other inhabitants to form relationships, such as the spiritual imaginary in which the promotion of the Communion of Saints may well have become a dominant unifying impulse. The regional associations glimpsed behind the distributions of sculpture decoration, represented by the groups discussed earlier, hint at similar conclusions, while the individuality of each piece and the presence of sepulchral monuments remind us that the creation of specific holy places through liturgical practice also created specific minster-centred communities. It is not intended to suggest that the specific associations revealed by the production of stone sculpture were inordinately important parts of the bigger picture; they are particularly important to historians because the surviving evidence allows us to say something substantive, but their utility lies chiefly in hinting at a dense web of connections maintained to create a variety of different communities, within which one of many imperatives was the occasional sourcing of sculptors and their models for the production of stone monuments.

Minster-based communities were thus not confined to specific minsters, but straddled several in ways that changed over time as their members formed and dissolved different kinds of relationship with one another. Moreover, while the liturgical communities centred on minsters were of fundamental importance to many of the local inhabitants of their regions, the spiritual motivations of those who commissioned hagiography and stone monuments are best understood as belonging to an elite section of society: the bishops, abbots and abbesses who ruled these minsters, and their peers, colleagues and confidants. Indeed, the communities discussed in the first three chapters of this book were probably dominated by that elite, although the liturgical communities, more than others so far discussed, might also have included some of the less socially influential inhabitants of the minsters. This has several implications, concerning the relationship of this elite to, in particular, other communities, such as the Mercian royal dynasty, but also to lay society more generally, both high and low. These areas will be explored in subsequent chapters, but first the position of bishops and their clergy within the communities identified in this chapter, and in particular in relation to the rulers of minsters in the diocese, needs to be addressed.

Chapter 4

The bishop and the lords of minsters

Thus far this book has identified several different religious communities within early medieval England, each defined according to ritualising collective activities, which brought people together in common endeavour, often articulated around imagined communities such as the Church of the English or the Church of Lichfield. Power and hierarchy have received less attention, except in specific circumstances. We have witnessed how hierarchy was articulated through the roles staked out within communities: a clear example is provided by the hierarchy of ecclesiastical offices, which Chad was so careful to maintain within the nascent English ecclesiastical community when he submitted to the authority and commands of Archbishop Theodore in 669, perhaps fearing that he would otherwise be expelled from it. We have also witnessed how a community might act in solidarity to subordinate someone outside its core membership: for example, the Mercian king Cœnwulf could not invoke sufficient spiritual authority when challenging the solidarity of the English ecclesiastical community, and so was unable to prevent the abolition of the archbishopric of Lichfield or the restoration of metropolitan authority to Canterbury in the early ninth century. Here, Cœnwulf was excluded from the core community, and thus was unable to enact his will, but, crucially, he was a member of the imaginary Church of the English, around which the English ecclesiastical community was articulated, and was therefore vulnerable to the powerful assertion of the latter's authority. Power and hierarchy are complex issues when we focus on the edges of communities in this way; such edges were often fuzzy, especially where imagined communities were envisioned more inclusively than the practical communities that organised around them. In these contexts we have to consider issues of inclusion, exclusion and subordination, and the practices that were worked out to negotiate these boundaries and to establish and maintain hierarchies across them.

This chapter seeks to explore such issues through the relationship between the diocesan community, ruled by the bishop, and minster-centred liturgical communities within the diocese, ruled by abbots and abbesses who were not necessarily a part of the diocesan community. Members of both forms of community might claim to belong to the Church of Lichfield as an imagined community of Christians, past, present and future. Crucially, members of both might also claim some degree of spiritual authority within this Church through the activities that defined their communities: the celebration of the liturgy, the sacramental activities of the clerics and the living of regulated religious lives at the cathedral and the minsters. The canons produced at councils of the English ecclesiastical community during the seventh, eighth and ninth centuries repeatedly stressed the bishop's spiritual lordship over the lords of other minsters, and the sacramental connection between a bishop and the clergy of his diocese ensured that the diocesan community extended into all minsters at which such clergy lived. But the lords of these minsters embodied a second source of spiritual lordship over both the clerics and the monks and nuns who had vowed to live regular lives under their care, and in their curation of any saints' cults within their churches' liturgies. The tensions inherent in this overlap resulted in several developments, two of which are explored here: firstly, the payment of ecclesiastical tribute, often called church-scot, and secondly, the bishop of Lichfield's relationship with a distinctive group of churches in the diocese known in the later medieval period as 'royal free chapels'.

Ecclesiastical tribute

Since the 1980s John Blair has been the foremost champion of an early parochial system based on minsters, to which the surrounding laity paid ecclesiastical tribute in return for pastoral ministration;[1] this concept, though not without its critics, has been widely accepted. Blair's latest restatement of the idea emphasises the relationship of such a system to secular territories of the seventh and eighth centuries.[2] He argues that the ecclesiastical territories of minsters (usually labelled *parochiae* by historians) were coincident with, or occupied a substantial part of, these secular territories; the simultaneous fragmentation of both kinds of territory during the tenth and eleventh centuries resulted in the more numerous, smaller estates recorded in the Domesday survey, on the one hand, and the later medieval system of local church parishes, on the other. Acceptance of this narrative has enabled the earlier territories to be reconstructed by a combination of estate geography, often from the evidence of Domesday Book, and later parochial geography, often from evidence of the dependence of later medieval chapels on nearby mother churches, or pensions paid from one church to another, indicative of earlier dependence. The identification of early minsters and their associated territories in this way has subsequently been attempted across much of the country, not least within the diocese of Lichfield, where Steven Bassett, Nick Higham and Jane Croom have each studied parts of the parochial landscape.[3]

However, the assumption on which this narrative is based is problematic, because even if there was a close connection between ecclesiastical and secular territories in the seventh and eighth centuries neither can necessarily be reconstructed using later evidence. Eric Cambridge and David Rollason have suggested that the reconstructed pattern represents 'a system of mother churches, probably imposed by royal authority

---

1 For example: J. Blair, 'Minster churches in the landscape', in D. Hooke (ed.), *Anglo-Saxon settlements* (Oxford, 1988), pp. 35–58; J. Blair, 'Introduction: from minster to parish church', in J. Blair (ed.), *Minsters and parish churches, the local church in transition 950–1200* (Oxford, 1988), pp. 1–19; J. Blair, 'Ecclesiastical organisation and pastoral care in Anglo-Saxon England', *Early Medieval Europe*, 4 (1995), pp. 193–212; Blair, *Church*.
2 Blair, *Church*, pp. 154–5.
3 Higham, *Origins*, especially pp. 126–81 (chapter 5); Bassett, 'Anglo-Saxon Shrewsbury', pp. 1–23; Bassett, 'Medieval ecclesiastical organisation'; Bassett, 'Church and diocese in the West Midlands'; S. Bassett, 'Anglo-Saxon Birmingham', *Midland History*, 25 (2000), pp. 1–27; S. Bassett, *Anglo-Saxon Coventry and its churches*, The Dugdale Society Occasional Papers 41 (Stratford-upon-Avon, 2001); J. Croom, 'The fragmentation of the minster *parochiae* of south-east Shropshire', in J. Blair (ed.), *Minsters and parish churches, the local church in transition 950–1200* (Oxford, 1988), pp. 67–81.

and as such not necessarily of pre-Viking origin', and, indeed, they would date its establishment to the tenth century.[4] Responding to this, Blair has taken a 'middle position': 'that there was indeed fundamental reorganisation in the tenth century, but that it probably did make use of earlier quasi-parochial structures of some kind'.[5] The difference between the two positions in part relates to the elements of church organisation that each chooses to focus on: Cambridge and Rollason emphasise the novelty of tithes as the primary contribution to church income in England in the tenth century, whereas Blair points to a coherent, if eccentric, system of church dues, 'church-scot' and the like, which first becomes visible in the late ninth century, but which, he argues, represents much earlier practices.[6] All three authors agree on the introduction of compulsory tithe payment to England from the 920s, and on the existence of earlier 'church dues' of some kind, but disagree on their implications.

These issues are reassessed in what follows. Of particular concern is the very existence of the early ecclesiastical territories essential to Blair's position, and the idea that their focal minsters were the ultimate beneficiaries of the early church dues as a reciprocal recognition of their role as the primary institutional vectors of pastoral care. Here, after criticising Blair's argument, it is proposed that ecclesiastical tributes such as church-scot represent specifically episcopal dues, which continued to be demanded in one form or another throughout the period as an acknowledgement of the bishop's spiritual lordship over the landholders of the diocese, including minster- or church-centred liturgical communities otherwise independent of the core diocesan community. Such acknowledgements, it is argued, were initially justified by reference to the obligatory hospitality owed to a bishop in his diocese to support his visitation of its population. They were organised in a variety of ways depending on the relationships between bishops and the churches of their dioceses, and evidence from the diocese of Lichfield and elsewhere in the Midlands is employed to demonstrate that a reorganisation in and after the mid-tenth century connected church-scot to the regnal administrative territories of hundreds and shires.

Blair's model of early minster foundation rests on the idea that minster estates were carved out of large secular territories, called variously *provinciae*, *regiones* or 'small shires' by scholars; these territories were assessed in quantities of hides, the unit by which kings organised and extracted royal renders. A major part of these renders, Blair suggests, comprised 'food-rents', which supported the royal court as it travelled around the kingdom.[7] Accordingly, the 'bundles of hides' given to early minsters within various *regiones* were essentially 'food-renders … split off from the rest and assigned to new recipients'; this acquisition of royal rights was distinctive of 'bookland', land conferred on minsters by charter 'in perpetual possession, with unrestricted rights of alienation'.[8] Blair also points to early evidence for ecclesiastical tributes levied in return

---

4   E. Cambridge and D. Rollason, 'The pastoral organisation of the Anglo-Saxon church: a review of the "minster hypothesis"', *Early Medieval Europe*, 4 (1995), pp. 87–104, at p. 100.
5   Blair, *Church*, p. 153.
6   Blair, *Church*, pp. 433–40.
7   Blair, *Church*, p. 154.
8   Blair, *Church*, p. 90.

for pastoral care, which is worth reproducing here: in his letter to Bishop Ecgberht Bede referred to the 'tributes' (*tributa*) owed and 'money' (*pecunia*) paid to the bishop by remote Northumbrian villages, and in his commentary on Ezra and Nehemiah he wrote of the priests and ministers who demanded 'tax' (*vectigal*) and received 'payment (*sumptus*) owing to their office';[9] in his penitential Archbishop Theodore ordered that 'ecclesiastical tribute' (*tributum ecclesiae*) be levied 'according to the custom of the province';[10] and the canons of the synod at *Clofesho* in 747 required that priests should undertake their office 'through the places and regions of the laity which are enjoined and committed to them by the bishops of the province'.[11] Blair suggests that this ecclesiastical tribute was levied in the same way as royal renders, assessed on the hide, and that it can be identified with *ciricsceat*, church-scot, 'a yearly render of grain from each homestead at Martinmas which the laws of King Ine of Wessex (688–726) make obligatory', and which appears in charters from the late ninth century onwards.[12] He concludes that minsters had direct control of much of this tribute through their right to royal renders from the estates they were given; moreover, given that the priests charged with pastoral care were based at minsters, Blair plays down the possibility that the episcopal administration of this tribute extended outside the estates attached to the bishops' own cathedrals and minsters.[13]

Aspects of this hypothesis can be criticised. First, it is by no means clear that the estates given to early minsters initially included the right to take specifically royal renders. The nature of such renders can be discerned by their appearance in contemporary charters, and they appear to have included a range of rents and services, summarised by Nicholas Brooks as follows: 'labour on public works, on royal vills and palaces and on churches, fines imposed by the popular courts and other profitable legal rights, and above all the rendering of royal *tributum* or *vectigal* which might be a food-rent or the actual feeding and housing of the king and his companions (nobles, bishops, reeves, officials and the keepers of his hounds, hawks and horses)'.[14] While these rights might be distributed variably among different landholders, they also included the three 'common burdens', common to all landholders, of army service, bridge work and fortress work. As Brooks has shown, the reservation of these three services in charters went hand-in-hand with clauses of immunity from all other royal exactions; the first example of such an immunity clause appears in a general privilege of 699 to all the churches and minsters of the kingdom of Kent, followed in 732 by its first appearance in a charter, again in Kent, relating to a specific land grant.[15] The

---

9 *EEE* 7; D. Hurst (ed.), *Opera exegetica (Beda Venerabilis)*, Corpus Christianorum series Latina 119a (Turnhout, 1969), pp. 236–392, at pp. 359–60 and 386.
10 Haddan and Stubbs, *Councils*, pp. 173–213, at p. 203.
11 Haddan and Stubbs, *Councils*, pp. 360–76, at p. 365.
12 Blair, *Church*, p. 157.
13 Blair, *Church*, pp. 156–7.
14 N. Brooks,'The development of military obligations in eighth- and ninth-century England', in P. Clemoes and K. Hughes (eds), *England before the Conquest: studies in primary sources presented to Dorothy Whitelock* (Cambridge, 1971), pp. 69–84, at p. 71.
15 Brooks,'Military obligations', pp. 75–6; S 20, S 23.

council at Gumley exempted Mercian minsters and churches in 749, and this privilege also contains the earliest specific reservation of the 'common burdens'.[16]

The crucial point here is that earlier minster estates were not initially immune from these renders; their lands were not special territories within which the king's food-rent and other rights had been diverted to the minster or bishop, but 'normal' estates, distinguished from lay estates only by the right of the holder to pass the land to an heir of his or her choosing, unencumbered by the competing claims of kin (the so-called 'bookright' accorded to 'bookland').[17] Several charters survive from the first half of the ninth century showing that even then important Mercian minsters, including Breedon-on-the-Hill, were willing to pay handsomely for immunity from various hospitality obligations owed to the king, obligations that were evidently unaffected by the more general immunities mentioned above.[18] Another example is provided by an early eighth-century letter written to Boniface by a Kentish abbess, Eangyth, who laments the oppression of her minster by 'obligations [*servitium*] to king and queen, bishops and reeves and princes and nobles'; the reference to bishops here will be taken up below.[19] Therefore ecclesiastical tribute, if it was treated like other royal dues, would not have been diverted to minsters simply by virtue of their landholdings.

A second objection to Blair's hypothesis concerns evidence for the render of church-scot to specific places, which appears from the late ninth century onwards. The early evidence for this render, which primarily comes from episcopal leases granted by the bishops of Winchester and Worcester, has recently been re-examined by Francesca Tinti.[20] Tinti highlights a distinction in the destination of church-scot between the Worcester leases of the later ninth century, in which nearby minsters are named, and the later leases of Bishop Oswald (961–92), in which the destination is not explicitly given, but which Tinti argues implies the bishop himself at Worcester, no matter how distant the lands from the cathedral;[21] she argues that these leases represent a transformation in the nature of church-scot, from a due used to support pastoral care at specific named minsters to a due (or rent) paid to the bishop as landlord of the leased estates.[22] This transformation, she suggests, occurred as tithe was introduced in the tenth century, a new due that was explicitly connected with the support of individual priests and their churches in tenth- and eleventh-century

---

16 S 92.
17 P. Wormald, 'On Þa wæpnedhealfe; kingship and royal property from Æthelwulf to Edward the Elder', in N.J. Higham and D.H. Hill (eds), *Edward the Elder 899–924* (London, 2001), pp. 264–79, at pp. 264–5.
18 S 193, S 197, S 207, S 215, S 1271. For discussion, see Kelly, *Charters of Peterborough Abbey*, pp. 209–11.
19 M. Tangl (ed.), *S. Bonifatii et Lullii epistolae*. Monumenta Germaniae historica epistolae, selectae 1 (Berlin, 1916), pp. 21–6 (No. 14).
20 F. Tinti, 'The "costs" of pastoral care: church dues in late Anglo-Saxon England', in F. Tinti (ed.), *Pastoral care in late Anglo-Saxon England* (Woodbridge, 2005), pp. 27–51.
21 The Winchester charters (S 1285 and S 1287) do not name the recipient of the church-scot to be paid from the leased lands.
22 Tinti, 'Pastoral care', pp. 42–9.

homilies.[23] Tinti's hypothesis agrees with that promoted by Blair in accepting a fundamental connection between the right to receive church-scot and the holding of land: 'church-scot seems to have been linked to the tenurial conditions of the land, from which it was to be paid, since its very origin', and the ecclesiastical administration represented by church-scot 'would have initially depended on the estates which belonged to the old minsters'.[24] According to Tinti, this explains why Bishop Oswald was able to appropriate the church-scot of minsters absorbed into the see of Worcester as a form of rent.

It is undeniable that the church-scot described by these leases was paid by landholders and calculated according to the number of hides of land they possessed.[25] However, even if the lands in the earliest leases had previously belonged to the minsters to which their church-scot was rendered, it is crucial to note that these minsters had also since been absorbed into the see of Worcester.[26] it is therefore impossible to determine from the leases alone whether church-scot had previously been connected with the minsters or with the bishop, as its collection could have been assigned to these minsters after their acquisition by the see; Oswald, in requiring the payment of church-scot to himself in the later leases, might simply have asserted a persistent episcopal right to this due. The notion that most minsters received church-scot before the late ninth century is thus not explicitly demonstrated by the leases, but is simply one argument that might invoke them in its support. An alternative argument, promoted here, views church-scot as one form of an ecclesiastical tribute specifically episcopal in nature, rendered by all landholders from the seventh century into the mid-tenth century and beyond.

This argument emphasises the clerical focus of Bede's references to ecclesiastical tributes and taxes, and thus their specific connection with the priests of the bishop's diocesan community, whether they lived at the cathedral, at minsters or at any other location. As a render intended to support the activities of the bishops, ecclesiastical tribute may well have resembled the secular renders invoked by Blair, but was plausibly administered by the bishops. Its collection was perhaps assigned to priests according to 'the places and regions of the laity which are enjoined and committed to them', as the synod at *Clofesho* put it in 747. It is certainly possible, as Blair suggests, that territories for the collection of royal renders often formed the framework for the collection of ecclesiastical tribute, 'according to the custom of the province', but these territories must be divorced at a conceptual level from the landholdings of the minsters, as argued above. Indeed, if we accept the parallel, then ecclesiastical tribute can be characterised as a form of the compulsory hospitality or 'guesting' explored by Alban Gautier, owed by landholders to the king and his men.[27] Some evidence to support this is provided by a dispute between the bishops of Hereford and

---

23 Tinti, 'Pastoral care', pp. 38–42.
24 Tinti, 'Pastoral care', pp. 49–50.
25 Tinti, 'Pastoral care', p. 42.
26 Tinti, 'Pastoral care', p. 43.
27 A. Gautier, 'Hospitality in pre-viking Anglo-Saxon England', *Early Medieval Europe*, 17 (2009), pp. 23–44, at pp. 35–43.

Worcester, resolved in 803, in which the bishop of Worcester claimed the episcopal right (*episcopali ius*) to provision of food (*pastus*) from the minsters of Beckford and Cheltenham, possessions of the bishopric of Hereford located within the diocese of Worcester; the bishop of Worcester claimed, moreover, that such provision had recently been commuted to a money payment.[28] The example shows that the form of such tributes could be flexible and open to negotiation; while many paid money or perhaps a food-rent some 'guested' the bishop instead (the obligatory nature of which was perhaps lamented by Eangyth in the quotation above). The bishop of Worcester may have been especially concerned to visit minsters within his diocese in person, as the very requirement to receive him embodied the subordination of the minster's lord to his episcopal authority.

At issue here, then, is the fundamental role of ecclesiastical tributes. Blair has suggested that these tributes, church-scot and its forebears, were 'distinctively English', and that there is 'a sense in which continental tithe and English church-scot were direct alternatives', tithe having been made compulsory in the Frankish kingdom by the late eighth century.[29] As mentioned above, Tinti has shown that the English evidence, attenuated though it is, makes an explicit connection between tithe, introduced to England in the early tenth century, and the funding of pastoral care undertaken at the churches to which it was due. Ecclesiastical tribute was certainly mentioned by Bede in the context of a bishop's spiritual obligations to the laity, but his concern was specifically those who rendered it in places that lacked any kind of local pastoral provision. Its role is thus not as distinct as that of tithe. Speculation on the obscure origins of church-scot led William Chaney to equate it with 'first-fruits', an offering supported by scriptural authority (like tithes), which, by the end of the sixth century, was often given to churches in western Europe as one of several voluntary offerings, also including wax, oil, food and money.[30] Tinti objects to this equation, noting that some tenth- and eleventh-century homilies mention both first-fruits and church-scot as separate dues.[31] However, it is quite plausible that the homilists were attempting to impose first-fruits, with its biblical rationale, on top of the existing customary render of church-scot without any knowledge of the context of the latter's seventh-century origin. Nevertheless, the argument presented here seeks instead to connect ecclesiastical tributes with renders initially due to the bishop to support his diocesan visitations. As such, these tributes are readily comparable to a Continental render, namely the 'circuit payment' (*circada*) or 'hospitality payment' (*parata*) paid by churches in Francia, often recorded for the first time in the tenth or eleventh centuries but 'perhaps surviving from the bishop's ancient public rights in parish churches'.[32]

---

28 S 1431; see also Sims-Williams, *Religion and literature*, pp. 138–9.
29 Blair, *Church*, pp. 435–6.
30 W.A. Chaney, 'Anglo-Saxon church dues: a study in historical continuity', *Church History*, 32 (1963), pp. 268–77; see also S. Wood, *The proprietary church in the medieval West* (Oxford, 2006), pp. 459–60.
31 Tinti, 'Pastoral care', pp. 48–9.
32 Wood, *Proprietary church*, p. 712.

The bishop and the lords of minsters

Tithe is discussed further in Chapter 6, but it is important here to demonstrate a persisting distinction between its role in England after its introduction in the tenth century, keyed to support for the pastoral care provided within the parish territories of churches, and the role of church-scot during the same period, which appears to have been articulated across the Midlands around the framework of the hundreds and shires, royal administrative territories established in the mid-tenth century.[33] Formalised renders had probably always represented the main form of the tribute due to bishops since the seventh century, outside the 'privileged' circle of those who offered him direct hospitality, but just as the royal guesting studied by Gautier was commuted in later centuries, so the commutation of provision owed to bishops dominated in later centuries, primarily in the form of church-scot. Later evidence for this annual grain render is variable but fairly comprehensive, and its association with hundred territories is consistent. For example, in Domesday Book church-scot is said to be due to Worcester from 'every hide of its land' in its estates in the ecclesiastical triple hundred of Oswaldslow.[34] Elsewhere we find that the church at Pershore was entitled to the church-scot from its ecclesiastical triple hundred, and the episcopal church at Aylesbury received the church-scot from eight surrounding hundreds.[35] Whereas the bishop's lands and the hundred of Oswaldslow were largely coterminous, the hundreds rendering to Pershore and Aylesbury contained lands belonging to other landholders as well; it is therefore possible to argue that the dues had been assigned to these churches on the basis of the hundred territories, and not on the basis simply of their landholdings, even if the churches themselves were not in the direct possession of the bishop.

Later evidence also supports the importance of hundredal administration of church-scot across other parts of the Midlands. For example, in the twelfth and thirteenth centuries an equivalent due, 'Scrifcorn', was collected across much of the ancient parish of the church of Leominster in Herefordshire, which was itself almost coterminous with the estate at Leominster held by Queen Edith in 1066 and, more importantly, the hundred of the same name.[36] In Northamptonshire the church on the royal hundredal estate at Fawsley was receiving church-scot from the two hundreds attached to it by the end of the eleventh century.[37] At an altogether larger scale, the cathedral church of St Mary, Lincoln, received 'Marycorn' from the landholding population of the shire of Lincoln by the mid-twelfth century.[38] All these customs appear to have been of some antiquity when they were first recorded. The collection

---

33 Molyneaux, *The formation of the English kingdom*; see pp. 141–72 for the establishment of hundreds and shires north of the Thames.
34 *DB Worcs.*, 2.80.
35 *DB Worcs.*, 9.7, *DB Bucks.*, 3a.1; see Tinti, 'Pastoral care', p. 48.
36 B. Kemp, 'Some aspects of the *parochia* of Leominster in the 12th century', in J. Blair (ed.), *Minsters and parish churches, the local church in transition 950–1200* (Oxford, 1988), pp. 83–95, at pp. 87–8.
37 M.J. Franklin, 'The secular college as a focus for Anglo-Norman piety: St Augustine's Daventry', in J. Blair (ed.), *Minsters and parish churches, the local church in transition 950–1200* (Oxford, 1988), pp. 97–105, at p. 99.
38 S. Bassett, 'Lincoln and the Anglo-Saxon see of Lindsey', *Anglo-Saxon England*, 18 (1989), pp. 1–32, at pp. 21–2.

of church-scot thus appears to have retained a connection with important churches, sometimes episcopal, but often also those at royal estate centres in receipt of the customs of one or more local hundreds.[39] On the basis of this evidence, geographically broad if locally specific, we can posit a reorganisation of church-scot across much of the Midlands in or after the mid-tenth century, when its collection was aligned with the newly established hundredal territories.

Evidence to support this pattern within the diocese of Lichfield is not earlier than the twelfth century, but can be found thereafter. In Warwickshire, when Henry I gave Stoneleigh church, at the centre of Stoneleigh hundred, to Kenilworth Priory in 1122, the grant included church-scot due to the church.[40] Elsewhere in the shire, an episcopal *actum* reporting a synodal judgement of 1160×1176 established the estates rendering a due called 'church-amber' to the church of Marton, which then belonged to the nuns of Nuneaton Priory; the estates listed were in the possession of several different landholders, and covered well over half the hundred of Marton.[41] The hundred was dominated by lay estates, interspersed with holdings of Coventry Abbey, and it is interesting to note that estates at Dunchurch, Leamington Hastings, Wolfhamcote, Napton and Ladbroke were each recorded with a priest in 1086, yet still owed church-scot to Marton in the later twelfth century.[42] These represent some of the larger estates in the hundred; other such estates, also recorded with priests in 1086 (Wolston, Bilton, Clifton-on-Dunsmore and Long Itchington), did not owe church-scot to Marton; if they ever had, the custom had since been redirected or had fallen away.[43] None of Coventry Abbey's estates paid, but it is notable that an estate at Rugby, discussed in Chapter 3 as a possible early minster site, did pay. Marton does not feature in the Domesday survey, except as the name of the hundred, but it was later in the hands of the earls of Warwick, who succeeded to the lands of the count of Meulan in Warwickshire, and he in turn had succeeded to several pre-Conquest comital estates in the shire; thus it had probably been a centre of some status, and the income of the hundred may have been attached to it.[44] It is also worth noting that the bishop's confirmation demonstrates that 'church amber' was considered to be a spirituality subject to his adjudication.

A hundredal pattern can also be observed in Shropshire: the collection of church scot, again called 'church amber', from Wrockwardine and Condover hundreds is recorded in a charter of Richard I dated 1189, confirming the gifts of Bishop Roger de

---

39 N. Neilson, *Customary rents*, Oxford Studies in Social and Legal History 2 (Oxford, 1910), pp. 193–6.
40 L.F. Salzman (ed.), *VCH Warwickshire*, vol. 6 (Oxford, 1951), pp. 229–40.
41 M.J. Franklin, *Coventry and Lichfield 1160–1182*, English episcopal *acta* 16 (Oxford, 1998), pp. 73–5 (No. 80); the estates were Rugby, Causton, Dunchurch, Thurlaston of the fee of the Earl of Warwick, Willoughby, Leamington Hastings, Hulla (in Leamington Hastings) of the fee of Abingdon, Grandborough of the fee of Walter Croc, Wolfhamcote, Flecknoe, Calcutt, Napton (Moysi's land), Ladbroke (William's land), Ladbroke of the fee of Henry Boscherville, Hodnell of Hugh son of Richard's fee, Hodnell (Gurmund's land), the third holding in Hodnell, Radbourne of the fee of Hugh of Arden, Shuckborough, and Hunningham.
42 *DB Warks.* 37.3, 39.1, 17.5, 16.31 and 18.9.
43 *DB Warks.* 12.4, 12.6, 14.2 and 42.3.
44 Salzman, *VCH Warwickshire*, vol. 6, pp. 170–3.

The bishop and the lords of minsters

Clinton to Buildwas Abbey in 1135.[45] It was suggested in Chapter 2 that the bishop's estate here related to an interest in the church of Wroxeter. Whether or not this was the case, there is consistency in the little evidence we have for this due for its collection from hundred territories across the breadth of the diocese. Moreover, while we have no evidence for the collection of church-scot at Lichfield cathedral, it is possible that the hundredal form of the territories across which it was collected influenced later claims to parochial superiority:[46] Steven Bassett has assembled evidence that the cathedral laid claim to rights in the churches of Shenstone, Walsall and Harborne during the twelfth and thirteenth centuries, all of which lay, like Lichfield, in Offlow hundred.[47] At Derby, the due was almost certainly paid to the king by the burgesses, as Domesday records that twelve thraves of wheat were to be paid on the feast of St Martin, equating to the borough's assessment of twelve carucates; as elements within royal administration, boroughs often lay outside the system of hundreds, but it is also worth noting that the two main churches of the borough were in the king's lordship.[48] It is thus plausible to argue that, as across the rest of the Midlands, so in the diocese of Lichfield, the payment of church-scot was reorganised in or after the mid-tenth century, to be collected on the basis of the newly instituted hundreds. Not all the churches in receipt of church-scot after this reorganisation were episcopal possessions; many were probably royal, and yet in some cases a continuing episcopal interest in the administration of the due can also be demonstrated. Like many minsters before them, the importance of all these churches lay in their status as clerical centres, and thus as habitations for members of the diocesan community, even if they lay outside the bishops' estates.

The arrangements for collecting church-scot after the mid-tenth century in the English Midlands do not match exactly with those made for collecting the contemporary Frankish circuit payments mentioned earlier, nor should we expect them to, as they emerged in different places and conditions. Nevertheless, they can be viewed as examples of the same kind of practice. More broadly, Susan Wood argues that all such obligations should be understood as 'extensions of the social practice of gift-giving: at one level to God or a saint, at another to bishop, abbot, or priest as a mark of respect; or perhaps as countergifts, token or substantial, for help provided, services rendered, or functions performed'.[49] This is a very broad definition of ecclesiastical obligations, which might also encompass tithe, but it highlights the significance of the relationships created through such renders. In the case of both the Frankish circuit payments and English church-scot, the focus of such relationships was the bishop, and by extension the diocesan community. As an important corollary of this argument, ecclesiastical tribute should not be understood as part of an early parochial system centred on minsters and linked to

---

45 Bassett, 'Anglo-Saxon Shrewsbury', p. 6; the relevant part of the charter is printed in Franklin, *Coventry and Lichfield 1072–1159*, pp. 10–11.
46 A late twelfth-century source records that 'wax scot, which is called plough alms' was owed to the cathedral from much of the estate at Lichfield: Greenslade, *VCH Staffordshire*, vol. 14, p. 135.
47 Bassett, 'Church and diocese in the West Midlands', p. 31 and note 57; Bassett, 'Anglo-Saxon Birmingham', p. 21 and note 86.
48 J.H. Round, '"Churchscot" in Domesday', *English Historical Review*, 5 (1890), p. 101. *DB Derbys.*, B1.
49 Wood, *Proprietary church*, p. 459.

territories associated with them; there is no certain evidence for the minster *parochiae* advocated by Blair and others, and it is more plausible in the light of the argument made here to conceive instead only of episcopal *parochiae*, essentially dioceses and any administrative parts into which they were divided. Pastoral connections were no doubt forged between many lay people and the liturgical communities at minsters, forming subordinate penumbras of the latter as discussed in Chapter 3, but there is no reason to limit these people to groups encompassed by specific minster territories.

In summary, throughout the period, from the seventh century to the eleventh, the annual render of ecclesiastical tribute at Martinmas or the direct guesting of the bishop can be understood to have created ritualised extensions of the diocesan community, incorporating the landholders of the diocese (including independent minster-and church-centred communities) through the creation of an explicitly hierarchical relationship; this spiritual lordship between them and the diocesan community's core membership was further articulated around the bishop's periodic (theoretically annual) procession through his bishopric and his regular visitations of priests based at various locations throughout his diocese. Our conception of the diocesan community now expands beyond its core clerical membership, discussed in Chapter 2: as ensouled individuals, the diocese's landholders formed a subordinate penumbra at the edges of the diocesan community, creating a dependent personhood that justified the clerics' fashioning of their own selfhood as spiritual shepherds, the essence of spiritual lordship. As ever, regular ritualising activities provide evidence of members of that community actively attempting to create and maintain these relationships.

Episcopal authority over the lords of minsters

Any argument concerning ecclesiastical tributes during the seventh, eighth and ninth centuries is necessarily speculative, given the state of the evidence, and any proposal perhaps overly hypothetical. Moreover, the evidence for collection of church-scot at minsters or churches at the centres of later hundreds demands further consideration of the relationships between the bishop and the lords of minsters in his diocese. This section demonstrates that the lords of minsters and important churches, whose own spiritual authority was rooted in their rulership of their own liturgical communities, were in turn made subject to the spiritual lordship of the diocesan bishop in a variety of ways beyond the payment of church-scot or the guesting of the bishop. Before the tenth century such relationships are difficult to discern with clarity, but a small amount of evidence can be invoked. A witness to Southumbrian bishops acting alongside prominent members of their diocesan communities is provided by the attestations attached to a decree from the Council of *Clofesho* in 803, in which each bishop is listed with a number of clergy and, notably, abbots, presumably from his diocese.[50] The five priests listed alongside Ealdwulf, bishop of Lichfield, were mentioned in Chapter 3, and the single accompanying abbot, Hygeberht, represents the retired former archbishop of the diocese. Other dioceses are more enlightening, as they include several abbots, some styled 'priest–abbots', and some of whom can be identified in other documents.

---

50   S 1431b.

For example, one of the four priest–abbots of the Leicester diocese was Beonna of *Medeshamstede* (Peterborough), and Thingferth of the Worcester diocese was probably abbot of Evesham;[51] notably, neither minster was, as far as is known, ever in the possession of the respective episcopal sees. More tentatively, Richard Gem has equated the two minsters represented by the priest–abbots of the diocese of Lindsey with the two 'congregations of the churches of those under vows' (*subnuncupatorum congregationes ecclesiae*) given alongside the abbots and abbesses of the diocese in the profession of Bishop Beorhtred in 836×839, suggesting, moreover, that these two congregations were singled out as possessions of the see.[52]

Gem's hypothesis remains speculation, but probably represents a common situation in which bishops' diocesan holdings comprised, in part, dependent minster-centred liturgical communities, as discussed in Chapter 2. Beonna plausibly represents a second phenomenon, in which the lords of independent liturgical communities were also important members of a bishop's diocesan community by virtue of being ordained as priests. In both situations we might envisage the possibility that the minsters at which they were based housed groups of priests and became collecting houses for ecclesiastical tributes. Other minster-centred liturgical communities were ruled by abbots and abbesses who remained independent of the diocesan community, but were probably associated with the see in other ways: some, like Thingferth, appear to have had some form of close relationship with their bishop, not easily definable, which ensured their attendance at Southumbrian synods; others were perhaps not so close, but were at least accustomed to render ecclesiastical tributes of some kind, perhaps through periodically guesting the bishop and his retinue. The implications of some of these different relationships can be explored further by focusing on the contours of the bishop's formal modes of authority, including his sacramental and disciplinary roles within his diocese, illuminated by later evidence. In what follows, the so-called 'royal free chapels' of the diocese of Lichfield are considered; their distinctive character was largely a phenomenon of the twelfth and later centuries, but their relationship to the bishop implies something of earlier centuries, especially when compared to a similar phenomenon in the diocese of Canterbury.

The royal free chapels of the diocese of Lichfield have not always received the attention they deserve.[53] Dorothy Styles produced the first detailed study of the Staffordshire examples, and J.H. Denton later produced a definitive 'constitutional study' of the wider English phenomenon; a third study by A.E. Jenkins focused

---

51   Keynes, *Councils of* Clofesho, p. 47; W.D. Macray (ed.), *Chronicon abbatiae de Evesham ad annum 1418* (London, 1863), p. 76.

52   R. Gem, 'The episcopal churches of Lindsey in the early 9th century', in A. Vince (ed.), *Pre-Viking Lindsey*, Lincoln Archaeological Studies 1 (Lincoln, 1993), pp. 123–7.

53   For example, D. Parsons, 'The Mercian church: archaeology and topography', in M.P. Brown and C.A. Farr (eds), *Mercia: an Anglo-Saxon kingdom in Europe* (London, 2001), pp. 50–68, has nothing to say about them. Alan Thacker suggested that the royal free chapels in the diocese of Lichfield represented the survival of early medieval secular minsters into the central Middle Ages: Thacker, 'Kings, saints and monasteries', p. 2; more recently, David Horovitz has reconsidered the possible significance of the royal free chapels: D. Horovitz, *Æthelflæd, Lady of the Mercians: the battle of Tettenhall 910AD; and other west Mercian studies* (Brewood, 2017), pp. 573–601.

particularly on their early medieval origins.[54] The label 'royal free chapel' was used only from the thirteenth century, although then with increasing frequency; beforehand, the term 'royal chapel' was applied not only to the royal free chapels of modern scholarship but also to the Chapel Royal and the king's private oratories and hospitals, nearly all of which, as non-parochial chapels on royal demesne, claimed some form of freedom from episcopal interference.[55] Moreover, by the thirteenth century, the label 'free chapel' was most commonly applied to chapels outside the jurisdiction of the local parish church, whether royal or no; crucially, these free chapels had no parochial duties of their own.[56] Nevertheless, Denton distinguishes a group of twenty-two royal chapels that were free, in the sense of having some form of exemption from episcopal interference, but, unlike the king's oratories and hospitals, also had parochial rights and responsibilities connected with surrounding populations; likewise, these royal free chapels (as they will hereafter be called, whether referring to the time before or after the term's historical introduction) were nearly always centred on a college of secular canons, ruled by a dean.[57] The diocese of Lichfield contained ten, a considerable fraction of the national total, at Stafford (St Mary's), Derby (a fusion of All Saints' and St Alkmund's), Penkridge, Tettenhall, Wolverhampton, Bridgnorth, Gnosall and Shrewsbury (St Mary's, St Michael's and St Juliana's).[58]

As a group of royal churches exempt from episcopal jurisdiction but with parochial responsibilities, these colleges formed a distinct group in the later medieval period, but Denton suggests that their distinctiveness had pre-Conquest origins and Jenkins argues for the coherence of the group of churches located in south Staffordshire from at least the tenth century.[59] They certainly fit into a wider pattern of superior churches used by kings and other members of the elite in their patronage of clerics during the tenth and eleventh centuries.[60] Eight out of the ten royal free chapels in the diocese of Lichfield are recorded in Domesday Book holding land as tenants-in-

---

54 Styles, 'King's chapels in Staffordshire'; J.H. Denton, *English royal free chapels 1100–1300. A constitutional study* (Manchester, 1970); A.E. Jenkins, 'The early medieval context of the royal free chapels of south Staffordshire', PhD thesis (University of Birmingham, 1988); see also D. Styles, 'The early history of Penkridge church', in *SHC* 1950/1, pp. 1–52.
55 Denton, *Royal free chapels*, pp. 2–8.
56 Denton, *Royal free chapels*, pp. 8–9.
57 Denton, *Royal free chapels*, pp. 12–14.
58 In addition to these eight, other royal free chapels identified by Denton were established at Bromfield (Shropshire), St Oswald's, Gloucester (Gloucestershire), St George in Oxford Castle (Oxfordshire), St Nicholas in Wallingford Castle (Oxfordshire), Waltham (Essex), St Martin-le-Grand London, Dover (Kent), Pevensey (Sussex), Staining (Sussex), Bonham (Sussex), Wimborne Minster (Dorset) and St Bryans (Cornwall); Edward I tried and failed to establish Tickhill (formerly Blyth; Nottinghamshire) and Hastings (Sussex) as royal free chapels.
59 Denton, *Royal free chapels*, p. 139; Jenkins, 'Royal free chapels', pp. 72–3 and 187–9.
60 J. Barrow, 'The clergy in English dioceses c.900–c.1066', in F. Tinti (ed.), *Pastoral care in late Anglo-Saxon England* (Woodbridge, 2005), pp. 17–26, at pp. 21–3; J. Barrow, *The clergy in the medieval world: secular clerics, their families and careers in north-western Europe, c.800–c.1200* (Cambridge, 2015), pp. 236–48, and 274–8.

chief: they are given their own sections or, in the case of the two churches at Derby (later one college), are listed in the initial borough section, and all are described either by reference to their body of clerics or by record of the church itself.[61] The two remaining churches may not yet have been founded: the college at Bridgnorth was transferred there from Quatford only in 1101, and a foundation charter for the latter is dated 1086, the year of the survey;[62] Gnosall appears as an estate held by the clerics at Penkridge, hinting that the college at the former was founded from the latter at some point after the survey.[63] The king's power over these churches was sometimes described explicitly; for example, All Saints' and St Alkmund's at Derby were 'in the king's lordship', while the clerics at Penkridge 'held from the king' and the land of Tettenhall church was 'the king's alms'. Of the other churches in the diocese given their own sections in Domesday Book, four were or became Benedictine abbeys (St Werburgh's at Chester, St Peter's at Shrewsbury, St Mary's at Burton and St Mary's at Coventry), and never claimed the freedom of royal free chapels;[64] St Alkmund's, Shrewsbury, was subsumed into Lilleshall Abbey, a house of Arrouaisian canons;[65] and St Chad's, Shrewsbury, was an episcopal college never claimed by the king. In 1086 the royal free chapels thus comprised the major part of the group of land-holding churches supporting communities of clergy, and were understood to lie directly within the king's lordship.

It is notable that, of these ten royal free chapels, only two (St Alkmund's, Derby, and Wolverhampton) were identified in Chapter 3 as possible early minster sites. The location of five of the royal free chapels at boroughs established as the focal settlements of shires in the second half of the tenth century is probably significant. Nevertheless, a number of these places (in addition to St Alkmund's and Wolverhampton) do appear to have possessed some significance from at least the tenth century: Derby and Stafford were royal strongholds ('burhs') in the early tenth century, when they were established by Lady Æthelflæd of the Mercians;[66] Penkridge was the location of a royal council in 958, and was described in a charter issued there as a 'famous place' (*locus famosus*);[67] and Shrewsbury was the site of a Mercian council in 901.[68] Beyond this, it is difficult to say much on the dates of these churches' foundations, whether precise or approximate, without archaeological evidence. Jenkins ascribes

---

61   At Derby, St Alkmund's church appears to have been given to All Saints' church, united under the title of the latter: W. Page (ed.), *VCH Derbyshire*, vol. 2 (Oxford, 1907), pp. 87–92.
62   E.W. Eyton, *Antiquities of Shropshire, volume I* (London, 1854), p. 109.
63   *DB Staffs.*, 7.18.
64   St Werburgh's was founded by Earl Hugh of Chester in 1093: Harris, *VCH Cheshire*, vol. 3, pp. 132–46; St Peter's was founded by Earl Roger of Shrewsbury in 1083: Gaydon, *VCH Shropshire*, vol. 2, pp. 30–37; Burton Abbey was founded in the early eleventh century by Wulfric: Greenslade, *VCH Staffordshire*, vol. 3, pp. 199–213; Coventry Abbey was founded by Earl Leofric and Lady Godgifu in 1043: W. Page (ed.), *VCH Warwickshire*, vol. 2 (Oxford, 1908), pp. 52–9.
65   Founded between 1145 and 1148: Gaydon, *VCH Shropshire*, vol. 2, pp. 70–80.
66   *ASC* (C) s.a.a. 913 (Stafford) and 917 (Derby).
67   S 667.
68   S 221.

Lichfield and the Lands of St Chad

most of the south Staffordshire churches to the 'Middle Saxon' period, although this is achieved by reconstructing mother parishes and assuming that they belonged to minsters of this early period, a methodology criticised earlier in this chapter and in Chapter 3.[69] There is probably some truth in her suggestion that the concentration of these distinctive churches in and around south Staffordshire is connected with the presence of large royal estates of long standing, initially a heartland of the Mercian kings.[70] However, it seems most likely that most of the royal free chapels originated in the royal endowment of churches on these lands in the tenth and eleventh centuries.

It is assumed here, following Denton, that the later status of the royal free chapels represents in part the legacy of their pre-Conquest situation, an assumption that the following discussion attempts to vindicate. Denton's study of these churches is largely concerned with the twelfth and thirteenth centuries, and makes clear that explicit assertions of the rights of royal free chapels and the nature of their exemption from episcopal jurisdiction followed on the papal reform movement of the second half of the eleventh century. Thereafter the increasing prominence of Canon Law, and an emphasis on exclusive episcopal right within the incipient conceptual space of 'spiritual' jurisdiction, inspired episcopal reorganisation, in particular the elaboration of the roles of archdeacons and rural deans. As ecclesiastical authority and jurisdiction were redefined and new prerogatives asserted where previously they had not been recognised, they came up against earlier customary relationships between the king's churches and the bishop; the royal free chapels therefore began to appear unusual only when they reacted defensively against the bishop's assertions, paradoxically conceiving a pre-existing 'exemption' from the bishop's 'right', even though the original nature of the royal free chapels, whatever that might have been, was not constructed in the light of such authority. A similar phenomenon occurred within the cathedral community, as the dean and chapter created an exempt peculiar to exclude the bishop's new officers from interfering with their customary relationships with the parishioners of the cathedral church.[71] Nevertheless, 'the defence of the royal chapels in the twelfth and thirteenth centuries was asserted as a defence of customary rights' – that is, rights asserted as of long standing.[72] Furthermore, the royal free chapels are unlikely to have *gained* many privileges 'as a result of a defensive policy in the face of increased episcopal vigilance', and thus the balance of episcopal rights and those of the royally backed chapels probably represents something of an earlier situation.[73]

The liberties later claimed by the royal free chapels are difficult to define precisely because of both the varying quality of the evidence across the different churches and the ambiguity that surrounds these liberties where they are described; often, especially during the twelfth century, it is merely stated that the churches should hold their 'land', 'customs' and 'possessions' 'liberally and freely', 'quietly', 'perpetually', 'without perturbation', 'free of all customs and exactions' and as 'one of the king's

---

69 Jenkins, *Royal free chapels*, pp. 24–87 (Chapter 2).
70 Jenkins, *Royal free chapels*, pp. 73–5.
71 Greenslade, *VCH Staffordshire*, vol. 3, pp. 143–5; Greenslade, *VCH Staffordshire*, vol. 14, pp. 154–5.
72 Denton, *Royal free chapels*, p. 141.
73 Denton, *Royal free chapels*, p. 136.

own chapels, which pertained to the crown'.[74] Thirteenth-century sources are sometimes more specific, and provide enough information to discern a core balance of rights between royal free chapels on the one hand and bishop on the other. Denton considers that the right of 'collation' or free appointment – belonging to the lord of the royal free chapel (either the king or his donee) in respect of the dean, and to the dean in respect of the canons – was 'the central right' of the royal free chapels' claims to freedom, and that the reservation of such right also implied freedom from the bishop's claims to payments and renders ('customs and exactions', 'procurations'), ancient or more recent, in his diocese.[75] From the mid-twelfth century the emerging system of advowson defined the 'institution' of a priest – putting him into his office – as a spiritual concern, performed by the bishop, while lay lords of churches were allowed only to choose ('present') the candidate. The king's right of collation in the royal free chapels evoked an earlier situation when these two actions had not yet been distilled out of the unitary act of appointment. Conversely, the bishop continued to insist on his right to honourable reception at the royal free chapels, and to celebrate orders, to preach in the churches, to confirm the young, to ordain clerics presented to him by the dean and to bless and provide chrism (oils used for anointing and consecration).[76]

A useful comparison can be made here with a group of important churches with parochial functions in the diocese of Christ Church, Canterbury, the archiepiscopal see, on which a late eleventh-century source known as the Domesday Monachorum provides valuable information.[77] One of several lists in this document identifies fourteen mother churches that owed certain renders to Christ Church cathedral before the arrival of Archbishop Lanfranc in 1070; Lanfranc reformed this arrangement, and so it is described as the 'old institution'.[78] Another list gives groups of daughter churches that were dependent on nine of these mother churches, as well as on two further mother churches that do not appear in the list of churches of the 'old institution' and one last mother church for which the name is missing.[79] The renders of the 'old institution' to the bishop comprised food-rents and payments for wine and chrism (in multiples of 7d for oil and 6d for wine), to be delivered at Easter, probably on Maundy

---

74 Denton, *Royal free chapels*, pp. 41–2 and 139.
75 Denton, *Royal free chapels*, pp. 136–7; see also at pp. 49 and 67 for examples from Bromfield and Waltham Holy Cross.
76 Denton, *Royal free chapels*, pp. 43–4 and 109; see also at pp. 155–6 (Appendix 2) for an important agreement between the bishop and the dean of Wolverhampton, and pp. 92–114 for a conflict between the bishops and the colleges that resulted in a similar agreement.
77 A translation of the lists is provided in T. Tatton-Brown, 'The churches of Canterbury diocese in the 11th century', in J. Blair (ed.), *Minsters and parish churches, the local church in transition 950–1200* (Oxford, 1988), pp. 105–18.
78 The fourteen mother churches were: Milton, Maidstone, Charing, Wye, Teynham, Wingham, Eastry, Lyminge, Appledore, Dover, Folkestone, two Broughtons and Ruckinge.
79 The two extra mother churches were Newington and Lympne; Tim Tatton-Brown ('Churches of Canterbury diocese', pp. 107 and 115) has suggested that the unidentified church is Eastry, although the daughter churches do not form a group near this church, and are in fact scattered across the diocese.

Lichfield and the Lands of St Chad

Thursday when the oils were blessed, and, in three cases, an additional payment of 600d to be made at Pentecost. Frank Barlow suggests that the food renders from these mother churches, which he calls 'old minsters', were contributions to the archbishop's Maundy gifts to the poor, 'that normally the old minsters collected chrism and wine from the archbishop for distribution among their daughter churches, and that, although they seem to have made payments to Canterbury on behalf of these, the arrangement was lucrative to the minsters'.[80] Nicholas Brooks asserts that this system was 'a jealously maintained relic of an age when the Kentish "monasteries" were true baptismal churches, taking a dominant role in the pastoral work of the diocese', along the lines of early medieval continental baptismal churches found in Gaul and Italy.[81] More recently, Blair has extended this interpretation, suggesting that this system was exclusive to Kent and that the eleventh-century chrism payments provide 'a faint aftertaste of the distinctly Italian flavour of Canterbury under Augustine'.[82]

Comparison with the royal free chapels indicates that the arrangement was less distinctive than this. Like the royal free chapels, the 'old institution' churches had varied origins, but most were located on old royal estates and some had been minsters founded in the seventh, eighth and ninth centuries; unlike the royal free chapels, many of them had since been passed into other hands, most of them to the archbishop.[83] Significantly, the only church of the 'old institution' to remain in direct royal lordship by the time the Domesday Monachorum was produced, St Martin's of Dover, later became a royal free chapel.[84] Both the Domesday Monachorum and the rights successfully claimed by later bishops of Coventry and Lichfield over the royal free chapels emphasise the blessing and provision of chrism, an important element of the bishop's sacramental powers. The arrangement in the Domesday Monachorum implies that the mother churches of the 'old institution' distributed chrism to their daughter churches.[85] We have no direct evidence that the royal free chapels in the diocese of Lichfield supplied chrism to the dependent chapels in their parishes (or 'deaneries', as they were called), but the fact that its supply was negotiated with the bishop indicates that it was an important issue: as with the mother churches of the 'old institution', the bishop's role as dispenser of the sacraments was not denied by the royal free chapels, but it might plausibly have been mediated via the colleges, thus barring direct episcopal access to their dependent chapels.

Pentecostal oblations can also be productively compared between the two groups

---

80   F. Barlow, *The English Church 1000–1066* (London, 1963), pp. 181–2.
81   Brooks, *Early history of the church of Canterbury*, p. 184.
82   Blair, *Church*, p. 69. Perhaps unsurprisingly, an alternative interpretation has been offered by Eric Cambridge and David Rollason (Cambridge and Rollason, 'Pastoral organisation of the Anglo-Saxon church', pp. 101–2).
83   Tatton-Brown, 'Churches of Canterbury diocese', p. 108.
84   Many of the daughter churches given for St Martin's, Dover, in the Domesday Monachorum were still part of its deanery in the 1291 papal taxation records: see Denton, *Royal free chapels*, p. 64.
85   The daughter churches of the 'old institution' do not appear in Lanfranc's extended list of churches representing his reorganisation.

of churches. An agreement in 1224 between the bishop of Coventry and Lichfield and the dean of Wolverhampton reserved to the bishop the customary oblations on the occasion of the Pentecostal procession;[86] among the churches of the 'old institution' list in the Domesday Monachorum 600d is payable by three to the bishop at Pentecost.[87] Such oblations were commonly required from the parishioners and clergy of daughter churches by their mother church, and were often rendered to a cathedral from across its diocese; later medieval evidence exists for such payments from the dioceses of Chichester, Worcester and Lichfield.[88] In the Lichfield diocese these oblations were known as 'Chad-farthings' by the thirteenth century, explicitly connecting them to the patronage of the diocesan saint.[89] Essentially, like the earlier ecclesiastical tributes, these payments expressed the spiritual lordship of the bishop as head of the diocesan community, and their reservation from the royal free chapels can be understood as a desire for acknowledgement of that lordship from churches that acted in other ways as independent spiritual lords. In Kent, the three mother churches owing Pentecostal payments, Milton, Dover and Folkestone, were not in the hands of the bishop when the 'old institution' was in operation, whereas the majority of the others had been acquired by the see over the preceding centuries.[90] Thus the archbishop would likewise appear to have desired a Pentecostal payment in acknowledgement of his spiritual lordship over these churches; in contrast, those churches held directly by the see were no longer independent spiritual lords, and their submission to the lordship of Christ Church was perhaps expressed annually by the participation of their clergy and parishioners in the Pentecostal procession at Canterbury, and their making of oblations there.

The concerns of the bishops of Coventry and Lichfield over their relationships with the royal free chapels of their diocese in the twelfth and thirteenth centuries are thus mutually comparable with the late eleventh-century concerns of the archbishop of Canterbury over the mother churches of his diocese. Both episodes post-date the period considered by this book, but both also hint at the contours of episcopal relationships with earlier independent minster-centred communities, for which little contemporary evidence survives. Bishops persisted in claiming a form of spiritual

---

86 The agreement is printed in Denton, *Royal free chapels*, pp. 155–6 (Appendix 2); see also at pp. 43–4.
87 The date of payment is only recorded for the first church in the list, Milton, but can be plausibly extrapolated to the other two churches from which the payment was due; Barlow, *English Church*, p. 180, focuses on the payment due from St Augustine's on Maundy Thursday, plausibly identifying it as representing Maundy hearth-pennies, but appears to have missed the reference to Pentecost in the 'old institution' list.
88 R. Phillimore, *The ecclesiastical law of the Church of England* (London, 1873), vol. 2, pp. 1598–9.
89 Greenslade, *VCH Staffordshire*, vol. 3, p. 150.
90 The 'new institution', whereby the customs of the mother churches were commuted to money payments, singles out Dover and Folkestone with amounts much larger than those paid by the other churches (Dover, 55s; Folkestone, 50s; 50s = 600d); the new institution was operational by the time the Domesday Book was produced, in which both churches were explicitly said to render 55s to the archbishop (*DB Kent*, P,15; 5,128), while by this time Milton had recently been given to St Augustine's, and was therefore no longer an independent spiritual lord.

Lichfield and the Lands of St Chad

lordship over the clergy in their diocesan communities that emphasised their sacramental and disciplinary roles: supplying chrism, ordaining clergy, and baptising, consecrating, preaching and correcting in their churches. This role compares closely to that outlined in the canons of the Council of *Clofesho* in 747, which present the bishop as the ultimate guarantor (and example) of correct religious life in his diocese, and encourage and empower him to visit the various parts of his diocese each year, inspecting the minsters within it in order to teach and correct error, examine candidates for ordination and monastic tonsure, ensure that all have access to the ministrations of a priest, monitor and correct priests in the undertaking of their office and institute the careful and reverent performance of the liturgy there.[91] The canons are not overly prescriptive, leaving scope for individual bishops to impose customs to accomplish them as he saw fit, but they are comprehensive, and the similarities to the episcopal rights claimed in the royal free chapels are striking enough to support the notion that the broad contours of this spiritual lordship continued to inform the self-image of bishops in the diocese of Lichfield.

The limits of the bishop's authority left space for a spiritual lordship claimed by the lords of liturgical communities, whose roles were concerned with the general governance and guidance of those communities, the management of their associated property and, in particular, the appointment of clergy to roles within them. The lord of the royal free chapels, the king, was a layman, but such was not unusual between the eighth and eleventh centuries. While the earliest minsters were usually established under the lordship of abbots and abbesses, some of them subsequently passed into the hands of lay people, and references to this are found from the mid-eighth century; Susan Wood has demonstrated that this usually represented the lords of minsters exercising their 'bookright' to pass them on to heirs of their own choosing.[92] The royal free chapels are thus good examples of the kind of liturgical communities that probably often provoked episcopal anxiety, whose membership included clergy (the dean and canons of the royal free chapels) but whose lords, whether religious or lay, were not themselves ordained, and were thus independent of claims made by the bishop over the core clerical members of the diocesan community. As landholders these lords were part of that subordinate penumbra at the edge of the diocesan community over which a bishop and his clergy might demand acknowledgements of their spiritual lordship, but the lordship claimed by these lords over their own congregations appears frequently to have caught episcopal attention and provoked responses intended to institute ritualising expressions of spiritual hierarchy: these perhaps included regular visitation, earlier versions of the chrism payments and Pentecostal oblations later demanded by Lichfield and Canterbury, and other acknowledgements now lost to us. Such anxieties perhaps also prompted bishops from the eighth century onwards to attempt to acquire independent liturgical communities in their dioceses, as discussed in Chapter 2, bringing them within the core diocesan community and integrating them more firmly into its hierarchies.

---

91   Haddan and Stubbs, *Councils*, pp. 362–76.
92   Wood, *Proprietary church*, pp. 239–44.

Conclusions

There is still a tendency to define episcopal authority in England prior to the papal reform movement of the later eleventh century in negative terms, characterised by a lack of proper governance. Frank Barlow thought that the bishops of the earlier eleventh century were 'hindered by a proprietary pattern ... [and] handicapped by the scarcity of institutions or agents of government'.[93] John Blair is sceptical of the efficacy of the *Clofesho* canons agreed three centuries earlier, citing a documented situation in which a bishop was involved in resolving the succession of a minster's lord and contending that 'the bishop's role looks tenuous'; while his right to involvement was acknowledged, he could not 'do more than protest or persuade'.[94] This chapter does not seek to suggest that English bishops of this period enjoyed the governmental abilities of their twelfth- and thirteenth-century successors, but it does mean to demand more recognition for protestation and persuasion as valid approaches to the imposition and negotiation of spiritual lordship, and to emphasise the importance of ritualised acknowledgements in maintaining such lordship. Moreover, after the initial emergence of the English ecclesiastical community and individual diocesan communities in the later seventh century, the broad shape of this lordship and the mechanisms of its assertion appear to have remained broadly similar across four centuries.

Nevertheless, this constancy was a symptom of dynamic equilibrium rather than of stability. The relationships between bishops and those who might hinder or threaten their spiritual lordship probably ebbed and flowed considerably. We might envisage a range of possible relationships between bishops and the lords of independent liturgical communities during the seventh, eighth and ninth centuries. At one end of this range the lord of one or more liturgical communities might resist the bishop's authority to a considerable degree, perhaps aided by appeals to royal or papal support and protection, governing resident clerics without too much oversight; elsewhere in England good examples are provided by the conflicts between successive Mercian royals and archbishops of Canterbury in the late eighth and early ninth centuries. At the other end of the range, small liturgical communities probably possessed neither the ability nor perhaps the will to resist the bishop's spiritual lordship, their resident clergy (often small in number) being easily governed by the bishop; the lords of such communities, perhaps members of local and regional elite families, may often have been persuaded to bequeath their minsters to bishops, thus contributing to the growth of episcopal holdings in the eighth and ninth centuries discussed in Chapter 2. Between these two poles, no doubt, lay many communities whose lords generally accepted the bishop's spiritual lordship while maintaining an acceptable degree of independence in the day-to-day management of the religious life of their minsters, some perhaps actively working alongside the bishop in promoting the interests of the diocesan community.

By the tenth and eleventh centuries we see something of a polarisation in the diocese of Lichfield and across much of the rest of England. Those minsters not acquired by the episcopal see appear to have emerged largely as parish churches

---

93 Barlow, *English Church*, p. 245.
94 Blair, *Church*, p. 114.

by the eleventh and twelfth centuries, joining many others founded in that period (see Chapter 6), most of which were served by individual priests. Alongside these were superior churches such as the royal free chapels, served by clerical communities, many, if not all, associated with royal landholdings; the monasteries at Burton-upon-Trent and Coventry were the only foundations in the diocese prompted by the Benedictine reform movement of the later tenth and early eleventh centuries, established respectively by Wulfric Spot and by Earl Leofric and his wife Godgifu. The bishop's relationships with these two kinds of church plausibly resembled those proposed above at either end of the range of independent liturgical communities. Between these extremes we might consider the mother churches that were assigned ecclesiastical tributes from hundredal territories in and after the mid-tenth century. Some were probably episcopal churches, such as Lichfield, but others were churches on royal estates, such as Wroxeter. In one sense they embody the very close integration of English ecclesiastical and regnal communities during this period: church-scot, argued here to represent an episcopal due, might be funnelled to churches on royal lands supporting clerical groups that the bishop could confidently hope to govern and that might have formed important administrative nodes of episcopal governance at this time, paralleling regnal developments. By the mid-tenth century the management of the English Church had become a collaborative project between king and bishops.[95]

---

95 Giandrea, *Episcopal culture in late Anglo-Saxon England*, pp. 35–69.

Chapter 5

The people

Thus far the communities introduced and explored in this book have been primarily religious in character, excepting only the regnal communities discussed in Chapter 1. However, as argued there, in order to develop a broader understanding of these religious communities they must be placed within the contexts of their interrelations and connections with other communities. This chapter introduces two further types of community, neither of which form the primary focus of this study, but both of which must be considered alongside the communities discussed in previous chapters. First, 'agricultural communities' are considered in the contexts of the landscapes in which they emerged and upon which they worked. These communities represent the different modes of organisation by which people farmed the lands of the diocese, and specifically the repetitive collective activities that brought people together throughout the turn of the agricultural year; they encompassed the majority of the population of the diocese throughout the period, although the nature of the evidence requires that we discuss them in only the most general of terms. More space in what follows is given to 'domainal communities', representing groups that were articulated around issues of landholding, possession and territorial lordship. Of course, the two kinds of community were nearly always tightly entangled, but they can be fruitfully separated for analytical purposes.

It has long been recognised that the material character of any landscape – its fields, pastures, settlements and woodlands – has many implications for our understanding of the people who lived and worked on it. The landscape itself thus forms the major source of evidence for an exploration of agricultural communities, which occupies the first part of this chapter. Recent scholarship has identified the seventh and eighth centuries with the beginnings of an agricultural expansion across England that has important implications for these communities, and is considered here through the importance of the distribution of different kinds of soil to the organisation of early medieval farming. The chapter then moves on to review some of the more pertinent scholarship on landholding in early medieval England, before undertaking an analysis of the place-names of the diocese that illuminates something of the dynamics of landholding practices during the period, in particular the ways in which they relied on collective action at local assemblies. A final discussion integrates both parts of the chapter by placing the place-names explored here within the broader context of the historic landscape of the diocese.

Agricultural communities and the historic landscape

Our understanding of the early medieval landscape of England begins with the fundamental role of mixed farming throughout the period and beyond. Essentially, arable farming – largely the production of various kinds of cereal – depended on the maintenance of livestock – sheep, cattle, pigs – whose manure brought nutrients to the cropland from various kinds of grazing, such as heaths and moors, crop stubble in the fields, floodplain marshlands and managed hay meadows. Our knowledge has recently gained focus thanks to an increasing array of archaeological, archaeobotanical and palynological investigations. A recent synthesis of this evidence by Mark McKerracher, based on a study region in the southern Midlands and East Anglia, gives detailed shape to an emerging consensus regarding the dynamics of agricultural productivity following the end of Roman rule in Britain in the early fifth century: the removal of imperial exploitation allowed a period of economic relaxation, until, in what he characterises as a significant transformation, 'arable farming expanded from the seventh century onwards, leading to greater harvests and hence more mills, granaries, ovens and charred plant remains in the archaeological record'.[1] That such expansion also occurred outside the confines of McKerracher's study region is implied by widespread palynological studies, indicating an increase in arable cultivation beginning in a period spanning the seventh to ninth centuries, the so-called 'long eighth century'.[2] This picture resonates with earlier scholarship that proposed an early medieval colonisation of heavier clay soils enabled by the gradual adoption of the heavy mouldboard plough, which could cut through and turn such soils, and accomplished by increasing cultivation of free-threshing wheat, which is better suited to the conditions offered by them.[3] However, by studying the relative proportions of cereal remains at different sites across a range of ecologies within his study region, McKerracher demonstrates that cereal production was also increased 'by "fine-tuning" other crop choices [such as barley, rye and oats] in response to local environmental conditions, whether moist and fertile or dry, poor and acidic'.[4] He also argues, albeit more cautiously, for an accompanying increase in the numbers of livestock during this period.[5] Thus McKerracher persuasively supports a more widespread agricultural expansion across England (and further afield), a model with important implications for the diocese of Lichfield, which is largely bereft of fertile clay soils.

Nevertheless, such soils can be found in some of the eastern parts of the diocese, notably in the Warwickshire 'Feldon' district and around the valleys of the Trent, Tame, Dove and Derwent rivers, and the only complete early medieval settlement excavated within the bounds of the diocese is located in such an area, at Catholme, on the edge of a gravel terrace above the Trent.[6] The settlement appears to have been established around the early seventh century, and continued in occupation until at least the late ninth century;[7] throughout this time an evolving complex of ditches defined and

---

1 M. McKerracher, *Farming transformed in Anglo-Saxon England: agriculture in the long eighth century* (Oxford, 2018), p. 93.
2 McKerracher, *Farming transformed*, pp. 80–3.
3 T. Williamson, *Shaping medieval landscapes: settlement, society, environment* (Macclesfield, 2003), pp. 118–22; D. Banham and R. Faith, *Anglo-Saxon farms and farming* (Oxford, 2014), pp. 44–50.
4 McKerracher, *Farming transformed*, p. 106.
5 McKerracher, *Farming transformed*, pp. 49–68.
6 McKerracher, *Farming transformed*, p. 123, refers to the settlement in support of seventh-century arable expansion outside his study region.
7 S. Losco-Bradley and G. Kinsley, *Catholme: an Anglo-Saxon settlement on the Trent gravels in Staffordshire* (Nottingham, 2002), pp. 120–3.

distinguished the enclosed plots of houses and ancillary buildings from trackways and animal enclosures.[8] The site fits well within a set of examples highlighted by McKerracher, which he calls 'paddock and droveway complexes', and which he explains as the result of a tendency to overwinter livestock within settlements rather than, as previously, in woodland or on wood pasture supported by hitherto marginal clay soils; such sources of winter fodder were under pressure from expanding arable cultivation but could be replaced with hay cropped from managed river meadows.[9] Indeed, this may explain why the settlement at Catholme was located in the midst of the river's alluvial floodplain: its wet meadowland soils were well suited to the growing of hay. The settlement was encompassed within the township territory farmed in the later medieval period from the village of Barton-under-Needwood, which was located to the west on the edge of a local spread of fertile clay soils; the settlements may have coexisted as two parts of a single agricultural organisation, or perhaps Barton in some sense replaced the settlement at Catholme. The place-name derives from *bær-tun*, 'barley farm', which later indicated a demesne farm or outlying grange, and the location of the township in the parish of Tatenhill may indicate the ultimate control of what was probably an early minster (as discussed in Chapter 3).[10] Again, this resonates with McKerracher's broader argument, in which he proposes that the expansion in arable cultivation was connected with the increasing influences of lords, both lay and ecclesiastical, in the organisation of the countryside.[11]

McKerracher's study can be placed within a broader historiography concerned with the expansion and development of English agricultural landscapes throughout the medieval period, but which otherwise often approaches its subject by projecting backwards from later centuries. Attention has focused on a distinction between two 'types' of countryside, 'champion' and 'woodland', which had emerged by the thirteenth century. Recently summarised by Tom Williamson, champion countryside

> possessed a settlement pattern of nucleated villages whose inhabitants practised highly communal forms of agriculture. The holdings of individual farmers – and usually the demesnes, or home farms, of manorial lords – lay intermingled as a multiplicity of small unhedged strips which were usually scattered evenly through two or three extensive open fields.[12]

In contrast, woodland countryside encompassed landscapes in which 'settlement was less nucleated in character and where villages existed they did so alongside other forms of habitation – hamlets, loose agglomerations of dwellings around small greens or extensive commons, and isolated farms standing in the midst of their own

---

8   Losco-Bradley and Kinsley, *Catholme*, pp. 115–20.
9   McKerracher, *Farming transformed*, pp. 33–48.
10 Horovitz, *Place-names*, p. 104.
11 McKerracher, *Farming transformed*, pp. 124–5.
12 T. Williamson, *Environment, society and landscape in early medieval England: time and topography* (Woodbridge, 2013), p. 125.

fields'.[13] The survival of many of the extensive open fields of champion countryside into the late eighteenth century, when most were enclosed under parliamentary acts, ensured that this medieval distinction remained part of the landscape character into recent times and is still partially visible to this day. The different landscapes have been mapped many times, most recently by Brian Roberts and Stuart Wrathmell, whose plot of relative 'settlement dispersion' is based on later nineteenth-century Ordnance Survey maps and confirms that champion countryside was largely confined to a band running from Northumberland, County Durham and eastern Yorkshire through the eastern Midlands to the south coast of Dorset; woodland countryside lay to either side.[14] The diocese of Lichfield was largely situated within the western region of woodland countryside, with only those areas of fertile clays – parts of the Trent, Tame, Dove and Derwent valleys and the Warwickshire Feldon – encroaching onto the western edge of the champion belt.

The historiography of scholarship devoted to comprehending and explaining the early medieval roots of this distinction is long, and this is not the place to revisit it.[15] It is, however, important to emphasise that the classic 'Midland system' of nucleated villages and extensive open fields in the champion region was a particularly discrete form of landscape that existed alongside a much more varied range of landscapes subsumed within the umbrella of woodland countryside. It was once thought that the champion landscape was a later medieval innovation that emerged from a homogenous background of dispersed settlements set in 'ancient' woodland landscapes, but this has been challenged by more recent scholarship. In their study of the medieval landscape of Whittlewood, an area displaying characteristics of woodland countryside within the champion belt, Richard Jones and Mark Page have demonstrated that dispersed farmsteads and hamlets were being founded at the same time as larger nucleated settlements.[16] This is crucial, as it demonstrates that the development of both champion and woodland landscapes can be understood as parts of the same extended process. Indeed, this is also implicit in the fact that open fields with their intermingled holdings were not limited to the champion regions, although they tended to more 'irregular' forms in woodland regions, often encompassing a smaller proportion of the landscape and representing only one element in a diversity of agricultural forms that also included enclosures, woodlands and various kinds of common pasture. Within the diocese of Lichfield David Hall has identified a number of different types of open field, from one-field systems ('town fields') in the west and north through various permutations of irregular fields to more regular two- and three-field systems on the fertile soils in the centre and east.[17]

---

13 Williamson, *Environment, society and landscape*, p. 125.
14 B.K. Roberts and S. Wrathmell, *An atlas of rural settlement in England* (London, 2000).
15 A thorough review can be found in Williamson, *Shaping medieval landscapes*, pp. 1–21.
16 R. Jones and M. Page, *Medieval villages in an English landscape: beginnings and ends* (Macclesfield, 2006); see also M. Page and R. Jones, 'Stability and instability in medieval village plans: case studies in Whittlewood', in M. Gardiner and S. Rippon (eds), *Medieval landscapes: landscape history after Hoskins, volume 2* (Macclesfield, 2007), pp. 139–52.
17 D. Hall, *The open fields of England* (Oxford, 2014), pp. 233–5, 242–5, 307–9, 314–18 and 330–3.

The people

In this book, champion and woodland landscapes are understood as the later medieval culmination of the expansion initiated in the long eighth century. The emergence of open fields and managed pastures within this evolution implies much about the nature of the agricultural communities that drove it. Following earlier scholars, Tom Williamson has associated open fields with plough-sharing (or 'co-aration'), in which the farmers of several holdings shared a plough because 'both the plough itself and the animals that pulled it together constituted … expensive pieces of equipment which were only used at limited times of the year';[18] the lands of these farmers were intermingled in order to ensure 'that the holdings of those who contributed shares to the common plough were distributed in an equitable manner across land of varying aspect and drainage potential, and lying at varying distances from the village'.[19] It is in such activities that we can recognise one form of agricultural community, defined by arrangements repeated every year and no doubt ritualised to varying extents, by which groups of farmers organised the passage of the plough and allotted the ploughed lands among themselves. Such communities might encompass a large number of farmers within a township centred on a nucleated village in the champion region, but in woodland regions might include only two or three, depending on the extent of open-field land and the size of the settlement from which it was farmed. Despite the importance of arable farming here, these groups must be distinguished from a second kind of agricultural community, formed from groups of farmers managing areas of common pasture, although both kinds were necessarily extensively entangled. In a champion township of the eastern Midlands membership of the two communities might overlap perfectly, those who organised the ploughing also arranging the grazing of the stubble and the allotment of shares in hay meadows. But other permutations were possible, especially in woodland regions, where, for example, several groups of plough-sharers might come together to manage the common pasturage of a town field or large heaths or moors.

Williamson views the distinctions between champion and woodland landscapes as the results of the impact of different hydrological, topographical and climatic factors on the activities of farmers as they gradually expanded the extent of arable cultivation over generations. He associates the relative dispersion of settlement (whether discretely clustered in villages or more dispersed more evenly across a range of settlement types) with the local availability of water, determined ultimately by the geological provision of subterranean aquifers accessed through wells and springs; settlements clustered in discrete nucleations only when the geology prevented extensive access to such water sources across the landscape.[20] In champion countryside supplies of ground water were limited to specific locations, concentrated by the distinctive geology along springlines or on valley floors, encouraging the growth of clustered villages; in woodland regions access to ground water was generally more

---

18 Williamson, *Environment, society and landscape*, p. 196. For earlier consideration of the importance of plough-sharing, see F. Seebohm, *The English village community* (London, 1890), and C.S. Orwin and C.S. Orwin, *The open fields* (Oxford, 1938).
19 Williamson, *Environment, society and landscape*, p. 197.
20 Williamson, *Environment, society and landscape*, pp. 184–95.

extensively available, allowing a greater dispersion of settlement. This is an important argument, as it contradicts an earlier consensus around a process of 'nucleation' from a pre-existing pattern of dispersed settlement in the champion region; instead, he argues, the phenomenon is better understood as the product of settlement expansion at a more limited number of sites than was possible in woodland regions.[21]

Williamson explains the comparative regularity and dominance of open fields in the champion region by the prevalence there of two kinds of soil: large blocks of difficult yet fertile clay and mudstone soils, which could be ploughed only when not too wet, thus limiting cultivation to a short ploughing window in the dry days of spring;[22] and light, freely draining soils formed in chalk, limestone and sands, which required the regular folding of sheep in some numbers, whose manure maintained soil fertility.[23] When combined with the discrete clustering of settlements into villages in these areas, both kinds of soil encouraged a greater degree of cooperation and collective effort among farmers than was necessary elsewhere, whether in the efficient mobilisation and use of the plough and its team or the collective management of hay meadows or a common herd of sheep. Outside of these champion regions, the more widespread availability of ground water encouraged a more dispersed settlement pattern, while soils were either more easily cultivated or too wet and/or acidic to encourage any concerted attempt, resulting in a greater variety of field systems intermingled with different kinds of pasture and woodland to support livestock. Thus the development of distinctive landscapes across England during the medieval period can be understood through the activities of the agricultural communities, of both plough and pasture, that inhabited them; communities that, from perhaps the seventh century, were driven to increase their arable productivity.

A detailed study of the interplay of medieval field systems and local soil types and hydrology in the diocese of Lichfield is beyond the scope of this book, although it would be a useful addition to the historiography of the subject, which tends to focus on landscapes further east.[24] Nevertheless, it is worth making some initial points on the distribution of soils throughout the diocese, and a map illustrating various useful distinctions based on the discussion above has been prepared from the data collected by the Soil Survey of England and Wales (see Figure 11). The significant

---

21 Williamson, *Environment, society and landscape*, pp. 162–5.
22 Williamson, *Environment, society and landscape*, pp. 196–201.
23 Williamson, *Environment, society and landscape*, pp. 204–5.
24 Notable contributions to an understanding of the historic landscapes of the north-western Midlands, in whole or in part, are provided by: Gelling, *The West Midlands*, pp. 172–83; Hall, *Open fields of England*; N.J. Higham, 'Patterns of settlement in medieval Cheshire: an insight into dispersed settlement', *Annual Report of the Medieval Settlement Research Group*, 2 (1987), pp. 9–10; Higham, *Origins*, pp. 202–7; A.D.M. Phillips and C.B. Phillips (eds), *A new historical atlas of Cheshire* (Chester, 2002), pp. 22–35; A.D.M. Phillips and C.B. Phillips (eds), *An historical atlas of Staffordshire* (Manchester, 2011), pp. 28–47; D. Sylvester, *The rural landscape of the Welsh borderland: a study in historical geography* (London, 1969); B.K. Roberts, 'Field systems of the West Midlands', in A.R.H. Baker and R.A. Butlin (eds), *Studies of field systems in the British Isles* (Cambridge, 1973), pp. 188–231.

expansion of arable cultivation across heavier clay soils using the heavy plough was less viable in much of the north-western Midlands than in areas further east. Outside of the Jurassic clays of the Feldon district, most of the heavier clay soils in the diocese of Lichfield derive from a glacial till called Reddish Till, which notably blankets the Shropshire and Cheshire Plains, but is also found on the South Staffordshire Plateau and across parts of the Midland Gap in mid-Staffordshire;[25] these soils are largely less fertile than similar soils in the eastern Midlands, which are derived from glacial till (Chalky Till) and from Jurassic and Cretaceous clays, because the wetter climate in the north-west Midlands tends to leach them of nutrients and lime.[26] Slightly better possibilities for arable expansion were offered by the clayey soils derived from Permo-Triassic mudstones, located in the Midland Gap adjacent to the Trent, Tame, Sow and Severn rivers, which do not become as waterlogged as the Reddish Till soils.[27] When not opened to tillage, clayey soils in the region supported a range of grassland and woodland habitats, and always offered a range of prospects for pasturage, although the wetter soils were likely to suffer more under the hooves of livestock.

A more reliable arable prospect was offered by the better-drained brown earths and sands of the diocese, which, although vulnerable to leaching, were drier and easier to work: those across the Midland Gap, derived from underlying Permo-Triassic sandstones;[28] those in the Shropshire and Cheshire Plains, developed out of glaciofluvial moraines;[29] and those associated with the distinctive Permo-Triassic sandstone outcrop of the Mid-Cheshire Ridge.[30] These did not necessarily require use of the heavy plough for effective cultivation, and so are likely to have been persistently farmed across many centuries. Arable expansion in these areas is often likely to have involved more intensive use of existing farmed landscapes and occupation of any remaining unoccupied niches in the local ecology; nevertheless, if more fertile – albeit more difficult – clay soils were opened to tillage nearby, brown earths and sands might also remain attractive as drier pastures, less vulnerable to the passage of livestock especially during winter. The brown earths developed in the Aeolian drift over the limestone of the Peak District were also attractive to farmers, although

---

25 J.M. Ragg, G.R. Beard, H. George, F.W. Heaven, J.M. Hollis, R.J.A. Jones, R.C. Palmer, M.J. Reeve, J.D. Robson and W.A.D. Whitfield, *Soils and their use in Midland and western England* (Harpenden, 1984), pp. 132–7 and 287–90 (Clifton and Salop Associations, derived from Reddish Till); pp. 156–9 and 190–3 (Evesham 2 and Denchworth Associations, derived from Jurassic clays).

26 T. Williamson, 'The distribution of "Woodland" and "Champion" landscapes in medieval England', in M. Gardiner and S. Rippon (eds), *Medieval landscapes: landscape history after Hoskins, volume 2* (Macclesfield, 2007), pp. 89–104, at p. 97; Williamson suggests that this occurs at precipitation levels above *c.*740mm per annum.

27 Ragg *et al.*, *Soils and their use*, pp. 319–23 (Whimple 3 Association).

28 Ragg *et al.*, *Soils and their use*, pp. 112–16, 120–4 and 323–7 (Bridgnorth, Bromsgrove and Wick 1 Associations).

29 Ragg *et al.*, *Soils and their use*, pp. 177–8, 248–52 and 323–7 (Ellerbeck, Newport 1 and Wick 1 Associations).

30 Ragg *et al.*, *Soils and their use*, pp. 112–16, 120–4 and 248–52 (Bridgnorth, Bromsgrove and Newport 1 Associations).

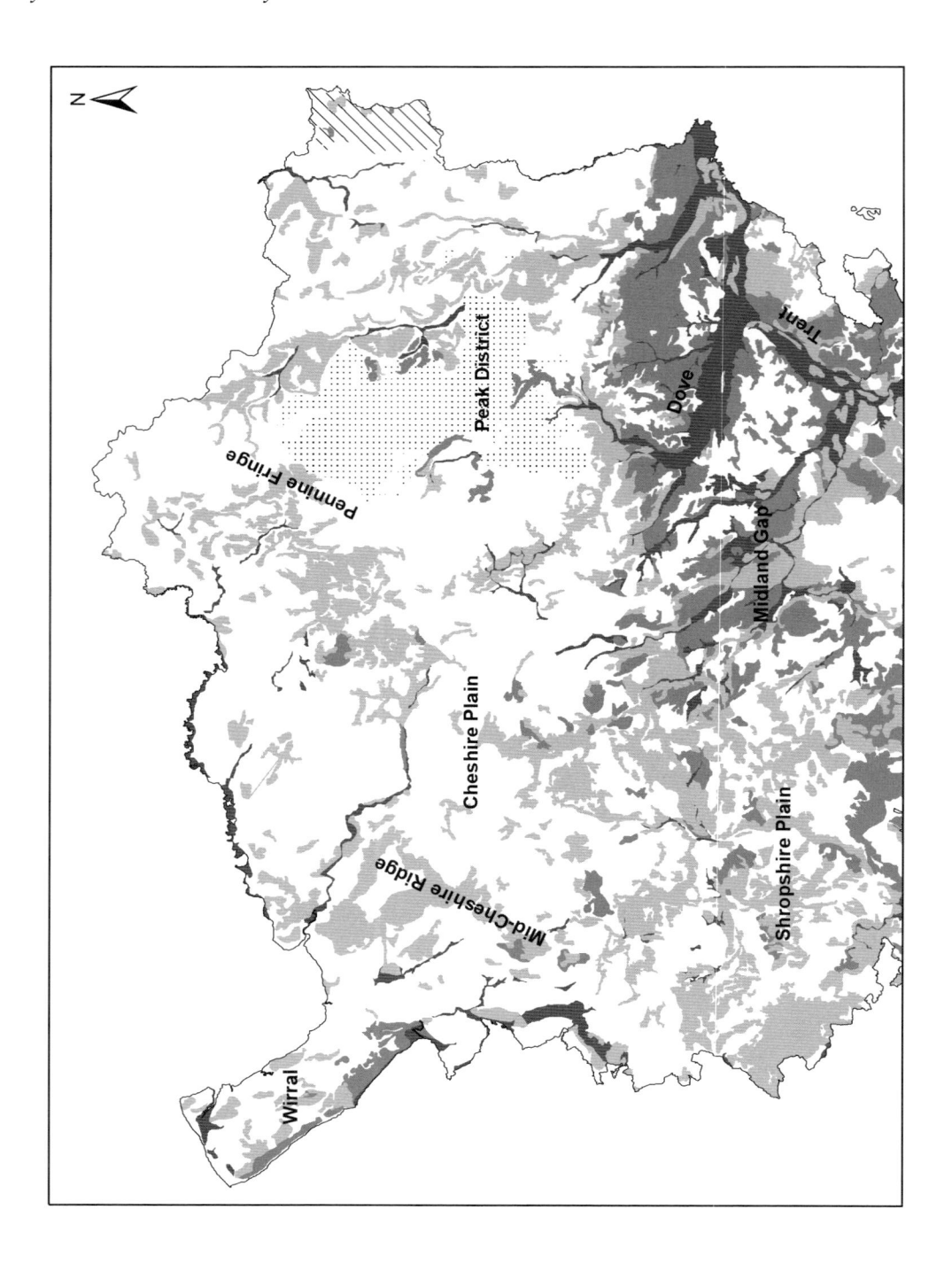

Lichfield and the Lands of St Chad

The people

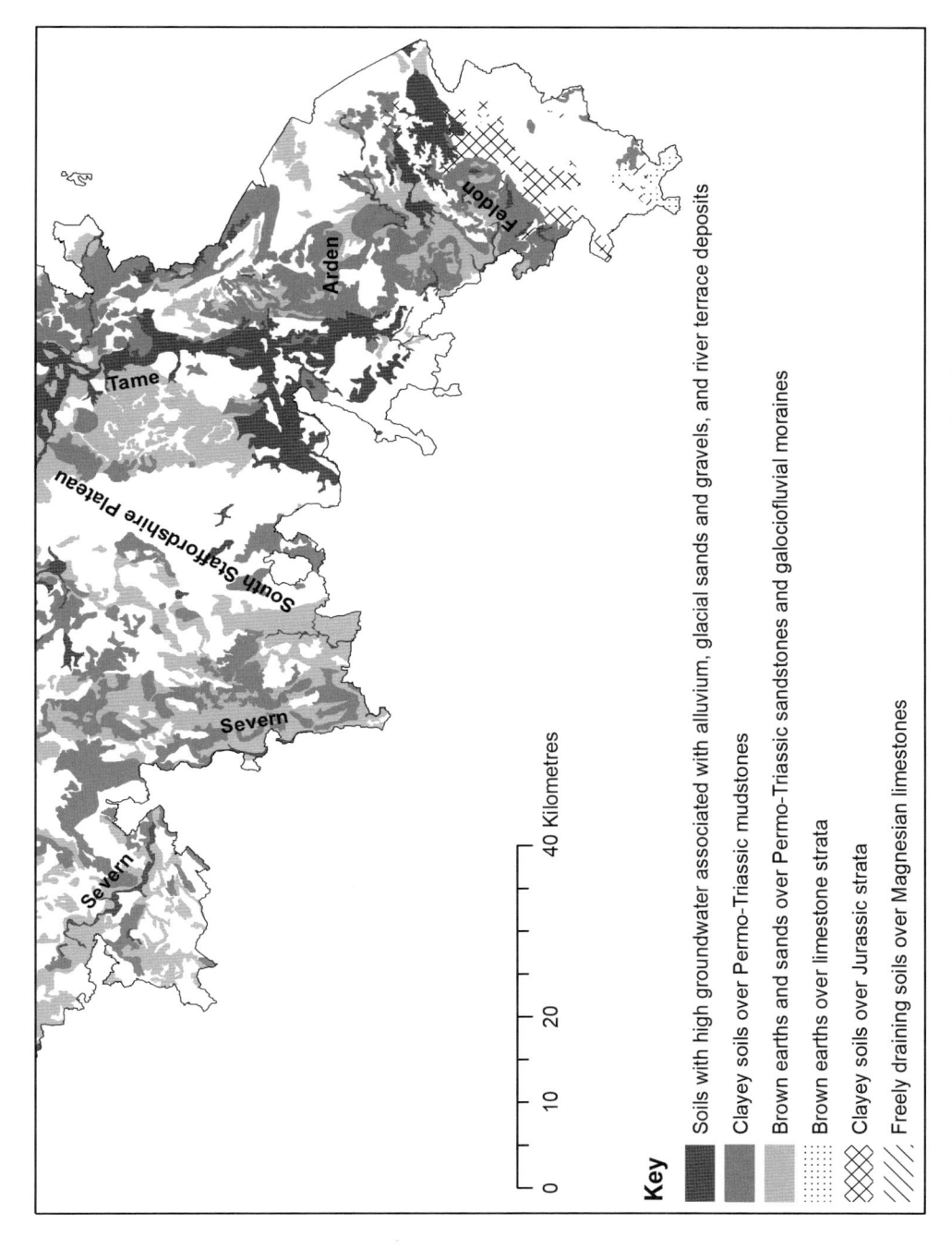

Figure 11 Distribution of various soil types amenable to cultivation across the diocese of Lichfield.

the greater wetness of the climate has tended to encourage the primacy of pastoral agriculture historically, especially as the soils are not easily damaged by livestock.[31] Finally, the soils with high groundwater associated with streams and river floodplains in eastern parts of the diocese were suited to both summer hay harvests and autumn grazing. Outside all these areas, soils of the Pennine Fringe on the edges of the Peak District, formed in head derived from underlying sandstones, mudstones and shales of Millstone Grit and Coal Measures, were largely unsuited to cultivation;[32] likewise, the acidic soils atop the Mid-Cheshire Ridge, and scattered across the sandstones and glaciofluvial moraines of the Midland Gap and the Shropshire and Cheshire Plains.[33] Overall, the diocese offered many possibilities for arable expansion from the seventh century onwards, though not to the same extent as lands further east. However, beyond the broad aggregation of their activities over many centuries in the landscapes they inhabited, the agricultural communities of the region must remain largely hidden from us, at least in this study.

In summary, this section has defined two kinds of agricultural community, arable and pastoral, present within the diocese, as no doubt throughout the rest of the British Isles and further afield at this time. The memberships of such communities in any given location overlapped to varying degrees depending on the extent of communal organisation in the ploughing of arable fields and the management of stock pastures. Following recent scholarship, it is suggested here that such decisions were often based on the geological and topographical capacities of the landscape. The territory encompassed by the diocese of Lichfield was not particularly conducive to the expansion of agrarian productivity, at least in comparison to other parts of England, but several general topographies, defined primarily by their soils, have been identified in which early medieval farmers were able to colonise newly farmed landscapes or, more often, expand and intensify pre-existing farmed landscapes. Such expansion appears to have occurred between the eighth and fourteenth centuries, and the remainder of this chapter considers the domainal communities that may have been primarily responsible for generating the drive towards greater arable productivity, before considering agricultural and domainal communities together in a concluding discussion.

Domainal communities and the possession of land

The discussion of lands held by minsters in Chapter 4 raised the spectre of 'bookland', a term with a distinct pedigree in early medieval documents but used with perhaps greater consistency by historians to refer to the distinctiveness of land possessed through grant of a charter or 'land-book', which could in theory be passed on by the holder to an heir of his or her choosing, free of any familial expectations of inheritance. 'In theory', because, as Julie Mumby has recently pointed out, expectant family

---

31 Ragg *et al.*, *Soils and their use*, pp. 225–8 (Malham 2 Association).
32 Ragg *et al.*, *Soils and their use*, pp. 90–2 and 109–12 (Bardsey and Brickfield 3 Associations).
33 Ragg *et al.*, *Soils and their use*, pp. 141–2, 152–5, 204–7, and 252–4 (Crannymoor, Delamere, Goldstone and Newport 4 Associations).

members did not always act as if their expectations were invalid, and holders of bookland might deliberately have sought to ensure that the land did not pass outside the family; Mumby warns that, on this issue, 'cautious expectations of fuzziness are in order'.[34] Historians have long taken a legalistic approach to the possession of land in early medieval England, understanding bookland as a specific form of tenure and contrasting it with 'folkland', a term with a more tenuous pedigree in contemporary documents, which is often used as a catch-all to represent other forms of tenure. Susan Reynolds has done more than most to embrace fuzziness and upset any notion of neat tenurial schemes, insisting that any understanding of medieval property must set it within the rights and obligations implied by ownership, rights and obligations that might be social and political as much as (or rather than) legal.[35] Nevertheless, this has not prevented historians from assuming that a broader tenurial system is there to be found, even if such a system remains vague; Wormald invokes 'norms of customary inheritance' to characterise the obligations that he assumes must have attached to folkland, thereby implying a specific 'customary' tenurial form.[36]

It is not intended here to deny the existence in early medieval England of recognised procedures regarding the inheritance of some types of folkland (quite the contrary), but the primary intent is to move away from a discussion of the ownership of land that characterises it primarily as a tenurial object attached to specific rights and obligations. Here, in line with the conceptual terminology promoted in this book, emphasis is placed on the collective contexts in which landholding was made meaningful, and on what are here called 'domainal communities', groups of people who acted together to articulate land as a possession, a domain, and through this to identify themselves as landholders. In this view, it is telling that so much of the discussion surrounding bookland and folkland relates to the manner of its inheritance or transmission from one landholder to another (through, for example, gift or purchase), and that the evidence presented in such discussions essentially comprises charters recording and attesting to actions taken, negotiated and decided in the ritualised fora provided by various assemblies.[37]

While bookland was created by royal grant, evidence marshalled by Catherine Cubitt demonstrates that both royal and church councils adjudicated disputes over such land during the eighth and ninth centuries, the involvement of the latter perhaps

---

34 J. Mumby, 'The descent of family land in later Anglo-Saxon England', *Historical Research*, 84 (2011), pp. 399–415, at p. 400.
35 S. Reynolds, *Fiefs and vassals: the medieval evidence reinterpreted* (Oxford, 1994), pp. 53–64.
36 Wormald, 'On þa wæpnedhealfe', p. 268.
37 For important elements within this contentious discussion see: P. Vinogradoff, 'Folkland', *English Historical Review*, 8 (1893), pp. 1–17; E. John, *Land tenure in early England: a discussion of some problems* (Leicester, 1964); E. John, 'Folkland reconsidered', in E. John (ed.), *Orbis Britanniae and other studies* (Leicester, 1966), pp. 64–127; P. Wormald, *Bede and the conversion of England: the charter evidence*, Jarrow Lecture (Jarrow, 1984); Wormald, 'On þa wæpnedhealfe'; S. Baxter and J. Blair, 'Land tenure and royal patronage in the early English kingdom: a model and a case study', *Anglo-Norman Studies*, 28 (2006), pp. 19–46.

emerging from the common association between bookland and minsters.[38] From the late ninth century church councils appear largely to have been subsumed within royal assemblies, as discussed in Chapter 1, but A.G. Kennedy has demonstrated that disputes over bookland were also adjudicated in local courts during this later period, primarily shire courts established in the second half of the tenth century, but perhaps others as well.[39] There is less certainty around the various types of folkland, as, without the evidence of charters and wills, which by definition pertains to bookland, it is largely invisible in our sources. Over a century ago Paul Vinogradoff plausibly described folkland as land 'held by folkright', which he glossed as 'common law, the law which keeps land in families'.[40] This is just as vague as Wormald's 'norms of customary inheritance', but the legal context that proved so inviting to both scholars at least points towards the legal fora in which folkland was given meaning. In an important article, Mumby has assembled the meagre evidence to suggest that what she calls 'family land' 'was passed across the generations within structurally complex kin groups through flexible succession practices';[41] this flexibility was facilitated in the later tenth and eleventh centuries by 'the public negotiation of competing claims and interests' at the hundred and shire assemblies.[42] It would be surprising if royal assemblies did not also offer an appropriate venue for adjudicating folkright, and they probably also did so during the centuries before English kings demanded the establishment of local hundred and shire courts. Evidence for precursors to the local courts is minimal, but Tom Lambert has recently argued forcefully for the importance of local assemblies in arbitrating legal disputes more generally in England between the sixth and tenth centuries.[43]

It is very difficult to construct a precise understanding of the domainal communities that came together at royal, ecclesiastical and local assemblies to promote, secure and defend their possession of land, even in those parts of England where evidence survives more plentifully. The bulk of surviving charters relating to places within the diocese of Lichfield is associated with the minster at Wolverhampton and the Benedictine monastery at Burton-upon-Trent.[44] Domesday Book presents a detailed survey of landholding across the region at the very end of the period, and will be used extensively in Chapter 6. The remainder of this chapter approaches the issue from a different direction. Compared with other forms of evidence for this period, place-names offer a relatively voluminous corpus that has been used in many different ways to explore a variety of issues in the early medieval history of England, as the major part of the national place-name stock appears to have its origins within this period. In what follows, some of the place-names likely to have been coined in the seventh,

---

38 Cubitt, *Anglo-Saxon church councils*, pp. 65–74.
39 A.G. Kennedy, 'Disputes about *bocland*: the forum for their adjudication', *Anglo-Saxon England*, 14 (1985), pp. 175–95.
40 Vinogradoff, 'Folkland', p. 11.
41 Mumby, 'The descent of family land', p. 412.
42 Mumby, 'The descent of family land', p. 415.
43 T. Lambert, *Law and order in Anglo-Saxon England* (Oxford, 2017), pp. 44–7 and 136–49.
44 Hooke, *Landscape of Anglo-Saxon Staffordshire*.

The people

eighth and ninth centuries in the diocese of Lichfield are identified and interrogated for what they illuminate of landholding practices among the domainal communities of the diocese. This exercise involves consideration of both the Brythonic and Old English place-names of the region.[45] A concluding discussion then ties the results into the themes explored in the first part of the chapter.

In a recent review, Alaric Hall has noted that the chronology and form we ascribe to language change is largely dependent on how stable we understand Old English place-naming practices to have been; he cites Margaret Gelling's assertion that many topographical names, at least in southern and eastern England, were in place by the fifth century, noting that they must therefore have remained stable from that time and, by extension, the vast majority of the population there must have spoken Old English from at least that time.[46] In contrast, Hall supports the view 'that place-names in large parts of Britain shifted only gradually to English, with competing names co-existing in variation perhaps for long periods, but with the establishment of a linguistically English place-name stock largely before the time of our earliest documentation'.[47] He thus accepts, as elsewhere does Gelling, that spoken Brythonic, or Primitive Welsh, had probably disappeared in most of England by the end of the ninth century; crucial in this respect is Gelling's observation that tenth-century boundary clauses for charters relating to the West Midlands 'indicate that with very few exceptions the smallest features of the landscape had English names by this time'.[48] We should, of course, be aware of the possibility that many such small-scale place-names were coined there and then by the people commissioned to walk the boundaries for the production of the charters, but the important point here is that the coining of such names was undertaken in the Old English language, and the sheer density of such names, on and off the boundaries, demonstrates that the vast majority of the population was speaking Old English by the tenth century.

Hall investigates the relative stability of place-names through a preliminary study of the loss to the modern English landscape of place-names in existing datasets, comprising charters of the seventh to eleventh centuries, Domesday Book and place-names appearing in texts up to and including Bede's *Ecclesiastical History*. Although the sample size is fairly small, two clear trends are revealed: the place-names of small places or topographical features are less stable than those of larger places or topographical features; and about a third of place-names recorded up to

---

45 The terminology used here to refer the Celtic languages of the British Isles is that proposed by John Koch, in which 'Brythonic' refers to the member of the Celtic language family spoken in much of western Britain in the early medieval period; for a convenient summary see J.T. Koch, *Cunedda, Cynan, Cadwallon, Cynddylan: four Welsh poems and Britain 383–655* (Aberystwyth, 2013), pp. 17–18.

46 A. Hall, 'The instability of place-names in Anglo-Saxon England and early medieval Wales, and the loss of Roman toponymy', in R. Jones and S. Semple (eds), *Sense of place in Anglo-Saxon England* (Donington, 2012), pp. 101–29, at pp. 103–4; Hall cites M. Gelling and A. Cole, *The landscape of place-names* (Donington, 2000), p. xix.

47 Hall, 'The instability of place-names', p. 103.

48 Gelling, *West Midlands*, p. 70.

Lichfield and the Lands of St Chad

the early eighth century are now lost, but this proportion declines through subsequent centuries, so that only about a tenth of place-names recorded in the eleventh century are lost.[49] This gradient implies a shift in the nature of place-naming practices across this period: by the eleventh century the names of even minor places were more likely to remain in use than they were three centuries earlier. Any plausible explanation of this stabilisation is unlikely to be simple, but we might expect it to relate to the expansion of agricultural production and the emergence of distinctive settlement and field patterns during this period, as discussed earlier. The place-names of the diocese of Lichfield have received much attention, but do not as a whole represent a dataset that can be analysed across time in the way that Hall demonstrates; many are recorded only once during the period, often in Domesday Book.[50] Nevertheless, certain kinds of place-name can be dated to the earlier centuries of the period to varying degrees of confidence, and can thus be considered more stable than contemporary names that, following Hall, must since have been lost; consideration of these older names alongside the places to which they were attached enables some exploration of the reasons for their greater stability.

Brythonic place-names

Of the corpus of place-names in the diocese possibly representing older coinages, those containing Brythonic elements comprise a good place to start, as the disappearance of Old Welsh as a significant spoken language in the diocese by the tenth century almost guarantees that these place-names were formed earlier. Lichfield itself provides a particularly useful place-name because different versions of it are attested over a comparatively long period. The place-name itself is first recorded in two eighth-century sources, Stephen of Ripon's *Life* of Bishop Wilfrid and Bede's *Ecclesiastical History*.[51] However, the first element of the name, **Lyccid*, appears in the early medieval Brythonic place-name 'Cair Luitcoit', a place mentioned in the Welsh poem *Marwnad Cynddylan* (possibly composed in the seventh century)

---

49 Hall, 'The instability of place-names', pp. 104–12.
50 Cheshire, Derbyshire and Warwickshire are covered by complete series of English Place-Name Society volumes, and almost all of the relevant parts of Shropshire are covered by the published parts of the incomplete series for that county: J.M. Dodgson, *The place-names of Cheshire*, five parts in seven volumes (Cambridge, 1970–97); M. Gelling and H.D.G. Foxall, *The place-names of Shropshire*, 6 vols (Nottingham, 1990–2012); K. Cameron, *The place-names of Derbyshire*, 3 vols (Cambridge, 1959); Gover *et al.*, *Place-names of Warwickshire*. Only Staffordshire remains seriously incomplete, represented thus far only by J.P. Oakden, *The place-names of Staffordshire, part 1* (Nottingham, 1984), although Horovitz, *Place-names of Staffordshire*, has gone a considerable way towards making up the deficit. See also M. Gelling, 'Some notes on Warwickshire place-names', *Transactions of the Birmingham and Warwickshire Archaeological Society*, 86 (1974), pp. 59–79, and M. Gelling, 'Some thoughts on Staffordshire place-names', *North Staffordshire Journal of Field Studies*, 21 (1981), pp. 1–20.
51 Stephen provides the forms *Onlicitfelda* (or *Anliccitfelda*) and *Lyccitfelda*, while Bede gives *Lyccidfelth* (or *Lyccitfeld*) and *Liccitfeld* (or *Liccidfeld*).

and also one of twenty-eight cities listed in the ninth-century *Historia Brittonum*.[52] An earlier form, 'Letocetum', itself probably a Latinised form of an ancient Brythonic original, *Letocaiton*, appears in the name of the nearby Roman station at Wall on Watling Street recorded in the late Roman Antonine Itinerary.[53] The Brythonic name simply means 'grey wood', and must originally have been descriptive of the local area. However, while the persistence of the name is uncontroversial, the fact that it appears at different times in the names of two places about two miles apart has raised questions about the ways in which the name was used and understood over this period.[54] Likewise, exactly what was meant by the name 'Cair Luitcoit' is ambiguous.

The Old English place-name provides a useful point from which to approach these questions. Douglas Johnson notes that the prefix *on* of Stephen of Ripon's 'Onlicitfelda' indicates that the place given to Chad by Wilfrid was 'in Lichfield', suggesting that the name was understood in the early eighth century to apply to a region rather than a specific settlement within it.[55] This is unsurprising, as Margaret Gelling has suggested that early usage of the term *feld* referred generally to open country, and more specifically to areas of common pasture, the term later attaching to settlements when they were founded within such areas.[56] However, Chris Lewis has suggested that *feld* was also used by English-speakers to rename Welsh territorial districts, citing the examples of Ergyng in south-west Herefordshire, which became Archenfield, and Tegeingl in north-east Wales, which became Englefield.[57] If Lichfield was named in this way, then the Brythonic element itself must also have referred to a region rather than a specific place within it, or at least did so at the moment when it was compounded with the Old English suffix *feld*. Gelling has argued that the specific form of the early medieval Brythonic name borrowed into Old English as *Lyccid* indicates a date for that borrowing around 675, and, while precision in this kind of argument is impossible, this would suggest that the Old English name was coined not long before or even at the time when Wilfrid was given the Lichfield estate by Wulfhere.[58]

If the early medieval Brythonic name referred to a region rather than a specific settlement, as is accepted here, then the identity of Cair Luitcoit must remain ambiguous, as it would have meant 'the city in the region of Luitcoit'. The remains of the Roman station at Wall offer an obvious candidate, but evidence has also been found for a fifth- or sixth-century settlement at Lichfield.[59] More pertinent to the present

---

52 H. Bradley, 'Etocetum or Letocetum?', *The Academy*, 756 (1886), p. 294; Koch, *Cunedda, Cynan, Cadwallon, Cynddylan*, pp. 236–7.
53 Bradley, 'Etocetum or Letocetum?'; the Roman name appears as *Etocetum*, but Bradley's emendation has gained scholarly consensus.
54 Greenslade, *VCH Staffordshire*, vol. 14, pp. 37–8; Gelling, *Signposts*, pp. 54 and 57–9.
55 Greenslade, *VCH Staffordshire*, vol. 14, p. 38.
56 Gelling, *Signposts*, pp. 127–8; M. Gelling, *Place-names in the landscape* (London, 1984), pp. 235–45; Gelling and Cole, *Landscape of Place-Names*, pp. 269–79.
57 C.P. Lewis, 'Welsh territories and Welsh identities in late Anglo-Saxon England', in N. Higham (ed.), *Britons in Anglo-Saxon England* (Woodbridge, 2007), pp. 130–43, at pp. 137–40.
58 Gelling, *Signposts*, p. 100.
59 Sargent, 'Early medieval Lichfield', pp. 7–12 and 23–5.

discussion is the fact that Wulfhere's grant presumably comprised something very similar to the Lichfield estate of twenty-five and a half hides recorded four centuries later in Domesday Book, and that this estate remained in episcopal possession throughout the intervening period.[60] The stability of the place-name at Lichfield might thus be plausibly associated with two important attributes. First, the size of the territory with which it was associated, in this case a large estate; this is noted more generally by Hall, who suggests that 'small places would be spoken of by smaller numbers of people, meaning that a new name could spread relatively easily through the speech community, whereas a new name for a famous place would face the greater challenge of being adopted by a larger and more dispersed speech community'.[61] This explanation is plausible, if perhaps not entirely satisfying, and can be afforded further nuance by the second significant attribute of the Lichfield place-name: the persistent association of the estate to which it referred with an elite landholder. Hall's 'dispersed speech community' might then be equated in part with people living on the estate, whose lives were entangled with various practices articulating explicit subordination to the bishop as landholder, thereby reproducing the integrity of the territory and its name.

This connection between large estates, elite landholders and place-names featuring Brythonic elements is also found elsewhere in the diocese. Penkridge offers another good example of a place-name for which a much earlier form survives, associated with another Roman station on Watling Street, two miles south of Penkridge, which was named 'Pennocrucium'; this name is itself a Latinisation of ancient Brythonic *Pennocroucion*, assembled from the elements *penno*, 'head, end, headland, chief', and *crug*, meaning 'hill, mound, tumulus', thus meaning 'headland tumulus', 'chief hill' or 'chief mound', and probably referring to a prominent tumulus in the area.[62] As with Lichfield, the distance between the two settlements associated with versions of the name, in this case borrowed into Old English without additional elements, suggests that it referred to a region or territory rather than a specific place, at least by the time of its borrowing; certainly, any association with the tumulus that inspired the original name must have been lost by this period. Domesday Book records Penkridge as a royal estate in 1086, with outlying members dispersed across a considerable region.[63] Other place-names in the diocese featuring Brythonic elements cannot be placed alongside any known Roman-period versions, but a significant proportion were associated with the centres of important royal, comital or episcopal estates in 1066 according to Domesday Book: Penkhull, Cannock, Kinver, Penn and Eccleshall in Staffordshire, Prees, Hodnet and Cound in Shropshire and Tarvin in Cheshire.[64] Others were held

---

60 *DB Staffs.*, 2,16 and 2,22.
61 Hall, 'The instability of place-names', p. 107.
62 Horovitz, *Place-names of Staffordshire*, pp. 21–2.
63 *DB Staffs.*, 1,7.
64 *DB Staffs.*, 1,27, 1,25, 1,16, 12,5–12,6, 2,10–2,13 and 2,20–2,21; *DB Salop.* 1,8, 4,1,4 and 4,3,16; *DB Chesh.*, B4; Tarvin derives from Welsh *terfyn*, a loanword from Latin *terminus* meaning 'boundary', possibly referring to the river Gowy, although Gelling suggests that it might have applied to a boundary region instead (Gelling, *West Midlands*, p. 65).

The people

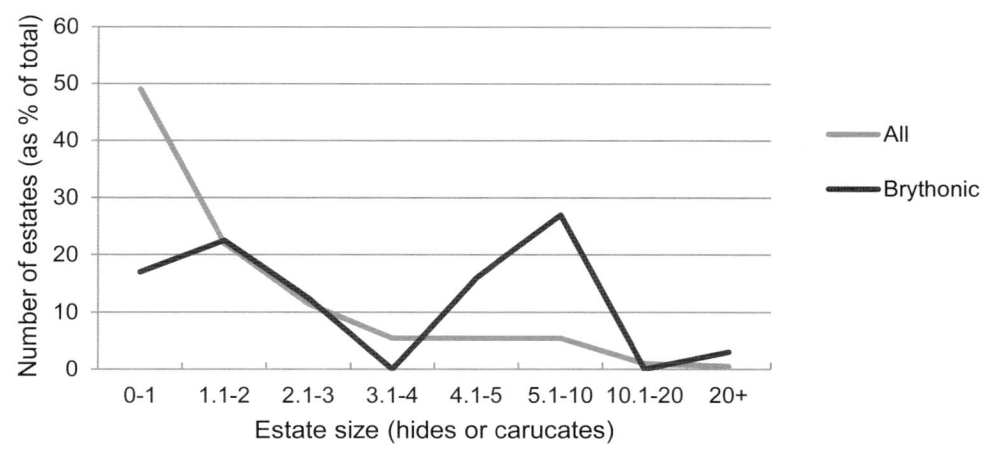

Figure 12 Distribution of sizes of estates with place-names containing Brythonic elements recorded in the Domesday survey, compared with the distribution of sizes of all recorded estates.

by thegns, but were of considerable size, such as Morfe, assessed at a sizeable five hides, or Barr, a nine-hide holding split into three three-hide thegn's estates.[65]

Figure 12 shows the distribution of sizes of estates with names featuring Brythonic elements in terms of hidage assessments recorded in the Domesday survey, calculated as a percentage of the regional corpus and compared with the distribution of sizes of all estates in a study region approximating to the diocese of Lichfield.[66] It should be noted that, where more than one estate has the same name, the separate hidages have been added together to represent the full size of the holding centred on the vill after which the estates were named. While the overall corpus is dominated by estates of a hide or less, falling off quite smoothly as estate-size increases, the curve representing Brythonic names clearly divides into two peaks and demonstrates that, while some of the estates appear to conform to the overall distribution of sizes, a significant proportion are distributed within the four- to ten-hide bracket. Even the smaller estates are, on average, slightly larger than the overall average, centring on one to two hides rather than nought to one; they include some of the place-names mentioned above, such as Hodnet, Penkhull and Cannock, as well as others, such as Gnosall and Cheadle in Staffordshire, and Cheadle in Cheshire.[67] Indeed, it may be significant that Penkhull,

---

65 *DB Staffs.*, 12,2, 12,25, 12,27 and 12,28.
66 For the purpose of this exercise, the study region is defined as the entire shires of Staffordshire, Derbyshire and Cheshire and the northern hundreds of Shropshire (Mersete, Baschurch, Hodnet, Wrockwardine, Shrewsbury, Patton and Alnothstree) and Warwickshire (Brinklow, Coleshill, Hunsbury, Marton and Stoneleigh).
67 Gnosall: *DB Staffs.*, 7,18, two hides and three virgates held by the clerics at Penkridge in 1066; Cheadle: *DB Staffs.*, 1,57 and 11,42, one carucate held by Wulfheah and one virgate held by Godgifu in 1066; Cheadle: *DB Chesh.*, 26,9, two hides held by Gamel in 1066.

Cannock and the two Cheadles were all recorded with substantially more ploughlands than hides, suggesting a degree of under-assessment.[68]

One final point worth noting here is the number of Brythonic place-names that were associated with areas of woodland. Most such names do not explicitly refer to woodland etymologically but are recorded in association with woods. The woods (*silvae*) at Morfe and Kinver were mentioned in an eighth-century charter, although the derivation of neither is absolutely secure: the former is assumed to be Brythonic, but has no obvious meaning, while the latter is probably descended from Brythonic *Cunobriga, 'hound hill'.[69] Brewood and Cannock also appear to derive from names for hills, the former being a compound from Brythonic *briga, 'hill' and Old English *wudu*, 'wood', the latter probably deriving from Welsh *cnwc*, 'hill, lump, hillock', but perhaps from the Old English loanword *cnocc*.[70] All these were later incorporated into medieval hunting forests that took their names. Some Brythonic names do refer explicitly to woodland. For example, Penkhull in Staffordshire derives from Brythonic *pencet*, 'end of the wood', added to Old English *hyll*, 'hill';[71] Cheadle (one in Staffordshire, one in Cheshire) is a tautologous compound of Brythonic *ceto*, 'wood', with Old English *leah*, also 'wood';[72] Prees in Shropshire derives from a Brythonic words meaning 'brushwood' or 'grove';[73] and *Letocaiton, 'grey wood', has already been discussed. Nevertheless, the predominance of hills or other prominent protrusions invoked to provide place-names within this corpus is impressive, and extends to other place-names that were never associated with woodland in our sources: for example, two place-names in Staffordshire, Penn and Barr, straightforwardly derive respectively from *penno, 'headland', and *barro, 'top, summit'.[74] Rarely a name appears explicitly to describe a wider landscape rather than some specific feature within it; for example, Hodnet in Shropshire derives from a Brythonic word meaning 'pleasant valley', although if modest in size that valley might itself be understood as a specific landscape feature.[75]

The underlying place-naming pattern that appears to apply to most, if not all, place-names featuring Brythonic elements involves the invocation of a distinctive topographical feature to label a broader territory containing that feature. Once the territorial name was established, other places within the territory might inherit it. This

---

68 Penkhull: two hides and 11 ploughlands; Cannock: one hide and 15 ploughlands; Cheadle, Staffs.: one virgate and four ploughlands; Cheadle, Chesh.: two hides and six ploughlands.
69 Horovitz, *Place-names of Staffordshire*, pp. 346–7 and 395–6; suggestions for Morfe include early medieval Brythonic *mor + *dref*, 'large village', Welsh *morfa*, 'marsh, upland moor', and Brythonic *morhev 'great summer-place', none of which is obviously relevant to the location; both elements of Kinver have mutated under the influence of Old English, the first from Old English *cyne*, 'royal', the second from *fare, fær*, 'road', so giving a false etymology of 'royal road'.
70 Horovitz, *Place-names of Staffordshire*, pp. 146 and 172–3.
71 Horovitz, *Place-names of Staffordshire*, p. 432.
72 Horovitz, *Place-names of Staffordshire*, p. 186.
73 Gelling, *West Midlands*, p. 68.
74 Horovitz, *Place-names of Staffordshire*, p. 433.
75 Gelling, *West Midlands*, p. 68.

appears to have happened with the woods in many of the examples given above, and probably also occurred with the river Penk, earlier the river Penkridge, which took its name from the territory through which it flowed.[76] Key to understanding the stability of these place-names is the fact that these territories were estates that persisted from their establishment to the eleventh century and beyond, often administered from a settlement that itself inherited the place-name. Some of these estates had existed since the seventh century, and, crucially, many were probably established at a time before the complete dominance of Old English in the region, when early medieval Brythonic was still in some sense a significant living language. In some instances the coining of a place-name may represent the moment when a Brythonic name was borrowed into Old English, especially in the case of names comprising compounds of Brythonic and Old English elements, but this may or may not have been the moment when the estate itself was created. Some estates, such as Lichfield and Penkridge, where earlier versions of the name were attached to nearby Roman stations, may already have existed in some form. Others were perhaps created in the eighth or even ninth centuries, named from features that already possessed names borrowed from Brythonic. Compound names such as Penkhull, in which the generic part of the name means 'hill' in Old English, demonstrate that the use of distinctive landscape features, especially hills, to name estates persisted among Old English speakers. The dynamics of estate-naming practices is arguably more important to understanding the greater stability of these place-names than a simple correlation with the size of the topographical feature referred to in the name, as Hall suggests, although the latter argument probably applies more effectively to Brythonic river-names, which have survived in considerable numbers across the region, as across much of England.

Old English place-names

It would be plausible to argue that a decent proportion of estates with entirely Old English names recorded in Domesday Book represented landholdings that were established during the seventh, eighth and ninth centuries, just like those discussed above featuring Brythonic elements. They are, however, more difficult to identify because Old English remained the spoken language of the region into the eleventh century, and thus Old English place-names could have been coined at any time during (or even a little beyond) the early medieval period. Nevertheless, place-name scholarship has identified a series of name elements that may, for various reasons, have been more productive of place-names earlier in the period than they were later,

---

76   Horovitz, *Place-names of Staffordshire*, p. 432; it is not possible to state when this back formation occurred, whether it was created by Brythonic speakers or Old English speakers. Cound in Shropshire may be another example of this phenomenon, as it forms the name of a settlement and a river; unfortunately Cound is of uncertain meaning, and thus it is not possible to decide whether it was initially applied to the river or some other feature. In an analogous example, Bede, in his *Ecclesiastical History* (ii.14), attaches the name of the kingdom of Elmet, described as such in the ninth-century *Historia Brittonum*, to a wood, describing the location of a minster 'in the forest of Elmet'.

and some of these will be considered here. Such scholarship often distinguishes between 'habitative' names, which make explicit reference to a settlement, and 'topographical' names, which refer instead to topographical features in the landscape. This categorisation is not particularly helpful here, as the place-names studied in this chapter were all used to name estates, usually including the administrative centre of the estate, and were all therefore habitative in function if not in explicit etymology. Indeed, Margaret Gelling has argued for the importance of topographical names attached to central settlements in large estates from an early period.[77] This is supported by the discussion of Brythonic names here, which demonstrates the predominance of prominent topographical elements in the names applied to estates from at least the seventh century.

Of the Old English topographical names that come closest to the hills and headlands of the Brythonic place-names, those formed with the element *dūn* are more likely than most to have been coined earlier rather than later. The word most commonly meant 'hill with a summit suitable for settlement', and Gelling suggests that it was not employed for major place-names much after 800, as it is not found in areas where Old English speaking was widespread only after the ninth century, such as Cornwall or the Weald of Kent and Sussex.[78] Place-names with this element can usefully be considered alongside those formed with the element *ēg*, meaning 'island, dry ground in a marsh', which again points to notably distinct, if less dramatic, topographical locations suitable for settlement; this word is particularly important when searching for earlier place-names, as it is overall not a particularly common element, especially in minor names and field names, but was the most common place-name element in the corpus of English texts composed before 735, and is therefore likely to have had a fairly exclusively early usage and to have proved quite stable subsequently.[79] Figures 13 and 14 show the distributions of sizes of estates in our region with names containing these two elements, as recorded in the Domesday survey, compared with the distribution of sizes of all recorded estates.[80] As with the Brythonic names, the graphs each display two peaks, one conforming with the overall distribution, although here with a slightly larger average estate size, and the other ranging across a bracket from four to ten hides and occasionally more. Some of the larger estates, such as Eyton-on-Severn and Long Eaton (incorporating *ēg*), and Repton and Bupton (incorporating *dūn*), were held by the earls or the bishop in 1066, but others, such as Caldy (incorporating *ēg*) and Edgmond, Spondon and Seisdon (incorporating *dūn*), were held by thegns. Likewise, some of the smaller estates, such as Puleston, Quarndon, Sandon and Cauldon (all incorporating *dūn*) were in royal or comital hands in 1066, while, again, others were in the hands of thegns. Overall, the name elements appear to follow very similar patterns to the Brythonic names, and thus similar explanations might be pursued.

---

77   Gelling, *Signposts*, pp. 118–26; Gelling, *Place-names in the landscape*; Gelling and Cole, *Landscape of place-names*.
78   Gelling, *Place-names in the landscape*, pp. 140–58; Gelling and Cole, *Landscape of place-names*, pp. 164–73.
79   Gelling, *Place-names in the landscape*, pp. 34–40; Gelling and Cole, *Landscape of place-names*, pp. 37–44.
80   The total regional corpus is identical to that used earlier.

The people

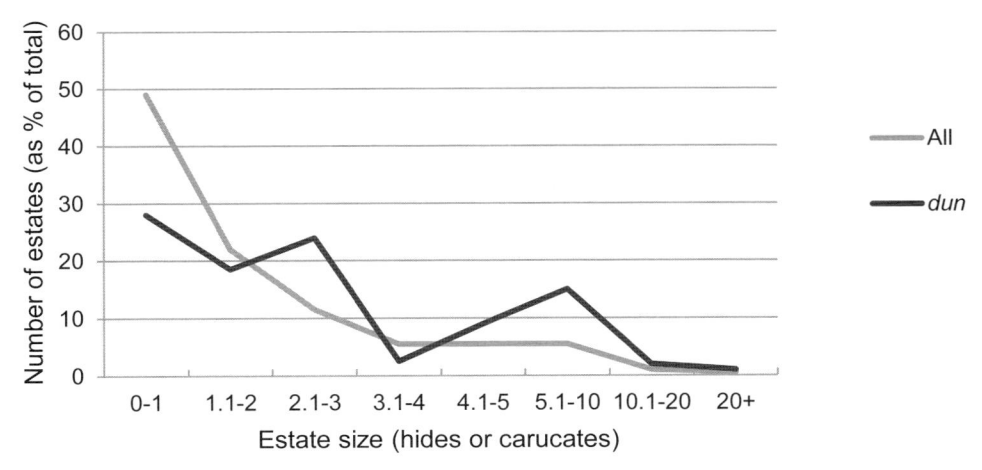

Figure 13 Distribution of sizes of estates with place-names containing *dūn* recorded in the Domesday survey, compared with the distribution of sizes of all recorded estates.

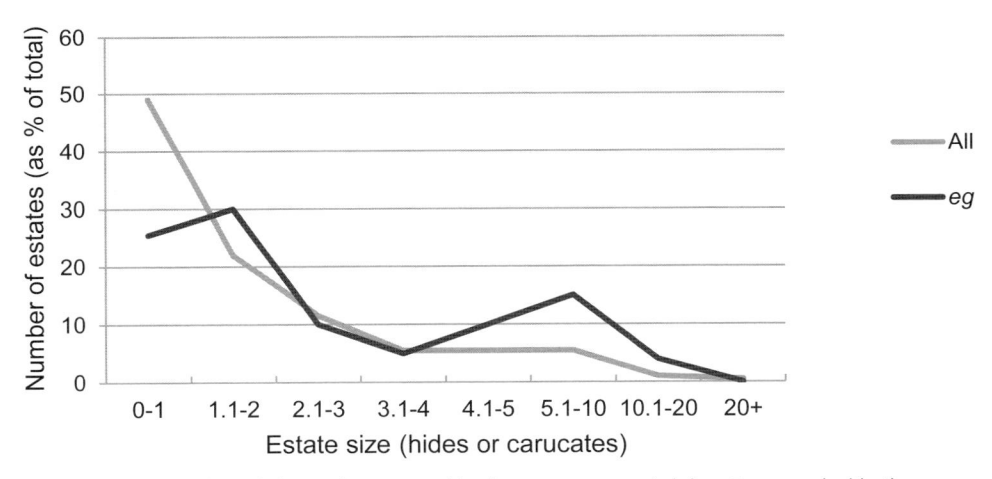

Figure 14 Distribution of sizes of estates with place-names containing *ēg* recorded in the Domesday survey, compared with the distribution of sizes of all recorded estates.

Other Old English place-names of use here include those formed with the element *hām*, meaning 'village, manor, homestead', which are moderately well represented across our study region. In one or two cases *hām* is compounded with a personal name and *-ingas*, the plural form of the patronymic suffix *-ing* and meaning 'people of n', forming place-names with the suffix *-ingahām*, 'homestead of the people of n'. Place-names containing both *-ingas* and *hām* are more densely distributed in regions to the south and east of the diocese of Lichfield, and used to be considered to mark the earliest settlement locations of the Angle and Saxon 'tribes' that apparently settled

Lichfield and the Lands of St Chad

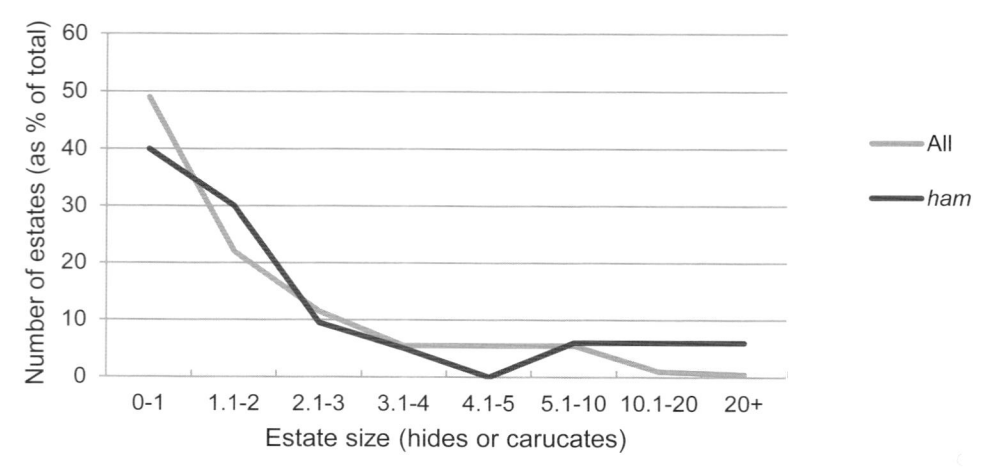

Figure 15 Distribution of sizes of estates with place-names containing *hām* recorded in the Domesday survey, compared with the distribution of sizes of all recorded estates.

there, described by Bede as the first of the 'English'.[81] Such an outdated framing of the fifth and sixth centuries is now viewed with deep suspicion, but the interpretation of these place-names is still bedevilled by the legacy of a historiography that took Bede too literally, and they have not yet been reinterpreted satisfactorily. This is not the place for such reinterpretation, but it is assumed that the broad consensus about the early coining of these place-names still holds some validity. A special form of the suffix -*ing* is also considered here: John McNeal Dodgson has suggested that 'a palatalized and assibilated form with the pronunciation -*indge*, -*inch* ... represents an archaic locative-inflected form of a common-noun or place-name containing the -*ing* suffix', having the meaning 'place connected with *n*', which Dodgson suggests was obsolete by 700;[82] some of these place-names are compounded with *hām*. The complete corpus of *hām* place-names in the diocese, including all the various compounds discussed above, lends itself to the sort of distribution analysis used above: the graph (see Figure 15) displays only a very modest second peak in the bracket from five hides to twenty and beyond, which comprises two huge Cheshire estates at Eastham (twenty-two hides) and Weaverham (thirteen hides), both held by Earl Edwin in 1066.

One other potentially early, and therefore more stable, place-name element is *burh*, 'defensible enclosure', 'stronghold', later 'defended manor house, town'.[83] As this

---

81   J.M. Dodgson, 'The significance of the distribution of English place-names in -*ingas*, -*inga*- in south-east England', *Medieval Archaeology*, 10 (1966), pp. 1–29, questions the primacy of -*ingas* place-names, but his argument continues to rely on comparison with furnished burial sites and notions of 'primary' and 'secondary' colonisation undertaken by the incoming migrants buried there.
82   Dodgson, *Place-names of Cheshire*, part 5.2 (1997), p. 279.
83   Gelling, *Signposts*, pp. 143–6; S. Draper, 'Burh enclosures in Anglo-Saxon settlements: case studies in Wiltshire', in R. Jones and S. Semple (eds), *Sense of place in Anglo-Saxon England* (Donington, 2012), pp. 334–51; J. Baker and S. Brookes, *Beyond the Burghal Hidage* (Leiden, 2013), pp. 96–7.

The people

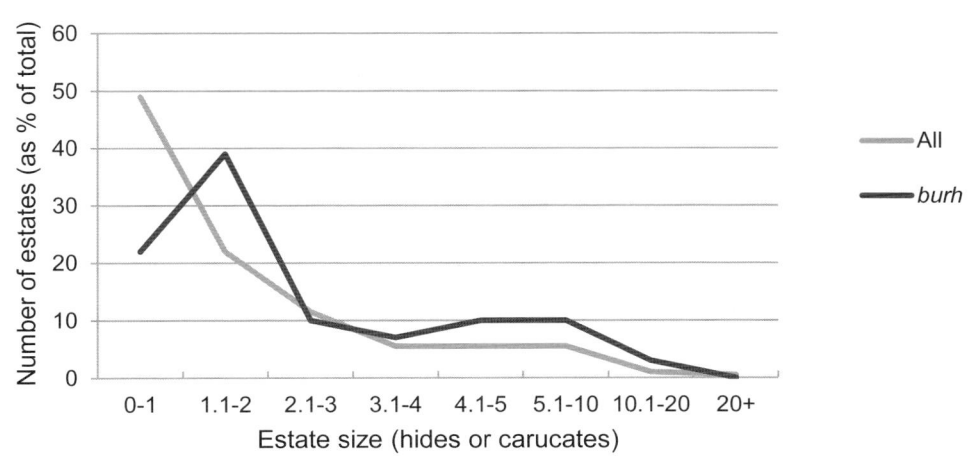

Figure 16 Distribution of sizes of estates with place-names containing *burh* recorded in the Domesday survey, compared with the distribution of sizes of all recorded estates.

semantic shift indicates, the word *burh* continued to be used in the formation of place-names throughout the early medieval period. John Blair has suggested that the word was specifically employed before the mid-eighth century to describe minsters, which probably formed the largest and most distinctive enclosed settlements in the contemporary landscape.[84] A distribution analysis of the occurrence of the term in Domesday Book across the region, as a simplex name or as the second element in a compound name, produces familiar results (see Figure 16): two peaks, the first suggesting a slightly larger than average size for the smaller territories and the second spread across a range of larger estates from four to ten hides. In 1066 most of the estates were held by thegns, and, of the minority held by the elite, only Lady Godgifu's estate at Kingsbury and the city at Shrewsbury were assessed at greater than four hides. Thus, we have in *burh* a corpus of significant place-names, many of which may have been coined in the ninth century or before and subsequently remained stable, but some of which were perhaps coined more recently, especially given the number of thegns among the landholders of these estates.

The place-names considered so far tended to name estates that were larger than the 'background' distribution of estates in the region, and a significant proportion also belonged to the elite in 1066. Overall we would expect the place-names against which these stand out to have been coined later, naming estates that were generally smaller, fewer of which were held by the elite. On the basis of previous research, we might expect many such smaller holdings to bear names formed with the elements *tūn* ('enclosure, farmstead, settlement, estate') and *lēah* ('wood, wood pasture');[85] while

---

84 Blair, *Church*, p. 250.
85 For *lēah*, see Gelling, *Place-names in the landscape*, pp. 198–207; Gelling and Cole, *Landscape of place-names*, pp. 237–42; and D. Hooke, 'Early medieval woodland and the place-name term *lēah*', in O.J. Padel and D.N. Parsons (eds), *A commodity of good names: essays in honour of Margaret Gelling* (Donington, 2008), pp. 365–76.

the former can be considered habitative and the latter topographical, they are more usefully considered together as both were evidently used extensively to name estates, as a glance at the index of any Domesday county would demonstrate. In a pioneer study of the terms *tūn* and *lēah*, Margaret Gelling has established the common geographical mutual exclusivity of the two terms, and the absence of both from later medieval settlement, perhaps from the twelfth century onwards, indicating that they were used in the same way but in landscapes of different character, and over a defined period.[86] Gelling notes the 'growing and quite impressive number of instances in which an "x's *tūn*" place-name is firmly connected with a man or woman mentioned in a charter of tenth- or eleventh-century date', suggesting that many of these names, and perhaps the settlements to which they were attached, should be associated with the landholding practices of these centuries.[87] Hall's observation that only around 10 per cent of place-names recorded in the tenth century have been lost would illuminate the persistence of these place-names in the record if *tūn* and *lēah* were particularly productive during a period centred on the tenth century.

However, based on a study of place-names in the Chilterns and Essex region, John Baker has recently speculated that *tūn* and *lēah* might also have been used frequently during the sixth and seventh centuries, but that they do not appear so much in early textual sources because the latter focused on minsters and meeting-places rather than on more mundane settlements.[88] If this was the case, then we might expect a proportion of the surviving corpus of place-names formed with these elements to date before the tenth century. Good examples are provided by Cheadle, in which *lēah* is compounded with a Brythonic element likely to date to the ninth century at the latest, and *Tomtūn*, thought to be an earlier name for Tamworth, which appears in a charter of King Æthelred dated 675×691, although its earliest witness dates to the twelfth-century.[89] If the 'x's *tūn*' usage studied by Gelling was also productive during this earlier period, it is possible to speculate that the estates concerned tended to have their names changed along with their owners until around the tenth century, although ultimately it is not possible to demonstrate this. The undoubted productivity of *tūn* and *lēah* in the tenth century and later unfortunately renders it impossible in most instances to separate earlier from later place-names. However, the element *feld* ('land without trees as opposed to forest, level ground as opposed to hills, or land without buildings') perhaps offers some insight into the early use of *lēah*, as it was probably used in similar circumstances in the earlier centuries, but did not proliferate to quite the same extent as *tūn* and *lēah* in the designation of estates during the tenth century and later.[90] Gelling notes that it increasingly appears in the names of large open arable fields from the tenth century, but that 'for most of the pre-Conquest period it was used indifferently of land which might

---

86 Gelling, 'Notes on Warwickshire place-names'.
87 Gelling, *Signposts*, p. 183.
88 J.T. Baker, *Cultural transition in the Chilterns and Essex region, 350 AD to 650 AD* (Hatfield, 2006), pp. 229–30.
89 Horovitz, *Place-names of Staffordshire*, p. 186; Kelly, *Charters of Peterborough Abbey*, pp. 178–85 (No. 4c).
90 Gelling, *Place-names in the landscape*, p. 235.

The people

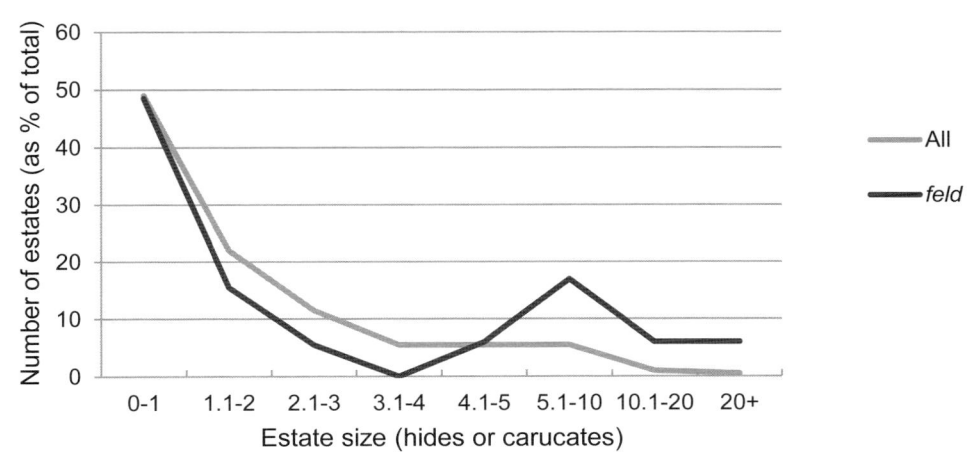

Figure 17 Distribution of sizes of estates with place-names containing *feld* recorded in the Domesday survey, compared with the distribution of sizes of all recorded estates.

or might not be under the plough';[91] in fact, she suggests, before the tenth century *feld* was predominantly associated with open, common pasture, onto which the arable fields later often 'encroached'.[92] Hooke has noted that *lēah* is glossed with both *silva* and *campus* in pre-Conquest texts, and as the latter term usually provides the Latin gloss for *feld*, there was evidently something of a continuum of meaning between the two terms, with the least open wood pasture (*lēah*) at one end, the most open country (*feld*) at the other, and a murky overlap somewhere in the middle.

Given this overlap, it is relevant to note that *feld* tends to group with *lēah*, as against *tūn*, geographically. Indeed, it is evident that both could be used across a range of differently sized territories: Hooke notes that *lēah* was employed to describe the large Weald of Kent and Sussex (*Andredesleage*), through parishes, manors and townships to 'local woods or patches of wood-pasture that gave their names to lesser medieval settlements or remained wood names'.[93] Lewis' hypothesis on the early use of *feld*, rehearsed earlier, suggests that it could also be applied to large territories such as Englefield as much as the open pastures or fields of individual townships evoked by Gelling. Indeed, the large numbers of *feld* place-names in our region indicates that the term continued to produce place-names after the seventh century, and perhaps predominantly during the later centuries, as did the even more numerous elements *tūn* and *lēah*. A distribution analysis of *feld* (see Figure 17) shows, as with those of the place-names considered above, a second peak indicating an over-representation of large estates against the regional background, and thus perhaps indicating some earlier estates. However, the first peak conforms more closely to the overall distribution, indicating that *feld* is less representative of larger territories than the

---

91 Gelling, *Place-names in the landscape*, p. 236.
92 Gelling, *Place-names in the landscape*, pp. 236–7.
93 Hooke, 'Early medieval woodland', pp. 368 and 374.

place-name elements discussed above; we might envision a more polarised situation here, in which *feld* was used to name a number of substantial territories across the early medieval period but was otherwise confined to the more modest estates of the tenth century and later dominated by name elements such as *tūn* and *lēah*.

Similar observations might be made about the place-name element *halh*, 'nook, hollow, dry ground in a marsh, administrative salient', which is common in our region and appears to fill a semantic gap left by *feld* and *lēah*, describing a landscape not particularly wooded, but confined in some way, so not open either. Gelling's research again suggests that, as with *feld*, *lēah* and *tūn*, *halh* began to be used in place-name formation early, but continued in use into the eleventh century.[94] Overall, by the time of the Domesday survey, evidence suggests that place-names featuring *tūn*, *lēah*, *feld* and *halh* were used similarly to denote estates (often naming the settlement from which they was administered) and were overwhelmingly attached to those assessed at around a hide or less, the smallest category used in the analyses above, but containing the largest number of holdings. However, while many of these names were no doubt coined in the tenth century and later, there is some reason to propose that a significant proportion were older.

John Blair has built on the recent work of several scholars to propose a category of 'functional -*tūnas*', represented by place-names compounded with the generic -*tūn* whose specifying elements related to the functions of those places within local clusters of linked settlements that acted as dependent holdings in relation to elite centres; Blair dates the formation of these place-names to the late seventh, eighth and earlier ninth centuries.[95] Given the similarities shared by *tūn* with *lēah*, *halh* and *feld* discussed here, it is possible that the other three elements should be viewed in a similar way. Nationally *lēah* was not infrequently compounded with some of the specific elements highlighted by Blair, such as *burh* ('stronghold'), *cniht* ('retainer'), *strǣt* ('metalled road'), directional elements and the products of farming.[96] The national evidence is less compelling for *feld* and *halh*; the former may have had a more restricted meaning in earlier centuries, as discussed above, and the same may be true of *halh*, although a possible functional use is discussed below. In summary, this section has identified several place-name elements across the diocese, some of which – *dūn*, *ēg*, *hām*, -*ingas*, *ingahām*, and -*ing* – are likely to denote estates established during the seventh, eighth and ninth centuries, while others – *tūn*, *lēah*, *halh* and *feld* – are likely to have been most productive during the tenth and eleventh centuries, and one – *burh* – probably remained productive throughout the period. However, there is no hard and fast boundary between these phases of place-naming, and it is also likely that some of the elements popular later were also used earlier, perhaps to name subordinate elements within estates. There is reason to suggest that the earlier place-names often survived as a result of their association with landholders among the elite, while the later place-names were more commonly associated with a lower stratum of the elite.

---

94 Gelling, *Place-names in the landscape*, pp. 100–11; Gelling and Cole, *Landscape of place-names*, pp. 123–33.
95 J. Blair, *Building Anglo-Saxon England* (Princeton, 2018), pp. 193–201.
96 Gelling, *Place-names in the landscape*, pp. 203–7.

The people

Eccles place-names

The final place-name element considered here, *eccles*, derives from Old English *eclēs*, a borrowing of early medieval Brythonic **eglēs*, which is derived ultimately from Latin *ecclesia*, meaning 'a body of Christians, a church'.[97] It was not considered with other Brythonic names earlier in the chapter because it presents rather unique difficulties. Place-names featuring this element survive in two distinct regional clusters, one of which straddles the northern Midlands, south Lancashire and the West Riding of Yorkshire; in contrast, there are no examples in the other ridings of Yorkshire, in Cumbria, the East Midlands, the central south or south-west of England, and only a few outlying examples in Norfolk, Kent and County Durham.[98] The second cluster is represented in a series of place-names quite extensively distributed across lowland Scotland, almost all located south of the Mounth, both in its simplex form and compounded with English and Gaelic elements.[99] The English cluster is represented in the diocese of Lichfield at Eccleshall in Staffordshire and Exhall in Warwickshire, in which *eclēs* is compounded with Old English *halh*; at Eccleston in Cheshire, where it is compounded with Old English *tūn*; and twice in north Derbyshire, where it is in simplex form.[100] In a seminal study of the place-name element in England, Cameron collected six examples of the simplex place-name and fourteen in which it is compounded with an Old English generic element; of the latter *tūn* and *halh* were the commonest, accounting for eight examples, but one further example is compounded with *feld* and another with *lēah*, and thus over two-thirds of the corpus of compounded names (and precisely half of the entire corpus) features one of these four generics.[101] Cameron omitted all but three examples of *eccles* names in Scotland, considering them problematic in that they might more easily derive from Gaelic *eaglais*.[102]

Given the clustered distributions, Cameron suggested that, in some cases, *eccles* might have been borrowed into Old English not as a Brythonic place-name but as a localised loan word, used meaningfully by Old English speakers, although he admitted that 'there is no independent evidence that it was ever taken over into colloquial use'.[103] Richard Sharpe has supported this idea, noting that the element is not attested among the early place-names of western Britain or Ireland: 'in Wales and Cornwall *eglwys* and *eglos* are slow to become productive of place-names, and in Irish the word *eclais*, common from an early date to mean an ecclesiastical institution, is late to appear as a place-name element'; thus the English place-names were not simply reproductions of Brythonic place-names, and *eccles* might indeed have been an Old English loan

---

97 Horovitz, *Place-names of Staffordshire*, p. 243; K. Cameron, 'Eccles in English place-names', in M.W. Barley and R.P.C. Hanson (eds), *Christianity in Britain, 300–700* (Leicester, 1968), pp. 87–92.
98 Cameron, 'Eccles', p. 89.
99 J. MacQueen, *Ninian and the Picts*, Fifteenth Whithorn Lecture (Whithorn, 2007), pp. 7–8 and 20.
100 Cameron, 'Eccles', pp. 87–8.
101 Cameron, 'Eccles', pp. 87–9.
102 Cameron, 'Eccles', p. 90.
103 Cameron, 'Eccles', pp. 88–9.

word 'being (however briefly) productive of place-names in English'.[104] However, this consensus has been challenged by two more recent studies by Carole Hough and Alan G. James, both of which argue that the *eccles* place-names in Old English and Gaelic were produced through being borrowed into these languages as place-names, rather than being formed through the use of a previously borrowed loan word.[105]

The two authors differ on the manner in which the word was borrowed into Old English place-names: Hough assumes that the word was applied to a church or specific church community, and hypothesises a set of original Brythonic place-names generally of simplex form, *eglēs, most of which have necessarily since been lost, as the word now exists mostly in Old English compound place-names; the latter were thus formed later, in relation to the original simplex place-names. James, on the other hand, treats the Brythonic word as a common noun used to describe any territory associated with an ecclesiastical community, which was, however, repeatedly misunderstood to denote a particular place by Old English speakers when hearing such territories described in this way by Brythonic speakers. Like Hough, James suggests that the compound place-names were formed in relation to a set of simplex names, although in this case these took the form *eclēs*, having already been borrowed into Old English from Brythonic. The two theories share a number of problems: they both require that a substantial number of simplex place-names have been lost while derivative place-names survive; they also assume that a geographical cluster of simplex names appears plausible, when it would presumably have been quite confusing to people living in the region. Nevertheless, James' suggestion that *eglēs* formed a Brythonic common noun is useful, and it is accepted here, following Cameron and Sharpe, that the word was borrowed into Old English as a common noun *eclēs* with the same meaning, thus allowing for a greater degree of comprehension between Brythonic and Old English speakers.

It is particularly notable that, of the entire corpus of English *eccles* place-names, half are compounded with *tūn*, *halh*, *feld* and *lēah*. As discussed earlier, these elements are characteristic of estates named in the tenth century and later, but the borrowing of Old English *eclēs* from Brythonic *eglēs* suggests that these names represent some of the earlier uses of these elements. Nevertheless, only half of Cameron's corpus of *eccles* place-names is represented by an estate in Domesday Book, and of these only two were assessed at five hides or more: the bishops of Chester's estate at Eccleshall (seven hides) and Eccleston (five hides), held by a thegn named Edwin in 1066.[106] The remaining estates were almost all held by thegns in 1066, excepting only Eccles in Norfolk, held by Earl Ralph, and Great and Little Eccleston in Amounderness, which were members of Earl Tostig's estate at Preston. The corpus is not therefore one for which early place-name stability looks likely, and it is possible that many members of

---

104 R. Sharpe, 'Martyrs and local saints in Late Antique Britain', in A. Thacker and R. Sharpe (eds), *Local saints and local churches in the early medieval West* (Oxford, 2002), pp. 75–154, at p. 147.
105 C. Hough, 'Eccles in English and Scottish place-names', in E. Quinton (ed.), *The church in English place-names* (Nottingham, 2009), pp. 109–24; A.G. James, 'Eglēs/Eclēs and the formation of Northumbria', in E. Quinton (ed.), *The church in English place-names* (Nottingham, 2009), pp. 125–50.
106 *DB Staffs.*, 2,10; *DB Chesh.*, 17,1.

the corpus defied the odds in surviving to be recorded in much later sources. It is, of course, not possible to quantify how many *eccles* place-names did not survive.

However, there is another possibility to explain the apparent stability of the surviving corpus or place-names: while not representing significant estate centres themselves, many of the places given *eccles* names might initially have been associated with such centres, especially if the Old English *eclēs* had the same meaning ascribed to Brythonic *eglēs* by James, namely an ecclesiastical territory or estate. A compound place-name can then be understood as signifying a connection with a nearby ecclesiastical estate centre, perhaps held directly by the ecclesiastical landholder in contrast to surrounding places held by dependent lay people; significantly, the place so-named need not have been the location of the ecclesiastical estate centre. These place-names might thus be fruitfully compared with Blair's functional dependencies, especially given the compounding of *eclēs* with *tūn* (four examples) and *lēah* (one example); moreover, the four examples compounded with *halh* hint at a specific functional use of this element. This resonates in part with Gelling's suggestion that the *halh* compounds might have utilised that element in its sense of 'administrative salient', although she supposed that all these places hosted churches and speculated that *halh* related to their protected or tax-exempt status, an interpretation that is not supported here.[107]

It is therefore proposed that most if not all *eccles* place-names represent places associated with religious centres, whether or not a community and its church were located at these places or elsewhere. As such, the use of Old English *eclēs* as a loan word is supported, and the period during which it was used was most plausibly centred on the seventh and eighth centuries, when a shift between the predominance of early medieval Brythonic and Old English was probably underway. It is possible that some of the religious centres concerned were very old, as earlier authors have proposed, and originally inhabited by entirely Brythonic-speaking communities. It is also possible that the process of language shift was in some instances accomplished through dramatic political events, as when Bishop Wilfrid appropriated 'consecrated places' (*loca sancta*) vacated by Britons in Northumbria.[108] However, it is important to note that use of the loan word does not necessarily require that we envision a decisive moment of language shift in all cases, as once it had entered Old English it could have been used in a variety of contexts. Many of the *eccles* place-names in the diocese of Lichfield might thus refer to religious centres that we have already encountered. Eccles House in Derbyshire lies less than a kilometre from the minster at Hope, while a second Eccles House is adjacent to Eccles Pike, close to the western edge of Hope's huge later medieval parish; neither place hosted a later medieval church or chapel. Exhall in Warwickshire, which later hosted a church of its own, was located at what was probably the northern extent of the later mother parish of the minster at Coventry. Eccleston in Cheshire also hosted a medieval church, but is notably only 3.5km south of Chester, where an early church cannot be ruled out; alternatively, it may have been a dependency of the minster at Bangor-is-y-Coed to the south. Finally, Eccleshall was

---

107 Gelling, *Signposts*, pp. 96–9; Gelling, *Place-names in the landscape*, p. 109.
108 *VW*, c. 17.

notably an important episcopal estate, and may have hosted a church from an early date, but it is also possible that its association with the cathedral at Lichfield explains the initial inclusion of *eclēs* in its name; it might thus offer a model for the way in which *halh* could be used to indicate a detached dependency.

Agricultural and domainal communities in the diocese of Lichfield

As outlined in Chapter 3, the word 'estate' has been used throughout this book to refer to the kind of landholdings called 'manors' after the Conquest, and labelled with a variety of terms beforehand, including the frustratingly flexible 'land'.[109] The meaning intended here by 'estate' is necessarily imprecise, given the partial understanding we have of such entities, but needs to be explored in a little more detail here if we are to grasp the interconnections between agricultural and domainal communities. Our understanding of early medieval estates in England has relied for some time on a model proposed by Rosamond Faith, which posits a directly farmed 'inland' and an outlying 'warland' inhabited by subordinate holders rendering various dues and services to the holder of the estate.[110] The model has recently been criticised by David Pratt because of the way it confuses the relationship between the landholder and warland inhabitants with the landholder's relationship to royal authority.[111] Faith had suggested that the dues and services of the warland, specifically a *feorm* comprising food rents and labour services, represented 'public obligations' formerly owed to the king from across large territories; these were then 'privatised' when the king granted out estates from these territories to landholders, whose own inlands were exempted from such obligations, including the geld or royal land tax that was imposed across all warlands in the tenth century.[112] It is this model of landholding that lies behind Blair's vision of the early estates given to minsters, and which was criticised in Chapter 4. Pratt has demonstrated that inlands were generally not exempt from the geld until they were made so during the reign of William I after the Norman Conquest, and has thereby brought into question the very nature of the warland inhabitants' relationship with the estate owner. Indeed, use of the term 'warland' in pre-Conquest contexts now seems ill advised, as it appears solely in post-Conquest evidence, denoting that part of an estate that was assessed to the king's geld, as against the recently exempted inland. It therefore has no directly attested connection with the pre-Conquest relationship between a landholder and the subordinate holders on his or her estate.

Use of the term 'inland' is retained here, despite the post-Conquest transformation in its meaning, as it was certainly used in the tenth and eleventh century to denote the part of an estate directly farmed by the landholder.[113] However, the problems with the

---

109 Lewis, 'The invention of the manor', pp. 145–6.
110 R. Faith, *The English peasantry and the growth of lordship* (Leicester, 1997), pp. 15–55 (inland), pp. 89–125 (warland).
111 D. Pratt, 'Demesne exemption from royal taxation in Anglo-Saxon and Anglo-Norman England', *English Historical Review*, 128 (2013), pp. 1–34.
112 Faith, *English peasantry*, pp. 89–92 and pp. 104–5 (in respect of royal *feorm*).
113 Pratt, 'Demesne exemption', p. 1, n.4.

term 'warland' are more substantial, and its use is now liable to provoke questionable assumptions, in particular an association with the supposed ancient public roots of the dues and services owed by its inhabitants. A number of alternative Old English words appear in the surviving documentary evidence to denote those parts of the estate not farmed directly, but here 'outland' (a modernised form of Old English *utland*) will be used, as it neatly complements 'inland' and is explicitly associated with *gafollands* in a charter of the tenth or eleventh century.[114] *Gafollands*, apparently more or less synonymous with *gesettlands* or *geneatlands*, were notable features of outland in the tenth and eleventh century;[115] these words point to an agreement to 'set' or fix certain dues and services by which an explicitly hierarchical relationship between an estate holder and the inhabitants of the outland (sometimes referred to as *geneats*) was articulated.[116] Primary among these dues was *gafol*, best translated as 'tribute', paid in cash or kind;[117] the various services owed could include labour on the landholder's defended residence, aiding with the landholder's hunt and with haymaking and harvest on the inland, carrying messages and transporting goods and provisions, and acting as a bodyguard for the landholder.[118] Other inhabitants of the outland, known as *geburs*, were more heavily burdened, again owing *gafol* of various kinds, but also ploughing services and two or three days' labour on the inland each week, often in acknowledgement of the fact that the landholder had provided certain resources to set these holders up on their holdings.[119] None of these services and tributes need be understood as ancient 'public' dues.

It should be apparent from this brief summary that the organisation of agricultural communities was fundamentally entangled with the ways in which a landholder's possession of his or her estate was articulated. While the farming of a set of arable fields might be organised collectively, with each farmer (including the estate's owner) allotted a share of the land, the labour required to farm these shares was unequally distributed. The landholder farmed with assistance from the estate's *geburs*, and occasionally the *geneats*, who also farmed their own holdings; these subordinate holders also had to take into account the various *gafols* they needed to produce for the landholder when organising the farming of their holdings, and the *geneats* had to maintain horses to fulfil various services. Moreover, we can readily recognise a kind of ritualised collective activity in the fixed and repetitive nature of many of the

---

114 S 108; the charter probably dates from the tenth or eleventh century in its surviving form, although it purports to be a charter of the late eighth century issued by the Mercian king Offa.
115 See Pratt, 'Demesne exemption', p. 23, for the equation of *gesettland* and *gafolland*.
116 This interpretation follows Faith, *English peasantry*, pp. 103–4, but removes her suggestion that 'tax liability' was implicated in the 'setting' of land in this way.
117 Faith, *English peasantry*, pp. 105–6.
118 Faith, *English peasantry*, pp. 107–12.
119 Faith, *English peasantry*, pp. 76–84. Faith styles *geburs* as inhabitants of the inland, but, while they worked regularly and frequently on the inland, their own holdings were farmed independently and were part of the outland; see the tenth-century survey of the estate at Tidenham, Gloucestershire (S 1555), which lists the yardlands of the *geneats* and *geburs* as *gesettlands* in explicit contrast to the inland.

dues and services owed by the subordinate holders, especially the *gafols* that were often rendered at certain points throughout the agricultural year, like the ecclesiastical tributes discussed in Chapter 4. It is here that we can posit a connection with the domainal communities of landholders, as there is some evidence to suggest that the fixing or 'setting' of the dues and services of the subordinate holders, often lumped together under the umbrella term 'customs' (*consuetudines*) was publicised and affirmed at the assemblies that constituted the domainal communities. Faith makes much of the 'law-worthiness' of independent farmers and their right to attend such assemblies and appeal to the folkright negotiated there; this is supported by the appearance of *gafol*-payers in late ninth- and tenth-century lawcodes, and by David Roffe's suggestion that the manorial values recorded in Domesday Book represent expressions of *gafol* in cash that were public knowledge at the large assemblies used by the commissioners.[120] Like the relation of ecclesiastical tribute-payers to diocesan communities, this subordinate penumbra of *gafol*-payers was necessary to domainal communities because possession of land meant little without the creation and maintenance of explicit territorial hierarchies among the inhabitants of early medieval landscapes. Indeed, without seeking to understand such relations it would make little sense for us to talk of 'estates'.

These relations can now be explored within the context of the place-names analysed earlier. Figure 18 shows all these place-names, excepting those containing *burh*, *tūn*, *lēah*, *feld* and *halh*, alongside the minsters identified in Chapter 3, and overlaid on the soil map introduced in the first part of the chapter. It is intended to indicate the locations of places whose place-names were probably coined before the tenth century and yet remained stable into the eleventh century and beyond. The vast majority of these place-names are located on the brown earths and sands that were most easily worked by the plough, although the clay soils over mudstone were evidently also moderately attractive, offering a satisfactory trade-off between greater fertility and more difficult ploughing. There are some interesting regional concentrations, such as the place-names containing *dūn* that cluster in the Peak District, probably due to the nature of the topography there, where flat hilltops adjacent to the many narrow steep-sided valleys offered some of the best locations for settlement; the grouping of settlements here vindicates the pastoral possibilities offered by the brown earths of the White Peak in the particularly wet climate of this region. Across the diocese settlements on larger blocks of more easily worked soils tend to be found on or towards their edges, often close to soils with high groundwater associated with streams and rivers, supporting a point made by McKerracher – that the best settlement locations offered access to several different soil types and the varied ecologies that they supported.[121] The minsters demonstrate a particular association with such intersections of soil types, notably emphasising the importance

---

120 Faith, *English peasantry*, pp. 116–21; Roffe, *Decoding Domesday*, pp. 243–4. Alfred and Guthrum's Treaty acknowledged the *ceorls* 'who live on *gafolland*', and one of Edgar's lawcodes required tithes to be paid from the inland and *geneatlande* of estates (F. Liebermann, *Die gesetze der Angelsachsen*, I (Halle, 1903), pp. 126 and 196–7).
121 McKerracher, *Farming transformed*, pp. 37–8.

of soils with high groundwater, attractive for the hay harvests and summer grazing they could offer. More generally, the map allows us to draw a connection between the most stable place-names and the areas in which a reliable harvest could most easily be farmed. It is worth noting that the map does not display a comprehensive distribution of settlements with stable place-names. That proportion of the corpus of place-names containing *burh*, *tūn*, *lēah*, *feld* and *halh* predating the tenth century cannot be distinguished from the remainder coined at a later date, and other place-name elements not considered in this chapter could also doubtless be added. Nevertheless, the overall shape of the distributions considered here is convincing, and other place-name elements might be expected simply to sharpen its focus.

This chapter has advanced the proposal that the relative stability of such place-names can be explained in part by their association with large estates held by the social elite. This has been supported by comparing their hidage assessments in Domesday Book to the diocesan 'background' and noting the significant number of elite landholders associated with them. It must be acknowledged, however, that all the place-names elements analysed here also feature in the names of smaller estates, more typical of the average size of the majority of estates in the survey, and that many, both large and small, were held by thegns and 'free men' (*liber homines*) rather than their social superiors. Thus, neither size nor status on its own would appear to represent sufficient explanation for place-name stability. It is possible that the estates represented by these place-names were once all towards the larger end of the range, but that some later fragmented through grant and exchange, although the clustering of these estates on certain soils would tend not to support such a theory, there being insufficient space to posit larger territories for many of the smaller estates. Alternatively, the estates always displayed a range of sizes, but were once nearly all held by the highest of the social elite, only later being distributed through grant and exchange to those lower down the social scale. This appears implausible, as it is not at all clear how such a homogeneous earlier landholding situation might be explained.

The explanation proposed here draws on that broached earlier in relation to the kinds of functional settlement discussed by Blair, and the settlements with *eccles* place-names. Essentially, we need to envision significant elite centres in the landscape, often administering comparatively large estates and held by bishops, abbots, abbesses, earldormen and kings, maintained across generations along with their place-names. Some smaller estates, often held by thegns or free men, became persistently associated with these centres to the extent that the longevity of the latter acted to stabilise the place-names of the former up to and beyond the tenth and eleventh centuries. This explanation might imply that the more stable place-name elements analysed in this chapter represent the surviving rump of a once more widespread corpus, some of which were later lost. This appears plausible in relation to the Brythonic place-names, which display a variety of forms related to prominent landscape features. However, it is also possible that some Old English place-name elements were always associated with elite settlements, and thus we might expect the current distribution to be more representative of the earlier corpus. *Burh* is an obvious example: as noted earlier, Blair has suggested that the word was particularly associated with minsters in the seventh and eighth centuries, and sites with defensible enclosures might be expected always to have been associated with the social elite. Either way, the model presented here offers a way to begin to connect place-name stability with the communities of the region.

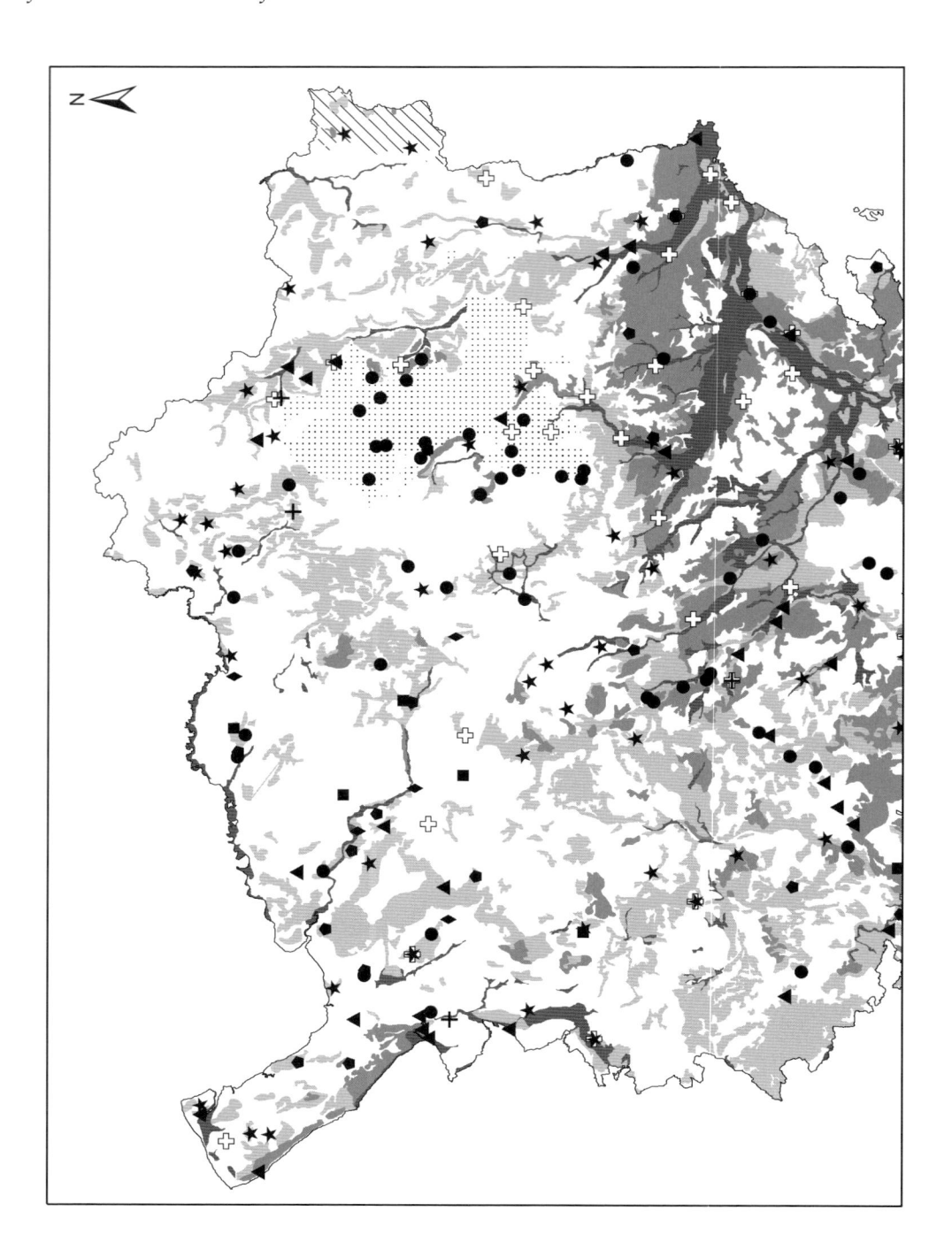

Lichfield and the Lands of St Chad

The people

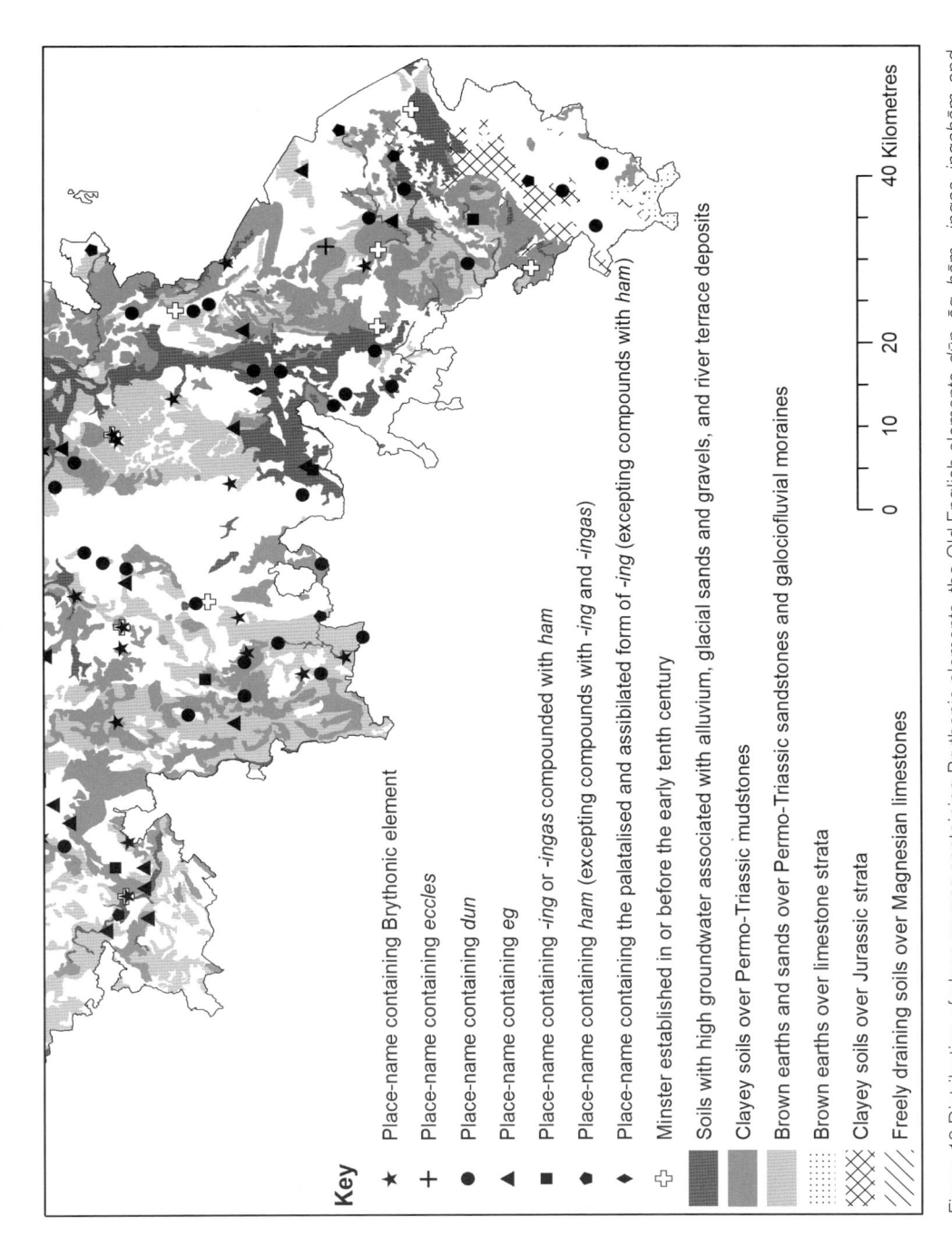

Figure 18 Distribution of place-names containing Brythonic elements, the Old English elements *dūn*, *ēg*, *hām*, *-ingas*, *ingahām*, and *-ing*, and the loan word *eclēs*, overlain on the distribution of different soil types.

The persistent association of some smaller estates with elite centres might be conceived in two ways. First, some such holdings may have initially comprised dependencies of large estates, their holders being servants of the estate's owner or members of that broader subordinate penumbra of outland farmers on the periphery of domainal communities. For example, the episcopal estate at Lichfield, bearing a name containing a Brythonic element, encompassed (among others) the townships of Hints, another place-name of Brythonic derivation, and Longdon, a *dūn* place-name (the 'long hill'), which became the centre of the manorial demesne after the Conquest.[122] Both were probably coined before the tenth century, and plausibly owe their stability to an active and persistent connection with the centre at Lichfield, which in this case lasted into the later medieval period. The functional settlements and *eccles* place-names probably offer other examples of this kind of situation, and John Blair has suggested that we understand the elite settlement morphology of the eighth and ninth centuries in terms of 'central clusters', 'specialised and defined mono-functional foci linked in complimentary groups'.[123] In the terminology developed earlier, we might conceive of specialised, possibly detached, parts of the estate's inland, and of subordinate holders on the outland whose customs had been fixed at an early date to ensure the certain provision of specific goods or services. The roles of estate reeves were probably important here: kings and bishops with extensive possessions could not, of course, attend every assembly in person, and probably relied on reeves to represent them, a subject recently explored by Tom Lambert;[124] the association of such reeves with the prestige of their royal and episcopal lords no doubt empowered them at assemblies to preserve the integrity their masters' landholdings (and their place-names) across generations. Many such holdings plausibly became estates in their own right later in the period, through grant, purchase or perhaps occasional loss.

It is, however, also likely that many of the smaller estates persistently associated with elite centres were never dependencies of those estates, but always independent of them. Such estates were probably more vulnerable to division or amalgamation through grant, exchange and the vagaries of inheritance, passing between different segments of one family, or sometimes into different families. Landholders belonging to such families did not necessarily have the political weight of royal status or the privilege of bookright to affect such processes, but they might attempt to gain access to such influence through seeking the patronage of the king, bishop or other political heavyweight; estates successfully shepherded by such means through several generations might, almost incidentally, also keep their earlier place-names. Nevertheless, the churn of estates through such conjunctions over time guaranteed that other landholders would not succeed as they had hoped. Many estates split and reformed, lost and gained owners, and some no doubt changed their names. Another strategy worth noting here has recently been explored by David Pratt: many of those who served the king might seek estates given on loan for the duration of

---

122 For Hints and Longdon see Horovitz, *Place-names of Staffordshire*, pp. 317–18 and 369.
123 Blair, *Building Anglo-Saxon England*, p. 193.
124 Lambert, *Law and order*, pp. 120–3 and 127–8.

The people

their service.[125] In remaining tightly associated with royal estates across substantial periods of time, many of these 'loanland' estates might also be expected to have kept their earlier place-names.

This discussion can do no more than hint at the kinds of community that inhabited the early medieval landscapes of the diocese of Lichfield; precision is impossible. Nevertheless, consideration of place-name corpora alongside a critical review of the broader field of scholarship has enabled some conclusions to be drawn. In particular, this chapter extends the criticism launched in Chapter 4 against the model of landholding that views the formation of estates as a result of the fragmentation and 'privatisation' of older 'small shires' or 'multiple estates', territories of 'extensive lordship' focused on royal centres;[126] this model relies on the idea that the tributes and services owed by dependent landholders were 'originally' owed to the king, an idea that is rejected here. The landscape revealed here was certainly dominated by large elite estates belonging to kings and bishops, and perhaps to ealdormen and some prominent minsters. However, there is no reason to assume that this dominance echoes an earlier royal monopoly on landholding before newly baptised kings started to grant bookland estates to their nascent religious elite; there is in practice no need to deny the likelihood that non-royal estates had existed throughout the period. The mechanisms discussed above to explain relative place-name stability would permit the existence throughout the period of a range of landholdings, different in size and internal complexity, and held by a variety of owners, from kings and bishops down through ealdormen and the rulers of minsters to the less exalted members of the elite, the thegns and free men.

The element crucial to understanding the definition and dynamics of landholding is the existence of the assemblies that constituted domainal communities: fora in which landholders ritually fashioned their own personhood by producing and reproducing their own claims to landholding and validating them through mutual acknowledgement. Here, smaller landholders mixed with royal and episcopal reeves. The locations of such assemblies are lost to us before the emergence of the royally mandated hundred and shire assemblies of the tenth and eleventh centuries, although some of these later assemblies may have maintained the meeting-places of earlier assemblies. This chapter has thus denied the formative role of primordial royal estates in the constitution of early medieval landholdings, but it does not ignore the importance of royal patronage in the dynamics of landholding, and, indeed, it must be remembered that royal assemblies constituted high-status domainal communities throughout the period. None of these elements should be confused with the territories across which kings continued to extract various tributes and services from independent landholdings over the same period, which were discussed briefly in Chapter 4. These territories, extensively distributed across the various regions of the kingdoms and usually administered by reeves, are here labelled 'regnal territories' and are discussed further in Chapter 6. There is no basis on which to assert that the local assemblies through which domainal communities of the seventh, eighth

---

125 Pratt, 'Demesne exemptions', pp. 23–4.
126 Faith, *English peasantry*, pp. 1–14.

and ninth centuries were constituted were necessarily commensurate with these regnal territories. This changed in the mid-tenth century, when regnal territories were superseded by hundreds and shires, which also became the basic units of assembly, although even then there is evidence to suggest that these assemblies were used creatively: there is evidence of several cases in which a number of hundreds or even shires assembled together in one large gathering, perhaps reproducing the outlines of earlier local or regional assemblies.[127]

It is beyond the scope of this book to explore the origins of the landholding patterns illuminated and discussed here. Such a study would involve an investigation of the period centred on 600, at the portal between late antique and early medieval Britain. Nevertheless, the agricultural expansion explored at the beginning of this chapter probably holds the key to understanding the development of these patterns. Regardless of the initial proportions of royal estates to those of other landholders, the imperatives driving the maintenance of land ownership through the regular assembly of domainal communities appear to have remained vibrant throughout the period, and may well have increased in intensity. If agricultural expansion can be understood as a result of landholders intensifying the productivity of their inlands and putting ever greater pressure on the subordinate holders of the outlands to produce greater tributes, as McKerracher essentially argues, then it must also be understood as a negotiated process in which the inhabitants of the outlands acted to resist the excesses of such pressure through the fixing of customs at the assemblies that drew all these people together. Solidarities within domainal communities probably focused on appealing to the patronage of ealdormen, and of royal and episcopal reeves, at the core of these communities, but they were perhaps also generated through the constitution of agricultural communities, the members of which shared interests generated through their geographical proximity in the management of common fields and pastures. The varying extents to which fields and pastures were farmed in common during this period correlates well with differences in the underlying soils and hydrology, but the specific forms of communal organisation that constituted many agricultural communities during this period ultimately emerged from such negotiations.

Nevertheless, regardless of such solidarities, the articulation of normative 'customs' within domainal communities enabled the explicit ascription of hierarchies, in which assertions of power involved attempts to impose customs of greater benefit to oneself than to the other party and to have them formally acknowledged, and thus fixed, at assemblies. The creation of the relationship between a subordinate penumbra of outland holders and a core group of landholders thus formed the basic rationale of a domainal community, the solidarity of that core group enabling the repeated assertion of dominance over the penumbra. However, that core group also formed a locus of negotiation and competition in its own right. Within regnal and diocesan communities, hierarchical norms were ultimately focused on a single person at the top in relation to which other positions might be staked out; in contrast, the domainal community looked to no such nexus of authority. Instead, a range of landholders at

---

127 H. Cam, 'Early groups of hundreds', in H. Cam (ed.), *Liberties and communities in medieval England* (Cambridge, 1944), pp. 91–106.

The people

the top end might compete for greater recognition among their fellows by seeking to increase the size, quantity and quality of their landholdings, and to win various privileges and immunities for those holdings from regnal and episcopal authorities.[128] Similar forms of competition might extend down through the rest of the community, even into the subordinate penumbra, some of whom may have had the connections or resources to pursue strategies of 'upward mobility', converting outland holdings into independent estates.[129] The desires and anxieties thus generated around status throughout domainal communities perhaps best explain the drive towards agricultural expansion during the period considered in this book. But if this chapter presents a more plausible vison of the dynamics of landholding and agricultural expansion than that offered by the model of fragmenting 'small shires', it leaves unanswered the many questions raised by the stabilisation of place-names of the tenth and eleventh centuries, which has traditionally been explained by the granting of thegns' estates out of such territories. These issues are tackled in the next chapter.

---

128 Elements of such competition emerge in the 'discourse' of landholding explored in S.T. Smith, *Land and book: literature and land tenure in Anglo-Saxon England* (Toronto, 2012).
129 Williamson, *Environment, society and landscape*, pp. 119–23, explores issues of upward and downward mobility, although he employs a notion of 'ancestral' folkland at odds with the model explored above.

Chapter 6

The parish

The stabilisation of place-names belonging to many small estates during the tenth and eleventh centuries, even as it occurred alongside the persistence of many larger estates held by kings, ealdormen and bishops that were named in earlier centuries, represents an important transformation within the diocese of Lichfield and across much of England. The process was contemporary with another significant phenomenon, the addition of a large number of churches to the landscape of existing minsters and episcopal churches. Some of these newer churches were significant in their own right, while others were smaller, often staffed by a single priest rather than a larger clerical group. Moreover, from the 920s the regnal authorities of the nascent kingdom of England imposed on the landholding population the compulsory payment of tithe to a select group of 'mother churches' distributed widely across the landscape in order to support the pastoral care of the population. The territory from which these tithes were drawn is commonly labelled the parish, the name by which it eventually came to be known. There was, however, always more to a parish than the payment of tithes, and this chapter seeks to understand the emergence of what is here called the 'parochial community' in the diocese of Lichfield. This community is defined generically through the regular collective attendance of its membership at a parish church and the formalised relationships that lay people established with their priests, in particular the payment of tithes, but also including other pastoral ministrations and burial in the church graveyard. As such, parochial communities involved large numbers of lay people with the liturgical and pastoral activities of ecclesiastical communities.

The chapter begins with a consideration of the broader context of tithe payment and its establishment in England. Thereafter, two main analyses are employed, the first considering the 'superior churches' of the diocese identifiable in the Domesday folios, the second the identity and form of 'mother parishes' within the diocese, in order to demonstrate the nature of the tenth- and eleventh-century transformation in the ecclesiastical landscape of the diocese. An important connection is illuminated between the estates of kings, ealdormen and bishops and the mother churches that were initially granted the tithes of the diocesan population. It is suggested that the mother parishes of these churches were created around a framework of 'regnal territories' that had been instituted in earlier centuries to administer and collect dues and obligations owed to the king, territories that were shortly after reorganised to create the hundreds and shires of the late tenth and eleventh centuries. Having emphasised the distinctions of the new ecclesiastical landscape when compared with that of the earlier minsters, the chapter considers how the transition from one arrangement to the other might be framed. Previous scholarship has drawn significant conclusions here, and this chapter engages particularly closely with John Blair's work on what he views as a 'secularisation' of religious life during this period. In contrast, the concluding discussion emphasises the close entanglement of secular and ecclesiastical communities throughout the period covered by this book, and suggests that the tenth-

The parish

century transformation involved the formal assumption of spiritual lordship by kings, ealdormen and (later) earls as part of a broader assimilation of regnal and spiritual forms of lordship that eventually resulted in the emergence of parochial communities associating a larger proportion of the diocesan population with liturgical and pastoral activity than had been the case in the earlier landscapes of minsters.

Churches and parishes

As noted briefly in Chapter 4, the annual payment of tithe, the tenth part of a farmer's annual agricultural produce, was mandated in England by royal decree only from the later 920s, beginning with a law-code issued by Æthelstan at about the time he began styling himself 'king of the English'; there is little evidence that it was paid before this time in any kind of regular or comprehensive way.[1] Tithe originated as a voluntary spiritual offering with a biblical basis, and appears first to have become a compulsory payment within the Carolingian kingdom in the mid-eighth century, when attempts were first made to enforce it, attempts that were continuously reiterated in subsequent Carolingian legislation.[2] As such, it should be viewed as a tributary render, like the ecclesiastical tributes discussed in Chapter 4; however, whereas the latter might be paid *at* certain churches, the continental tithe payment soon became a render paid *to* a specific church, a common idea being that it should go to the church where the tithe-payer received the sacraments and baptised their children.[3] Francesca Tinti notes that instructions for the clergy and homilies written in England in the late tenth and eleventh centuries explicitly connected tithe to the maintenance of the clergy and their churches, as well as the relief of the poor.[4] Nevertheless, while the English tithe was certainly a *church* due rather than an *episcopal* one, the question regarding to which particular churches it should be paid remained important.

John Blair has demonstrated that English legislation between the 920s and 1020s repeatedly insisted that tithe be paid to churches styled 'old minsters' or the particular minsters 'to which it belonged'; Edgar's Andover Code (959×972) makes clear that this category excluded churches that thegns might build on their 'booklands', but concedes that such a church, if it had a graveyard, should be given a third of the thegn's 'own' tithe, probably that from his inland.[5] The law does not preclude the possibility that churches might also be built on non-booked holdings, but denies the latter any right to tithe.[6] Blair has assembled textual and archaeological evidence to demonstrate that the foundation of such estate-churches became increasingly popular in the second half of the tenth century and through the eleventh, before declining

---

1 Blair, *Church*, pp. 435–6 and 440–1; F. Tinti, 'Pastoral care', pp. 32–3.
2 Wood, *Proprietary church*, pp. 459–61.
3 Wood, *Proprietary church*, pp. 462–3.
4 Tinti, 'Pastoral care', pp. 35–42.
5 Blair, *Church*, pp. 441–5.
6 A law-code of Cnut implies that folkland might be treated much like bookland at assemblies determining its inheritance if the previous holder had fulfilled all obligations owing to the king: Liebermann, *Die gesetze der Angelsachsen*, p. 366 (II Cnut, 79).

in the earlier twelfth.[7] Such churches were often initially constructed in timber, and usually adjacent to the hall complexes of their builders, or sometimes on plots located within the expanding towns; their appearance in considerable numbers across two centuries or so has been compared to the appearance of 'mushrooms in the night' by Richard Morris.[8] This period also witnessed the formalisation of churchyard burial in consecrated ground; outside the cemeteries of the earlier minsters much of the population had previously been buried in grounds unassociated with churches or churchmen, but after the mid-tenth century many estate-churches soon attracted graveyards, or were built in pre-existing cemeteries, a phenomenon also associated in some places with a phase of memorial stone sculpture production.[9] From the late tenth century stone masons were also occupied in building or rebuilding estate-churches in stone, and from the mid-eleventh century incorporated some stylistic influences and building techniques borrowed from the larger Romanesque projects of the Norman conquerors.[10] The intensity of this activity appears to have varied across the country, being particularly prevalent in the east, and Blair has suggested that in the north-western parts of England (including much of the diocese of Lichfield) 'small churches were still mostly non-permanent structures in 1100'.[11]

Legislative protection of tithes owed to 'old minsters' thus correlated with the proliferation of estate-churches. This protection may have lasted largely intact up to the Conquest, but thereafter evidence suggests that many Norman lords alienated the remaining two-thirds of their inland tithes to distant monastic foundations, often in Normandy, indicating that the original recipients of these tithes had lost any control over them; likewise, from the twelfth century onwards the tithes of the outlands, which previously had presumably gone to the 'old minsters', were more commonly associated with local churches.[12] Nevertheless, the post-Conquest fragmentation of large parishes centred on the 'old minsters' was not an entirely comprehensive phenomenon. The reconstruction of earlier 'mother parishes' from later references to dependent chapels within them demonstrates a continuing element of parochial hierarchy, as well as offering a plausible means of identifying some of the 'mother churches' that were probably intended by the 'old minsters' of Edgar's law.[13] These mother churches can in one sense rightly be considered to be the earliest parish churches, at least if we define the parish solely by reference to the collection of tithes across a distinct territory. However, before the Conquest mother churches must have coexisted with a number of estate-churches within their territories, some of which were in receipt of a portion of their lords' tithes, which acted as alternative

---

7   Blair, *Church*, pp. 385–96 and 402–7.
8   R. Morris, *Churches in the landscape* (London, 1989), Chapters 4 and 6.
9   Blair, *Church*, pp. 463–71.
10 Blair, *Church*, pp. 411–17.
11 Blair, *Church*, pp. 417–22, at p. 420.
12 Blair, *Church*, pp. 447–8.
13 S. Bassett, 'Boundaries of knowledge: mapping the land units of late Anglo-Saxon and Norman England', in W. Davies, G. Halsall and A. Reynolds (eds), *People and space in the Middle Ages, 300–1300* (Turnhout, 2006), pp. 115–42.

foci of spiritual provision for certain portions of the inhabitants; this situation renders a stable understanding of parochial communities during this period more difficult to articulate.[14] Only in the twelfth century did the parish as a discrete community, constituted by the annual payment of all its inhabitants' tithes to its central church in return for the regular pastoral care of its priest, emerge as the dominant type.

We can thus envisage a pre-Conquest hierarchy of churches: at the top were the 'old minsters' granted a near-monopoly on tithe in the laws and apparently defined in part by their large size and possession of a graveyard. These probably correlated to a significant extent with the mother churches ruling mother parishes identifiable from later records. Nevertheless, these facts do not tell us much about the origins of the 'old minsters' or their broader social contexts. To approach these issues we begin here with an analysis of the larger and more significant churches of the diocese of Lichfield, in order to define more closely the attributes that might have characterised the 'old minsters'. It is now commonly appreciated that Domesday Book hints at the presence of a large number of substantial churches staffed by colleges of clerics across late eleventh-century England, which previous scholarship has labelled 'secular minsters' or 'superior churches', emphasising their presence alongside the Benedictine monasteries that dominate the historiography of the tenth and eleventh centuries in much of western Europe.[15] In a seminal article John Blair set criteria for identifying them and presented maps showing 311 superior churches across Domesday England, while admitting that this total almost certainly represented an underestimate of the type.[16] His criteria included all churches recorded with more than one priest and all holding land independently, together with those holding more than one hide or carucate of land within a parent estate; this essentially distinguishes all churches that appeared in some way larger than the 'classic' estate-church served by a single priest, although he also admitted that the smaller superior churches 'shade imperceptibly into the ranks of larger manorial churches'.[17]

Table 2 lists superior churches within the diocese of Lichfield identifiable from Domesday evidence. Blair's criteria have been attenuated to omit any church holding land within a parent estate unless it has more than one priest;[18] this is intended to focus the group on those churches displaying evidence for a group of priests rather than the single pastoral priest of the classic estate-church, and also recognises that we do not sufficiently understand how much land within an estate was considered appropriate to support such a priest or what considerations might have caused such an amount to vary, and therefore whether Blair's limit of one hide or carucate realistically distinguishes different types of church. The results of this exercise are not, of course, comprehensive: there may well be some clerical groups who were represented in Domesday Book, if at all, by the record of only one priest, but the method here errs on

---

14　Blair, *Church*, pp. 426–504, provides an essential discussion.
15　J. Blair, 'Secular minster churches in Domesday Book', in P. Sawyer (ed.), *Domesday Book: a reassessment* (London, 1985), pp. 104–42.
16　Blair, 'Secular minster churches', pp. 107–11.
17　Blair, 'Secular minster churches', p. 119.
18　Blair, 'Secular minster churches', p. 106.

Lichfield and the Lands of St Chad

Table 2
'Superior churches' identified in Domesday Book within the diocese of Lichfield.

Church location	Holder TRW	Holder TRE	Relevant elements of Domesday Book entry
Staffordshire			
Lichfield	Bishop of Chester	The Church	5 canons
Burton	St Mary's of Burton		'Abbey' (*abbatia*)
Stafford	Canons of Stafford		13 prebendary canons, holding from the king in alms
Wolverhampton	Samson and the canons of Wolverhampton		
Tettenhall	Priests of Tettenhall		Holding from the king in alms
Penkridge	Clerics of Penkridge		9 clerics
Norbury	Earl Roger	Auti, a free man	2 priests
Warwickshire			
Stoneleigh	King William	King Edward	2 priests
Leek Wootton (*Optone*)[1]	King William	King Edward	2 priests; the holding was a member of the estate at Stoneleigh
Coventry	Church of Coventry		'Abbey' (*abbatia*)
Kingsbury	King William	Countess Godgifu	2 priests
Monks Kirby	Geoffrey de la Guerche	Leofwin, freely	2 priests
Long Itchington	Christina		2 priests
Derbyshire			
Derby		One church	'in the king's lordship'; 7 clerics
Derby		A second church	'likewise the king's'; 6 clerics
Repton	King William	Earl Ælfgar	2 priests
Bakewell	King William	King Edward	2 priests
Shropshire			
St Peter's, Shrewsbury	St Peter's	St Peter's	'Minster' (*monasterium*), Earl Roger building an 'abbey' (*abbatia*) there
St Mary's, Shrewsbury	St Mary's	St Mary's	
St Michael's, Shrewsbury	St Michael's		
St Chad's, Shrewsbury	St Chad's	St Chad's	
St Alkmund's, Shrewsbury	St Alkmund's	St Alkmund's	The church holds 12 canons' houses
St Juliana's, Shrewsbury	St Juliana's		
Ellesmere	Earl Roger	Earl Edwin	2 priests
Wroxeter	Earl Roger, Rainald from him	Thored, a free man	4 priests
Cheshire			
Farndon	Bishop of Chester	Bishop of Chester	2 priests and 1 'priest of the vill'
St John's, Chester	Bishop of Chester	Bishop of Chester	The church holds 8 houses, one for the *matricularius* and 7 for the canons
St Mary's, Chester	Bishop of Chester		'Minster' (*monasterium*), next to St John's church
St Werburgh's, Chester	St Werburgh's	St Werburgh's	The church holds 13 houses, one for the *custos* of the church, 12 for the canons
Acton	Earl Hugh, William Malbank from him	Earl Morcar	2 priests
Runcorn (recorded under the estate at Halton)	Earl Hugh, William son of Nigel from him	Orm, a free man	2 priests

1   The equation of *Optone* with Leek Wootton, which is not otherwise recorded in the Domesday survey, is based on the fact that twelfth-century evidence gives the latter an assessment of three hides, identical to *Optone*, and that Leek Wootton was a mother church in the twelfth century, befitting the two priests recorded in Domesday Book (it was granted to Kenilworth Priory with chapels at Leamington, Ashow, Lillington, Milverton and Cubbington): *VCH Warks*. vol. 6, 167–70.

The parish

the side of caution in order to exclude single-priest estate-churches. The diocese's two pre-Conquest Benedictine monasteries, at Burton and Coventry, are also included as they appear as independent landholders in Domesday Book.

The group includes all the superior episcopal churches explored in Chapter 2: the cathedral at Lichfield and the three western churches at Chester, Farndon and Shrewsbury. It also includes the nine pre-Conquest churches that emerged later in the medieval period as 'royal free chapels', as discussed in Chapter 4.[19] All churches for which we have documentary evidence of foundation (or perhaps refoundation) during the tenth and eleventh centuries appear in the group: that at Bakewell endowed by Uhtred in 949;[20] that at Wolverhampton founded by Wulfrun in the later tenth century;[21] the Benedictine monastery at Burton founded by her son Wulfric *c*.1000;[22] and that at Coventry founded by Earl Leofric and his wife Godgifu in 1043.[23] St Werburgh's church in Chester is known to have been in existence by 958, when King Edgar granted it various lands in Cheshire.[24] It is also notable that the shire towns at Chester, Derby and especially Shrewsbury appear to have acted as magnets for superior churches, a fact also noted in Chapter 4 in relation to the royal free chapels. The group contains fifteen churches (out of thirty-one in total) that were recorded as independent landholders with their own sections in Domesday Book. Of the remainder, which were recorded in parent estates, four were held TRE by the bishopric, three by King Edward, four by members of the Mercian comital family (Godgifu, Ælfgar, Edwin and Morcar) and four by named thegns or free men (Auti, Leofwin, Thored and Orm), while for one no information is provided; the dominance of the highest stratum of the elite among these holders is thus impressive.[25]

This dominance is also notable if we compare this corpus of superior churches with that of the earlier minster churches identified in Chapter 3. There is a noticeable lack of overlap between the two corpora, with only eight churches appearing in both.[26] Of these eight, the information for 1066 recorded in Domesday Book demonstrates that one was among the holdings of the bishopric (Lichfield), four were independent churches (Wolverhampton, Burton, Coventry and Derby St Alkmund), one belonged to King Edward (Bakewell), one to Earl Ælfgar (Repton) and one to a thegn, Thored (Wroxeter); the range of holders thus epitomises that displayed by the corpus of superior churches more generally, again focusing on the elite. However, the same

---

19 Stafford, Wolverhampton, Tettenhall, Penkridge, the two Derby churches (combined into one royal free chapel at All Saints) and St Mary's, St Michael's and St Juliana's, Shrewsbury.
20 S 548.
21 S 860 and S 1380.
22 S 906 and S 1536.
23 S 1000.
24 S 667.
25 Bishopric: Lichfield, Farndon, Chester St John, Chester St Mary. King Edward: Stoneleigh, *Optone*, Bakewell. Comital family: Kingsbury, Repton, Ellesmere, Acton. Thegns: Norbury (Staffs.), Monks Kirby, Wroxeter, Runcorn.
26 Lichfield, Repton, Andresey/Stapenhill (at Burton), Northworthy (Derby St Alkmund), Coventry, Wroxeter, Bakewell and Wolverhampton.

range is not reproduced among the whole corpus of earlier minster churches, thirty-seven of which were located on estates that were recorded in Domesday Book.[27] Of these, four were independent churches in 1066, while, of the rest, twenty were represented by one or more priests (sometimes alongside a church) recorded among the estate population of 1086 and thirteen were not explicitly represented in the relevant estate at all.[28] By definition, the four minsters that had become independent churches by 1066 appear in the corpus of superior churches, but, among the thirty-three earlier minsters churches located on parent estates in 1066, 25 per cent of those held by King Edward appear in the corpus of superior churches, as do 33 per cent of those held by Earl Ælfgar, 11 per cent of those held by the bishop, and only 7 per cent of those held by thegns.[29] The last figure is particularly striking, because thegns held 45 per cent of the thirty-three minster churches on parent estates.

The earlier minsters that can be recognised as later superior churches were thus disproportionately drawn from among those held by the elite in the eleventh century, especially the king and comital family. The lower percentage of episcopal minsters among the superior churches is probably related to the dominance of the cathedral at Lichfield among the episcopal holdings, discussed in Chapter 2. It is perfectly plausible that a good proportion of the earlier minsters were of no great size or importance in the seventh, eighth or ninth centuries, and need not have become so in the tenth and eleventh centuries. Nevertheless, it is perhaps surprising that twenty-three of the thirty-one superior churches (74 per cent) do not currently display any evidence for the presence of earlier minsters. It should be noted that others have argued for the greater antiquity of some of those twenty-three solely on the basis of the large extents of their reconstructed mother parishes, which have been associated

---

27   Polesworth cannot be associated with any Domesday estates, and may have been located within the estate of the borough of Tamworth, which was omitted from Domesday Book. Bangor-is-y-Coed may have been located within the estate at Worthenbury, but this cannot be empirically demonstrated.
28   The independent churches were Burton (for Andresey/Stapenhill), Coventry, Wolverhampton and Derby St Alkmund. Churches represented by priests (and sometimes churches) in the estate entries were located at Lichfield, Fauld (for Hanbury), Walton (for Stone), Norbury (Derbys.), Repton, Wirksworth, Bradbourne, Bakewell, Wroxeter, Sawley (for Wilne), Prees, Eccleshall, Tachbrook, Bupton (for Longford), Brewood, Baswich, Hope, Spondon, Ashbourne and Newton (for Blackwell). Churches not represented in any way within the relevant estate entries were located at Berkswell, Eyam, Rugby, Sandbach, Over, Tarvin, Upton (for Overchurch), Leek, Tean (for Checkley), Okeover (for Ilam), Alstonefield, Barton-under-Needwood (for Tatenhill), Aston-on-Trent.
29   King Edward held Wirksworth, Bakewell, Hope and Ashbourne. Earl Ælfgar held Repton, Leek and Barton-under-Needwood (for Tatenhill). The bishop held Lilchfield, Sawley (for Wilne), Prees, Eccleshall, Tachbrook, Bupton (for Longford), Brewood, Baswich and Tarvin. Thegns held Walton (for Stone), Norbury (Derbys.), Bradbourne, Wroxeter, Spondon, Newton (for Blackwell), Berkswell, Eyam, Rugby, Sandbach, Over, Upton (for Overchurch), Tean (for Checkley), Alstonefield and Aston-on-Trent. Churches located on estates at Fauld (for Hanbury) and Okeover (for Ilam) were held by the independent churches at Chester St Werburg and Burton respectively.

The parish

with earlier minster *parochiae*, an idea criticised and dismissed in Chapter 4.[30] It is also possible that future archaeological work will admit some of these churches to the corpus of earlier minsters. However, it is difficult to believe that the proportion of superior churches without earlier antecedents, currently almost three-quarters of the corpus, will be reduced radically by such work. In summary, the predominance of independent churches and churches held by the royal, comital or episcopal lords (twenty-six of thirty for which information is given, or 87 per cent) among the superior churches indicates that the status of these churches was much more likely to have related to the status of their lords than to their antiquity as liturgical communities.[31]

Of course, while the 'superiority' of these churches must have been apparent to contemporaries, we cannot necessarily connect them directly to the 'old minsters' whose tithes were protected in the laws. We can point to hierarchies of status according to various attributes, but it is not possible to draw a definite line between different *kinds* of church recorded in Domesday Book. Within the corpus of superior churches it is tempting to make more of the distinction between independent churches and those on parent estates, but this should be resisted. Indeed, it was suggested in Chapter 4 that many of the independent churches that later became royal free chapels originated as churches founded at the centres of royal estates. Within the corpus of royal estate-churches, differences between those that did and did not emerge later as royal free chapels were perhaps negligible in the tenth and eleventh centuries. For example, a single priest is recorded among the population of the royal estate at Condover in 1086, representing the presence of St Andrew's church there;[32] nearby, in Berrington, a thegn named Thored held half a hide from St Andrew's church by service (*per servitium*).[33] Thus Condover church was itself a landholding entity, despite apparently being recorded as part of the royal estate. In fact, the presence of the priest among the estate population probably indicates only that he (or rather, his church) held land within that estate. The church holding was on the outland, a subordinate holding in a hierarchical relationship with the lord of the estate. Later in the medieval period such holdings in England were called 'glebe lands', and were usually held free of tributary dues, owing only spiritual service to the lord.[34] The case of Condover demonstrates that a church seated on such a holding need not be prevented from holding estates elsewhere, and the largest of such churches were probably largely indistinguishable from the independent churches of Domesday Book.

Indeed, even the distinction between superior churches and the single-priest estate-churches against which they have been defined should not be pushed too far. Instead we should envisage a spectrum on which most churches were located

---

30 See, for example, Bassett, 'Anglo-Saxon Shrewsbury', which argues for the antiquity of St Mary's and St Chad's churches at Shrewsbury.
31 Blair, 'Secular minster churches', pp. 114–25, discusses the varied origins of superior churches over a period from the seventh century to the eleventh.
32 *DB Salop.*, 4,1,2.
33 *DB Salop.*, 4,3,14.
34 Wood, *Proprietary church*, pp. 437–44.

during the tenth and eleventh centuries, distinguished by degree rather than kind. This can be demonstrated by further consideration of glebe holdings, which are often discussed in relation to the active endowment of new or pre-existing estate-churches at the lower end of this spectrum. Blair dates this phenomenon to the period of estate-church rebuilding beginning in the late tenth century, tentatively suggesting that it represents 'a shift from priests maintained in thegnly households to priests holding earmarked lands'.[35] While this is plausible, we must acknowledge that the assignment of part of an estate to the support of a church has a longer history in England, and in identifying such shares in the information recorded in Domesday Book we must consider the whole spectrum of churches, whether or not they can otherwise be defined as superior in any way. For example, the collegiate clerical group at the royal church of Tettenhall, which was recorded as an independent church in Domesday Book and emerged as a royal free chapel in the later medieval period, held two hides of land in 1086, distinguished from a royal estate there assessed at two and a half hides, from which it was probably initially endowed. The church at Baschurch, which also hosted a collegiate group but was recorded within an estate entry, held two and a half hides of a three-and-a-half-hide royal estate.[36] Moving a little down the scale, we find the royal churches at Ashbourne and Hope recorded within estate entries, each holding one carucate from estates assessed at three carucates and ten carucates respectively.[37] Still further down the scale, the church on Earl Morcar's five-hide estate at Great Ness, which was a daughter church of Baschurch, held a virgate (quarter of a hide).[38] Finally, the single priests recorded at so many estates probably represent holdings similar to those of the *villani* with whom they were listed, perhaps a virgate or half-virgate in size. Such a continuum recalls Æthelred II's lawcode of 1014, which, excepting the smallest 'field-churches', recognised all churches in the kingdom to be 'minsters', reckoned only by size ('head', 'rather smaller' and 'smaller still').[39]

Nevertheless, Edgar's laws imposed a clear distinction between 'old minsters', which were allowed to take tithe, and others, which could not. The spectrum of churches discussed above does not enable the certain identification of this distinction among the churches of the diocese of Lichfield in the tenth and eleventh centuries, despite describing a clear hierarchy based on other attributes. This is clearly problematic if we want to identify parochial communities based on the payment of tithe, as defined in the introduction to this chapter. The next section therefore turns to later evidence for mother parishes, territories within which tithe was paid to central mother churches. It should be noted that henceforth, and despite Æthelred's terminology, the tenth- and eleventh-century churches studied here will all be called 'churches' rather than minsters, whether or not they can be defined as superior on the basis of the attributes discussed above. Thus the churches of this chapter are clearly distinguished from the earlier minsters considered in Chapter 3. This is not intended to forestall any

---

35   Blair, *Church*, pp. 407–10, at p. 410.
36   *DB Staffs.*, 1.2, 1.3 and 7.5; *DB Salop.*, 4.1.3; Bassett, 'Wroxeter', p. 12.
37   *DB Derbys.*, 1.14 and 1.29.
38   *DB Salop.*, 4.1.17.
39   Liebermann, *Die gesetze der Angelsachsen*, p. 264 (VIII Æthelred, 5.1).

The parish

connections or commonalities between earlier and later periods, but recognises that the introduction of mandatory tithe payments in the earlier tenth century, the associated formation of parochial territories and the great expansion of churches across England in the subsequent two centuries present significant differences from the earlier situation and demand an analysis that clearly distinguishes between them.

Churches, estates and 'regnal territories'

If the payment of tithe to the church of one's priest formed a key ritual around which a parochial community was defined, as argued here, then an analysis of the geography of parochial territories forms an obvious route to understanding the formation and development of such communities. There are, however, problems inherent in the later date of most of our evidence for parochial geography: the parochial arrangements of the tenth and eleventh centuries have to be 'reconstructed', and our knowledge must remain partial. After briefly discussing these issues, this section presents the results of such a reconstruction. The subsequent analysis demonstrates the importance of the mother parish, which contained not only the estate directly supporting its mother church, but also the estates of other landholders; it is suggested that such mother parishes allow our closest approach to the churches that would have been recognised in the tenth and eleventh centuries as 'old minsters' according to Edgar's laws. Given that the extent of such a mother parish must have been informed by more than simply the bounds of the estate supporting its mother church, the remainder of the section explores various possibilities for the creation of these mother parishes by comparing the parochial geography of the diocese to other kinds of territory that existed at the time, and advocates the primacy of 'regnal territories', across which royal reeves administered the dues and services owed by landholders to the king.

As described earlier, the law-codes appear to indicate a situation after the introduction of compulsory tithe payments in which early mother churches ('old minsters') received the tithe of many local landholders, but that among these landholders those with bookland were able to divert a third of their inland tithes to their own churches if the latter had graveyards; landholders who did not fulfil these conditions were presumably not allowed to divert any tithe to their churches, if they had them. However, between the Conquest and the early twelfth century many smaller estate-churches were able to acquire all the tithe from their host estates, from both inland and outland, and some may also have acquired the tithe from other estates. This post-Conquest transformation established a denser parochial geography in which many mother parishes had been substantially reduced from their original extents and were now situated within a meshwork of newly won parishes. However, subsequent parochial fission later in the twelfth and thirteenth centuries was often more successfully resisted, generating documentation in which mother churches and their dependent chapels or daughter churches are explicitly identified. Even where such dependencies did eventually gain their independence, such records can be used to reconstruct the earlier extent of mother parishes, and such reconstruction has been attempted by many scholars across different parts of England; the results of this exercise across the diocese of Lichfield are shown in Figure 19, excluding only

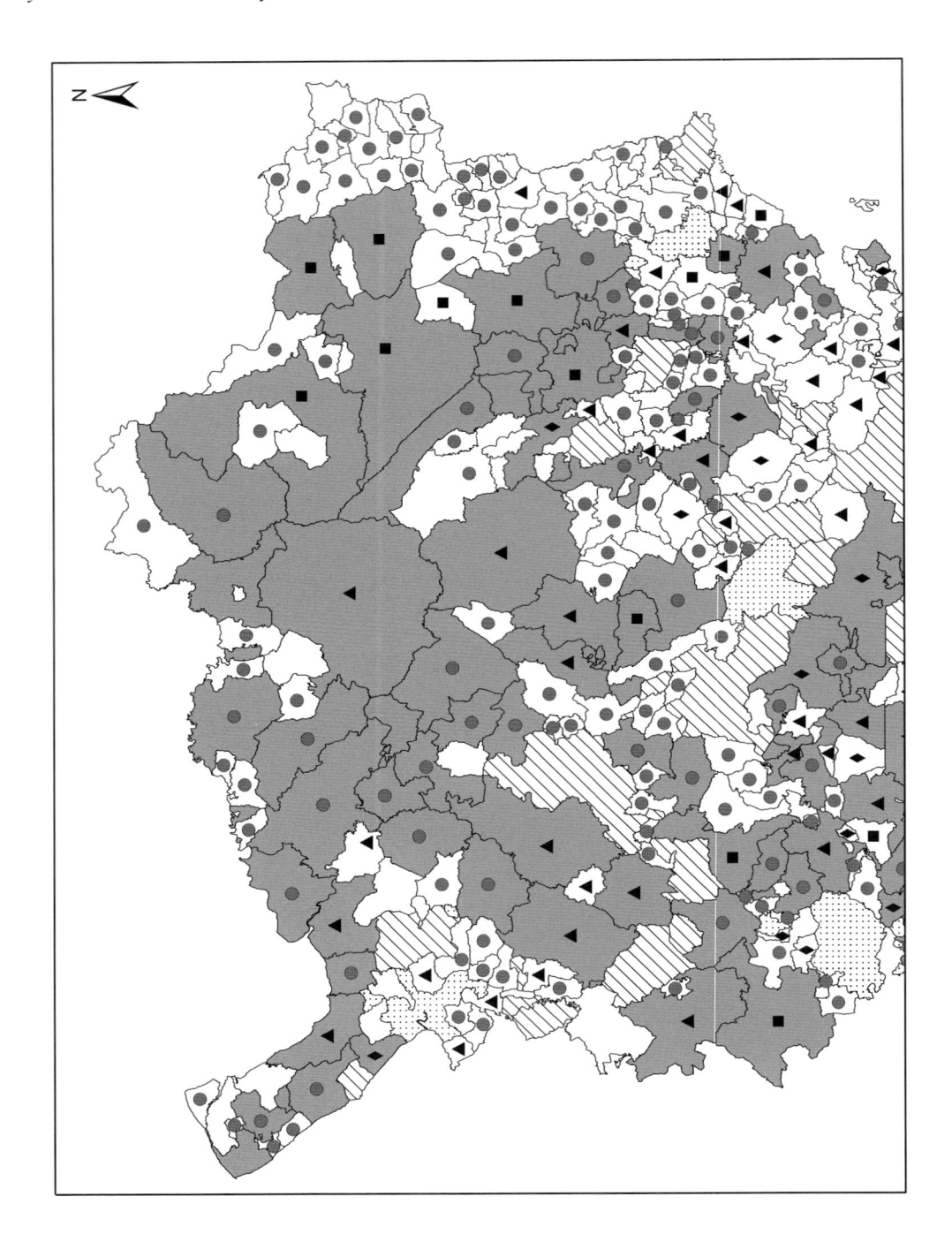

Lichfield and the Lands of St Chad

The parish

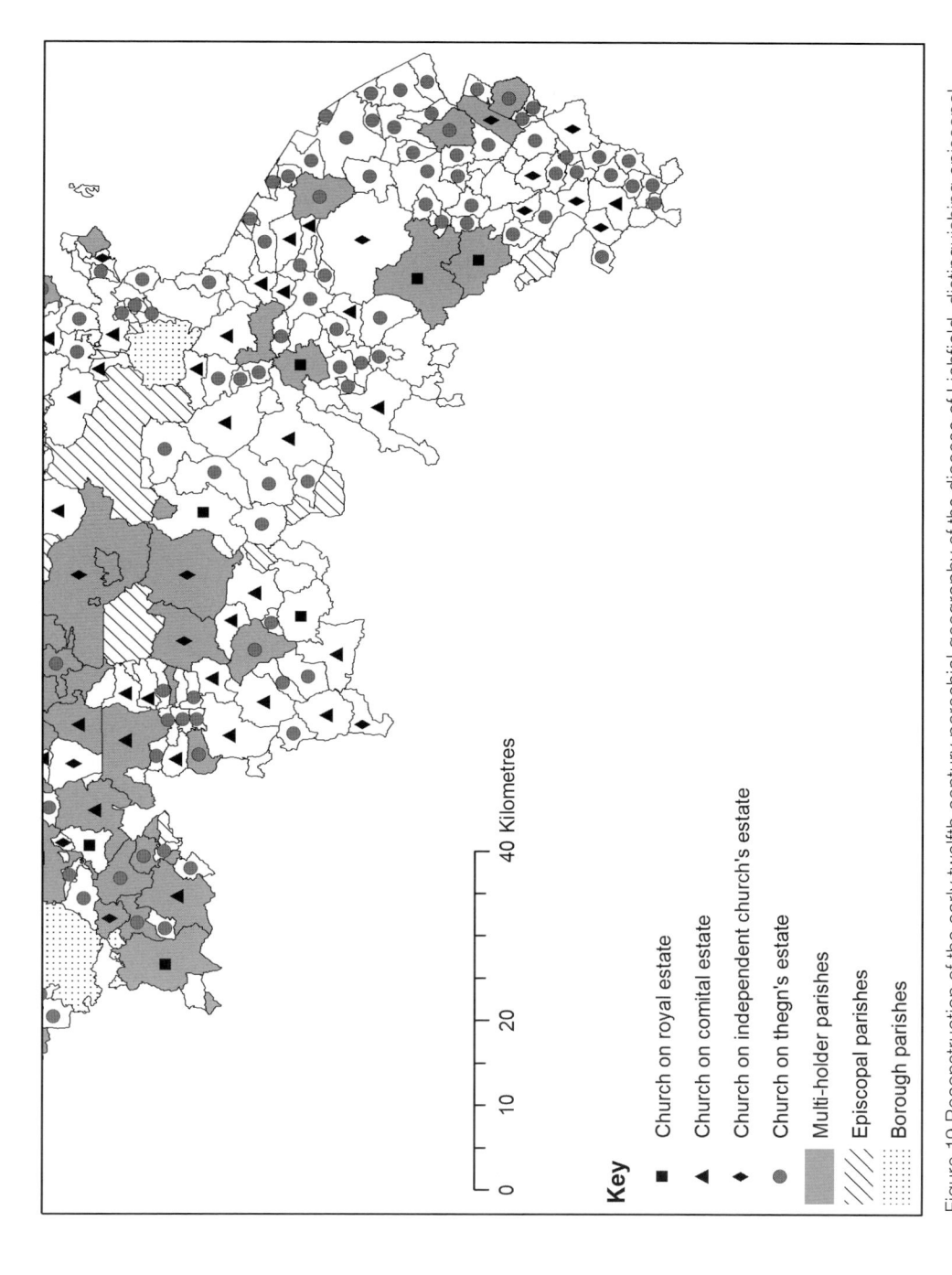

Figure 19 Reconstruction of the early twelfth-century parochial geography of the diocese of Lichfield, distinguishing episcopal, borough and multi-holder parishes from the surrounding mesh of one- or two-holder parishes.

Key
■ Church on royal estate
▲ Church on comital estate
♦ Church on independent church's estate
● Church on thegn's estate
▨ Multi-holder parishes
▨ Episcopal parishes
▨ Borough parishes

the parishes of borough churches, which were often entangled in complex ways.[40] It must be noted, given the post-Conquest transformation discussed above, that such reconstructions, even at their most successful, can only be accepted to represent the situation in the early twelfth century, and it must also be accepted that no exercise of this nature will be entirely successful owing to the partial nature of the evidence. Further analysis is necessary to provide suggestions as to which parishes constituted mother parishes with rights to tithe during the tenth and eleventh centuries.

Here, such analysis proceeds by laying the reconstructed parochial geography over the distribution of estates recorded for 1066 in Domesday Book. Specifically, this exercise distinguishes between parishes in which only one or two landholders possessed an estate ('one- or two-holder parishes') and parishes in which three or more landholders held distinct estates ('multi-holder parishes').[41] The category of one- or two-holder parishes is intended to demonstrate a connection between parochial geography and domainal geography, and thus to indicate churches that were likely to have been located within mother churches centred elsewhere in the tenth and eleventh centuries, but which were held after the Conquest by lords of significance sufficient to be able to gain independent parishes for them. The inclusion of two-holder parishes within this category is intended to account for the likelihood of a degree of fuzziness in the analysis: the parochial geography shown in Figure 19 was still developing in the early twelfth century, and it is unlikely that the domainal geography of the mid-eleventh century will straightforwardly illuminate the rationale of parochial formation in all cases. We simply do not know the precise histories of the estates recorded in Domesday Book through the tenth, eleventh and twelfth centuries, histories that probably included the splitting and amalgamation of estates that later informed the bounds of parishes. Such fuzziness might also encompass parishes formed around single estates that had nevertheless been divided into three, four or more parts through grant or inheritance by 1066, but the greater the number of estates in a parish the more likely that some other factor besides landholding informed its extent, and for the purposes of analysis the line has to be drawn somewhere. Nevertheless, cases in which three or more landholders held estates centred in the same vill have been treated as if they represented one landholder, to both account for the probability of earlier division and acknowledge the likelihood that all the inhabitants of the vill went to the same church regardless of which estate they lived on. Multi-holder parishes are considered most likely to represent mother churches of the tenth and eleventh centuries, which were granted the tithes of the estates of other landholders in the vicinity. The original mother parishes of many of these churches were doubtless initially larger, before other churches within them gained parochial independence in

---

40   The map uses parish boundaries first recorded in the nineteenth-century tithe surveys. In cases where explicit indications of parochial hierarchy are missing, more speculative arguments based upon the payment of pensions and the like have been avoided, as such payments could be made for a number of reasons, not only parochial dependence.

41   Cases in which all estates in a parish are ascribed to the same lord TRE have not been counted among the multi-holder parishes, as the record may represent two or more estates created after the Conquest out of a single pre-Conquest estate.

The parish

the post-Conquest transformation discussed above; many of the latter are probably represented by one- or two-holder parishes.

This analysis also indicates a connection between early mother parishes and the lords of their churches that extends the analysis of superior churches earlier in the chapter. The distribution of one- or two-holder parishes correlates well with estates held by named thegns and free men (*liber homines*) in 1066, although some were held by the king and members of the comital family at that time. For example, estates at Rolleston and Elford in Staffordshire, which had earlier been bequeathed by Wulfric to members of his family, were held in 1066 by Earl Morcar and Earl Ælfgar respectively.[42] A smaller proportion of the churches on thegns' estates were associated with multi-holder parishes, which were far more likely to be associated with churches on the estates of the elite: the king, members of the comital family and the lords of independently recorded churches. Parishes associated with the bishop's churches are distinguished separately on Figure 19. Some of the bishop's larger estates, such as Lichfield, were spread across several parishes; we might suspect in each of these cases that one large mother parish had subsequently been divided.[43] Most episcopal parishes belong to the one- or two-holder category, demonstrating a clear connection with the associated estate, but there were multi-holder parishes at Longford, Ellastone, Wybunbury, Prees, Tarvin, Farndon and Wilne. Overall, the landholders associated with the churches of multi-holder parishes occupied the same high status as those associated with most of the superior churches. Likewise, if we consider churches located on the sites of the earlier minsters identified in Chapter 3, we find that all four of those held by the king in 1066 had multi-holder parishes, as did all three of those held by Earl Ælfgar, eight out of nine of those held by the bishop and two of the six recorded as independent churches, but only three of the fifteen held by thegns. This is especially important, as it indicates that there is no reason to equate early mother parishes with earlier minsters, and reinforces the significance of the correlation between mother parishes and the elite lords of their mother churches in the tenth and eleventh centuries.

It is perhaps tempting at this point to equate Edgar's 'old minsters' with the holdings of the elite when tithe payment was imposed in the early tenth century. However, this would not explain why some of the estates held by that elite did not host mother churches, nor would it illuminate the processes whereby particular parochial territories were assigned to mother churches. The remainder of this section explores possible influences on the formation of mother churches, and thus the rationale for the parochial geography illustrated in Figure 19. Outside the estates hosting their mother churches, mother parishes largely encompassed estates held by thegns in 1066, although very occasionally we find comital estates, or some of the smaller holdings

---

42 *DB Staffs.*, 10.3 and 10.6.
43 Staffordshire: Lichfield (parishes of Lichfield, Longdon, Armitage, Norton Canes, Whittington, Weeford, Hints, Statfold, Pipe Ridware and Yoxall); Eccleshall (parishes of Eccleshall, Adbaston, Ellenhall and Seighford); Great Haywood (parishes of Colwich and Stowe); Derbyshire: Sawley (parishes of Wilne and Long Eaton, with two additional estates held by thegns in the former parish). Under Sawley the Domesday survey recorded two churches, perhaps located at Wilne and Long Eaton: *DB Derbys.*, 2.1 and 2.2.

of the bishop. Any explanation of the specific forms taken by mother parishes must be based on complementary connections between those estates and their mother churches. It is possible in some cases that the estate was held dependently, as some form of loanland, from the estate that hosted the mother church, and thus that landholding remains the most plausible explanation for the extent of the parish. However, a substantial proportion of the thegns holding these estates across the diocese are described as 'free' or are said to hold 'freely', explicitly indicating that no such dependent connection existed in 1066, although of course it may have done earlier.[44] Other possibilities must therefore be explored, and the following discussion considers three different entities: hundreds, territories defined by soke and 'regnal territories' defined by a more comprehensive set of obligations to the king, the last of which is considered to be the most likely basis for mother parishes.

Hundreds

The hundreds established in the mid- to late-tenth century constitute an obvious possibility, which can nevertheless be disposed of quickly, as mother parishes and hundreds do not generally correlate. However, there are some close geographical relationships between mother parishes and hundreds that should not be dismissed, particularly in Shropshire and Cheshire. Nick Higham has indicated a number of cases in which the territory covered by a Cheshire hundred was divided between two mother parishes, one focused on a church in secular hands in 1066, the other on a church held by the bishop. A good example is provided by Warmundestrou hundred, most of which was occupied by the parishes of the episcopal church at Wybunbury and the comital church at Acton.[45] In fact, Higham does not suggest a direct connection between the hundred and the mother parishes, but instead proposes that the estates at Wybunbury and Acton were once commensurate with their parishes, and that they represent two halves of an earlier unitary estate that gave form to the hundred. In contrast, it was suggested in Chapter 2 that the bishop's estate at Wybunbury had always been quite small, and was perhaps used to give the bishop access to the saltworks at Nantwich. It is certainly plausible that in some cases the establishment of mother parishes, probably in the first half of the tenth century, and the establishment of hundred territories in the second half were implemented with reference to similar concerns, especially in Cheshire and in Shropshire, where hundred dues were often rendered at the estate centres hosting mother churches. However, mother parishes were generally more numerous than the hundreds, even in these regions, and, as stated above, their boundaries were often not precisely commensurate. Neither territory directly explains the other, nor is it sufficient to explain the creation of either through straightforward invocation of earlier landholding arrangements.

---

44 S. Baxter, 'Lordship and justice in late Anglo-Saxon England: the judicial functions of soke and commendation revisited', in S. Baxter, C. Karkov, J.L. Nelson and D. Pelteret (eds), *Early medieval studies in memory of Patrick Wormald* (Farnham, 2009), pp. 397–8.

45 Higham, *Origins*, pp. 140–6.

The parish

Soke
A more convincing possibility is provided by the dues and services owed to the king or his representative by landholders. Tom Lambert has recently provided a comprehensive analysis of these obligations from the seventh century onwards, clarifying that they need to be understood in terms of two distinct spheres of action: first, military services, notably the three 'common burdens' of service in the army, building and repairing fortifications, and building bridges, which were often reserved in charters from the eighth century onwards; and, second, the provision of various dues and services to the royal household and its members, many of which were the subjects of immunity clauses granted to bookland holders in those same charters.[46] It is the second set of dues and services that concerns us here. As mentioned briefly in Chapter 4, eighth- and ninth-century charters indicate that these often comprised a food rent and/or the provision of hospitality to the king or his retainers and servants ('guesting'), assorted services such as carrying messages or guarding the king, and the fines and forfeitures resulting from litigation against people living or apprehended on the estate. These feature among the 'warland' services described by Rosamond Faith; however, as discussed in Chapter 5, in using this term Faith anachronistically projects a post-Conquest situation, in which the inlands of tenants-in-chief had been exempted from the geld while their outlands continued to pay it, back into the pre-Conquest past. This encourages an analytical confusion of domainal obligations owed from the outlands of estates to landholders (Old English *inwaru*, 'inward service') with regnal obligations owed from the estate to the king (Old English *utwaru*, 'outward service'), which were usually assessed on both outland *and* inland before the Conquest, as David Pratt has recently demonstrated.[47] This confusion has coloured much subsequent scholarship, but had in fact long been a bugbear of previous scholarship because of the use of the word *soca* by the Domesday scribe (and presumably the survey commissioners and inquisitors before him) to label dues and services of all kinds.

This is not the place for a comprehensive treatise on 'soke', but it must be touched upon briefly as regnal dues so-named may have provided the primary influence on the formation of mother parishes sought here. The term *soca* first appeared in the later tenth century, and David Roffe has summed up its wide semantic range, noting that it 'articulated nothing more than a relationship in which customary dues were rendered; it could refer to a whole host of dues from the render of a quitrent from an acre of land on the one hand, to the regalian rights of the king in the shire on the other'.[48] Nevertheless, two more specific meanings are often recognised by scholars, which resonate with the distinction between domainal and regnal dues made here. A domainal usage is visible in the parts of Domesday Book derived from Circuit VI of the survey, in which discrete parcels of land owing inward renders to an estate were indicated with a marginal 'S' signifying 'sokelands'. A regnal usage, indicating outward renders from an estate to the king, or more usually his local representative, is

---

46 Lambert, *Law and order*, pp. 114–24.
47 Pratt, 'Demesne exemption', pp. 21–2.
48 D. Roffe, *Domesday: the inquest and the book* (Oxford, 2000), p. 30.

visible throughout Domesday Book in a host of estate entries in which *soca* is said to be rendered out of the estate to another lord, often the king or the earl.

The regnal sense of the term *soca* is further complicated by its relationship to the legalistic jingle *saca et soca*, 'sake and soke', found in Domesday Book and in grants of privileges in charters and writs, as there is some debate over whether they can be treated as synonymous;[49] it appears most likely that 'sake and soke' referred more specifically to the fines and forfeitures included within the larger bundle of dues and services that comprised regnal soke, although use of the term may nevertheless have sometimes implied the latter.[50] Inasmuch as such bundles of renders had long formed the substance of immunities in charters, the word *soca* was a comparatively late label for an earlier phenomenon, although in the case of 'sake and soke' the shift from a discourse of freedom *from* fines and forfeitures to grants *of* them is noteworthy.[51] Moreover, the overall nature of regnal renders probably changed over time, as food rents and compulsory hospitality declined during the tenth century, perhaps compensated by an increasing emphasis on the efficiency of extracting fines and forfeitures through the hundred and shire courts.[52]

The two senses of soke, domainal and regnal, need to be kept separate when analysing Domesday Book and other documents, but this has often proved difficult. The reeves of royal estates, or those to which sake and soke had been granted, were responsible for administering both regnal and domainal soke, and so estate entries in Domesday Book might refer to both in ways that do not always make the distinction clear. Furthermore, some of the services that contributed to regnal soke were very similar to services that contributed to domainal soke. The eleventh-century estate-management manual *Rectitudines Singularum Personarum*, possibly associated with the Benedictine monastery at Bath, distinguishes clearly between the services owed by the thegn (who appears here to hold a bookland estate) and the *geneat*, the most independent member of the outland population.[53] Among the duties required of each, both must help to maintain animal-hedges (*deorhege*), probably referring to enclosures used for hunting; fulfil guard duties (*weard*); and help to build and maintain fortified enclosures. These activities differed only in that they related to the estate and household of the king in the thegn's case and to the lord of the estate in the case of the *geneat*, although even that difference blurs when we consider *geneats* on royal estates.

Historians have also invoked the twelfth-century 'Kalendar' drawn up for Abbot Samson of Bury St Edmunds, which lists various fixed sums due from 'socage' lands labelled 'hidage', 'wardpenny', 'averpenny', 'sheriff's aid', 'hundred aid' and the like

---

49 For example, see J. Tait, 'Review of *The Domesday inquest* by Adolphus Ballard', *English Historical Review*, 23 (1908), pp. 122–6; Roffe, *Domesday*, pp. 30–4. The interpretation employed here does not agree with Roffe's understanding of the use of the terms.
50 C.A. Joy, 'Sokeright', MA thesis (Leeds, 1972), pp. 56–62.
51 Lambert, *Law and order*, pp. 323–5.
52 Gautier, 'Hospitality in pre-Viking Anglo-Saxon England', pp. 42–3; Lambert, *Law and order*, pp. 242–53.
53 Liebermann, *Die Gesetze der Angelsachsen*, pp. 444–53.

The parish

– all cash payments by which services had probably been commuted.[54] These were paid by free men to the eight and a half hundreds that the abbey had acquired, and thus represent regnal soke; more broadly, similar dues were still being collected by royal agents across much of the country in the thirteenth century.[55] However, their similarity to the services imposed on outland inhabitants, such as the guarding and carrying services commuted by 'wardpenny' and 'averpenny', prompted C.A. Joy to propose in her seminal 1974 study of 'sokeright' that such outland services had 'originally been rendered to the king as part of the royal farm', thus compounding the confusion of domainal and regnal services by positing a remote period of earlier unity.[56] Joy's conclusions encouraged the thesis criticised in Chapter 5, in which the inhabitants of the outland were viewed as landholders whose ancient renders to the king had subsequently been 'privatised', a theory later reiterated by Faith.

The maintenance of a clear analytical separation between domainal and regnal soke avoids these problems and enables a plausible interpretation of mother parishes to be offered here. A series of charters and writs from the tenth century onwards demonstrates that 'sake and soke' was granted by the king to his earls and closest thegns over their estates.[57] Moreover, Stephen Baxter has proposed that 'the king could also grant estates to officials without issuing a royal diploma, and it is probable that many of the estates to which [regnal] soke was rendered in Domesday England were "comital" estates of this kind'.[58] Those most likely to hold their estates with 'sake and soke' by the mid-eleventh century would be the king, his earls and important thegns, along with the bishops whose estates had enjoyed similar privileges for centuries. These privileges are thus a possible influence on the assignment of tithe in the early tenth century. However, 'sake and soke' may not have been enough on its own; Edgar's law on estate-churches implies as much insofar as the possession of bookland (and therefore almost certainly 'sake and soke') gave the thegn only limited rights to his inland tithes. As Blair notes, a statement in Domesday Book concerning Stori, a landowner in Derbyshire and Nottinghamshire, to the effect that he was able to found a church 'in his land and his soke' and to direct tithe to it without anyone's permission, appears in the text 'as though an unusual anomaly needing special mention'.[59] Moreover, the elite stratum of people whose estates most commonly hosted mother churches is very narrow, dominated by king, earls and bishops and excluding many thegns whose estates were recorded in Domesday Book, suggesting that we should envisage territories from which a more comprehensive bundle of regnal dues and services were rendered as the forms around which mother parishes were shaped in the tenth century.

---

54 R.H.C. Davis, *The kalendar of Abbot Samson of Bury St Edmunds and related documents* (London, 1954), pp. xxxii–xlvii.
55 Neilson, *Customary Rents*, pp. 114–53 (Chapter 7).
56 Joy, 'Sokeright', p. 223.
57 Joy, 'Sokeright', pp. 120–34.
58 Roffe, *Domesday*, pp. 32–3; Baxter, *The earls of Mercia*, p. 239; Baxter's uninflected use of the term soke in this quotation is perhaps ill-advised, given his own assertion of the plurality of meanings inherent in this word (at pp. 210–11), also emphasised by Joy, 'Sokeright', p. 134.
59 Blair, *Church*, pp. 449–50; see *DB Derbys.*, B16.

'Regnal territories'

'Regnal territories' were introduced briefly in Chapter 5 as entities across which royal reeves administered and received tributes and services owed to the king from independent landholders; it was also noted there that they were reorganised after the mid-tenth century to create the hundreds and shires, for which much better evidence exists. Indeed, the main difficulty facing the analysis of regnal territories is lack of a contemporary name for them and of anything more than circumstantial evidence for their existence. The discussion of soke above introduces the notion of a more comprehensive form of regnal soke, encompassing the fines and forfeitures included in grants of 'sake and soke' but including other dues and services as well; evidence for the latter is not easily identified outside of the reservations in charters, discussed in Chapter 4 in relation to guesting and food-rents, and various unique documents from later centuries such as the *Rectitudines Singularum Personarum* mentioned earlier in this chapter. Nevertheless, some later evidence can be used to draw the outlines of earlier customary organisations that appear to follow the forms set out in these attenuated sources, and which can therefore be invoked as later iterations of earlier arrangements. The remainder of this section explores such evidence from the diocese of Lichfield.

The most compelling example concerns an estate at Leek (probably the location of an earlier minster) that was in the king's hands in 1086 and had been held by Earl Ælfgar before the Conquest.[60] The bounds of its ancient parish contained six estates recorded in Domesday Book besides Leek itself (Figure 20).[61] Five of these were recorded at the end of the section detailing the king's landholdings in what appears to be a list of estates that were 'waste' in 1086 (that is, they rendered nothing to the lord who owned them) but were held by named thegns in 1066, and one of them (Rudyard) had appeared half a century earlier in the will of Wulfric Spot.[62] The sixth estate, at Cheddleton, is recorded among the estates of Earl Roger of Shrewsbury and possessed a dependent member at nearby Basford, both elements being held by a thegn named Godwin before the Conquest.[63] Leek was subsequently granted to the earl of Chester, along with two of the earlier thegns' estates (Endon and Rushton), which appear as part of the fee of Leek in an early thirteenth-century survey.[64] Several

---

60 *DB Staffs.*, 1,21.
61 Leek's ancient parish included chapelries at Horton, Cheddleton and Ipstones.
62 Consall (Wulfheah), Endon (Dunning), Rownall (Wulfmer), Rudyard (Wulfmer), Rushton (Wulfgeat); *DB Staffs.*, respectively 1,56, 1,61, 1,62, 1,63, 1,64. Wulfric Spot's will (S 1536) gives to Burton, *inter alia*, 'Darlaston ['Deorlafestun'] and what belongs to it, namely Rudyard ['Rudegeard'] and my little estate at Cotwalton ['Cotewaltune']'.
63 *DB Staffs.*, 8,30, 8,31.
64 N. Tringham, 'An early 13th-century survey of the earl of Chester's fee of Leek', *Staffordshire Studies*, 5 (1993), pp. 1–12; see also N. Tringham, 'Leek before the Conquest', in P. Morgan and A.D.M. Philips, *Staffordshire histories: essays in honour of Michael Greenslade* (Keele, 1999), pp. 5–12. Endon is not mentioned explicitly in the survey, but was probably part of the holding at Longsdon; Rushton had been divided into two holdings, later called Rushton James and Rushton Spencer.

of the holdings into which the fee was by then divided were required to provide hospitality to the earl's servants and to aid in the earl's hunt at Hollinhay near Leek by building part of the hunting enclosure there; these services are notably similar to the kind that might form part of both domainal and regnal soke, discussed earlier. Two of the holdings owing this service in Leek's parish, Ipstones and Wall, were not recorded in Domesday Book, but probably originated as parts of the estate at Leek; notably, the service was not owed by the two earlier thegns' estates within the parish, Endon and Rushton, which were added to the fee after 1086. The service was also owed by five holdings that were probably earlier parts of the estate at Rocester, again held by the king in 1086 (and Earl Ælfgar before the Conquest), and also subsequently acquired by the earl of Chester;[65] these holdings were part of the Leek fee by the early thirteenth century, while the rest of the estate at Rocester had been granted to the priory there, founded by the nephew of an earlier earl, and of which the current earl held the advowson.[66] Finally, the same service was owed by the lord of the estate at Cheddleton, which had no post-Conquest connection with the earls of Chester.

It is possible to suggest that this hunting service was first imposed on the various holdings at some point before the Conquest: in the case of Cheddleton, an early connection, subsequently persistent, would explain the service in the absence of any later connection, while the absence of the service from holdings added to the fee in the late eleventh or twelfth century would also suggest that its original imposition belonged to an earlier context. Cheddleton may once have belonged to the estate at Leek, explaining its presence in Leek's parish; its subsequent separation from the estate may not have been sufficiently thorough so as to remove all service due. However, Rocester was certainly a significant estate in its own right before the Conquest and unlikely earlier to have formed part of Leek, so the service owed by those parts of it that were later placed in the fee of Leek cannot be explained in the same way. A better suggestion is that the estates of Leek and Rocester together, along with the estate at Cheddleton, were once all contained within the same territory, upon the entirety of which the service was originally imposed; within the estate of Leek it was a domainal service owed by holdings on the outlands, while outside Leek it was a regnal service owed by the estates held by thegns. Within the parish of Leek, the five thegns' estates recorded among the royal holdings in Domesday Book may have owed this regnal service initially, but post-Conquest acquisition by the king had perhaps 'laundered' them; likewise, those parts of the estate at Rocester granted to the priory are likely to have been freed of such service. The territory thus described encompassed much of the valley of the river Churnet, from its headwaters near Leek to its confluence with the river Dove at Rocester.

---

65   Waterfall, Denstone, Calton, Quixhill and Roston. A holding at Denstone recorded in Domesday Book (*DB Derbys.*, 1,55) was probably a separate estate, located in the parish of Alton. Sokeland at Roston belonging to Rocester was recorded in the section concerning an estate held by Henry de Ferrers at Roston (*DB Derbys.*, 6,57), but evidently belonged to the king's estate at Rocester.

66   *DB Staffs.*, 1,17 (and see *DB Derbys.*, 6,53 and 6,57 for Rocester's sokelands in Snelston and Roston respectively). See Tringham, 'An early 13th-century survey', pp. 1–2 and 7, for the earl's association with the priory.

Lichfield and the Lands of St Chad

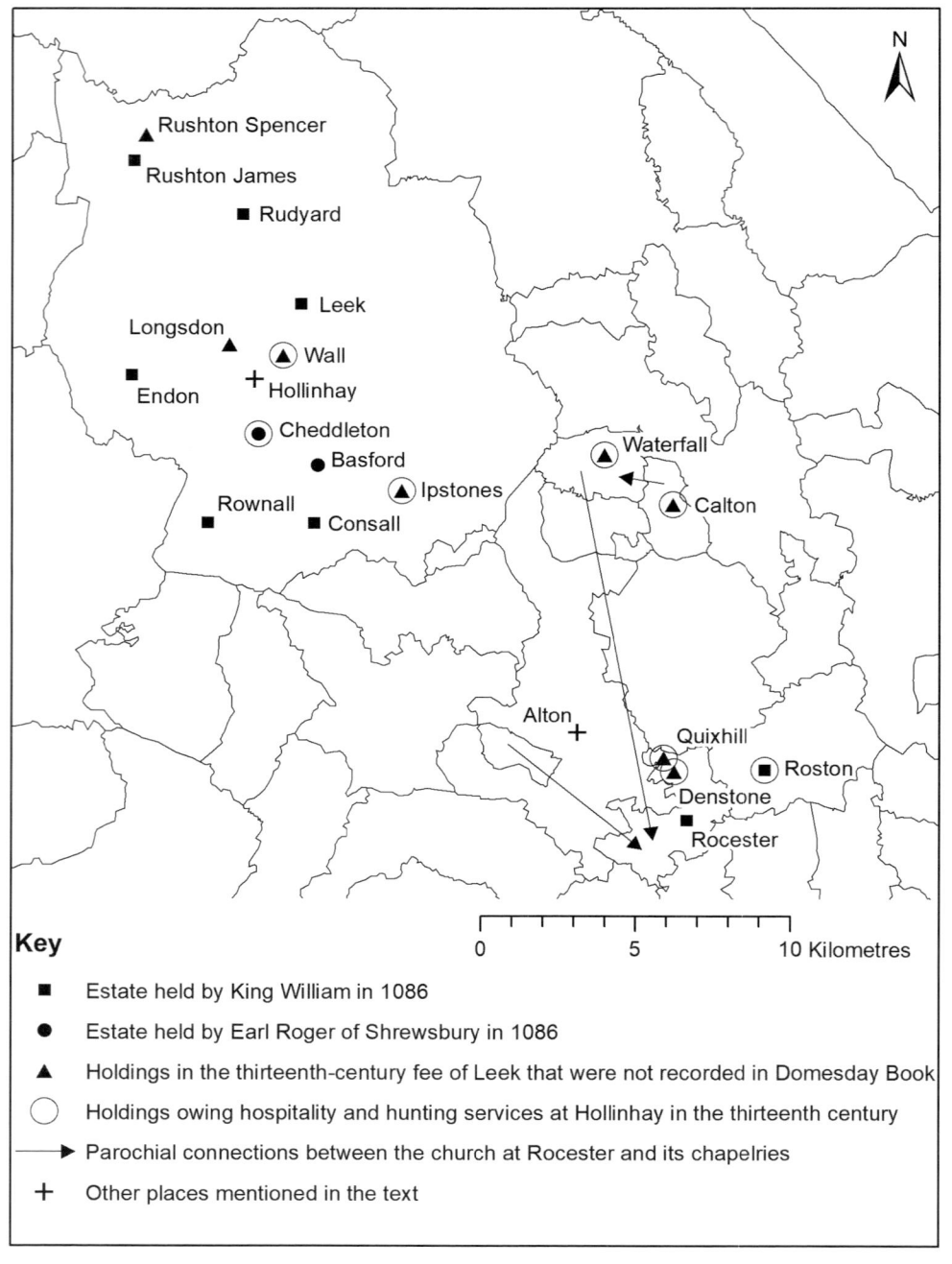

Figure 20 The thirteenth-century fee of Leek, including holdings owing hospitality and hunting services at Hollinhay, and also showing estates in the parishes of Leek and Rocester recorded in Domesday Book.

The parish

Thus, the mother parish of Leek may conform to a regnal territory within which the reeve of the estate organised and collected regnal dues and services; in comital hands by 1066, Leek had either been a royal estate at an earlier time or had been granted regnal privileges over the surrounding territory because of the comital status of its holder. The only part of the regnal territory outside the parish of Leek was contained within the estate at Rocester, which formed a second comital focus within the territory; Rocester perhaps had sufficient significance to warrant its own parish when tithe was assigned, encompassing the estate but nothing else.[67] Unfortunately, evidence for the kinds of regnal service recorded at Leek is exceptional, and so a more widely applicable theory concerning regnal territories must rest largely on extrapolation to explain broader patterns. It does at least appear plausible to extend the logic of these possibilities to the parochial geography of the diocese more broadly: one- or two-holder parishes centred on royal and comital estates may have been justified by the status of these estates' holders, while multi-holder parishes under the same lordship may well represent the outlines of earlier regnal territories. Our appreciation of the full extent of many of these territories is probably hampered by the presence of many of the one or two-holder parishes, which were probably created soon after the Conquest and cannot now be assigned to an earlier mother parish.

One further corpus of later evidence can be invoked to support the theory outlined here, and also enables consideration of an episcopal mother parish. Sources dating from the twelfth and later centuries have been employed to elucidate peace-keeping organisations articulated around 'serjeants of the peace' in the Welsh border shires of Cheshire and Shropshire, as well as in northern England, which appear to stand partly in the place of 'tithing' and 'frankpledge' organisations that fulfilled similar roles in other English shires.[68] The details of such organisation are largely irrelevant here, but a key element within them was the perambulation of peace serjeants around the territories that had been assigned to them, during which they were able to call upon food-rents and hospitality services known as 'puture' (*putura*) rendered from the estates of specific landholders, a form of obligation clearly very similar to elements of pre-Conquest regnal soke.[69] In Cheshire the peace serjeants answered to the earl across much of the shire, but of particular interest here are six baronial fees that maintained their own organisations of peace serjeants within their own holdings.[70] In most cases, one or more estates within each fee, including the later baronial *caput*, were held in 1066 by a member of the Mercian comital family, or, if this family held nothing within

---

67 Much of the Rocester estate emerged in later written sources within the parish of Rocester, although Roston lay in the parish of Norbury. A separate estate at Denstone had been held by a thegn named Iwar in 1066, together with another at nearby Alton; both appeared in the list of King William's 'waste' manors in Domesday Book, and may also have lain within the regnal territory discussed here, subsequently 'laundered' of their hunting obligations by royal acquisition after the Conquest.

68 R. Stewart-Brown, *The serjeants of the peace in medieval England and Wales* (Manchester, 1963).

69 Stewart-Brown, *Serjeants of the peace*, pp. 81–2.

70 Stewart-Brown, *Serjeants of the peace*, pp. 19–22.

Lichfield and the Lands of St Chad

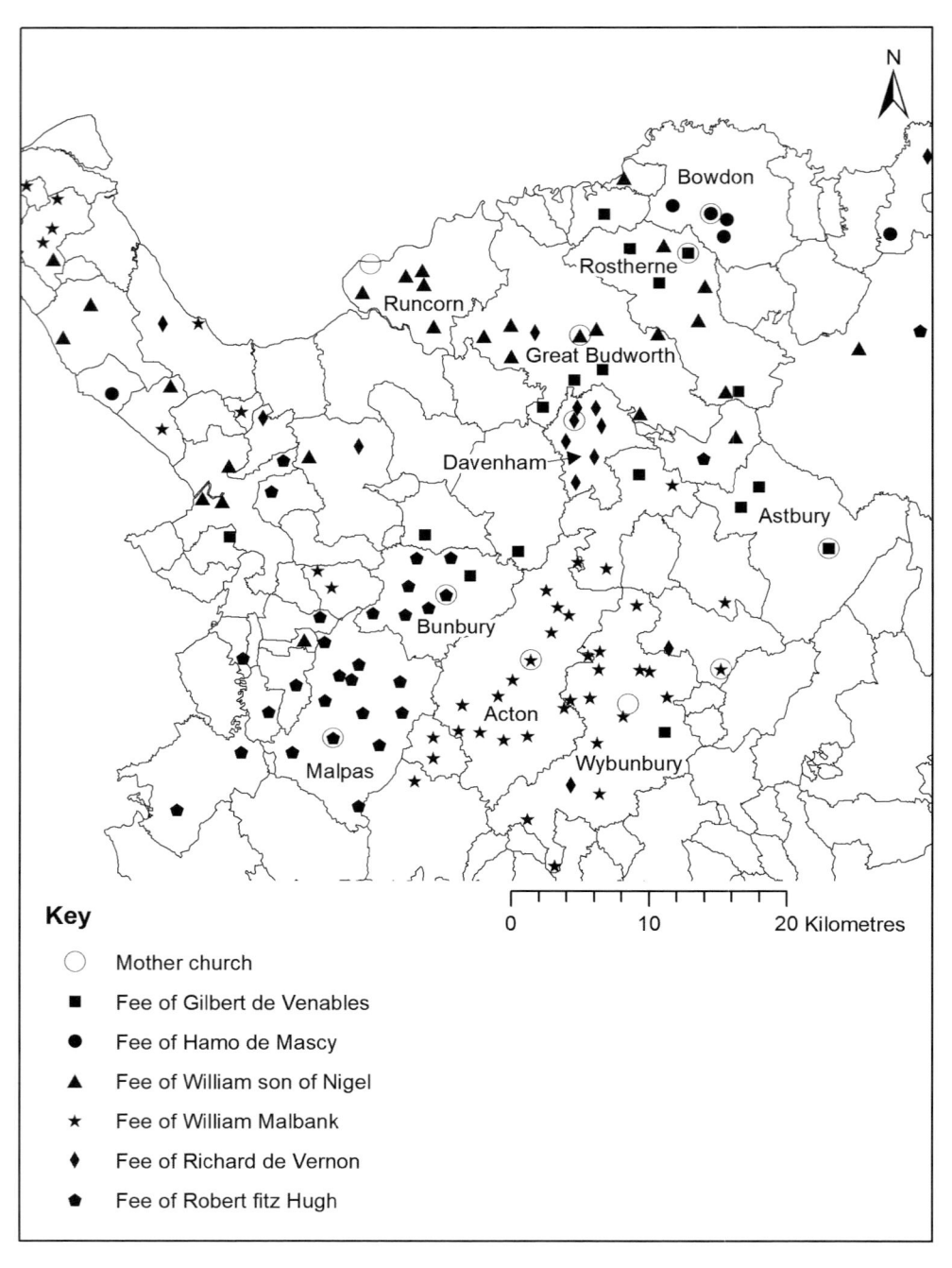

Figure 21 Cheshire fees of six barons recorded in Domesday Book, overlain on a reconstruction of the early twelfth-century parochial geography to demonstrate relationships with mother parishes.

The parish

the fee, then by a thegn, probably of some significance;[71] the remaining estates within the fee were held by various other thegns. When plotted on a map, the core areas of several of these fees correlate very closely with mother parishes, with only a little intermixing of the distributions (Figure 21); in each case the associated mother church was located either at the *caput* of the fee or on an estate held by the baron's pre-Conquest forebear. It can therefore be proposed that the post-Conquest lords of these fees were given sets of estates representing the remnants of earlier regnal territories, and that they were able to make use of customary connections between the head estates and their other landholdings to develop the peace serjeant organisations that emerge in the evidence of later centuries. Indeed, it is quite possible that these organisations represent later iterations of pre-Conquest arrangements.

The Malbank barony centred on Nantwich, one of those with its own peace serjeants, is particularly notable because it correlated very closely with the mother parishes of Wybunbury and Acton, introduced earlier.[72] Acton was held by Earl Morcar in 1066, the only estate in the fee held by a member of the comital family, and was also an administrative centre for salt production at nearby Nantwich;[73] it therefore represents the most likely candidate for the central estate of a regnal territory encompassing the two mother parishes. It was argued earlier that the hundred of 'Warmundestrou', also largely coterminous with the fee and the two mother parishes, is unlikely to have informed the territories of the latter, which were probably created a little earlier; here, the hundred is best understood as a later iteration of the earlier regnal territory, created when such territories were superseded by hundreds and shires after the mid-tenth century. The mother parish of Wybunbury was much larger than the episcopal estate at its centre, and it is proposed here that the extent of the parish represents the result of negotiations over the allocation of tithe within a regnal territory in which the earl and bishop both had some kind of interest, probably articulated around the saltworks at Nantwich. It was suggested in Chapter 2 that the bishop's estates at Wybunbury, Tarvin, Farndon, Ellastone and Longford were closely entangled in various ways with nearby royal estates, and it is doubtless no coincidence that this group also represents the majority of episcopal multi-holder parishes, all of which were plausibly the product of negotiations over tithe between

---

71 The only exception to this concerns the fee of Gilbert de Venables, which featured two notable oddities: first, it contained an estate at Alpraham in Bunbury parish, previously held by Earl Edwin, that we might expect to have found in the fee of Malpas, which otherwise dominates that parish; second, it appears to contain the core estates of two significant pre-Conquest thegns, Godwin (who had held the fee's *caput* at Kinderton), and Wulfgeat (who had held the mother churches at Rostherne and Astbury). The fees of Gilbert de Venables and William son of Nigel (who acquired mother churches at Runcorn – representing an estate at Halton – from Orm son of Gamal and Great Budworth from Edward) were also notably intermixed, perhaps hinting at the earlier division of a larger entity.

72 For the Malbank fee see *DB Chesh.*, 8; for Wybunbury see *DB Chesh.*, B8.

73 *DB Chesh.*, 8,16.

agents of the two authorities.[74] Elsewhere, however, one- or two-holder parishes such as Lichfield and Eccleshall were clearly informed by the bishop's landholdings, many of which had probably been immune from almost all regnal obligations for centuries, and were thus located outside the distribution of regnal territories across the rest of the diocese.

Regnal territories and the regnal community

Consideration of episcopal, royal and comital mother parishes has enabled some provisional conclusions to be drawn concerning the regnal territory; however, it remains a speculative entity, for the most part not directly visible, illuminated indirectly by evidence such as that for Leek's hospitality and hunting services and Cheshire's peace serjeants. The following discussion seeks to develop our understanding of these territories by placing them within the context of the regnal community. First, to reiterate, it is proposed here that territories for the collection of tithe – mother parishes – were assigned during the first half of the tenth century on the basis of pre-existing territories used by reeves to organise, administer and collect regnal dues and services from landholders; these were usually centred on royal or comital estates, also administered by these reeves, at which a church to be supported by the tithes often either already existed or was soon established. The only general exceptions to this were, apparently, churches on other royal, comital and episcopal estates within these territories, which established their own parishes (although they may have done so at a later date, perhaps even after the Conquest), and episcopal churches based on estates that were largely immune from regnal exactions other than the three military services, the 'common burdens'. Together, it is proposed, these churches represent the 'old minsters' of Edgar's law. Some of them had probably existed for centuries, but others were more recently established; the criterion that united both was the high status of their tenth-century ownership and their relations to regnal administration.

The notion of regnal communities was introduced in Chapter 1 to describe the groups who assembled regularly at the courts of kings to assert and validate the power of the king and their own authority, a ritualising form of activity that stabilised from the late seventh century onwards. In a recent review, Tom Lambert has proposed that kings used two 'parallel hierarchies' of subordinates to assert their royal power, articulated around distinct sets of obligations mentioned earlier, associated respectively with military activity and the support of the royal household.[75] First, military activity was enabled through networks focused on ealdormen, whose leadership roles were exercised both on their own account and as part of the larger armies that a king might assemble; their places within a regnal community essentially reproduced that of earlier sub-kings, but were subject to 'firmer expectations of loyalty and obedience'

---

74 We might suspect that the estates at the centre of the remaining episcopal multi-holder parishes at Prees and Wilne had also been entangled with nearby estates in similar fashion. Chapter 2 also pointed to regnal entanglements with episcopal estates at Chester and Shrewsbury, but the corresponding parishes have not been analysed here.

75 Lambert, *Law and order*, pp. 114–24.

The parish

in their relationships to the king.[76] Ealdormen drew upon their own military retinues to fulfil these roles, but were also able to draw more broadly upon the kind of military service assessed on landholders that was reserved in so many charters from the eighth century onwards, and thus were implicated in cultivating a subordinate penumbra of landholders with military obligations at the edges of the regnal community. It is likely that, from an early period, such ealdormen asserted their authority within specific regions of a kingdom, which are labelled 'comital territories' here. There is some evidence for such territories within the bounds of the diocese of Lichfield, generally named after topographical features on which they were focused in some way: they included the 'Tomsæte' of the river Tame, the 'Pencersæte' of the river Penk, the 'Wreocensæte' of the Wrekin or Wroxeter and the 'Pecsæte' of the Peak District.[77]

The second network of subordinates, parallel to the first, comprised the reeves of regnal territories.[78] Such people are almost invisible in textual sources, but Lambert makes clear that the meagre evidence emphasises their administrative roles, whether on royal estates, organising the activities of the inland populations and the renders of those on the outlands, or within regnal territories, receiving food rents, organising services and collecting the legal fines imposed at assemblies that were owed to the king. It is possible that reeves also organised the guesting of royal servants on other landholders' estates within the regnal territories. Surviving charters, especially from the ninth century, show that ealdormen and the lords of minsters were willing to lavish gifts and money on the king in order to be freed from the guesting of royal servants of different kinds (called *fæstingmen* in the charters, meaning men entrusted with specific duties), implying that it was regularly demanded of them during this period.[79] The general lack of evidence renders it almost impossible to provide any detail here, but the importance of reeves in the administration of these activities is plausible. Within a regnal community, reeves were probably themselves fairly peripheral figures, more likely to be visited by the court on its circuit than to visit it elsewhere. They are perhaps best viewed as a subordinate penumbra of privileged landholders on the edge of the regnal community: their landholdings were not their own but the king's, yet this connection no doubt conferred upon them a certain status at the assemblies attended by local and regional domainal communities.

Lambert, building on work by George Molyneaux, has suggested that the tenth century witnessed profound changes in the ways in which kings asserted their authority in the localities.[80] He proposes that the establishment of burhs in the earlier part of this period, followed by hundreds and shires during the second half of the century, imposed a more intense and standardised set of connections between the royal court and the localities. Whereas previously the assemblies attended by domainal and other forms of community had been free of formal royal oversight,

---

76   Lambert, *Law and order*, pp. 114–19, at p. 117.
77   Gelling, *West Midlands*, pp. 83–5 and 140; Hooke, *Landscape of Anglo-Saxon Staffordshire*, pp. 10–13.
78   Lambert, *Law and order*, pp. 119–23.
79   Gautier, 'Hospitality', pp. 39–42.
80   This paragraph is based on Lambert, *Law and order*, pp. 242–53. See also Molyneaux, *Formation of the English Kingdom*, pp. 116–94.

even if in some cases dominated by royal reeves and others with royal support, the hundred and shire assemblies represented a more direct connection between the royal court and local societies. These new assemblies were not under royal control in any formal sense, because they still facilitated the negotiation of claims and imposition of judgements through appeal to group consensus, but each was intended to have a presiding figure, the hundredman of the hundred and the sheriff of the shire, who was effectively a member of the regnal community and whose role was in part framed by the legislative programmes of tenth-century kings. Lambert also notes an important difference between these two roles: whereas the sheriff acted as the superior of the reeves of regnal territories, and was responsible for the organisation and collection of regnal services and renders across his shire, the hundredman was not a royal administrator, but assumed the title as a man of paramount standing among the attendees of the assembly. Unlike the reeves of regnal territories, both hundredmen and sheriffs were usually substantial landholders in their own right, and therefore potentially more effective in conveying the king's directives at assemblies and ensuring that the legal innovations of the period were implemented. Indeed, Lambert suggests that kings were motivated in part by frustration at the general inability of the reeves of regnal territories to achieve similar goals.[81]

Lambert's focus is on such legal innovations, but his conclusions can be applied to two of the issues explored by this book. First, the tenth and eleventh centuries appear to have witnessed a distinct reduction in the complexity of regnal dues and services claimed from landholders: as Alban Gautier has demonstrated, the requirements of formalised guesting appear to have dwindled during this period, perhaps being often commuted to a money payment, like the 'hidage' of later records, and paling in significance next to the payment of the geld, which was introduced as a regular 'tax' in the early eleventh century.[82] This coincided with a transition towards the organisation and imposition of regnal dues and services in the context of the shire, as the shire customs recorded for some shires in Domesday Book attest.[83] The sheriffs' administration of considerable territories probably necessitated the simplification of a host of more varied arrangements for tasks such as guard-duties and the support of the king's servants, perhaps resulting in the 'hidage', 'wardsilver', 'sheriff's aid' and 'hundred aid' recorded in thirteenth-century hundred rolls as many were commuted for cash.[84] These processes offer a compelling context for the stabilisation of place-names associated with smaller estates during this period, discussed in Chapter 5. Both the expanding size of administrative territories and the corresponding integration of their larger populations into the organisational purview of a smaller number of people – the sheriffs and their agents – required a greater standardisation of geographical knowledge. This was particularly the case in the administration of the geld, which appears to have been assessed on and collected from the inhabitants of each vill rather than though the landholders whose estates often encompass several such vills.

---

81 Lambert, *Law and order*, pp. 246–7.
82 Gautier, 'Hospitality', pp. 42–3; for hidage, see Neilson, *Customary Rents*, pp. 115–20.
83 Roffe, *Decoding Domesday*, pp. 127–32, and 271–3.
84 Neilson, *Customary Rents*, pp. 124–37.

The parish

Second, this tenth-century transformation affected the roles of the reeves of regnal territories. As sheriffs assumed the organisation of regnal dues and services, simplifying many of them, the roles of both regnal territories and their reeves in this regard became largely obsolete. Such reeves may initially have remained important in the collection of fines and forfeitures from the assemblies, even if they now had to account for these to a local superior, the sheriff. However, grants of 'sake and soke' to other landholders within these territories may have rendered this a fairly peripheral duty. Moreover, in later centuries such collections were undertaken by others of the sheriff's subordinates such as the hundred bailiffs, again suggesting obsolescence in this regard.[85] Reeves based on royal estates became almost solely concerned with the management of those estates, while the hospitality and hunting services recorded centuries later at Leek represent a diminished vestige of their once more substantial role in the wider area outside these estates. The later peace serjeants of Cheshire and Shropshire hint at the possibility of a continuing role of some kind for the regnal territories of these western shires, but these organisations were also assigned to specific officers rather than the reeves of their central estates.

It is important to note that shrieval administration superseded only that of the reeves' regnal territories, and not the earldormen's or earl's military roles. For example, in an Anglo-Saxon Chronicle annal for 1016 Eadric was styled ealdorman of the Magonsæte, a Mercian comital territory only partially coincident with shire boundaries.[86] Nevertheless, the sheriff probably mustered and led all the thegns in his shire owed from all lands that were not held by other lords with regnal privileges (at the very least with 'sake and soke'), either on his own account or in response to a summons from king or earl, and in that sense sheriffs were more involved with military service than the reeves of regnal territories are likely to have been.[87] Sheriffs may also have been more involved with the politics of land and patronage, given the greater geographical extent of their shires. They perhaps looked after estates that had been forfeited to the king following legal judgements and those for which judgements on the manner of inheritance had not yet been made; this might explain, for example, the lists of thegns' estates, 'waste' in 1086, given at the end of the king's section in the Domesday Book for Staffordshire.[88] In summary, the assignment of tithes to mother churches was perhaps one of the last phenomena in which the regnal territories played a significant role before they were largely superseded by shires. Unlike churchscot, a due owed to the head of the diocesan community and his servants, which was apparently reorganised in the Midlands with the establishment of shires and hundreds in the later tenth century, the bounds of mother parishes largely fossilised those of

---

85 H.M. Cam, *The hundred and the hundred rolls: an outline of local government in medieval England* (London, 1930), pp. 137–94.
86 *ASC* (E), s.a. 1016. The territory of the Magonsæte encompassed Herefordshire and southern Shropshire.
87 R.P. Abels, *Lordship and military obligation in Anglo-Saxon England* (London, 1988), pp. 119–31 and 179–84. The shire customs of Herefordshire and Shropshire mention the sheriffs of those shires leading contingents into Wales (*DB Heref.*, C 10; *DB Salop.*, C4).
88 *DB Staffs.*, 1,33 to 1,64.

earlier regnal territories, as tithe was owed from the outset to specific churches often located at their hearts. Finally, it is also worth noting that the specific territories thus fossilised should not necessarily be projected back to the seventh century, as they may represent only the most recent iteration of entities that had themselves morphed and developed since the establishment of kingdoms in England, depending on the methods by which hospitality services and the like were administered.

A parochial transformation

This chapter has proposed that a set of mother churches was established across the diocese in the first half of the tenth century through the allocation of compulsory tithe payments from the landholding population. These churches were not necessarily all newly founded, but their tenth-century status owed far more to their regnal and comital lords at that time than to their histories as earlier minsters, and it is certainly likely that a significant proportion, at least, had been established more recently. Indeed, the clear primacy of the central core of the regnal community, the kings, ealdormen and (later) earls, in the creation of a denser network of churches than was provided by the earlier minsters raises questions about the relationships between bishops and the highest lay lords in the land during this period. Clearly, beginning in the 920s there was a transformation in the provision of pastoral care throughout the diocese, and in the organisation of those who claimed responsibility for providing it. This concluding discussion asks broader questions about how this transformation should be framed, engaging in particular with recent work on the 'secularisation' and 'expropriation' of earlier religious centres across early medieval England, before finishing with an exploration of the emergence of coherent parochial communities by the end of the period considered by this book.

John Blair has characterised the period from the mid-ninth century to the late eleventh as one of 'secularisation'. He expresses this concept in various ways, but generally sees an increasing involvement of lay people in the affairs of minsters: 'places which were minsters – if perhaps with lay residential functions – at the start of the period appear by the end of it as secular places containing residually important churches.'[89] At the beginning of this process Blair invokes the attested election of lay lords of minsters (often of royal status, such as Offa and his wife Cynethryth) and traces what he refers to as the subsequent 'laicisation of ecclesiastical culture', in which, for example, minsters were 'annexed' by lay residences as formerly peripatetic households settled down, and ecclesiastical practices such as the erection of memorial sculpture were used in explicit reference to lay people and their self-perceptions through depictions of hunting scenes and the like.[90] Even so, Blair admits that '"secularisation" is a vague word: there may have been a big difference between influences which purists thought morally suspect, and interference which minsters themselves perceived as threatening'.[91]

It is the attitudes of such 'purists' that appear to inform Blair's framing of this period and, more generally, the way he defines minster 'communities'. It cannot be doubted

---

89   Blair, *Church*, p. 323.
90   Blair, *Church*, pp. 122–4, 129, 282–6 and 321–2.
91   Blair, *Church*, p. 282.

The parish

that Bede and some of his contemporaries were very worried about the interactions of monastic life, lived according to appropriate Rules, with the world outside the minster. Bede famously castigated the lax life of many minsters founded by nobles in his letter to Bishop Ecgberht of York, written in 734, in which he characterised their founders as lay people, even if they claimed to be otherwise when ruling over their new houses.[92] Blair traces this concern through Boniface, an important English missionary in Francia writing in the 740s, and within the canons of the Council of *Clofesho* in 747, both of which also acknowledged the dangers of minster landholdings and revenues in lay hands.[93] These issues need to be kept analytically separate from what Blair calls the 'struggle for episcopal governance' during this period, which aimed to manage and increase the provision of pastoral care to the laity in general. In pursuit of this, bishops appear to have acquired other minsters within their dioceses (a phenomenon discussed in Chapter 2), but Blair suggests that they may not have been acting solely from pastoral motivations: 'bishops were also aristocrats, and what is presented as diocesan reform could have contained elements of aristocratic encroachment.'[94] Elsewhere, Blair may demonstrate what he means by 'aristocratic encroachment' when discussing the ways in which minsters and their lands were exchanged or granted by one lord to another in the eighth and ninth centuries: 'the concerns of those in power seem more political and financial, less engaged with the minster communities in their own right.'[95] Blair's primary concern thus appears to lie with the 'minster community', free from political and financial concerns, and if even the motivations of bishops might be distorted by aristocratic concerns we must assume that such communities were threatened not simply by lay lordship but by any rulership that neglected maintenance of a regulated monastic life.

Blair therefore appears to judge the development of minsters across the period according to a purist definition of their composition, in which groups of monks or nuns lived regulated lives isolated from other social influences. This definition has an ambiguous relationship to his ideas about the integration of life in minsters with secular life, which, he acknowledges,

> exposed it to charges of worldliness from within its own ranks, but also enabled it to support such high culture and scholarship as the art and learning of Wearmouth-Jarrow, or the friendship networks of Aldhelm and Boniface ... minsters were opulent not because they housed particularly self-indulgent form of the religious life, but because gold, bright colour, and intricate ornament were integral to the society which bred them.[96]

The apparent paradox between a monasticism isolated from its social world and one thoroughly entangled with it is resolved by distinguishing between different kinds

---

92 *EEE*, pp. 414–17.
93 Blair, *Church*, pp. 108–17.
94 Blair, *Church*, p. 117.
95 Blair, *Church*, p. 129.
96 Blair, *Church*, p. 136.

of lay influence. For example, 'involvement of lords and patrons in the activities of religious communities ... could be both supportive and creative';[97] but 'whereas the secular great of the late seventh century had interacted with monastic culture by patronising it, their descendants of the late eighth and ninth were increasingly prone to bend its economic and material assets to their own ends'.[98] Thus, as Bede would no doubt approve, an independent 'monastic culture' remains definitive of minsters in Blair's eyes, and also enables a narrative of their decline:

> the comprehensive running-down of assets, going beyond the worst fears of observers before 850, signals ... a progressive takeover of the minster sites themselves, which left few communities (except, from the 960s, the reformed ones) in autonomous control of big endowments.[99]

In Blair's narrative, the 'minster community' becomes the dominant institution from which all else is judged, meaning that the right kind of secular patronage could be 'supportive' and 'creative', but the wrong kind was 'encroachment', a destructive interference that annexed minsters to other ends. However much Blair is willing to admit of the complexity of relations between minsters and broader society, the form of his argument creates the sense of a 'pure' minster community, in which the material forms of lay culture and the social structures that defined it had just enough influence to produce something distinctive, which might sometimes fall short of the more zealous reformers, but not enough influence to threaten the independence of such a community: 'minster culture was immune from reformers' attacks until, in the ninth century, it started to dissolve back into an aristocratic society which, having learnt so much from it, was less and less prepared to tolerate its financial and institutional autonomy.'[100] Any deviation from the regulated and isolated life of the minster becomes a form of 'secularisation', reducing complexity to a binary dynamic. However, the idea that 'minster culture' was separated from aristocratic society, sufficiently that it might later dissolve *back* into it, overlooks the fact that minsters had always been sites on which several different forms of community intersected, both religious and lay. In this book, both lay and religious elements are recognised as parts of a single 'culture' (an ill-defined word perhaps best avoided), and the focus is moved away from an evaluation of degrees of secularisation towards an analysis of the demands made and opportunities offered by different forms of community at minsters and elsewhere.

The notion of a specific 'minster community' has been rejected in this book in favour of multiple intersecting communities based (in part) at minsters. While the intentional imposition and maintenance of a regulated way of life within groups of monks and nuns at minsters offers a clear definition of the kind of ritualising community sought by this study, and while Rules appear to have formed important elements within extended ecclesiastical communities, discussed in Chapter 2, the individual existence of such communities appears to have been fairly short-lived. For example, when the

---

97 Blair, *Church*, p. 323.
98 Blair, *Church*, p. 285.
99 Blair, *Church*, p. 323.
100 Blair, *Church*, p. 136.

The parish

Lastingham Narrative was written in the later seventh or earlier eighth century, the Rule that Chad had established at Barrow a few decades earlier existed only in 'traces', presumably having been superseded by something else.[101] Until the Benedictine Rule was mandated as a 'universal' standard by King Edgar in the tenth century (following earlier Carolingian practice), it is not really possible to define specific monastic communities that persisted across time-scales longer than one or two generations, as the manner of life within them was profoundly connected to the decisions made by the rulers of those communities, which were themselves likely to alter as one generation followed the next.[102] Even the great cathedrals did not maintain a uniform practice: Archbishop Wulfred's 'renewal' of monastic life at early ninth-century Canterbury was mentioned in Chapter 3, as was the possibility that Bishop Æthelwald did something similar at Lichfield.[103] Of course, the varied and changing existence of such communities needs to be kept analytically separate from the fact that the imagined monastic community or *familia* was a common normative ideal in contemporary society;[104] the fact remains that many different forms of community might be articulated around it in different ways. Instead, in Chapter 3 it was argued that liturgical communities, based around the rituals of the altar, and often of the nearby shrines of saints, provided a more persistent form of minster-based community throughout the period; even if these changed and developed to some extent over the centuries, as they must have in many cases, they were more concretely grounded by the altars and shrines that defined them, and it is often the presence of churches and the saints associated with them in the later medieval period that provide clues to the sites of earlier minsters. It is these communities that formed the most stable religious centres of minsters.

Furthermore, the argument in this chapter has minimised the significance of the 'independence' of communities based at minsters and churches. The primary members of liturgical communities were the clerical groups who served the altars and saints' cults, and such groups do indeed appear to have persisted at minsters even when other elements of regulated monastic life dwindled, as appears to have occurred from the later eighth century and through the ninth.[105] The so-called 'division of the *mensa*', mentioned briefly in Chapter 2, in which the ruler of a cathedral or minster separated lands for the support and provision of the clerical group living there from the rest of the church's endowment, was undertaken from at least the eighth century, and Thomas Pickles has suggested that the place-name 'Preston' (*prēosta-tūn*), found fairly widely across England, may indicate holdings that were set aside for clerics.[106] Pickles frames such activities within a narrative partly influenced by Blair's, suggesting that the division of the endowment in this way was particularly

---

101 *HE*, iv.3.
102 Foot, *Monastic life*, pp. 48–69.
103 Langefeld,'*Regula canonicorum* or *Regula monasterialis vitae*?', pp. 27–32.
104 See Foot, *Monastic life*, pp. 172–84, although note that she largely equates the imagined community with the population actually living at a minster.
105 Blair, *Church*, pp. 124–6.
106 T. Pickles, 'Biscopes-tūn, muneca-tūn and prēosta-tūn: dating, significance and distribution', in E. Quinton, *The church in English place-names* (Nottingham, 2009), pp. 39–107.

Lichfield and the Lands of St Chad

likely to be undertaken by those who had 'expropriated' earlier minsters – either kings attempting to get back what they or their predecessors had previously given away or bishops attempting to enhance the resources of their sees.[107] It is not intended here to deny that such expropriations occurred throughout this period, especially as it is well documented in some cases. However, such acquisitions can be understood in other ways, as will shortly be explored, and in any case we must remain alive to the likelihood that the lords of minsters made specific arrangements to support the clerical groups serving their altars in more general and widespread circumstances.

The idea of expropriation as a general explanatory idea demonstrably oversimplifies more complex and varied circumstances where evidence survives. As ever, the diocese of Lichfield is bereft of textual sources that might furnish specific examples to illustrate this, but an example from the diocese of Worcester makes the point. In 804 Æthelric, a layman, bequeathed a minster at Westbury-on-Trym to his mother Ceolburh for her lifetime, and afterwards to the bishop, thereby hoping to gain the bishop's support for Ceolburh's undisturbed possession.[108] Here, the minster was used as any land grant might be, to encourage alliance over shared interests, and the context of the grant, a church council, clearly represents a particularly elite domainal community, of which Æthelric and the bishop were members, in the midst of the kinds of negotiation through which it was defined. It is also notable that Æthelric was a layman and yet also lord of the minster at Westbury, which had been given to him by his kinsmen; the land had been given to Æthelric's father Æthelmund, an ealdorman, by King Offa in the late eighth century, and Æthelric's bequest to his mother illustrates how tightly bound up with family inheritance arrangements the minster had become.[109] This can be considered expropriation only if one assumes that minster estates, privileged by charters, were not usually implicated in domainal communities, or that the 'community' of a minster should have been sole arbiter of its next lord. The former is clearly erroneous, as charters were themselves products of domainal communities and were used by their members to indicate privileged possession, while the latter, a norm asserted at many church councils of the period, was often more honoured in the breach.

Indeed, in many places across early medieval western Europe, the idea that the *familia* of a monastery might have control of the endowment and the right to elect its next lord was espoused in writing but not necessarily followed in practice: monastic founders, their families and unrelated people who later ruled these monasteries often tended to act as if they possessed the monastery's lands and could choose their own heirs, even if in some cases this was explicitly associated with the expressed agreement of the 'community'.[110] In England minsters had comprised important elements within domainal communities, and abbots and abbesses important members, since kings first began to establish them by granting land for the purpose to bishops and other nobles, and were thus from the beginning very probably implicated in the kinds of

---

107 Pickles, 'Biscopes-tūn, muneca-tūn and prēosta-tūn', pp. 44–7.
108 S 1187; see Sims-Williams, *Religion and literature*, pp. 174–6. Æthelric had arranged for a copy of the document to be kept at Lichfield cathedral with Bishop Ealdwulf.
109 S 139.
110 Wood, *Proprietary church*, pp. 118–39 and 181–90.

The parish

family-based negotiation (among others) that domainal communities often supported. The *familia* may have formed an important norm within monastic practice, but the minster's lord was the more consistently significant figure in the domainal sphere. This significance is also visible elsewhere, as, for example, in the tendency for authors in the eighth century to write histories of the abbots and abbesses of minsters, rather than their communities more generally, and for the saints' cults articulated around such people to become the liturgical foci of minsters. It is hardly surprising in such circumstances to witness a tendency for fewer lords of minsters to become avowed abbots and instead to remain laymen, as did Æthelmund and his son Æthelric. Finally, we must admit that there is little formal difference between, on the one hand, minsters owned by laymen and focused on the maintenance of a liturgical centre and, on the other, the tenth- and eleventh-century estates of kings and ealdormen within which holdings were assigned to the support of priests for the maintenance of a church.

It is not the intention here to deny the impressive exuberance of minsters founded in the seventh century, nor the religious dedication of their founders; it is clear that those who founded the earliest minsters almost always became or assigned them abbots or abbesses. Nevertheless, from the very beginning minsters were implicated in domainal communities (among others), and Bede's accusations of pretence regarding the abbatial status of some nobles are an early (and disapproving) recognition of this. A later increase in lay lordship is thus unsurprising, as is the topographical trend traced by Blair, in which lay lords increasingly constructed permanent dwellings within or adjacent to minsters;[111] this is especially visible among royal lords who developed a series of favoured centres on the peripatetic circuits of their courts, but Blair himself suggests that it 'is likely to have proceeded at the level of noble as well as royal households, perhaps more quickly in cases when the former ware sedentary already'.[112] Ultimately, it is very limiting to view these processes through the 'minster community' as a kind of institutionalised fixed variable. Minsters are far better treated as material loci within which several different forms of community intersected. This book has attempted to construct an understanding of minsters in which the presence of a regulated monastic life and the rule of a formally religious lord are not strictly necessary, and emphasis has been placed instead on the maintenance of liturgical foci at the centre of minster settlements, which no doubt took a variety of forms. This has the advantage of corresponding to the kinds of place that actually persisted throughout the seventh, eighth and ninth centuries and, moreover, allows a more direct focus on the different kinds of community that conjoined around minsters in a variety of ways without agonising over the extent of monastic purity displayed by those living there.

Of course, a drive towards a purer monastic life is visible again and again throughout the period, promoted by individual abbots and abbesses, and within the English ecclesiastical community at church councils. The membership of the latter included many significant lords of minsters, but many more lords were not included, and were more concerned with other forms of community. The minsters identified in Chapter 3 in the diocese of Lichfield probably represent a range of different circumstances. On the one hand, places such as

---

111 Blair, *Church*, pp. 281–6.
112 Blair, *Church*, p. 285.

Lichfield and the Lands of St Chad

Lichfield and Repton were respectively very important episcopal and royal centres from their foundations, and remained so into the eleventh century and beyond. Others held by royal and comital lords by the tenth century had become significant administrative centres associated with regnal territories and were accordingly assigned the tithes of these areas in and after the 920s. Yet others remained within the hands of thegnly families, and were essentially the forerunners of the estate-churches that would be founded in great numbers in the two centuries centred on 1050. Indeed, it is plausible that grants, exchanges and inheritance arrangements, negotiated through and validated at local and regional assemblies, accounted for the persistence of a good proportion of the earlier minsters, conceivably from the seventh century through to the eleventh. We can recognise in these examples the range of independent liturgical communities discussed in the conclusion to Chapter 4, but, whereas there the focus was on the bishop's relationships with such communities, here we are focused on the lords of those communities. A similar range of status among these lords persisted into the tenth and eleventh centuries, but crucially the assignment of compulsory tithe payments from the 920s acted to elaborate a distinction between kings, ealdormen and a few choice thegns at the upper end of the elite, who ruled a newly established group of mother churches, and a larger group of more lowly thegns whose estate-churches were largely bereft of formal support.

The evidence discussed in this chapter indicates that many of the bishop's churches were also allocated tithe payments, but the dominance of lay lords over the mother churches of the diocese is impressive. It was acknowledged in Chapter 1 and Chapter 4 that the agency of bishops from at least the reign of Æthelstan cannot often be disentangled from that of the regnal community. Consequently, it is perhaps unsurprising that the arrangements in place across regnal territories for the collection of dues and services were first exploited for ecclesiastical ends during this period. Again, this view modifies an element of Blair's argument, which proposes that ecclesiastical tributes piggy-backed on arrangements for regnal resource collection from a much earlier period. However, the establishment of tithe-funded mother churches does not simply represent assistance offered by kings and their agents to an episcopal project. The royal and comital lords of these mother churches occupied the same position as the lords of independent minsters in earlier centuries. They were thus themselves spiritual lords, insofar as they governed the groups of priests responsible for their churches, and indeed appointed those priests, as well as having overall lordship of the property assigned to their support. The people who assumed such lordship might have taken a position in relation to the diocesan community that was potentially threatening to a bishop's authority, as discussed in Chapter 4, but which might also have been ameliorated by the establishment of good working relations between them. The reorganisation of church-scot in the later tenth century may represent an attempt by bishops to renew their grip on acknowledgements of spiritual lordship from across the diocese. It is also plausible that the newly mandated assemblies, first those in burhs, then, from the later tenth century, those of hundred and shire around which church-scot collection was rearticulated, played important roles in negotiations between the bishop and the increasing number of high-status independent spiritual lords in his diocese.

It is likely that the beginnings of this transformation in claims to spiritual lordship should be dated to a realignment of regnal and spiritual authority during the early years of the tenth century. It is now widely accepted that King Alfred attempted to create a new regnal community in the 'kingdom of the Anglo-Saxons', which incorporated not only all the old 'Saxon' provinces south of the Thames (sometimes called 'Greater Wessex'), but also those parts of the Mercian kingdom not under the rule of Danish kings, and that he bequeathed this project to his son and successor, King Edward the Elder.[113] Nicole Marafioti has argued that Edward's enshrinement of his father's body in the New Minster, newly constructed in Winchester, was intended to make of Alfred's body a spiritual object similar to that of a saint, representing in some way a new covenant between God and Alfred's dynasty.[114] Matthew Blake and I have argued that Edward's sister Æthelflæd, Lady of the Mercians, also attempted to constitute a new Mercian kingdom during the second decade of the tenth century, in part by appeal to the power of sanctity, although in her case the Northumbrian St Oswald provided the primary holy object.[115] Following Oswald's enshrinement at Gloucester, she appears to have honoured a series of Mercian saints revered at existing minsters within the diocese of Lichfield by dedicating churches to them in her newly established burhs across the region; we might speculate that the specific saints involved – St Beorhthelm, St Ealhmund and St Eadgyth – were chosen in part to facilitate connections with the lords of the minsters that hosted their cults. More broadly, the assimilation of regnal and spiritual lordship in this period, largely as a response to the disruption of earlier regnal and spiritual communities, appears to have prompted a trend from the 920s for kings and ealdormen to assume the roles of spiritual lords by founding churches on their estates and assigning them the tithes of the associated regnal territories; that royal assemblies and church councils were essentially coterminous from at least the 920s must have further enabled this trend.

The realignment and closer integration of regnal and ecclesiastical communities during this period needs to be recognised as an integral part of the formation and intensification of the English regnal community recently illuminated by George Molyneaux and Tom Lambert. As this chapter has demonstrated, this involved a transformation in ecclesiastical geography across the diocese of Lichfield, establishing a large group of mother churches that were more densely distributed than the earlier minsters, and, while some of the latter were reinvigorated as mother churches, the majority were not. This had profound implications for the relationships between the purveyors of religious ministrations and much of the population of the diocese, and involved the constitution of something we can recognise as a parochial community. The liturgical communities at the centres of the earlier minsters no doubt developed a subordinate penumbra of Christians spiritually dependent on their liturgical and sacramental ministrations, which, as discussed in Chapters 3 and 4, probably comprised varying portions of the surrounding populations, but also included associations with more distant clients. The establishment of tithe-collecting mother churches within regnal territories must have refocused spiritual relationships, fusing regnal connections within these territories with new, or at least renewed, ties of spiritual

---

113 S. Keynes, 'Edward, king of the Anglo-Saxons', in N.J. Higham and D.H. Hill (eds), *Edward the Elder 899–924* (London, 2001), pp. 40–66.
114 N. Marafioti, 'Seeking Alfred's body: royal tomb as political object in the reign of Edward the Elder', *Early Medieval Europe*, 23 (2015), pp. 202–28.
115 Blake and Sargent, '"For the protection of all the people"', pp. 120–54.

lordship, and in many cases severing established ties with minsters elsewhere. Tithes were explicitly intended to support the provision of pastoral care, and the populations of these new parochial territories were thus subsumed as dependants within the liturgical communities of the mother churches, many of them perhaps newly established, creating a large and more coherent subordinate penumbra of parishioners whose souls were now bound to the priests of their assigned mother parishes. In distinct contrast to the notion of 'secularisation', this transformation might be better characterised as the 'spiritualisation' of formerly secular relationships and territories. However, neither formulation is particularly useful, as the parochial communities that resulted from this process were, for the most part, an entirely new phenomenon.

The pastoral effectiveness of this transformation cannot be closely evaluated, at least within the diocese of Lichfield, due largely to a lack of relevant evidence: we simply cannot know how closely the priests of the mother churches engaged with their flocks. However, one corpus of evidence previously considered in this book can be usefully revisited. It was noted in Chapter 3 that the Trent Valley Group of stone sculpture appears to have declined and disappeared in or after the early decades of the tenth century. This sculpture, it was argued, was produced throughout the ninth and early tenth centuries at minsters to fulfil liturgical and memorial roles. Much of it plausibly embodied connections between liturgical communities and their spiritual dependents, in particular members of the elite able to acquire the services of sculptors and, in some cases, the exemplars informing their sculptures. Such connections were not necessarily forged because of any particular regnal or domainal tie, and we must envisage a wider variety of contexts in their formation, encompassing extended networks of friendship, lordship of various kinds and other more ephemeral forms of association. These eclectic sets of connection were refashioned and replaced by the more tightly defined relationships of parishioners with their mother churches, defined through the claims these churches had on the produce of landholdings within their parishes, and thus through the regular contact implicated in attendance at such churches in order to render such dues, to receive the pastoral ministrations owed in return and ultimately to be buried there. Moreover, many members of the elite who might perhaps earlier have sought the patronage of a minster may, from the early tenth century, have invested their spiritual impulses in their own estate-churches. Finally, the proliferation of mother churches throughout the diocese must have marked an expansion of the bishop's diocesan community, as more priests were put into office; consequently, the clerical groups at the mother churches were probably smaller on average than those that once inhabited the minsters, their members often less well connected with those who might sponsor liturgical elaboration. All these considerations might serve to explain the disappearance of the Trent Valley Group of stone sculpture.[116] This phenomenon thus marked the beginnings of the parochial communities that would define the dominant form of spiritual relationship among the population for centuries to come.

---

116 The production of stone sculpture appears to have emerged again from the mid-tenth century in certain areas: in the diocese of Lichfield the Pennine Fringes Group was very much associated with the large mother parishes of that region, as discussed in Chapter 3. Its overall distribution and style marks it as quite distinct from the earlier Trent Valley Group, as does the location of a significant proportion of its members outside the bounds of churchyards. I intend to explore its significance elsewhere.

Conclusion

This book has provided a regional study that engages with broader debates concerning religious culture and the role of bishops in England between the seventh and eleventh centuries, both as a contribution to those debates and because such engagement is necessary if we are to develop compelling understandings of the fragmentary evidence from the diocese of Lichfield. A framework of 'communities' has structured this understanding, and several specific communities have been defined, both lying within and, in some cases, extending beyond the diocese. The theoretical frame used by this study requires that every encounter be understood dialectically, as a moment in which two processes act together: on the one hand, a process of personification, in which an understanding, a reality, is created about a person, be that oneself or another, defined through certain norms; on the other hand, a process of subjectification, in which the implications of that reality also come into existence, creating new possibilities. From an analytical perspective the personified reality is revealed to be imaginary, its defining norms changeable. To focus on ritualised communities in the past is to focus on the ways in which people have tried to narrow and constrict the possibilities present within encounter, and so to create a more solid reality for themselves and those in solidarity with them. To understand historical change is to understand how they ultimately failed to do so. While social meaning of any kind fundamentally depends on shared norms, whether elaborated in communities or apprehended more fluidly in the looser associative fields with which they coexist, people are never caught forever in the vice-like grip of just one way of knowing themselves and the world surrounding them: subjective experience always opens out beyond a singular conduit to personhood, often at moments when the contradictory vectors of different communities intersect within their overlapping memberships. The conviction, or even just the hunch, that meaningful solidity is founded on shifting foundations drives an apparent paradox: people have always had to act to keep their worlds the same, just as much as they have acted to change them.

This concluding section explores the implications of these insights in the context of the early medieval diocese of Lichfield, in order to offer a sense of the shape that these issues might give to the history of the period. The norms of consensual decision-making in assemblies studied by Susan Reynolds, and of regulated monastic life that inform John Blair's definition of minsters, had to be created and continually maintained through ritualised enactments. The analyses in this book enable a way of understanding such effort by focusing on the intersections of different communities and associative fields at specific places created in the historic landscape of the region. Such intersections forced novel encounters within communities, introduced tensions and opportunities into their dynamics, and prompted their members to renegotiate their relationships with their fellows. Some might even dissolve existing solidarities and seek new ones. The study also highlights how those working to create communities might wield certain shared norms to entrench power, cultivating hierarchical relationships articulated around various kinds of normative lordship. These lordships – spiritual, regnal, domainal – embodied influential images of certain kinds of lord – a bishop, a king, a landholder – that proved attractive not only to those who styled themselves in these images, but also to those whose membership of communities required explicit dependence upon them, and who formed the subordinate penumbras that constituted the edges of several of the communities studied here. Such hierarchies could no more be taken for granted than could any other communal norm. Where regular ritualised activities proved insufficient to maintain them, power of some other variety might be asserted. Moreover, hierarchical norms were generated not only through the imposition of power but through resistance to such acts, and the negotiation of resulting tensions. The following provides some concluding discussion of spiritual lordship, as embodied in bishops and their clergy, and also in the lords of liturgical communities, both religious and lay. Such lordship forms the centre of this book's analysis, in part because spiritual politics is still underappreciated in accounts of this period, which often give primacy to the authority of kingdoms and kings, but also because it was fundamental to the projects of bishops across the five centuries considered here.

Spiritual lordship ultimately relied upon a very specific conduit to personhood: the constitution of the soul subject to God, perhaps the most ubiquitous normative image of the period. However, the manner of its constitution varied across different communities. We can begin with liturgical communities, which intersected with every other religious community studied in these pages. The Roman missionaries who arrived in Kent in 597 were first based at a church in Canterbury previously used by the Kentish queen Bertha, and thereafter the setting up of churches containing altars and other liturgical spaces was a pre-requisite for any other kind of community.[1] Chapter 3 demonstrated the central importance of liturgical communities in constituting the religious places of the diocese of Lichfield, which began to proliferate across the landscape with land grants to establish churches and minsters from the mid-seventh century, including the cathedral at Lichfield in 669. While individual liturgies varied, all were articulated around a normative notion of the People of God. Baptism into this imagined community invoked a spiritual lordship subjecting lay people to the ministrations of clerics and those who governed them, which proved crucial to the crystallisation of the other ecclesiastical communities studied here, centred on bishops and priests, abbots and abbesses. Liturgical ceremonial was probably the most formalised of all collective rituals invoked in this study to define community, and it was argued in Chapter 3 that the liturgical community approaches most closely to the notion of an ecclesiastical community constituted in a single place. Even then, we can identify subordinate penumbras of lay people spiritually dependent on these communities, many of whom lived elsewhere and visited only periodically. The creation of parochial communities from the tenth century transformed this situation by integrating a territorially coherent and locally based penumbra of spiritually subordinate laity into a new iteration of liturgical community; however, the cores of such communities were often substantially reduced in comparison with the earlier minsters, commonly comprising a single priest.

---

1   *HE*, i.26.

Conclusion

As outlined above, it is often the intersection of different forms of community that accounts for changes and developments within them. Liturgical communities were fundamental to all other ecclesiastical communities studied here, but do not by themselves explain the developments of the period. Indeed, perhaps the most significant phenomenon was the creation from the late seventh century of a set of ecclesio-regnal communities constituted by the intersection of the English ecclesiastical community, the various diocesan communities and the associated regnal communities, including that of the Mercians. Of these, the evidence makes clear that regnal communities had emerged in England by the end of the sixth century, possibly much earlier, and were articulated around the politics of the royal assembly and armed muster, firmly within the mould of post-Roman kingship that had developed across western Europe in the fifth and sixth centuries.[2] These kingdoms were variously enmeshed in relationships of dominance and dependency, and their dynastic dynamics were distinctly unstable. They were loose entities, created within widespread associative fields that enabled people to buttress and enhance their own selfhood by organising as royal companions around people claiming royal status. In turn, the latter competed with each over the attributes of kingliness, a set of developing norms defining regnal authority in, for example, summoning assemblies (or armies), demanding food for oneself and one's servants (guesting) and protecting one's subjects.[3] Throughout much of the seventh century fragile overkingships waxed and waned across England, but the situation changed dramatically in the 670s and 680s.

The English ecclesiastical community was created within associative fields of Christian spirituality that had developed in England over the course of the seventh century. From the 670s bishops managed to buttress the spiritual authority implicit in their claims to ecclesiastical rank by forging a greater degree of solidarity with each other. This was by no means a simple or inevitable endeavour, as demonstrated by Chad's conflict with Wilfrid and its escalation around the authority claimed by Theodore, explored in Chapter 2, and indeed by Wilfrid's subsequent troubles with the archbishop. The coalescence of the English ecclesiastical community was in part aided by more intense contact with Rome, the highest authority among the People of God in this part of the world, but it relied fundamentally upon mutually productive intersections with regnal communities. Through much of the seventh century kings asserted and negotiated their authority at various types of royal assembly, and bishops did likewise as members of regnal communities. However, the establishment of a more formal ecclesiastical assembly in the 670s constituted an imagined English Church within the nascent English ecclesiastical community, supporting a more independent assertion of spiritual lordship. By reinforcing each other's authority from distinct positions, regnal and ecclesiastical lords both delimited and stabilised their intersecting communities. The kings of the late seventh century appear to have been viewed as embodiments of the 'nations' (*gentes*) they ruled, but, as discussed in Chapter 1, the very idea of such nations was promoted by the bishops, whose

---

2   G. Halsall, *Barbarian migrations and the Roman West 376–568* (Cambridge, 2007), pp. 488–94.
3   Lambert, *Law and order*, pp. 57–62.

bishoprics conformed with these kingdoms.[4] The regnal communities of the later seventh century onwards were thus fundamentally different entities to those of the preceding period, symbiotically intersecting with the English ecclesiastical and diocesan communities, and vice versa, to the extent that the new formation can most usefully be understood as a mesh of intersecting ecclesio-regnal communities. Successive iterations of these communities were to define elite social life for the next four centuries and more.

It is important to conceive of a single elite creating and maintaining these communities, some of whom fashioned a religious selfhood, others lay, but whose life courses were regularly and deeply entangled. Their imposition of power over others was achieved mutually, by establishing tribute payments that were entrenched through their ritualisation in assemblies of various types, or in the domestic contexts of guesting practices. These created overlapping subordinate penumbras at the edges of their communities. It has long been accepted that kings did this from an earlier period, although the details are obscure even in regions with some evidence for it, and certainly in the diocese of Lichfield; we must assume that earlier iterations of the regnal territories discussed in Chapter 6 were established by earlier kings. More contentious here is the argument made in Chapter 4 that ecclesiastical tributes, church-scot and the like, represented an episcopal version of regnal dues and services rather than a support system for minster-based pastoral care. We cannot know how such tributes were collected before the hundredal reorganisation of the late tenth century, but it is probable that bishops relied primarily on the churches and minsters they added to their holdings to support the core of their diocesan community, in the same way that kings relied on the reeves of their estates to administer regnal dues and services. The use of the same methods by kings and bishops to establish respectively their regnal and spiritual authorities represents more than simply borrowing from one community to another: it was the politics of a single ecclesio-regnal elite in action. We must be careful not to conceive of politics solely within a lay mode, of accepting the distinction made at the time between a People of God and the peoples of the world, and thus of framing ecclesiastical politics as a worldly departure from the spiritual 'ideals' of the Church, a form of secularising corruption. This perspective, criticised in Chapter 6, prevents us from recognising the fact that the pursuit of spiritual goals (including lordship) was as inherently material and thus as political as chasing secular ambitions.

A more explicitly political view of spiritual activity also allows us to confront issues of participation and control. In particular, the act of baptism no doubt provoked all sorts of spiritual contemplation, especially in the newly converted, but it also constituted a specific conduit to selfhood. In becoming one of the People of God, one submitted to God's all-knowing judgement of oneself and one's sins, but crucially one did so within ecclesiastical communities ruled by one's spiritual superiors: certainly within one's own liturgical or (later) parochial community, but also within the larger diocesan and English ecclesiastical communities. Baptism thus embodied membership within

---

4   Lambert, *Law and order*, pp. 104–10, suggests that the fines paid to the king in the law codes of the late seventh century represented an acknowledgement that an offence against the community was an offence against the king representing it.

Conclusion

the intersecting English ecclesio-regnal communities, and for most people outside the cores of these communities that membership was a dependent one within their various subordinate penumbras. More broadly, a spiritual life of some kind was a necessary corollary of any kind of political participation, even within the most local of contexts. The claims of core members of the English ecclesiastical and diocesan communities to work on behalf of the English Church, an imagined community encompassing the entire Christian population of the lands occupied by 'English' kingdoms, actively enabled attempts to impose and entrench dependent relationships on others notionally within that community.

At the core of these communities, tensions between regnal and spiritual lords coexisted with mutual support in what might be considered, for the most part, a dynamic equilibrium, although in considering the archbishopric of Lichfield Chapter I appraised a particularly dramatic episode in this relationship: in appealing to the spiritual requirements of his royal position, Offa managed to wield considerable agency within the English ecclesiastical community, splitting the metropolitan see, before his successor Cœnwulf was more successfully resisted by the renewed solidarity of the English bishops. More broadly, the immanence of a spiritual selfhood in elite politics provided a means to negotiate power and control, and it is not surprising to see it repeatedly used in this way. In particular, within the overlapping associative fields stretching from Britain to Rome there developed across the eighth and ninth centuries a normative ideal of *correctio*, the 'correction' of incorrect behaviour by aligning it with specific interpretations of biblical injunction.[5] We see this at work in reorganisations of liturgical communities at Canterbury and possibly Lichfield in the early ninth century, but also in the involvement of the English ecclesiastical community in wider initiatives, shared with Frankish and Italian bishops, to correct the Church as a society of Christians, visible in the visit of papal legates to Britain via Francia in 786. In England bishops were more invested in this project than kings, the primary royal support for such a project lying with Charlemagne's court in Francia. Again, *correctio* was more than simply an 'internal' spiritual issue, but had political implications connected to the very conception of a political community and the roles of bishops and kings in governing it. *Correctio* should be understood as an explicit example of a more general tendency to assert and control political agency through appeal to spiritual correction, also visible in Bede's earlier criticisms of 'false' minsters. In the tenth century, the closer integration of the English ecclesiastical and regnal communities effectively enabled the assimilation of spiritual correction as a normative principle for the latter as much as it had been for the former, establishing the imagined community of the English 'people' as the focus of attempts at Christian improvement from across various elements of the elite.

The transformations of the tenth century within the English ecclesio-regnal communities mark an important development. In the early tenth century the deliberate employment of lay lordship over minsters, itself nothing new, by the royal

---

5 See M. Innes, *Introduction to early medieval western Europe, 300–900* (London, 2007), pp. 456–65, for a useful summary, and for the historiographical suggestion of the term 'correction' over the more common 'reform'.

lords of Wessex and Mercia, with their New Minsters at Winchester and Gloucester respectively, created conditions subsequently utilised in the proliferation of mother churches on royal and comital estates from the 920s across the nascent kingdom of England. By the end of the period, parochial communities were developing that assimilated the spiritual lordship wielded by bishops, clergy and the lords of mother churches within coherent territorial entities, grounding the kinds of relationship that had for centuries been formed across greater distances and within more fluid contexts of network and encounter. We can only imagine that Chad would have envied his eleventh-century successors' increased capacity to guide the spiritual lives of so many of the diocese's inhabitants. Again, we must understand this transformation as part of the broader developments of governance that characterised this period, many of which mutually reinforced one another. As sheriffs increased the reach of regnal authority, implementing innovations in legal practice through the newly regulated borough, hundred and shire courts, so priests were developing a more intense liturgical engagement with the populations of the mother parishes, attempting to impose more regularly that spiritual guidance that ensured a 'correctly' constituted English *gens*, the paramount image of political community. These increasing degrees of integration among the overlapping memberships of intersecting ecclesio-regnal communities employed the ritualising fora and media used for centuries – assemblies, tributes – to delimit the creation of dominant meanings to a much greater extent than had previously been accomplished, and so created more tightly controlled worlds.

Throughout the period studied here, English ecclesio-regnal communities constantly intersected with domainal communities. This book has emphasised the importance of such communities, usually constituted through local and regional assemblies, in driving the agricultural expansion that characterised the period from the seventh century into the eleventh and beyond. The tributes claimed by domainal lords from members of the subordinate penumbras on the outlands formed crucial elements in approaches taken by agricultural communities to organise their activities. At the same time, members of agricultural communities used their membership of domainal communities to negotiate and authorise 'customs' that regulated agrarian commons of both arable and pastoral kinds. Similar domainal communities no doubt predated the period considered in this book, but it is important to acknowledge the results of their intersection with evolving ecclesio-regnal communities from the seventh century onwards. The roles of kings, ealdormen and bishops as foci of patronage probably affected the processes and outcome of assemblies regarding issues such as inheritance and gift. This resulted in a tendency for larger-scale landholding in the most fertile areas to concentrate among the higher end of the elite. Some royal and comital estates persisted throughout the period, as discussed in Chapter 5, but others were accumulated at later dates. Outside the highest elite strata, the organisation of domainal communities through attendance at specific assemblies and the use of specific normative customs may themselves have been more stable than the identities of the landholders constituted by them, as various landholding dynasties and interest groups waxed and waned over the centuries.

This book has stressed that, between the seventh and tenth centuries, minsters and cathedrals should be viewed as loci of intersecting communities and their politics rather than simply discrete communities in their own right. The spiritual lordships of bishops over their diocesan communities and of abbots and abbesses over their liturgical communities, the domainal lordship asserted by bishops and the lords of minsters as major landholders and the regnal lordship wielded by kings and their closest family and agents frequently intersected at these places in the bodies of people who might occupy two or three of these roles at once. Participation in ecclesio-regnal and domainal communities was necessary to succeed as a member of the elite, and this book has repeatedly asserted that involvement in regnal and domainal communities did not 'secularise' the spiritual attributes conferred by involvement in ecclesiastical communities, even if participation in the latter might involve claims to spiritual purity through rejection of worldly influence; to suggest otherwise mistakes material participation in communities for the ideologies they articulated. The communities studied in this book were formed through attempts to build and negotiate solidarity around common interests, entrenched through ritualised material practices that staked out the normative limits of idealised relationships, many of them hierarchical. From the seventh to the tenth centuries, these communities intersected at cathedrals and minsters, which were increasingly represented on the itineraries of kings, ealdormen and bishops, and at the various assemblies of differnt scales whose meeting-places are often so elusive. In the tenth century, as royal and ecclesiastical authorities actively sought to integrate and control these communities, boroughs emerged as new foci of intersection and assembly, alongside royally mandated hundred and shire assemblies, while mother parishes imposed a new territorial coherence. But while these communities and places were conceived by a desire to stabilise and entrench, the ongoing process of their historical becoming, and the transformations they underwent, demonstrate the constant presence of possibility and contingency.

This concluding discussion has offered the outlines of an early medieval history framed around community that might apply to much of England, reflecting the location of the diocese of Lichfield within the English ecclesiastical community and one of the 'English' regnal communities. Likewise, previous chapters have attempted to advance our understanding of the north-west Midlands by engaging in dialogue with scholarship concerning the broader English context, or that of other regions within it. Finally, however, it is worth focusing on the distinctiveness of the region itself, and to what extent such distinctiveness allows the extrapolation of conclusions drawn from this case study to other regions that were encompassed by English ecclesio-regnal communities. The physical geography of the north-west Midlands rendered much of the region less welcoming to attempts to expand agricultural production that characterised much of the period in other parts of England, as discussed in Chapter 5; it was one of the least densely populated parts of England recorded in Domesday Book. Supporting the self-image evoked by the various forms of lordship studied here would thus have demanded correspondingly larger areas of land, and given the advantages conferred on those with central roles in the communities considered here – bishops, kings, ealdormen, abbots, abbesses, the more influential thegns – it is unsurprising to find that these people dominated the lordship of land and churches in this region more than they did in most other parts of England. It is therefore possible to suggest that the patterns evident in the evidence considered here, and the conclusions built on them, such as the hundredal organisation of church-scot and the correlation of mother churches with regnal and comital lordship, have survived to a greater degree than in other regions. Elsewhere, to the east and south, the opportunities offered to members of lower strata in the elite enabled them to establish a larger proportion of lordships over landholdings and churches, and thus to disrupt the clarity of earlier patterns over subsequent centuries. However, the conclusions built on these patterns – the significance of ecclesiastical tributes to diocesan lordship, the existence and significance of regnal territories – should be considered equally valid in other areas encompassed by the larger ecclesio-regnal communities studied here, even if the evidence for them has been disrupted by later developments.

The implications of the region's distinctiveness are not limited to its effects on the evidence available to us. It must have been apparent in many ways to those who lived within it and outside it during the period studied here, especially those whose movements regularly took them across its borders. Lindy Brady has explored such early medieval perspectives in recent work on the 'Anglo-Welsh Borderland', a region she is happy to define quite vaguely and that, in many respects, encompasses much of the diocese of Lichfield.[6] Brady demonstrates that the region was conceived in texts from the eighth to eleventh centuries as distinct in several ways from the 'core' regions of England to the south and east, and shared attributes with the regions of Wales to the west. Indeed, alliances between Welsh rulers and Mercian kings and earls made significant contributions to political conjunctures throughout the period. That such an unpromising region should support the political ambitions of such men is notable, even if the extension of those ambitions to the south-east, where they might be rooted in more productive soils, seems often to have appeared necessary to them. Such explicit distinctiveness resonates with the 'Mercian' name, which means 'border people'. Chapter 1 highlighted evidence that the diocese of Lichfield continued to be known as the Church of the Mercians, even when the same name could be applied to the expanded Midland dominance of Mercian kings in the eighth and ninth centuries. The diocese lay at the edge of several of the communities that were important to many of its inhabitants: it was the most north-westerly of bishoprics in the Southumbrian half of the English ecclesiastical community; its minster churches, which focused the intersection of several different communities for much of the period, lay at the extremity of the kinds of landscape able to support the lordships of their rulers; and the diocese's mother parishes were larger than most in England, often containing long stretches of windswept upland. Many members of these communities must have had cause to realise and to lament their liminality at times, just as some do today; indeed, this book began with a lament for the deficiencies of the Mercian hole. And yet the edge can never be entirely overlooked. After all, a bishop of the Church of the Mercians once competed with Canterbury for pre-eminence in Southumbrian England. It is thus distinctly appropriate that studying the meagre evidence offered by this borderland should offer insights that challenge and disrupt conclusions drawn from the greater abundances of the lands to the south and the east.

---

6   Brady, *Writing the Welsh borderlands*.

Bibliography

Abels, R.P., *Lordship and military obligation in Anglo-Saxon England* (London, 1988).
Acta Sanctorum (eds), 'Vita secunda Sanctae Wenefredae, et ejusdem translatio', *Acta Sanctorum*, Nov., I (1887), pp. 708–31.
Bailey, R.N., *Corpus of Anglo-Saxon stone sculpture, volume IX: Cheshire and Lancashire* (Oxford, 2010).
Bailey, R.N., *Viking-Age sculpture* (London, 1980).
Baker, J.T., *Cultural transition in the Chilterns and Essex region, 350 AD to 650 AD* (Hatfield, 2006).
Baker, J. and Brookes, S., *Beyond the Burghal Hidage* (Leiden, 2013).
Banham, D. and Faith, R., *Anglo-Saxon farms and farming* (Oxford, 2014).
Barlow, F., *The English Church 1000–1066* (London, 1963).
Barrow, J., 'The clergy in English dioceses c.900–c.1066', in F. Tinti (ed.), *Pastoral care in late Anglo-Saxon England* (Woodbridge, 2005), pp. 17–26.
Barrow, J., *The clergy in the medieval world: secular clerics, their families and careers in north-western Europe, c.800–c.1200* (Cambridge, 2015).
Barrow, J., 'Demonstrative behaviour and political communication in later Anglo-Saxon England', *Anglo-Saxon England*, 36 (2007), pp. 127–50.
Barrow, J., 'Playing by the rules: conflict management in tenth- and eleventh-century Germany', *Early Medieval Europe*, 11 (2002), pp. 389–96.
Bartlett, R. (ed.), *Geoffrey of Burton: life and miracles of St Modwenna* (Oxford, 2002).
Bassett, S., 'Anglo-Saxon Birmingham', *Midland History*, 25 (2000), pp. 1–27.
Bassett, S., *Anglo-Saxon Coventry and its churches*, The Dugdale Society Occasional Papers 41 (Stratford-upon-Avon, 2001).
Bassett, S., 'Anglo-Saxon fortifications in western Mercia', *Midland History*, 36 (2011), pp. 1–23.
Bassett, S., 'Anglo-Saxon Shrewsbury and its churches', *Midland History*, 16 (1991), pp. 1–23.
Bassett, S., 'Boundaries of knowledge: mapping the land units of late Anglo-Saxon and Norman England', in W. Davies, G. Halsall and A. Reynolds (eds), *People and space in the Middle Ages, 300–1300* (Turnhout, 2006), pp. 115–42.
Bassett, S., 'Church and diocese in the West Midlands: the transition from British to Anglo-Saxon control', in J. Blair and R. Sharpe (eds), *Pastoral care before the parish* (Leicester, 1992), pp. 13–40.
Bassett, S., 'Lincoln and the Anglo-Saxon see of Lindsey', *Anglo-Saxon England*, 18 (1989), pp. 1–32.
Bassett, S., 'Medieval ecclesiastical organisation in the vicinity of Wroxeter and its British antecedents', *Journal of the British Archaeological Association*, 145 (1992), pp. 1–28.
Bately, J.M., 'Old English prose before and during the reign of Alfred', *Anglo-Saxon England*, 17 (1988), pp. 93–138.
Baxter, S., *The earls of Mercia: lordship and power in late Anglo-Saxon England* (Oxford, 2007).
Baxter, S., 'Lordship and justice in late Anglo-Saxon England: the judicial functions of soke and commendation revisited', in S. Baxter, C. Karkov, J.L. Nelson and D. Pelteret (eds), *Early medieval studies in memory of Patrick Wormald* (Farnham, 2009), pp. 397–8.
Baxter, S. and Blair, J., 'Land tenure and royal patronage in the early English kingdom: a model and a case study', *Anglo-Norman Studies*, 28 (2006), pp. 19–46.

Baylis, H., 'Prebends in the cathedral church of Saints Mary and Chad in Lichfield', *Transactions of the Lichfield Archaeological and Historical Society*, 2 (1960/61), pp. 38–52.

Bergius, G.C.C., 'The Anglo-Saxon stone sculpture of Mercia as evidence for continental influence and cultural exchange', PhD thesis (Durham, 2012).

Biddle, M. and Kjølbye-Biddle, B., 'Repton and the Vikings', *Antiquity*, 66 (1992), pp. 36–51.

Biddle, M. and Kjølbye-Biddle, B., 'The Repton stone', *Anglo-Saxon England*, 14 (1985), pp. 233–92.

Birch, W. de G., *Liber Vitae: register and martyrology of New Minster and Hyde Abbey Winchester* (London and Winchester, 1888).

Bischoff, B. and Lapidge, M. (eds), *Biblical commentaries from the Canterbury school of Theodore and Hadrian* (Cambridge, 1994).

Blair, J., *Building Anglo-Saxon England* (Princeton, 2018).

Blair, J., *The church in Anglo-Saxon society* (Oxford, 2005).

Blair, J., 'Ecclesiastical organisation and pastoral care in Anglo-Saxon England', *Early Medieval Europe*, 4 (1995), pp. 193–212.

Blair, J., 'A handlist of Anglo-Saxon saints', in A. Thacker and R. Sharpe (eds), *Local saints and local churches in the early medieval West* (Oxford, 2002), pp. 495–565.

Blair, J., 'Introduction: from minster to parish church', in J. Blair (ed.), *Minsters and parish churches, the local church in transition 950–1200* (Oxford, 1988), pp. 1–19.

Blair, J., 'Minster churches in the landscape', in D. Hooke (ed.), *Anglo-Saxon settlements* (Oxford, 1988), pp. 35–58.

Blair, J., 'A saint for every minster? Local cults in Anglo-Saxon England', in A. Thacker and R. Sharpe (eds), *Local saints and local churches in the early medieval West* (Oxford, 2002), pp. 455–94.

Blair, J., 'Secular minster churches in Domesday Book', in P. Sawyer (ed.), *Domesday Book: a reassessment* (London, 1985), pp. 104–42.

Blake, M. and Sargent, A., '"For the protection of all the people": Æthelflæd and her burhs in northwest Mercia', *Midland History*, 43 (2018), pp. 120–54.

Bradley, H., 'Etocetum or Letocetum?', *The Academy*, 756 (1886), p. 294.

Brady, L., *Writing the Welsh borderland in Anglo-Saxon England* (Manchester, 2017).

Breeze, A., 'Bede's *castella* and the journeys of St Chad', *Northern History*, 46/1 (2009), pp. 137–9.

Brett, M., 'Theodore and the Latin canon law', in M. Lapidge (ed.), *Archbishop Theodore: commemorative studies on his life and influence* (Cambridge, 1995), pp. 120–40.

Brooks, N., 'The development of military obligations in eighth- and ninth-century England', in P. Clemoes and K. Hughes (eds), *England before the Conquest: studies in primary sources presented to Dorothy Whitelock* (Cambridge, 1971), pp. 69–84.

Brooks, N., *The early history of the church of Canterbury* (Leicester, 1984).

Brown, M.P., *The Book of Cerne. Prayer, patronage and power in ninth-century England* (London, 1996).

Brown, M.P., 'Mercian manuscripts? The "Tiberius" group and its historical context', in M.P. Brown and C.A. Farr (eds), *Mercia: an Anglo-Saxon kingdom in Europe* (London, 2001), pp. 278–91.

Brown, M.P. and Farr, C.A. (eds), *Mercia: an Anglo-Saxon kingdom in Europe* (London, 2001).

Bryant, R. (ed.), *Corpus of Anglo-Saxon stone sculpture, volume X, the western Midlands* (Oxford, 2012).

Cam, H.M., 'Early groups of hundreds', in H. Cam (ed.), *Liberties and communities in medieval England* (Cambridge, 1944), pp. 91–106.

Cam, H.M., *The hundred and the hundred rolls: an outline of local government in medieval England* (London, 1930).

Cambridge, E. and Rollason, D., 'The pastoral organisation of the Anglo-Saxon church: a review of the "minster hypothesis"', *Early Medieval Europe*, 4 (1995), pp. 87–104.

Cambridge, E. and Williams, A., 'Hexham Abbey: a review of recent work and its implications', *Archaeologia Aeliana*, Fifth Series, 23 (1995), pp. 51–138.
Cameron, K., 'Eccles in English place-names', in M.W. Barley and R.P.C. Hanson (eds), *Christianity in Britain, 300–700* (Leicester, 1968), pp. 87–92.
Cameron, K., *The place-names of Derbyshire*, 3 vols (Cambridge, 1959).
Campbell, A. (ed. and trans.), *Chronicon Æthelweardi* (London, 1962).
Campbell, J., 'Bede's *reges* and *principes*', in J. Campbell (ed.), *Essays in Anglo-Saxon history* (London, 1986), pp. 85–98.
Carver, M.O.H., 'Excavations south of Lichfield cathedral', *Transactions of the South Staffordshire Archaeological and Historical Society*, 22 (1981), pp. 35–69.
Chaney, W.A., 'Anglo-Saxon church dues: a study in historical continuity', *Church History*, 32 (1963), pp. 268–77.
Charles-Edwards, T.M., 'Wales and Mercia, 613–918', in M.P. Brown and C.A. Farr (eds), *Mercia: an Anglo-Saxon kingdom in Europe* (London, 2001), pp. 89–105.
Christie, R.C., *Annales Cestrienses, or Chronicle of the Abbey of St Werburg, at Chester*, The Record Society for Lancashire and Cheshire 14 (n.p., 1887).
Clark, R., 'The dedications of medieval churches in Derbyshire: their survival and change from the Reformation to the present day', *Derbyshire Archaeological Journal*, 112 (1992), pp. 48–61.
Coatsworth, E. (ed.), *Corpus of Anglo-Saxon stone sculpture, volume VIII, western Yorkshire* (Oxford, 2008).
Colgrave, B., *Felix's life of Saint Guthlac* (Cambridge, 1956).
Colgrave, B., *The life of Bishop Wilfrid by Eddius Stephanus. Text, translation, and notes* (Cambridge, 1927).
Colgrave, B. and Mynors, R.A.B. (eds), *Bede's Ecclesiastical History of the English People* (Oxford, 1969).
Collingwood, W.G., *Northumbrian crosses of the pre-Norman age* (London, 1927).
Cox, B., 'The place-names of Leicestershire and Rutland', PhD thesis (University of Nottingham, 1971).
Cramp, R., 'Anglo-Saxon sculpture of the Reform period', in D. Parsons (ed.), *Tenth-century studies, essays in commemoration of the millennium of the Council of Winchester and Regularis Concordia* (London, 1975), pp. 184–99.
Cramp, R., 'New directions in the study of Anglo-Saxon sculpture', *Transactions of the Leicestershire Archaeological and Historical Society*, 84 (2010), pp. 1–25.
Cramp, R., 'Schools of Mercian sculpture', in A. Dornier (ed.), *Mercian studies* (Leicester, 1977), pp. 191–233.
Crook, J., *The architectural setting of the cult of saints in the early Christian West c. 300–1200* (Oxford, 2000).
Croom, J., 'The fragmentation of the minster *parochiae* of south-east Shropshire', in J. Blair (ed.), *Minsters and parish churches, the local church in transition 950–1200* (Oxford, 1988), pp. 67–81.
Cubitt, C., *Anglo-Saxon church councils c.650–c.850* (Leicester, 1995).
Cubitt, C., 'The clergy in early Anglo-Saxon England', *Historical Research*, 78/201 (2005), pp. 273–87.
Cubitt, C., 'Memory and narrative in the cult of early Anglo-Saxon saints', in Y. Hen and M. Innes (eds), *The uses of the past in the early Middle Ages* (Cambridge, 2000), pp. 29–66.
Cubitt, C., 'Universal and local saints in Anglo-Saxon England', in A. Thacker and R. Sharpe (eds), *Local saints and local churches in the early medieval West* (Oxford, 2002), pp. 423–53.
Darlington, R.R. and McGurk, P., *The chronicle of John of Worcester, volume II, the annals from 450 to 1066* (Oxford, 1995).
Davies, W., *An early Welsh microcosm: studies in the Llandaff charters* (London, 1978).
Davies, W., 'Middle Anglia and the Middle Angles', *Midland History*, 2/1 (1973), pp. 18–20.

Davis, R.H.C., *The kalendar of Abbot Samson of Bury St Edmunds and related documents* (London, 1954).
Denton, J.H., *English royal free chapels 1100–1300. A constitutional study* (Manchester, 1970).
Depreux, P., 'Gestures and comportment at the Carolingian court: between practice and perception', *Past and Present*, 203, supplement 4 (2009), pp. 57–79.
Dodgson, J.M., *The place-names of Cheshire*, five parts in seven volumes (Cambridge, 1970–97).
Dodgson, J.M., 'The significance of the distribution of English place-names in *-ingas*, *-inga-* in south-east England', *Medieval Archaeology*, 10 (1966), pp. 1–29.
Dornier, A., 'The Anglo-Saxon monastery at Breedon-on-the-Hill, Leicestershire', in A. Dornier (ed.), *Mercian studies* (Leicester, 1977), pp. 155–68.
Dornier, A. (ed.), *Mercian studies* (Leicester, 1977).
Draper, S., 'Burh enclosures in Anglo-Saxon settlements: case studies in Wiltshire', in R. Jones and S. Semple (eds), *Sense of place in Anglo-Saxon England* (Donington, 2012), pp. 334–51.
Dugdale, W., *Monasticon Anglicanum*, ed. J. Caley, H. Ellis and B. Bandinel, 6 vols in 8 parts (London, 1817–30).
Dümmler, E. (ed.), *Alcuin epistolae*, Monumenta Germaniae historica, epistolae Carolini aevi 4 (Berlin, 1895).
Dumville, D.N., 'The Anglian collection of royal genealogies and regnal lists', *Anglo-Saxon England*, 5 (1976), pp. 23–50.
Dumville, D.N., 'Essex, Middle Anglia and the expansion of Mercia', in D.N. Dumville (ed.), *Britons and Anglo-Saxons in the early Middle Ages* (Aldershot, 1993), Essay IX.
Dumville, D.N., 'The terminology of overkingship in Anglo-Saxon England', in J. Hines (ed.), *The Anglo-Saxons from the Migration Period to the eighth century: an ethnographic perspective* (Woodbridge, 1997), pp. 345–73.
Everson, P. and Stocker, D. (eds), *Corpus of Anglo-Saxon of stone sculpture, volume V, Lincolnshire* (Oxford, 1999).
Everson, P. and Stocker, D. (eds), *Corpus of Anglo-Saxon stone sculpture, volume XII, Nottinghamshire* (Oxford, 2016).
Eyton, E.W., *Antiquities of Shropshire, volume I* (London, 1854).
Faith, R., *The English peasantry and the growth of lordship* (Leicester, 1997).
Fanning, S., 'Bede, imperium, and the Bretwaldas', *Speculum*, 66/1 (1991), pp. 1–26.
Farmer, D.H., *The Oxford dictionary of saints* (Oxford, 1978).
Featherstone, P., 'The Tribal Hidage and the ealdormen of Mercia', in M.P. Brown and C.A. Farr (eds), *Mercia: an Anglo-Saxon kingdom in Europe* (London, 2000), pp. 23–34.
Feilitzen, O. von, *The pre-Conquest personal names of Domesday Book* (Uppsala, 1937).
Fell, C., 'Saint Æthelþryð: a historical dichotomy revisited', *Nottingham Medieval Studies*, 38 (1994), pp. 19–34.
Fernie, E., *The architecture of the Anglo-Saxons* (London, 1982).
Fernie, E., 'The eastern parts of the Anglo-Saxon church of St Wystan at Repton: function and chronology', *The Antiquaries Journal*, 98 (2018), pp. 95–114.
Finberg, H.P.R., *The early charters of the West Midlands* (Leicester, 1961).
Foot, S., *Athelstan: the first king of England* (New Haven, 2011).
Foot, S., *Monastic life in Anglo-Saxon England, c.600–900* (Cambridge, 2006).
Foot, S., *Veiled women: female religious communities in England, 871–1066*, 2 vols (Aldershot, 2000).
Ford, W.J., 'Some settlement patterns in the central region of the Warwickshire Avon', in P.H. Sawyer (ed.), *English medieval settlement* (London, 1979), pp. 143–63.
Franklin, M.J., *Coventry and Lichfield 1072–1159*, English episcopal *acta* 14 (Oxford, 1997).
Franklin, M.J., *Coventry and Lichfield 1160–1182*, English episcopal *acta* 16 (Oxford, 1998).

Bibliography

Franklin, M.J., 'The secular college as a focus for Anglo-Norman piety: St Augustine's Daventry', in J. Blair (ed.), *Minsters and parish churches: the local church in transition 950–1200* (Oxford, 1988), pp. 97–105.
Gautier, A., 'Hospitality in pre-Viking Anglo-Saxon England', *Early Medieval Europe*, 17 (2009), pp. 23–44.
Gaydon, A.T. (ed.), *VCH Shropshire*, vol. 2 (London, 1973).
Gelling, M., *Place-names in the landscape* (London, 1984).
Gelling, M., *Signposts to the past: place-names and the history of England* (London, 1978).
Gelling, M., 'Some notes on Warwickshire place-names', *Transactions of the Birmingham and Warwickshire Archaeological Society*, 86 (1974), pp. 59–79.
Gelling, M., 'Some thoughts on Staffordshire place-names', *North Staffordshire Journal of Field Studies*, 21 (1981), pp. 1–20.
Gelling, M., *The West Midlands in the early Middle Ages* (Leicester, 1992).
Gelling, M. and Cole, A., *The landscape of place-names* (Donington, 2000).
Gelling, M. and Foxall, H.D.G., *The place-names of Shropshire*, 6 vols (Nottingham, 1990–2012).
Gem, R., 'A B C: How should we periodise Anglo-Saxon architecture?', in L.A.S. Butler and R.K. Morris (eds), *The Anglo-Saxon church: papers on history, architecture, and archaeology in honour of Dr H M Taylor*, CBA Research Report 60 (London, 1986), pp. 146–55.
Gem, R., 'Architecture of the Anglo-Saxon church, 735 to 870: from Archbishop Ecgberht to Archbishop Ceolnoth', *Journal of the British Archaeological Association*, 146 (1993), pp. 29–66.
Gem, R., 'The episcopal churches of Lindsey in the early 9th century', in A. Vince (ed.), *Pre-Viking Lindsey*, Lincoln Archaeological Studies 1 (Lincoln, 1993), pp. 123–7.
George, G. (ed.), *An old English martyrology*, Early English Text Society 116 (London, 1900).
Giandrea, M.F., *Episcopal culture in late Anglo-Saxon England* (Woodbridge, 2007).
Gilbert, J., *Common ground: democracy and collectivity in an age of individualism* (London, 2014).
Gittos, H., *Liturgy, architecture, and sacred places in Anglo-Saxon England* (Oxford, 2013).
Gould, J., *Lichfield: archaeology and development* (Birmingham, 1976).
Gould, J. and Gould, D., 'St Michael's Churchyard, Lichfield', *Transactions of the South Staffordshire Archaeological and Historical Society*, 16 (1975), pp. 58–61.
Gover, J.E.B., Mawr, A. and Stenton, F.M., *The place-names of Warwickshire* (Cambridge, 1936).
Greenslade, M.W., *Saint Chad of Lichfield and Birmingham* (Birmingham, 1996).
Greenslade, M.W. (ed.), *VCH Staffordshire*, vol. 3 (London, 1970).
Greenslade, M.W. (ed.), *VCH Staffordshire*, vol. 14 (London, 1990).
Greenslade, M.W. and Johnson, D.A. (eds), *VCH Staffordshire*, vol. 6 (London, 1979).
Griffiths, D.W., 'Anglo-Saxon England and the Irish Sea region AD 800–1100: an archaeological study of the lower Dee and Mersey as a border area', PhD thesis (Durham, 1991).
Grosjean, P., 'Codices Gothani appendix', *Analecta Bollandiana*, 58 (1940), pp. 177–204.
Grosjean, P., 'De codice hagiographico Gothano', *Analecta Bollandiana*, 58 (1940), pp. 90–103.
Haddan, A.W. and Stubbs, W. (eds), *Councils and ecclesiastical documents relating to Great Britain and Ireland: volume III, the English Church 595–1066* (Oxford, 1871).
Hadley, D.M., *The Vikings in England. Settlement, society and culture* (Manchester, 2006).
Hadley, D.M. and Buckberry, J., 'Caring for the dead in late Anglo-Saxon England', in F. Tinti (ed.), *Pastoral care in late Anglo-Saxon England* (Woodbridge, 2005), pp. 121–47.
Hall, A., 'The instability of place-names in Anglo-Saxon England and early medieval Wales, and the loss of Roman toponymy', in R. Jones and S. Semple (eds), *Sense of place in Anglo-Saxon England* (Donington, 2012), pp. 101–29.
Hall, D., *The open fields of England* (Oxford, 2014).
Hall, R.A. and Whyman, M., 'Settlement and monasticism at Ripon, north Yorkshire, from the 7th to 11th Centuries AD', *Medieval Archaeology*, 40 (1996), pp. 62–150.

Halsall, G., *Barbarian migrations and the Roman West 376–568* (Cambridge, 2007).
Harmer, F.E., *Anglo-Saxon writs* (Manchester, 1952).
Harris, B.E. (ed.), *VCH Cheshire*, vol. 3 (London, 1980).
Harris, B.E. with Thacker, A.T. (eds), *VCH Cheshire*, vol. 1 (Oxford, 1987).
Harvey, S., *Domesday: book of judgement* (Oxford, 2014).
Hawkes, J., 'Constructing iconographies: questions of identity in Mercian sculpture', in M.P. Brown and C.A. Farr (eds), *Mercia: an Anglo-Saxon kingdom in Europe* (London, 2001), pp. 230–45.
Hawkes, J., 'The legacy of Constantine in Anglo-Saxon England', in E. Hartley, J. Hawkes and M. Henig (eds), *Constantine the Great: York's Roman emperor* (London, 2006), pp. 104–14.
Hawkes, J., *The Sandbach crosses: sign and significance in Anglo-Saxon sculpture* (Dublin, 2002).
Hawkes, J. and Sidebottom, P., *Corpus of Anglo-Saxon stone sculpture, volume XIII: Derbyshire and Staffordshire* (Oxford, 2018).
Higgitt, J., 'The dedication inscription at Jarrow and its context', *Antiquaries Journal*, 59 (1979), pp. 346–74.
Higham, N.J., *An English empire: Bede and the early Anglo-Saxon kings* (Manchester, 1995).
Higham, N.J., 'Northumbria's southern frontier: a review', *Early Medieval Europe*, 14/4 (2006), pp. 391–418.
Higham, N.J., *The origins of Cheshire* (Manchester, 1993).
Higham, N.J., 'Patterns of settlement in medieval Cheshire: an insight into dispersed settlement', *Annual Report of the Medieval Settlement Research Group*, 2 (1987), pp. 9–10.
Hill, D., 'Mercians: the dwellers on the boundary', in M.P. Brown and C.A. Farr (eds), *Mercia: an Anglo-Saxon kingdom in Europe* (London, 2001), pp. 173–82.
Hill, D. and Worthington, M., *Offa's Dyke: history and guide* (Stroud, 2003).
Hill, P.H., *Whithorn and St Ninian: the excavation of a monastic town 1984–91* (Stroud, 1997).
Hobbes, T., *Leviathan* [1651], trans. and ed. N. Malcolm, *Thomas Hobbes: Leviathan* (Oxford, 2012).
Hollis, S., 'The Minster-in-Thanet foundation story', *Anglo-Saxon England*, 27 (1998), pp. 41–64.
Holmes, M., 'Archaeological excavations at Polesworth abbey, Warwickshire, 2011–2013', unpublished report, MOLA No. 15/31 (Northampton, 2015).
Hooke, D., 'Early medieval woodland and the place-name term *lēah*', in O.J. Padel and D.N. Parsons (eds), *A commodity of good names: essays in honour of Margaret Gelling* (Donington, 2008), pp. 365–76.
Hooke, D., *The landscape of Anglo-Saxon Staffordshire: the charter evidence* (Keele, 1983).
Hooke, D., 'Wolverhampton: the foundation of the minster', in J. Maddison (ed.), *Medieval archaeology and architecture at Lichfield*, Transactions of the British Archaeological Association 13 (1993), pp. 11–16.
Horovitz, D., *Æthelflæd, Lady of the Mercians: the battle of Tettenhall 910AD; and other west Mercian studies* (Brewood, 2017), pp. 573–601.
Horovitz, D., *The place-names of Staffordshire* (Brewood, 2005).
Horstmann, C., *The Life of Saint Werburge of Chester by Henry Bradshaw*, Early English Text Society 88, vol. 1 (London, 1887).
Horstmann, C., *Nova Legenda Anglie* (Oxford, 1901).
Hough, C., 'Eccles in English and Scottish place-names', in E. Quinton (ed.), *The church in English place-names* (Nottingham, 2009), pp. 109–24.
Hummer, H.J., *Politics and power in early medieval Europe. Alsace and the Frankish realm, 600–1000* (Cambridge, 2005).
Hunter-Blair, P., 'Some observations on the *Historia Regum* attributed to Symeon of Durham', in N. Chadwick (ed.), *Celt and Saxon: studies in the early British border* (Cambridge, 1963), pp. 63–118.
Hurst, D. (ed.), *Opera exegetica (Beda Venerabilis)*, Corpus Christianorum series Latina 119a (Turnhout, 1969).

Innes, M., *Introduction to early medieval western Europe, 300–900* (London, 2007).
Innes, M., *State and society in the early Middle Ages: the middle Rhine valley, 400–1000* (London, 2000).
Insley, C., '"Ottonians with pipe rolls"? Political culture and performance in the kingdom of the English, c.900–c.1050', *History*, 102 (2017), pp. 772–86.
James, A.G., 'Eglēs/Eclēs and the formation of Northumbria', in E. Quinton (ed.), *The church in English place-names* (Nottingham, 2009), pp. 125–50.
Jenkins, A.E., 'The early medieval context of the royal free chapels of south Staffordshire', PhD thesis (University of Birmingham, 1988).
Jewell, R., 'Classicism of Southumbrian sculpture', in M.P. Brown and C.A. Farr (eds), *Mercia: an Anglo-Saxon kingdom in Europe* (London, 2001), pp. 246–62.
John, E., 'The division of the *mensa* in early English monasteries', *Journal of Ecclesiastical History*, 6/2 (1955), pp. 143–55.
John, E., 'Folkland reconsidered', in E. John (ed.), *Orbis Britanniae and other studies* (Leicester, 1966), pp. 64–127.
John, E., *Land tenure in early England: a discussion of some problems* (Leicester, 1964).
Jones, A., 'Lichfield cathedral close: archaeological evaluation (stages 1–4) 1989–1990', Birmingham University Field Archaeology Unit unpublished report (Birmingham, 1990).
Jones, G., *Saints in the landscape* (Stroud, 2007).
Jones, R. and Page, M., *Medieval villages in an English landscape: beginnings and ends* (Macclesfield, 2006).
Joy, C.A., 'Sokeright', MA thesis (Leeds, 1972).
Kelly, S.E., *Charters of Abingdon abbey, Part I*, Anglo-Saxon Charters 7 (Oxford, 2000).
Kelly, S.E., *Charters of Peterborough Abbey*, Anglo-Saxon Charters 14 (Oxford, 2009).
Kemp, B., 'Some aspects of the *parochia* of Leominster in the 12th century', in J. Blair (ed.), *Minsters and parish churches: the local church in transition 950–1200* (Oxford, 1988), pp. 83–95.
Kendrick, T.D., *Anglo-Saxon art to AD 900* (London, 1938).
Kennedy, A.G., 'Disputes about *bocland*: the forum for their adjudication', *Anglo-Saxon England*, 14 (1985), pp. 175–95.
Kettle, A.J. and Johnson, D.A., 'The cathedral of Lichfield', in *VCH Staffs.*, vol. III, pp. 140–98.
Keynes, S.D., *An atlas of attestations in Anglo-Saxon charters, c.670–1066* (Cambridge, 2002).
Keynes, S., *The councils of* Clofesho, Vaughan Paper 38 (Leicester, 1993).
Keynes, S., *The diplomas of King Æthelred 'the Unready' 978–1016* (Cambridge, 1980).
Keynes, S., 'Edward, king of the Anglo-Saxons', in N.J. Higham and D.H. Hill (eds), *Edward the Elder 899–924* (London, 2001), pp. 40–66.
Keynes, S., 'Regenbald the Chancellor (*sic*)', *Anglo-Norman Studies*, 10 (1988), pp. 185–222.
Keynes, S., 'Wulfhere', in M. Lapidge, J. Blair, S. Keynes and D. Scragg (eds), *The Blackwell encyclopaedia of Anglo-Saxon England* (Oxford, 1999), pp. 490–1.
Kirby, D.P., 'Bede's native sources for the *Historia Ecclesiastica*', *Bulletin of the John Rylands Library*, 48 (1966), pp. 341–71.
Kirby, D.P., *The earliest English kings*, rev. edn (London, 2000).
Kirby, D.P., 'Welsh bards and the border', in A. Dornier (ed.), *Mercian studies* (Leicester, 1977), pp. 31–42.
Koch, J.T., *Cunedda, Cynan, Cadwallon, Cynddylan: four Welsh poems and Britain 383–655* (Aberystwyth, 2013).
Lambert, T., *Law and order in Anglo-Saxon England* (Oxford, 2017).
Lang, J. (ed.), *Corpus of Anglo-Saxon stone sculpture, volume III, York and eastern Yorkshire* (Oxford, 1991).
Lang, J. (ed.), *Corpus of Anglo-Saxon stone sculpture, volume VI, northern Yorkshire* (Oxford, 2002).

Langefeld, B., '*Regula canonicorum* or *Regula monasterialis vitae*? The Rule of Chrodegang and Archbishop Wulfred's reforms at Canterbury', *Anglo-Saxon England*, 25 (1996), pp. 21–36.

Lapidge, M., *Anglo-Saxon litanies of the saints*, Henry Bradshaw Society 106 (London, 1991).

Lapidge, M. (ed.), *Archbishop Theodore: commemorative studies on his life and influence* (Cambridge, 1995).

Lapidge, M., 'The career of Archbishop Theodore', in M. Lapidge (ed.), *Archbishop Theodore: commemorative studies on his life and influence* (Cambridge, 1995), pp. 1–29.

Lewis, C.P., 'The invention of the manor in Norman England', *Anglo-Norman Studies*, 34 (2012), pp. 123–50.

Lewis, C.P., 'Welsh territories and Welsh identities in late Anglo-Saxon England', in N. Higham (ed.), *Britons in Anglo-Saxon England* (Woodbridge, 2007), pp. 130–43.

Liebermann, F., *Die gesetze der Angelsachsen, I* (Halle, 1903).

Losco-Bradley, S. and Kinsley, G., *Catholme: an Anglo-Saxon settlement on the Trent gravels in Staffordshire* (Nottingham, 2002).

Love, R.C., *Goscelin of Saint-Bertin: the hagiography of the female saints of Ely* (Oxford, 2004).

Lumby, J.R., *Polychronicon Ranulphi Higden monachi Cestrensis* (London, 1876).

McKerracher, M., *Farming transformed in Anglo-Saxon England: agriculture in the long eighth century* (Oxford, 2018).

MacQueen, J., *Ninian and the Picts*, Fifteenth Whithorn Lecture (Whithorn, 2007).

Macray, W.D. (ed.), *Chronicon abbatiae de Evesham ad annum 1418* (London, 1863).

Marafioti, N., 'Seeking Alfred's body: royal tomb as political object in the reign of Edward the Elder', *Early Medieval Europe*, 23 (2015), pp. 202–28.

Matthew, H.C.G. and Harrison, B. (eds), *Oxford Dictionary of National Biography* (Oxford, 2004).

Mellows, W.T., *The chronicle of Hugh Candidus, a monk of Peterborough* (London, 1949).

Moffett, C., 'Archaeological investigations at the Anglo-Saxon church of St Andrew, Wroxeter: 1985–6', *Transactions of the Shropshire Archaeological and Historical Society*, 66 (1989), pp. 1–14.

Molyneaux, G., *The formation of the English kingdom in the tenth century* (Oxford, 2015).

Moore, M.E., *A sacred kingdom: bishops and the rise of Frankish kingship, 300–850* (Washington, DC, 2011).

Morris, J. *et al.* (ed.), *Domesday Book*, 34 vols (Chichester, 1974–86).

Morris, R., *Churches in the landscape* (London, 1989).

Mumby, J., 'The descent of family land in later Anglo-Saxon England', *Historical Research*, 84 (2011), pp. 399–415.

Neilson, N., *Customary rents*, Oxford Studies in Social and Legal History 2 (Oxford, 1910).

Nelson, J.N., 'England and the continent in the ninth century: III, rights and rituals', *Transactions of the Royal Historical Society*, 6th series, 14 (2004), pp. 1–24.

Oakden, J.P., *The place-names of Staffordshire, part 1* (Nottingham, 1984).

Orwin, C.S. and Orwin, C.S., *The open fields* (Oxford, 1938).

Ozanne, A., 'The Peak dwellers', *Medieval Archaeology*, 6/7 (1962/3), pp. 15–52.

Page, M. and Jones, R., 'Stability and instability in medieval village plans: case studies in Whittlewood', in M. Gardiner and S. Rippon (eds), *Medieval landscapes: landscape history after Hoskins, volume 2* (Macclesfield, 2007), pp. 139–52.

Page, R.I., 'Anglo-Saxon episcopal lists', *Nottingham Medieval Studies*, 9 (1965), pp. 71–95, and 10 (1966), pp. 2–24.

Page, W. (ed.), *VCH Derbyshire*, vol. 2 (Oxford, 1907).

Page, W. (ed.), *VCH Warwickshire*, vol. 2 (Oxford, 1908).

Parsons, D., 'The Mercian church: archaeology and topography', in M.P. Brown and C.A. Farr (eds),

Bibliography

Mercia: an Anglo-Saxon kingdom in Europe (London, 2001), pp. 50–68.
Phillimore, R., *The ecclesiastical law of the Church of England* (London, 1873).
Phillips, A.D.M. and Phillips, C.B. (eds), *An historical atlas of Staffordshire* (Manchester, 2011).
Phillips, A.D.M. and Phillips, C.B. (eds), *A new historical atlas of Cheshire* (Chester, 2002).
Pickles, T., 'Biscopes-tūn, muneca-tūn and prēosta-tūn: dating, significance and distribution', in E. Quinton, *The church in English place-names* (Nottingham, 2009), pp. 39–107.
Plummer, C., *Venerabilis Bedae opera historica* (Oxford, 1896).
Pössel, C., 'The magic of early medieval ritual', *Early Medieval Europe*, 17 (2009), pp. 111–25.
Pratt, D., 'Demesne exemption from royal taxation in Anglo-Saxon and Anglo-Norman England', *English Historical Review*, 128 (2013), pp. 1–34.
Radford, C.A.R., 'The church of Saint Alkmund', *Derbyshire Archaeological Journal*, 96 (1976), pp. 26–61.
Ragg, J.M., Beard, G.R., George, H., Heaven, F.W., Hollis, J.M., Jones, R.J.A., Palmer, R.C., Reeve, M.J., Robson, J.D. and Whitfield, W.A.D., *Soils and their use in Midland and western England* (Harpenden, 1984).
Ray, K. and Bapty, I., *Offa's Dyke: landscape and hegemony in eighth century Britain* (Oxford, 2016).
Reynolds, S., *Fiefs and vassals: the medieval evidence reinterpreted* (Oxford, 1994).
Reynolds, S., *Kingdoms and communities in Western Europe 900–1300* (Oxford, 1984).
Roach, L., *Kingship and consent in Anglo-Saxon England, 871–978: assemblies and the state in the early Middle Ages* (Cambridge, 2013).
Roberts, B.K., 'Field systems of the West Midlands', in A.R.H Baker and R.A. Butlin (eds), *Studies of field systems in the British Isles* (Cambridge, 1973), pp. 188–231.
Roberts, B.K. and Wrathmell, S., *An atlas of rural settlement in England* (London, 2000).
Rodwell, W., 'Archaeological excavation in the nave of Lichfield cathedral: an interim report', unpublished report (Lichfield Cathedral Library, 2003).
Rodwell, W., 'Archaeology and the standing fabric: recent studies at Lichfield cathedral', *Antiquity*, 63 (1989), pp. 281–94.
Rodwell, W., 'The development of the choir of Lichfield cathedral: Romanesque and Early English', in J. Maddison (ed.), *Medieval archaeology and architecture at Lichfield*, Conference Transactions of the British Archaeological Association 13 (Oxford, 1993), pp. 17–35.
Rodwell, W., 'An interim report on archaeological investigations in the nave of Lichfield cathedral', unpublished report, Lichfield Cathedral Library (Lichfield, 2000).
Rodwell, W., 'Lichfield cathedral: interim report on archaeological excavations in the north quire aisle', unpublished report, Lichfield Cathedral Library (Lichfield, 1994).
Rodwell, W., 'Lichfield cathedral: interim report on archaeological excavations in the south quire aisle and the consistory court', unpublished report, Lichfield Cathedral Library (Lichfield, 1992).
Rodwell, W., Hawkes, J., Howe, E. and Cramp, R., 'The Lichfield Angel: a spectacular Anglo-Saxon painted sculpture', *The Antiquaries Journal*, 88 (2008), pp. 48–108.
Roffe, D., *Decoding Domesday* (Woodbridge, 2007).
Roffe, D., *Domesday: the inquest and the book* (Oxford, 2000).
Roffe, D., 'From thegnage to barony: sake and soke, title, and tenants-in-chief', *Anglo-Norman Studies*, 12 (1990), pp. 157–76.
Rollason, D.W., 'The cults of murdered royal saints in Anglo-Saxon England', *Anglo-Saxon England*, 11 (1983), pp. 1–22.
Rollason, D.W., 'Lists of saints' resting-places in Anglo-Saxon England', *Anglo-Saxon England*, 7 (1978), pp. 61–93.
Rollason, D.W., *The Mildrith legend. A study in early medieval hagiography in England* (Leicester, 1982).

Rollason, D.W., *The search for St Wigstan, prince-martyr of the kingdom of Mercia*, Vaughan Paper 27 (Leicester, 1981).
Rosser, G., *The art of solidarity in the Middle Ages* (Oxford, 2015).
Round, J.H., '"Churchscot" in Domesday', *English Historical Review*, 5 (1890), p. 101.
Rumble, A.R., '*Ad Lapidem* in Bede and a Mercian martyrdom', in A.R. Rumble and A.D. Mills (eds), *Names, places and people. An onomastic miscellany in memory of John McNeal Dodgson* (Stamford, 1997), pp. 307–19.
Rumble, A.R. '"Hrepingas" reconsidered', in A. Dornier (ed.), *Mercian studies* (Leicester, 1977), pp. 169–71.
Rushforth, R., *Saints in English calendars before AD 1100*, Henry Bradshaw Society 117 (London, 2008).
Salzman, L.F. (ed.), *VCH Warwickshire*, vol. 6 (Oxford, 1951).
Sargent, A., 'Early medieval Lichfield: a reassessment', *Transactions of the Staffordshire Archaeological and Historical Society*, 46 (2013), pp. 1–32.
Sargent, A., 'Lichfield and the lands of St Chad', PhD thesis (Keele, 2012).
Sargent, A., 'A misplaced miracle: the origins of St Modwynn of Burton and St Eadgyth of Polesworth', *Midland History*, 41 (2016), pp. 1–19.
Savage, H.E., *Book of Alan Asseborn: an address given on the festival of St. Chad* (Lichfield, 1922).
Savage, H.E. (ed.), 'The Great Register of Lichfield cathedral known as Magnum Registrum Album', in *SHC* 1924, pp. xi–404.
Savage, H.E., *The Lichfield Chronicle: an address given on the festival of St. Chad* (Lichfield, 1915).
Sawyer, P.H., *Anglo-Saxon charters: an annotated list and bibliography* (London, 1968).
Sawyer, P.H. (ed.), *The charters of Burton Abbey*, Anglo-Saxon Charters 2 (Oxford, 1979).
Seebohm, F., *The English village community* (London, 1890).
Sharpe, R., 'Martyrs and local saints in Late Antique Britain', in A. Thacker and R. Sharpe (eds), *Local saints and local churches in the early medieval West* (Oxford, 2002), pp. 75–154.
Sidebottom, P.C., 'Schools of Mercian stone sculpture in the north Midlands', PhD thesis (University of Sheffield, 1994).
Sims-Williams, P., *Religion and literature in western England 600–800* (Cambridge, 1990).
Smith, K., 'From dividual and individual selves to porous subjects', *The Australian Journal of Anthropology*, 23 (2012), pp. 50–64.
Smith, S.T., *Land and book: literature and land tenure in Anglo-Saxon England* (Toronto, 2012).
Stewart-Brown, R., *The serjeants of the peace in medieval England and Wales* (Manchester, 1963).
Story, J., 'After Bede: continuing the Ecclesiastical History', in Stephen Baxter, C.E. Karkov and J. Nelson (eds), *Early medieval studies in memory of Patrick Wormald* (Farnham, 2009), pp. 165–84.
Stubbs, W. (ed.), *Memorials of St Dunstan, archbishop of Canterbury* (London, 1874).
Styles, D., 'The early history of the king's chapels in Staffordshire', *Transactions of the Birmingham Archaeological Society*, 60 (1936), pp. 56–95.
Styles, D., 'The early history of Penkridge church', in *SHC* 1950/1, pp. 1–52.
Styles, T., 'Whitby revisited: Bede's explanation of *Streanaeshalch*', *Nomina*, 21 (1998), pp. 133–48.
Swanton, M., *The Anglo-Saxon Chronicles* (London, 2000).
Sylvester, D., *The rural landscape of the Welsh borderland: a study in historical geography* (London, 1969).
Tait, J., *The chartulary of Chester Abbey*, Chetham Society New Series 79 (Manchester, 1920).
Tait, J., 'Review of *The Domesday inquest* by Adolphus Ballard', *English Historical Review*, 23 (1908), pp. 122–6.
Tangl, M. (ed.), *S. Bonifatii et Lullii epistolae*, Monumenta Germaniae historica, epistolae selectae 1 (Berlin, 1916).
Tatton-Brown, T., 'The churches of Canterbury diocese in the 11th century', in J. Blair (ed.), *Minsters and parish churches: the local church in transition 950–1200* (Oxford, 1988), pp. 105–18.

Bibliography

Taylor, H.M., 'Anglo-Saxon architecture and sculpture in Staffordshire', *North Staffordshire Journal of Field Studies*, 6 (1966), pp. 7–11.

Taylor, H.M. and Taylor, J., *Anglo-Saxon architecture*, vol. 2 (Cambridge, 1965), pp. 510–16.

Thacker, A.T., 'Early ecclesiastical organization in two Mercian burhs', *Northern History*, 18 (1982), pp. 199–211.

Thacker, A.T., 'Kings, saints and monasteries in pre-Viking Mercia', *Midland History*, 10 (1985), pp. 1–25.

Thompson, V., *Dying and death in later Anglo-Saxon England* (Woodbridge, 2004).

Tinti, F., 'The "costs" of pastoral care: church dues in late Anglo-Saxon England', in F. Tinti (ed.), *Pastoral care in late Anglo-Saxon England* (Woodbridge, 2005), pp. 27–51.

Tinti, F. (ed.), *Pastoral care in late Anglo-Saxon England* (Woodbridge, 2005).

Tinti, F., *Sustaining belief: the church of Worcester from c.870 to c.1100* (Farnham, 2010).

Tönnies, F., *Gemeinschaft und gesellschaft* [1887], trans. and ed. J. Harris and M. Hollis, *Community and civil society* (Cambridge, 2001).

Tringham, N., 'An early 13th-century survey of the earl of Chester's fee of Leek', *Staffordshire Studies*, 5 (1993), pp. 1–12.

Tringham, N., 'Leek before the Conquest', in P. Morgan and A.D.M. Philips, *Staffordshire histories: essays in honour of Michael Greenslade* (Keele, 1999), pp. 5–12.

Tringham, N., 'St Edith of Polesworth and her Cult' (forthcoming).

Tringham, N. (ed.), *VCH Staffordshire*, vol. 9 (London, 2003).

Tringham, N.J. (ed.), *VCH Staffordshire*, vol. 10 (Woodbridge, 2007).

Vinogradoff, P., 'Folkland', *English Historical Review*, 8 (1893), pp. 1–17.

Vleeskruyer, R., *The life of St Chad. An Old English homily* (Amsterdam, 1953).

Warner, D.A., 'Rituals, kingship and rebellion in medieval Germany', *History Compass*, 8 (2010), pp. 1209–20.

Wharton, H., *Anglia Sacra*, Part 1 (London, 1691).

Whitelock, D., *Anglo-Saxon wills* (Cambridge, 1930).

Whitelock, D. (ed.), *English historical documents c. 500–1042*, vol. 1 (London, 1955).

Williamson, T., 'The distribution of "Woodland" and "Champion" landscapes in medieval England', in M. Gardiner and S. Rippon (eds), *Medieval landscapes: landscape history after Hoskins, volume 2* (Macclesfield, 2007), pp. 89–104.

Williamson, T., *Environment, society and landscape in early medieval England: time and topography* (Woodbridge, 2013).

Williamson, T., *Shaping medieval landscapes: settlement, society, environment* (Macclesfield, 2003).

Wilson, D.M., *Anglo-Saxon art, from the seventh century to the Norman Conquest* (London, 1984).

Wood, S., *The proprietary church in the medieval West* (Oxford, 2006).

Woolf, A., 'Imagining English origins', *Quaestio Insularis*, 18 (2017), pp. 1–20.

Wormald, P., *Bede and the conversion of England: the charter evidence*, Jarrow Lecture (Jarrow, 1984).

Wormald, P., 'Bede, the *Bretwaldas*, and the origins of the *gens Anglorum*', in P. Wormald, D. Bullough and R. Collins (eds), *Ideal and reality in Frankish and Anglo-Saxon society: studies presented to J.M. Wallace-Hadrill* (Oxford, 1983), pp. 99–129.

Wormald, P., 'On þa wæpnedhealfe: kingship and royal property from Æthelwulf to Edward the Elder', in N.J. Higham and D.H. Hill (eds), *Edward the Elder 899–924* (London, 2001), pp. 264–79.

Wormald, P., 'The Venerable Bede and the "Church of the English"', in G. Rowell (ed.), *The English religious tradition and the genius of Anglicanism* (Wantage, 1992), pp. 13–32.

Yorke, B., 'Political and ethnic identity: a case study of Anglo-Saxon practice', in W.O. Frazer and A. Tyrrell (eds), *Social identity in early medieval Britain* (Leicester, 2000), pp. 69–90.

Index

Acton 78, 220, 230, 239
Advowson 171, 235
Ælfflæd, queen 129
Ælfgar, earl of Mercia 78, 220–2, 229, 234–5
Ælfheah, bishop of Lichfield 44
Ælfthryth, abbess of Repton 127
Ælfwine, bishop of Lichfield 43
Ælfwine, subking in Northumbria 55
Ælle, king of Sussex 22
Æthelbald, king of Mercia 34, 81, 128
Æthelberht, king of Kent 20, 22, 48
Æthelflæd, Lady of the Mercians 115, 126
   building of burhs 82, 169, 251
   Mercian political identity 110, 251
   Mercian saints 126, 138–9, 251
Æthelfrith, king of Northumbria 147
Æthelheard, archbishop of Canterbury 37–40, 47
Æthelmund, ealdorman in Mercia 134, 248–9
Æthelmund, name on inscription at Overchurch 144
Æthelred II, king of England 42, 144, 224
Æthelred, king of Mercia 27–8, 30, 80, 125, 200
Æthelred, king of Northumbria 13
Æthelred, Lord of the Mercians 82, 110, 115, 143
Æthelric 248–9
Æthelstan, king of England 126, 143
   integration of English ecclesiastical and regnal communities 47, 250
   introduction of compulsory tithe payment 217
   royal style 20
   royal councils 41–3,
Æthelwald, bishop of Lichfield 120–3, 153, 247
Æthelwold, bishop of Winchester 44
Æthelwulf, ealdorman of Berkshire 137
Æthelwulf, king of Wessex 41
Agricultural communities 10, 177, 181–6, 207–8, 214, 258
Agricultural landscapes 10, 79, 177–186, 206–11, 214, 258–60
   animal enclosures 179–80, 232, 235

   commons 61, 179–82, 191, 201, 214, 258
   cereal production 177–8
   fields 177–82, 186, 190, 196, 200–1, 207, 214
   hay production 178–9, 181–2, 186, 207, 209
   heavy mouldboard plough 178, 181–3, 186, 208
   settlement dispersion 179–82, 190
   wood pastures 179, 199, 201
   woodlands 177, 179–180, 182–3, 194
Aidan, bishop of Lindisfarne 49, 52–4, 80
Alan of Ashbourne 11–12, 53, 120–2
   see also Lichfield, Lichfield Chronicle
Alcuin 37–9
Aldhelm 83, 245
Alfred the Great, king of the Anglo-Saxons 133, 250–1
Alhflæd 29
Alhfrith, subking in Northumbria 55–7
Alhred, king of Northumbria 135
Allington 77
Alstonefield 101n45, 103, 106, 147
Ancient countryside *see* Agricultural landscapes, settlement dispersion
Andresey 132, 134
Angles 18, 24–5
   see also East Anglia; Mercia; Middle Anglia; Northumbria
Anglian genealogies 12–14, 18, 32n87, 46–7
Anglo-Welsh borderland 2, 77, 237, 260
Annales Cestrienses 126
Arable communities *see* Agricultural communities
Archdeacons 121, 170
Archenfield 191
Arden 133, 185
Asfordby 101n45,
Ashbourne 101n45, 106, 147, 224
   see also Alan of Ashbourne
Ashford 143
Ashton 76, 79

273

Assemblies *see* Church councils; English royal councils; Hundreds, hundred courts; Local assemblies; Mercian royal councils; Muster; Royal assemblies; Shires, shire courts
Astbury 238, 239n71
Aston-on-Trent 101n45, 106, 147, 151
Augustine, archbishop of Canterbury 22, 39, 48, 147, 172
Auti 220–1
Averpenny *see* Regnal soke
Aylesbury 163

Bægloc 147
Bakewell 96–7, 142–3, 145, 150, 220–1
Bangor-is-y-Coed 146–147, 151, 205
Baptism 45, 152, 172, 254, 256–7
Barking 34n91, 52
Barr 193–4
Barrog, 146
Barrow (Cheshire) 76–7, 79
Barrow (Lincolnshire) 53–4, 58, 84, 247
Barrow (unlocated) 35
Baschurch 150, 224
Basford 234
Baswich 65–6, 146, 151
Beckford 162
Bede 51, 60, 83, 124n136
   commentary on Ezra and Nehemiah 159, 161–2
   concern for monastic purity 245–6, 249, 257
   Historia Abbatum 52
   Historia Ecclesiastica gentis Anglorum 1, 45, 54–6, 88–9, 125, 140, 198
   letter to Archbishop Ecgberht 159, 161–2
   place-names 189–90, 195n76
   promotion of the English Church 19–21
   discourse of provincial kingship and *imperium* 21–5
   see also Chad; Dinooth; Episcopal List Tradition; Lastingham Narrative; Leicester, diocese; Mercian episcopal memorandum; St Chad, shrine at Lichfield; St Cuthberht
Beonna, abbot of Medeshamstede 167
Beorhtfrith 129
Beorhtred, bishop of Lindsey 167

Beorhtwulf, king of Mercia 13, 128–129
Berhtgisl, bishop of Dunwich 19, 59n59
Berkswell 146–7, 152
   see also St Milred
Bernicia 23
Berrington 150, 223
Bertha, queen 254
Bettisfield 66, 67n88, 68, 72–3
Betton 66, 72
Bicton 72
Bilton 164
Birmingham 120
Birstall 101n45
Bishops 6, 9–10, 24–5, 44–7, 83–5, 173–6, 250-60
   see also Canons; Canterbury, archbishopric; Canterbury, diocese; Chester, diocese; Chester-le-Street, diocese; Chichester, diocese; Church councils; Church of Lichfield; Diocesan communities; Domesday Book, estate of the bishop of Chester; Dorchester, diocese; Dunwich, diocese; Ecclesiastical tributes; Ecclesio-regnal communities; Elmham, diocese; English Church; English ecclesiastical communities; Episcopal List Tradition; Expropriation; Extended ecclesiastical communities; Hereford, diocese; Independent ecclesiastical communities; Landholding; Lastingham Narrative; Leicester, diocese; Lichfield, archbishopric; Lichfield, diocese; Lindisfarne, diocese; Lindsey, diocese; Liturgical communities; London, diocese; Mercia, diocese; Mercian episcopal memorandum; Minsters; Mother parishes; Northumbria, diocese; Papacy; Parochial communities; Priests; Rochester, diocese; Royal assemblies; Royal free chapels; Secularisation; Spiritual lordship; Textual communities; Whithorn, diocese; Winchester, diocese; Worcester, diocese; York, archbishopric; York, diocese
Bishops Tachbrook 66, 67n87, 68, 74, 146
Blackwell 101n45, 147–8
Boniface 83, 85, 160, 245

Index

Book of Cerne 153–4
Book of Walter of Whittlesey 139
Bookland 36, 158–60, 186–8, 213, 231–2
  relation to tithes 217, 225, 233
  see also Church councils; Ecclesiastical tributes; Landholding
Bookright see Bookland
Bosel, bishop of the Hwicce 27
Bowdon 238
Bradbourne 96, 97n32, 142
Brailsford 79
Breedon-on-the-Hill 62n70, 128, 160
  stone sculpture 97, 100, 101n45, 141–2, 154
Brescia 109
Brewood 65–6, 75, 146, 194
Bridgnorth 168–9
Broughton 66, 72
Brunloc 147
Buildwas 66, 75, 77, 79–80, 165
Bunbury 238, 239n71
Bupton 65–6, 74, 75n113, 79, 146, 196
Burhs 82, 139, 143, 169, 241, 250–1
  see also Place-names
Burials 1, 111–117, 125, 128–131, 133, 136–7
  charcoal 114, 136
  churchyard 216, 218
  eaves-drip 114
Burston 140
  see also St Ruffin
Burton in Wirral 66, 73, 75
Burton-upon-Trent, St Mary's abbey 1, 169, 176, 188, 220–1
  hagiography 90–2, 94, 132–4
  see also St Modwynn
Burwardestone 66, 88n67, 72–3, 74n109
Bury St Edmunds 90, 232

Cælin 49, 60n64
  see also Ceawlin, king of Wessex
Caldecote 66, 75
Caldy 196
Calendars 53, 89–91, 150
Calton 235n65
Cannock 78, 192–4
Canon law 36, 38–9, 57, 83, 156, 170
  canons of the Council of Clofesho (747) 159, 174–5, 245
  canons of the Council of Hertford (672) 20–1, 28
  see also Church councils
Canons (clergy) 38, 121, 168, 169, 171, 174
  Lichfield cathedral 66, 82, 111, 121–3, 220
  St Alkmund's church, Shrewsbury 220
  St Chad's church, Shrewsbury 67, 72
  St John's church, Chester 67, 73, 220
  St Mary's church, Stafford 220
  St Mary's church, Wolverhampton 144, 220
  St Werburgh's church, Chester 126–7, 220
Canterbury 27, 34n91, 49, 56, 142, 254
  Christ Church 91
  renewal 121–2, 247, 257
  school 19, 21
  source of Bede's information 17–19
  see also Canterbury, archbishopric; Canterbury, diocese
Canterbury, archbishopric 14, 37–41, 156, 260
  see also Æthelheard; Augustine; Ceolnoth; Church councils; Deusdedit; Dunstan; Jænberht; Lanfranc; Sigeric, Theodore; Wigheard; Wulfred
Canterbury, Diocese 23, 35, 167, 171–5
  see also Domesday Monachorum
Castor 97, 154
Cathedrals see Canons, Lichfield cathedral; Lichfield, cathedral church
Catholme 178–9
Cauldon 196
Ceatta 90, 120
Ceawlin, king of Wessex 22
Cedd, abbot of Lastingham and bishop of Essex 48–54
  see also Lastingham Narrative; Rules, monastic; St Cedd
Ceolburh 248
Ceollach, bishop of Mercia 15, 17
Ceolnoth, archbishop of Canterbury 41, 142
Ceolred, king of Mercia 125
Chad 1, 9, 48–61, 255, 258
  biography 48–9
  bishop of Mercia 15, 17, 26
  extended ecclesiastical community 48, 53–5, 59–60, 84–5, 87
  oratory at Lichfield 111
  relationship with Archbishop Theodore and Bishop Wilfrid 19–20, 54–60, 156

275

see also Lastingham narrative; Lichfield;
　　Rules, monastic; St Chad
Champion countryside see Agricultural
　　landscapes, settlement dispersion
Charlemagne, king of Francia 37, 109, 257,
　　see also Francia
Charters 1, 121, 135, 207, 248
　　Æthelstan A, draftsman-scribe 42–3
　　alliterative charter group 42–3
　　associated with Bakewell 143
　　associated with Burton-upon-Trent 188
　　associated with Coventry 141
　　associated with Quatford 169
　　associated with Repton 127–8
　　associated with Wolverhampton 144–5, 147, 188
　　associated with Stone 139–40
　　boundary clauses 189
　　Dunstan B, draftsman-scribe 42–3
　　papal charters 38–9
　　place-names 189, 194, 200
　　witnessed at church councils 20, 31, 35–6, 40
　　witnessed at English royal councils 42–3, 169
　　witnessed at Mercian royal councils 27, 30–1,
　　　　33–5, 169
　　see also Bookland; Division of the mensa;
　　　　Ecclesiastical tributes, church-scot;
　　　　Landholding; Privileges and immunities;
　　　　Regnal soke; Regnal territories
Chartley 78
Chatsall 66, 75
Cheadle (Cheshire) 193–4, 200
Cheadle (Staffordshire) 193–4, 200
Checkley 101n45, 103–6, 147
Cheddleton 234–5
Cheltenham 162
Cheshire Plain 183–4, 186
Chespuic 66, 67n88, 68, 72
Chester 67, 77, 82, 147, 221
　　diocese 64, 68–9, 77, 79, 204, 220
　　St John's church 62, 66–70, 73–6, 82, 84,
　　　　220–1
　　St Mary's monastery 220
　　St Werburgh's abbey 127, 169
　　St Werburgh's church 77, 126–7, 220–1
　　see also Goscelin of St Bertin, Life of
　　　　St Wærburh; Hugh, earl of Chester;
　　　　St Wærburh

Chester-le-Street, diocese 42
Chesterton 101n45, 103, 148
Chichester, diocese 173
Chillington 66, 67n88, 75
Chilterns 200
Chrodegang of Metz 121
Church-amber see Ecclesiastical tributes
Church councils 4, 14, 20–1, 33, 35–7, 40–1,
　　44–6, 167, 248–9, 255
　　672, Hertford 19–20, 23, 28
　　679, Hatfield 21, 23
　　702/3, Austerfield 30
　　747, Clofesho 31, 85, 159, 161, 174, 245
　　781, Brentford 35
　　787, Chelsea 37
　　803, Clofesho 38, 123, 135, 166
　　816, Clofesho 31
　　825, Clofesho 35, 40
　　836, In cræft 41
　　839, Æt astran 41n133
　　845, London 41n133
　　adjudication of bookland cases 36, 187–8
　　canons 21, 28, 36, 83, 85, 156, 159, 174,
　　　　245
　　papal councils 27
　　stabilising effects on kingdoms 23–5, 28–9
　　see also Diocesan synods; Synod of Whitby
Church dues see Ecclesiastical tributes
Churches see Ecclesiastical landscapes;
　　Estate-churches; Minsters; Mother
　　churches; Superior churches
Church of Lichfield 11, 38, 44, 47, 83, 121
　　as imagined community 80–1, 85, 156
　　see also Church of the Mercians; Diocesan
　　　　communities; Lichfield, diocese
Church of the Mercians 9, 80, 85, 260
　　see also Church of Lichfield; Diocesan
　　　　Communities; Lichfield, diocese
Church-scot see Ecclesiastical tributes
Clergy see Bishops; Canons; Priests
Clifton-on-Dunsmore 164
Clipshead 101n45, 148
Clofesho see Church councils
Cnut, king of England 91, 129, 140, 217n6
Coenred, king of Mercia 129
Coenwald, bishop of Worcester 43–4
Coenwulf, king of Mercia 13, 35–6, 135

Index

dissolution of the archbishopric of Lichfield 38–40, 47, 156, 257
Colman, bishop of Lindisfarne 49, 55–6
Colwich 66, 78
Comital estates 164, 229, 237, 240, 258
Comital territories 241, 243
Common burdens 159–60, 231, 240
Communion of Saints 153, 155
Communities *see* Agricultural communities; Diocesan communities; Domainal communities; Domestic communities; Ecclesio-regnal communities; English ecclesiastical community; Extended ecclesiastical communities; Independent ecclesiastical communities; Liturgical communities; Minster-based communities; Parochial communities; Regnal communities; Textual communities
Community, theory of:
   associative field 10, 44, 153–5, 253, 255, 257
   gesellschaft and gemeinschaft 5–6
   habitus 8
   hierarchy 5–7, 156
   shared norms 5–9, 44–5, 153, 187–8, 214, 253–5
   subject/person dialectic 7–9, 44–5, 153, 166, 213, 253–4
   subordinate penumbra 153, 166, 174, 208–15, 241, 251–2, 254–8
Conchubran, *Life* of St Monenna 90, 92, 132–4
Condover 80, 150, 223
   see also Hundreds
Consall 234n62, 236
Correctio 257
Cotswold Hills 97, 142
Cound 192, 195n76
County Durham 180, 203
Coventry 107, 140–1, 150, 205
   St Mary's abbey 91, 140–1, 164, 169, 176, 220–1
   see also Geoffrey, prior of Coventry; St Osburh
Crakemarsh 78
Cranwell 101n45
Cropthorne Group 97, 100, 107, 142
Cumbria 203

Curborough Brook 110–1
Customs *see* Domainal soke; Ecclesiastical tributes; Landholding; Regnal soke; Rules, monastic
Cuthberht, priest 123n133
Cyneberht, bishop of Lindsey 17–18
Cynebil 49
Cynesige, bishop of Lichfield 44
Cynethryth, queen of Mercia 244
Cynewaru, abbess 128, 142

Danish invasions *see* Vikings
Danish polities 62, 251
Darliston 70
Davenham 238
Deans, rural 170
Deira 23, 49, 55
Denstone 235n65, 236, 237n67
Derby 67, 90, 134–7, 165, 169, 221
   All Saints' church 168–9, 220
   St Alkmund's church 99, 135–7, 168–9, 220–1
   stone sculpture 99–100, 101n45, 106–7, 135–6, 147–8, 150
   St Werburgh's church 148
   see also St Ealhmund; Royal free chapels
Deusdedit, archbishop of Canterbury 25
Dewsbury 146
Dinooth, abbot 147
Diocesan communities 9, 48, 60–1, 80–5, 252, 255–9
   subordination of landholders 156–8, 161, 165–6, 243
   subordination of independent liturgical communities 166–7, 173–6, 250
   see also Church of Lichfield; Church of the Mercians; English ecclesiastical community; Spiritual lordship
Diocesan synods 85
Diuma, bishop of Mercia 14–16, 18, 26, 29
Division of the *mensa* 68–9, 247–8
Dodington 71
Domainal communities 10, 177, 186–9, 206–8, 212–5, 258–9
   reeves 212, 214, 241
   rulers of minsters 248–9
   see also Domainal lordship; Domainal soke; Landholding

Domainal lordship 10, 177, 208, 214–15, 250, 254, 258–60
  see also Domainal communities; Domainal soke; Landholding
Domainal soke 231–3
  customs 208, 212, 214, 258
  dues and services 206–8, 231
  gafol 207–8
  guard services 207, 232–3
  hunting services 207, 232, 235–6
  see also Domainal communities; Domainal lordship; Landholding
Domesday Book 9–10, 87, 157, 208, 242–3, 259
  church-scot 163–5
  estate of the bishop of Chester 61–84
  parochial geography 228–40
  place-names 189–90, 192–3, 195–202, 204, 209
  royal free chapels 168–9
  superior churches 216, 219–224
  see also Canons, Lichfield cathedral; Chester, St Werburgh's church; Derby, St Alkmund's church; Landholding; Wolverhampton
Domesday Monachorum 171–3
Domestic communities 60
Dorchester, diocese 42
Dover 172–3
Draycott 64
Dunchurch 164
Dunstan, archbishop of Canterbury, bishop of Worcester and abbot of Glastonbury, 44
Dunwich, diocese 19, 23, 38
  see also Berhtgisl

Eadberht Præn, king of Kent 38
Eadberht, ealdorman in Mercia 25
Eadhere, priest 123n133
Eadred, king of England 143
Eadric, ealdorman of the Magonsæte 243
Eafa, ealdorman in Mercia 25
Ealdormen 25, 32, 39, 213–4, 240–3, 258–9
  foundation of mother churches 10, 216–7, 244, 249–51
  see also Æthelmund; Æthelwulf; Eadric
Ealdwine (alias Wor), bishop of Lichfield 15, 17, 31

Ealdwulf, bishop of Lichfield 40, 123, 166, 248n108
Ealhmund, son of King Alhred of Northumbria 134–5
Eangyth, abbess 160, 162
Eanmund, abbot of Breedon-on-the-Hill 128
Eardwulf, king of Northumbria 13–14, 135
Earls see Mercia; Northumbria
East Anglia 22–3, 28, 47, 90, 124, 178
  see also Dunwich, diocese; Elmham, diocese
East Saxons see Essex
Eastham 198
Eccles (Norfolk) 204
Eccles House 205
Eccles Pike 205
Ecceshall 65–6, 146, 192, 203–5, 240
  stone sculpture 97, 100, 101n45, 103, 108, 146, 150
Ecclesiastical landscapes 86, 175–6, 216–18, 250–2, 259
  see also Burials; Estate-churches; Liturgical communities; Minsters; Mother churches; Shrines; Superior churches
Ecclesiastical tributes 10, 157–62, 165–7, 176, 256, 260
  Chad-farthings 173
  chrism 171–2, 174
  church-scot 158–66, 176, 250, 256, 259
  circuit payment (circada) 162, 165
  first-fruits 162
  food-rents 158–9, 162, 171
  guesting 161, 163, 166–7, 256
  hides 159, 161, 163
  hospitality 158, 160–1, 163
  hospitality payment (parata) 162
  Marycorn 163
  Maundy gifts 171–2, 173n87
  Pentecostal oblations 172–4
  scrifcorn 163
  tithes 158, 160–3, 216–9, 224–5, 228–9, 233, 239–40, 243–4, 250–2
  see also Lichfield, prebends
Ecclesio-regnal communities 45, 255–60
Eccleston 203–5
Ecgberht, archbishop of York 159, 245
Ecgberht, holy man 49–52
Ecgberht, king of Wessex 40–1

Index

Ecgbert, king of Kent 25, 124n136
Ecgfrith, king of Mercia 13, 37, 39
Ecgfrith, king of Northumbria 18, 25–6, 55
Edgar, king of England 42–4, 77, 115, 126, 221, 247
   see also Lawcodes
Edgmond 150, 196
Edith, queen 71, 163
Edmund, king of England 126
Edward 239n71
Edward the Confessor, king of England 41, 64, 72, 77–8, 220–2
Edward the Elder, king of the Anglo-Saxons 41, 78, 143, 251
Edward the Martyr 147
Edwin, earl of Mercia 71, 73, 78, 198, 220–1
Edwin, king of Northumbria 22, 45
Edwin, thegn 204
Elfin 79
Elford 229
Ellastone 65–6, 70, 74–5, 78, 229, 239
Ellesmere 71, 220
Elmham, diocese 42
Ely 88n2, 91–2, 125, 139
   see also Eormenhild, abbess of Ely
Endon 234–6
Englefield 191, 201
English Church 3, 9, 11, 25–6, 44, 89, 176
   as imagined community 9, 12, 20, 26, 35–6, 44–7, 255–7
   creation of more dioceses 28
   promotion by Archbishop Theodore 19–21, 26
   see also English ecclesiastical community
English ecclesiastical community 9, 12, 20–1, 44–7, 153–4, 255–60
   as textual community 38–40, 44
   intersection with extended ecclesiastical communities 60
   intersection with Mercian regnal community 33, 37, 40, 46–7, 255–60
   intersection with English regnal communities 21–2, 24–5, 33, 45–7, 255–60
   relation to spiritual lordship 45, 156, 175, 255–60
   see also English Church; Spiritual lordship
English royal councils 20, 41–3, 46–7, 188, 213, 251
   941x946, London 46

   958, Penkridge 169
   989x990, London 46
Eorcenberht, king of Kent 124
Eormenhild, abbess of Ely 124–5, 127n149, 139
   see also St Wærburh
Episcopal List Tradition 12–19, 26–7, 30–3, 56n47
Ercall Magna 150
Ergyng 191
Essex 22–3, 25, 35, 48, 50, 53–4
   see also London
Estates *see* Bishops; Landholding
Estate-churches 217–21, 223–8, 250–2
   see also Burials, churchyard; Ecclesiastical landscapes; Ecclesiastical tributes; Parochial communities
Evesham 34n91, 91, 129
   see also Thingferth, abbot of Evesham
Exestan *see* Hundreds
Exhall 203, 205
Expropriation 244–9
Extended ecclesiastical communities 48, 60–1, 153, 246–7
   focused on Chad 53–4, 59–60, 84, 87, 246–7
   focused on Wilfrid 59–60
   focused on Wærburh 126, 137, 148
Eyam 96–9, 142
Eyton 66, 67n88, 68, 71n100, 74, 77
Eyton-on-Severn 196

Fæstingmen 241
Familia 123, 247–9
Farnborough 66, 75
Farndon 62, 66, 70–1, 73–7, 82, 84, 220–1
   parochial geography 229, 239
Fauld 126, 222n29
Fawsley 163
Feldon district 178, 180, 183, 185
Felix, *Life of St Guthlac* 31, 127, 138
Field systems *see* Agricultural landscapes
Finan, bishop of Lindisfarne 49
Fines and forfeitures *see* Regnal soke
Fletton 97, 154
Folkland 187–8, 215n129, 217n6
   see also Landholding
Folkright 188, 208
   see also Landholding

279

Lichfield and the Lands of St Chad

Food-rents *see* Ecclesiastical tributes; Regnal territories
Francia 8, 37, 45, 83, 127, 153, 245, 247, 257
   art 94, 100, 107, 108–9, 148
   bishops 24, 55–6
   ecclesiastical tributes 162, 165, 217
   ecclesiastical and sepulchral architecture 110, 130–1, 172
Frankpledge 237
Freeford 122
Frithuric, subking in Mercia 128

Gaul 24, 55–6, 131, 172
gens Anglorum see English Church
gentes see Peoples
Geoffrey, abbot of Burton-upon-Trent, *The Life and Miracles of St Modwenna* 92–3, 132–3
Geoffrey de la Guerche 220
Geoffrey, prior of Coventry 122
Geology *see* Soils; Water
Gilbert de Venables 238, 239n71
Gilling 17
Glastonbury 44, 111
Gloucester 108, 145
   New Minster 251, 258
Gnosall 168–9, 193
Godgifu 141, 176, 199, 220–1
Godwin 234, 239n71
Goscelin of St Bertin, *Life* of St Mildburh 128
   Life of St Wærburh 88n2, 124–6
Great Army *see* Vikings
Great Budworth 238, 239n71
Great Haywood 65–6, 75, 78
Great Ness 150, 224
Gregory the Great, pope 20, 38–9, 48, 89
Gresford 67n88, 71n100, 72–4, 76–8
Gruffydd ap Llywelyn, king of Wales 77
Guilden Sutton 66, 73
Gwytherin 150
Gyrwe 27

Hadrian, abbot 19, 21
Hadrian, pope 38–9
Hædda, abbot of Breedon-on-the-Hill 128
Hagiography 52, 59, 87–94, 152, 155
   see also St Beorhthelm; St Chad; St Eadgyth;
St Ealhmund; St Modwynn; St Osburh;
St Wærburh; St Wigstan; St Wulfhad
Hamo de Mascy 238
Hanbury 88, 124–7, 151
   see also St Wærburh
Handsacre 122
Hanmer 66, 73–4
Harborne 122n130, 165
Headda, bishop of Lichfield 15, 17, 30–1, 53, 120
Henry Bradshaw 126, 127n149
Henry de Ferrers 79, 235n65
Hereford, diocese 11, 31–4, 38, 42, 161–2
Hexham 56n47, 109, 111, 117
Hickling 101n45
Hidage *see* Regnal soke
Hild, abbess of Whitby 30, 133
Hints 122n130, 212
Historia Brittonum 191, 195n76
Historia Regum 13, 31, 135
Hodnet 150, 192–4
Holt 74
Hope 101n45, 103, 143, 147, 205, 224
Hopwell 64
Horton 234n61
Hospitality *see* Ecclesiastical tributes; Regnal territories
Hrepingas 128
Hugh Candidus, Peterborough Chronicle 89, 92–3, 120, 124, 132, 134, 137, 139, 140
Hugh de Nonant, bishop of Coventry and Lichfield 80n136
Hugh, earl of Chester 127, 169n64, 220, 234–5
Humber 14, 62, 103
Humberht, ealdorman in Mercia 128, 142
Humbrians 23
   see also Northumbria
Hundreds 43, 214, 216, 230, 234, 239, 241–2
   association with church-scot 163–6, 176, 243, 250, 256, 259
   Bury St Edmunds, eight and a half hundreds 233
   Condover 79, 164
   Exestan 77–8
   hundred aid 232, 242
   hundred bailiff 243
   hundred courts 188, 213–4, 232, 242, 250, 258–9
   hundredman 242

Index

Marton 164
Oswaldslow 163
Warmundestrou 230, 239
Wrockwardine 79, 80n138, 164
  see also Domesday Book; Ecclesiastical tribute; Local assemblies; Mother churches; Regnal soke; Regnal territories; Shires
Hwicce 16, 26, 30, 32, 61–2
  see also Worcester, Diocese
Hwita, bishop of Lichfield 15, 34–5, 80–1
Hygebald, bishop of Lindisfarne 14
Hygebald, abbot in Lindsey 51–2
Hygeberht, archbishop of Lichfield 37–8, 40, 123, 166

Ilam 101n45, 103–6, 137–9, 147, 150, 152
  see also St Bertram
Immin, ealdorman in Mercia 25
Imperial list 22–3, 25–6
imperium see Overkingship
Independent ecclesiastical communities 81–5, 158, 166–7, 173–6, 221–4, 228–9, 250
Ingleby 100n36, 101n45, 108, 148
Inheritance 186–8, 212, 217n6, 228, 243, 248–50, 258
  see also Domainal communities; Landholding
Iona 48
Ipstones 234n61, 235–6
Ireland 15, 17, 49–51, 138
  Irish bishops in Britain 26,
  Irish missionaries in Britain 22, 48
  Irish hagiography *see* Conchubran, *Life* of St Monenna
  Irish liturgical customs 55
  Irish place-names 203
  see also Aidan; Ceollach; Colman; Diuma
Irish Sea 2, 151
Isle of Wight 25, 140
Italy 45, 94, 100, 109, 153, 172, 257

Jænberht, archbishop of Canterbury 37, 39–40
Jarrow 48, 51–2, 245
Jaruman, bishop of Mercia 15, 17, 19, 26
John of Worcester, Chronicle 12, 92, 135
Jutes 24–5
  see also Kent

Kalendar of Abbot Samson 232–3
Kempsford 134–5
Kent 22–3, 25n47, 26, 35, 37–9, 52, 54–6, 254
  minsters and mother churches 159, 171–3
  Weald 196, 201
  see also Æthelberht; Anglian genealogies; Bertha; Canterbury; Domesday Monachorum; Eadberht Præn; Eangyth; Ecgberht; Eorcenberht; Eormenhild; Tiberius Group
Kentish Royal Legend 52, 124–5
Kingdom of the Anglo-Saxons 250–1
Kingsbury 199, 220
Kingship, post-Roman 255
Kinver 192, 194

Ladbroke 164
Land-book *see* Charters
Landholding:
  berewicks 64–5, 68, 70–1
  capita 64, 75, 78, 237–9
  carucates 64
  divided vills 62, 66, 68, 70–80, 193, 228
  estates 61–85, 157–61, 191–215, 219–43, 248–52, 258
  free men 76, 209, 213, 220–1, 229, 233
  gafollands 207–8
  geburs 207
  geneats 207, 232
  geneatlands 207–8
  gesettlands 207
  hides 64–5, 75, 194
  hunting services 232, 235–6
  inland 64, 206–8, 212, 214, 217–8, 225, 231, 233, 241
  integrated estates 62, 70–1, 73–6, 78, 81–2, 84
  labour services 64, 206–7
  less integrated estate complexes 62, 68, 70–7, 81–2
  loanland 213, 230
  manor 62–4, 197–8, 201, 206
  multiple estates 213
  outland 207, 212, 214–5, 218, 223, 225, 231–3, 235, 241, 258
  ploughlands 64–5, 75, 194
  sokeland 64–5, 68, 71, 231, 235n65

281

Lichfield and the Lands of St Chad

villani 224
vills 64, 133, 159, 242
see also Domainal communities; Domainal soke; Ecclesiastical tributes; Privileges and immunities
Lanfranc, archbishop of Canterbury 171
Lastingham 17, 26, 49, 55, 84
Lastingham Narrative 17, 27, 29, 48–54, 58, 60, 88, 247
see also Chad, relics
Lawcodes 208, 217–18, 224–5, 229, 233, 240, 256n4
Lay lordship 41, 171, 244–5, 249–50, 257–8
Leamington Hastings 164
Leek 147, 151, 234–7, 240, 243
stone sculpture 101n45, 103–4, 108, 147
Leek Wootton 220
Leeton 70
Leicester, diocese 11, 15–16, 28–35, 42, 80–1, 135, 167
see also Mercia, diocese; Torhthelm; Werenberht
Leo III, pope 38–9
Leofric, abbot of Burton-upon-Trent 132n181
Leofric, earl of Mercia 140–41, 176, 221
Leofwin 220–1
Leominster 163
Lichfield 1, 48–55, 58, 111–12, 150–1, 247, 250, 257
cathedral church (St Mary and St Chad) 9, 62, 70, 110–123, 131, 136, 220–2, 254
estate 65–6, 68, 74, 78, 82, 192, 195, 229
Lichfield Chronicle 11–12, 53, 120–2, 140
parochial geography 229, 240
St Chad's church *see* Stowe
St Mary's church (in the city) 122–3
St Peter's church 53, 116, 120
St Michael's church, Greenhill 111, 122–3
place-name 190–2, 195, 212
prebends 67n87, 70, 122–3
sepulchral chapel 112–120, 152
see also Canons, Lichfield cathedral; Chad; Lichfield, archbishopric; Lichfield, diocese; St Chad; Stone sculpture
Lichfield, archbishopric 12, 37–40, 46, 156, 257
see also Hygeberht
Lichfield, Diocese 1, 9, 11, 15–16, 20, 28, 30–5, 42–5, 60–85, 175–6, 256, 260

diocesan bounds 2–3, 61–2
see also Ælfheah; Ælfwine; Æthelwald; Chad; Church of Lichfield; Church of the Mercians; Cynesige; Ealdwine (*alias* Wor); Ealdwulf; Ecclesiastical tributes; Headda; Hugh de Nonant; Hwita; Mercia, diocese; Mercian episcopal memorandum; Roger de Clinton; Royal free chapels; Winfrith
Lilleshall abbey 134, 150, 169
Lincoln, St Mary's church 163
see also Lindsey, diocese
Lindisfarne 49, 53–4, 111
diocese 14, 49, 55–6
see also Aidan; Colman; Finan; Hygebald; Northumbria, diocese; York, diocese
Lindsey 15–16, 25–6, 51, 53, 84
diocese 11, 15–18, 27–9, 31–34, 38, 42, 167,
see also Mercia, diocese
Litanies 91
Little Buildwas 77
Little Eton 66, 72
Liturgical communities 9, 86–7, 152–6, 166–7, 173–6, 247–8, 250–2, 254–5
see also Spiritual lordship; St Chad; Stone sculpture; St Wærburh; St Wigstan
Local assemblies 4, 177, 188, 213–14, 241–2, 250, 258
see also Hundreds, hundred courts; Shires, shire courts
London 23, 35, 39–41, 168n58
diocese 19, 35, 43n145
see also Church councils; English royal councils; Mercian royal councils
Long Eaton 64, 196, 229n43
Long Itchington 164, 220
Longdon 122, 212
Longford 66, 79–80, 146, 229, 239
Longner 66, 72
Longsdon 234n64, 236
Lordship *see* Domainal lordship; Lay lordship; Regnal lordship; Spiritual lordship
Lulla, priest 123n133

Magonsæte 16, 32, 62, 128, 243
see also Hereford, diocese
Malbank barony 220, 238–9

Malpas 71, 74n109, 239n71
Markfield 61
Marmion family 132
Martimow 61n69
Martinmas 159, 165–6
Marton (Shropshire) 66
Marton (Warwickshire) 164
   see also Hundreds
Marwnad Cynddylan 190
Masham 146
Mayfield 78
Medeshamstede see Peterborough
Mediterranean 94, 100
Meole 66, 71–2, 80n136
Mercia 1–2, 260
   earldom see Ælfgar; Edwin; Leofric
   renewed tenth-century polity 108, 110, 115, 138–9, 169, 251, 257–8
   see also Æthelflæd, Lady of the Mercians; Æthelred, Lord of the Mercians; Mercia, diocese; Mercia, kingdom
Mercia, diocese 1, 11, 14–18, 21, 25–33, 48–9, 255–6
   see also Ceollach; Chad; Diuma; Episcopal List Tradition; Hereford, diocese; Jaruman; Lastingham Narrative; Leicester, diocese; Lichfield, diocese; Lindsey, diocese; Mercian episcopal memorandum; Seaxwulf; Trumhere; Winfrith; Worcester, diocese
Mercia, kingdom 1, 11, 25–6, 29, 31–2, 80–1, 170, 255–6
   see also Æthelbald; Æthelred; Anglian genealogies; Beorhtwulf; Ceolred; Cœnred; Cœnwulf; Cynethryth; Ecgfrith; Mercian royal councils; Offa; Penda; Regnal communities; Regnal lists; Wiglaf; Wigmund; Wulfhere
Mercian episcopal memorandum 17–19, 21–2, 25–6, 29n67, 49
Mercian royal councils 33–6, 187
   737x740, *Bearuwe* 35
   748, London 34
   749, Gumley 34, 80–1, 160
   775 or 777, Gumley 35
   779 Hartleford 35
   780, Tamworth 34
   901, Shrewsbury 169
   Brentford 34
Mercians see Mercia
Mercne mere 61n69
Merewalh, subking of the Magonsæte 128
Merovingian kingdoms see Francia
Mickley 70
Mid-Cheshire Ridge 183–4, 186
Middle Anglia 15–17, 25–32, 50
   see also Leicester, diocese; Mercia, diocese
Midland Gap 183–4, 186
Mildrith, abbess of Minster-in-Thanet 124
Millenheath 70
Minster-based communities 84–6, 93, 151–2, 154–5, 247
   see also Diocesan communities; Extended ecclesiastical communities; Independent ecclesiastical communities; Liturgical communities
Minster-centred communities see Liturgical communities
Minster community, as historiographical concept 53, 86, 245–9
Minster-in-Thanet 52, 124
Minsters 3–4, 6, 85–6, 154–5, 246–50, 253–4, 258–60
   comparison with Mother churches 229, 251
   comparison with Superior churches 221–3
   identification within the historic landscape 86–7, 123–4, 137, 141, 149–50, 157–61
   integration within Diocesan communities 81–4, 166–7, 173–5, 256
   narrative of golden age and decline 10, 244–6
   parochiae 157, 165–6, 222–3
   place-names 199–200, 205–6, 209
   topographical siting 110–12, 131, 151–2, 208–9
   see also Bookland; Burials; Communion of Saints; Division of the *mensa*; Ecclesiastical landscapes; Ecclesiastical tributes; Expropriation; Hagiography; Lastingham Narrative; Lay lordship; Liturgical communities; Minster-based communities; Minster community; Pastoral care; Privileges and immunities; Rules, monastic; Secularisation; Shrines; Spiritual lordship; Stone sculpture

Missionaries 22, 29, 48, 52, 89, 245, 254
Monastic Rules *see* Rules, monastic
Monks Kirby 220
Monn, priest 123n133
Morcar, earl of Northumbria 78, 220–1, 224, 229, 239
Morfe 193–4
Mother churches 10, 86–7, 157–8, 176, 250–2, 258–9
   see also Burials, churchyard; Domesday Monachorum; Ecclesiastical landscapes; Ecclesiastical tributes, tithe; Estate-churches; Liturgical communities; Mother parishes; Royal free chapels; Serjeants of the Peace
Mother parishes 10, 86–7, 157–8, 171, 216–20, 224–30, 233–40, 243–4, 251–2, 258–60
   see also Ecclesiastical landscapes; Ecclesiastical tributes, tithe; Minsters, *parochiae*; Mother churches; Parochial communities; Regnal territories; Royal free chapels; Serjeants of the Peace
Mounth 203
Muster 243, 255
   see also Royal assemblies

Nantwich 78, 230, 239
Napton 164
Norbury (Derbyshire) 101n45, 106, 146–7, 150, 237n67
Norbury (Staffordshire) 220
Norfolk 203–4
Northumbria 26–9, 32, 37, 48, 51, 55, 159, 205
   earldom *see* Morcar; Tostig
   see also Northumbria, archbishopric; Northumbria, diocese; Northumbria, kingdom
Northumbria, archbishopric *see* York, archbishopric
Northumbria, diocese 14, 18, 26, 49–50, 52, 55–7
   diocesan bounds 62
   see also Chad; Lindisfarne, diocese; York, diocese
Northumbria, kingdom 22–3, 25
   see also Ælfwine; Æthelfrith; Æthelred; Alhfrith; Alhred; Anglian genealogies; Bernicia; Deira; Ealhmund; Eardwulf; Ecgfrith; Edwin; Oswald; Oswiu; Regnal lists
Northumbrians *see* Northumbria
North-west Midlands 1–2, 9–10, 12, 48, 183, 259
Northworthy *see* Derby
Nuneaton Priory 164

Offa's Dyke 2
Offa, king of Mercia 13, 35–40, 46, 109, 244, 248, 257
Oftfor, bishop of the Hwicce 30
Old English Martyrology 89
Onslow 66, 72
Oratories 83, 111, 168
Orm, son of Gamal 220–1, 239n71
Oscytel, archbishop of York and bishop of Dorchester 42
Oswald, bishop of Worcester 160–1
Oswald, king of Northumbria 22, 48
   see also St Oswald
Oswiu, king of Northumbria 22, 25–6, 29, 48, 52, 55–8
Oundle 30
Over 107, 143–4
Overchurch 100, 143–4, 150–1
Overkingship 22–8, 31–2, 35–6, 48, 55, 81n142, 255
   see also Subkingship
Owine 50–3

Palynological studies 178
Papacy 38–40, 145, 170, 175, 257
   see also Gregory the Great; Hadrian; Leo III
Parishes *see* Mother parishes
Parochial communities 10, 216–17, 219, 225, 244, 251–2, 254, 256–8
Pastoral care 86, 158–60, 162–3, 216, 219, 244–5, 252
   see also Ecclesiastical tributes; Minsters, *parochiae*; Mother parishes
Pastoral communities *see* Agricultural communities
Pavia 109
Peada, subking of the Middle Angles 29, 31, 52
Peak District 1, 96–7, 183–6, 208, 241
   see also Stone Sculpture, Peak Group

Index

Pecsæte 241
Pencersæte 241
Penda, king of Mercia 25–6, 29, 50n13
Penkhull 192–5
Penkridge 168–9, 192, 195, 220
Penn 192, 194
Pennine Fringe 184–6
   see also Stone Sculpture, Pennine Fringes Group
Peoples, as imagined communities 24–5, 255–6
Pershore 163
Peterborough 27, 68, 128, 139, 142, 167
   see also Hugh Candidus, Peterborough Chronicle
Place-names 78, 128, 132–3, 140, 144, 152, 179, 247
   Brythonic 190–5, 203–5
   functional -tūnas 202, 205, 209, 212
   Gaelic 203–4
   Old English 195–206
   relation to diocesan bounds 61–2
   Scandinavian 144
   stability 188–90, 208–13, 242
Polesworth 90, 132–4, 151, 222n27
   see also St Eadgyth
Prebends *see* Lichfield
Prees 66, 70, 146, 192, 194, 229, 240n74
Preston 204, 247
Priests 29, 81–4, 121–3, 171, 250, 252
   see also Bishops; Canons; Cuthberht; Diocesan community; Domesday Book; Eadhere; Estate-churches; Ecclesiastical tributes; English ecclesiastical community; Liturgical communities; Lulla; Minsters; Monn; Mother churches; Parochial communities; Shrines; Spiritual lordship; Superior churches; Wigferth
Privileges and immunities 80, 145, 159–60, 215, 232–3, 237, 243, 248
Proprietary church 175
   see also Lay lordship
Puleston 196
Putta, bishop of the Magonsæte 27

Quarndon 196
Quatford 169
Quixhill 235n65

Radenoure 66, 67n88, 68, 71n100, 72
Rædwald, king of East Anglia 22
Ralph, earl of East Anglia 204
Ranulph Higden, *Polychronicon* 126,
Reading 137
Rectitudines Singularum Personarum 232, 234
Reculver 146
Redcliff 66–8, 73
Reeves 159–60, 212–4, 225, 232, 234, 237, 240–3, 256
Regnal communities 10, 22, 33, 45–7, 176, 240–4, 250–1, 255–60
   see also Royal assemblies; Regnal lordship; Regnal soke; Regnal territories
Regnal lists 13–14, 18, 46
Regnal lordship 10, 45, 214–15, 217, 250–1, 254, 257–60
   see also Regnal communities; Regnal soke; Regnal territories
Regnal soke 159, 231–7
   averpenny 232–3
   customs 164, 242, 243n87, 258
   dues and services 216, 225, 231–4, 237, 240, 242–3, 250, 256
   fines and forfeitures 159, 231–2, 234, 241, 243, 256n4
   geld 64, 73, 206, 231, 242
   guard services 231–3, 242
   hidage 232, 242
   hides 64, 158–9
   hundred aid 232, 242
   hunting services 232, 235–7, 240, 243
   puture 237
   sheriff's aid 232, 242
   wardpenny 232–3
   wardsilver 242
   see also Common burdens; Regnal communities; Regnal lordship; Regnal territories
Regnal territories 213–4, 216, 225, 234–44, 250–1, 256, 260
   food-rents 158–60, 206, 231–2, 234, 237, 241, 255
   hospitality and guesting 160–1, 163, 231–2, 234–7, 240–4, 255–6
   small shires 158, 213, 215
   socage lands 232

warland 206–7, 231
  see also Privileges and immunities; Regnal communities; Regnal lordship; Regnal soke
Repton 90–1, 126–32, 136, 141–2, 150–1, 220–1, 250
  mausolea 117, 128–32, 152
  place-name 128, 196
  stone sculpture 97, 101n45, 104–8, 131–2, 148
  see also St Wigstan
Resting-place lists see Secgan; Hugh Candidus, Peterborough Chronicle
Richard de Vernon 238
Richard I, king of England 80n136, 164
Ripon 48, 111
  see also Stephen of Ripon, *Life of Bishop Wilfrid*
Rivers 132–3, 149, 151–2, 179, 186, 208
  Anker 90, 133
  Blythe 152
  Churnet 151, 235
  Cound 195n76
  Dee 68, 70, 74, 77, 82, 151
  Derwent 90, 102, 134, 151, 178, 180
  Dove 78, 101–2, 151, 178, 180, 235
  Gowy 192n64
  Manifold 152
  Mersey 3, 61–2
  names 195
  Penk 195, 241
  Ribble 3, 61–2
  Severn 16, 183
  Soar 102
  Sow 101, 183
  Tame 90, 178, 180, 183, 241
  Tean 101
  Trent 27, 90, 101–2, 127, 131–2, 151, 178, 180, 183
Robert fitz Hugh 67n88, 238
Robert, prior of Shrewsbury, *Life* of St Winifred 150
Rocester 78, 235–7
Rochester, diocese 23, 35, 43n145
Roger de Clinton, bishop of Coventry and Lichfield 79, 122, 164–5
Roger, earl of Shrewsbury 169n64, 220, 234

Rolleston 229
Romanesque architecture 112–4, 118, 218
Rome 19, 38–40, 45–6, 57, 109, 255, 257
  destination of English bishops 25, 30, 38
  sepulchral architecture 130–1
Rossall 66, 72
Rostherne 239n71
Roston 235n65, 236, 237n67
Rothley 101n45
Rownall 234n62, 236
Royal assemblies 41, 188, 213, 251, 255
  see also English royal councils; Mercian royal councils; Regnal territories
Royal free chapels 10, 167–74, 176, 221, 223–4
Rudyard 234, 236
Rugby 96, 97n32, 142, 151, 164
Rules, monastic 6, 83–4, 156, 245–7, 249, 253
  Aidan 53–4
  Cedd and Chad 51, 53–4, 245, 247
  St Benedict 121, 247
  see also Chrodegang of Metz
Runcorn 220, 239n71
Rushton 234–6

Sake and soke 232–4, 243
Sandbach 97–100, 107, 143–4, 150, 154
  see also Stone sculpture, Sandbach Group; Stone sculpture, Trent Valley Group
Sandon 196
Sawley 64, 66, 70, 146, 229n43
Saxons 18, 24–5
  see also Essex; Sussex; Wessex
Scalpcliff Hill 132
Seaxburh, abbess of Ely 124, 127n149
Seaxwulf, bishop of Mercia 14–18, 27–30, 32–3, 52–3, 58
Secgan 89–91, 120, 128–9, 132, 134
Seckington 128
Secularisation 10, 216, 244–6, 252
Secular minsters see Superior churches
Seighford 65
Seisdon 196
Selly Oak 76
Serjeants of the peace 237–40, 243
  see also Regnal soke, puture
Shelford 101n45
Shelton (Nottinghamshire) 101n45

Index

Shelton (Shropshire) 66, 72
Shenstone 165
Sheriffs 77, 242–3, 258
   see also Regnal soke, sheriff's aid
Shires 43, 163, 169, 216, 234, 239–43
   bounds 61, 243
   shire courts 41, 188, 213–4, 232, 242, 250, 258–9
   see also Domesday Book; Local assemblies; Hundreds, hundred courts; Regnal soke
Shrewsbury 71, 76–7, 82, 169, 199, 221
   St Alkmund's church 150, 169, 220
   St Chad's church 62, 66–70, 72–6, 82, 84, 169, 220–1
   St Juliana's church 168, 220
   St Mary's church 168, 220
   St Michael's church 168, 220
   St Peter's abbey 150, 169, 220
   see also St Winifred
Shrines 88, 94, 150, 152–4, 247, 251
   see also Burials; Ecclesiastical landscapes; Minsters; Repton, mausolea; St Bertram; St Chad, shrine at Lichfield; St Eadgyth; St Ealhmund; Stone sculpture; St Osburh; St Wærburh; St Wigstan
Shropshire Plain 183–6
Sigeric, archbishop of Canterbury 144–5
Soils 178–80, 182–6, 208–11
   see also Water
Soke *see* Domainal soke; Regnal soke; Sake and soke
South Saxons *see* Sussex
South Staffordshire Plateau 183
Southumbria 14, 18, 35, 37, 47, 260
   see also Canterbury, archbishopric; Church councils
Spiritual jurisdiction 170
Spiritual lordship 9–10, 45–6, 156–8, 166, 173–5, 217, 250–2, 254–60
   see also Diocesan communities; English ecclesiastical community; Liturgical communities
Spondon 101n45, 106, 147–8, 151, 196
St Benedict *see* Rules, monastic
St Beorhthelm 92–3, 138–9, 251
St Bertelin 137–8
   see also St Beorhthelm

St Bertram 137–8
   see also St Beorhthelm
St Cedd 51, 54, 58–9, 90
St Chad 53–4, 58–60, 84–5, 87–8, 90, 150
   landholder in Domesday Book 68–70
   liturgical community 123
   Old English *Life* 88–9
   relics 116, 120
   shrine at Lichfield 115–20, 152
   well at Stowe 111
   see also Calendars; Hugh Candidus, Peterborough Chronicle; Litanies; *Secgan*
St Chad, church dedications 75, 84
   see also Birmingham; Bishops Tachbrook; Brailsford; Brewood; Caldecote; Canons; Eccleshall; Farndon; Hanmer; Lichfield; Longford; Over; Prees; Shrewsbury; Stafford; Stowe; Wilne; Wybunbury
St Cuthberht 133, 136
St Eadgyth 90, 92, 132–4, 251
St Ealhmund 90, 92–3, 134–6, 251
St Edmund, king and martyr of East Anglia 90
St Guthlac 31, 127
St Gwenfrewi *see* St Winifred
St Milred 146–7
St Modwynn 90, 92, 94, 132–4
St Monenna, abbess of Killevy 132, 134
St Osburh 92, 140–1
St Oswald 109, 116, 147, 251
   see also Gloucester, New Minster
St Ruffin 93, 139–40
St Wærburh 88, 90–4, 124–7, 137, 139, 148
   see also Calendars; Litanies
St Wigstan 88, 90–3, 127–32, 148, 152
   see also Calendars
St Winifred 150
St Wulfhad 93, 139–40
Stafford 67, 139, 168–9, 220
   see also St Bertelin
Stapenhill 132, 134
Stapleford 107
Statfold 78, 122
Stephen of Ripon, *Life of Bishop Wilfrid* 30, 48, 54–60, 190–1
Stipershill 133

Stone 93, 139–40, 151
  see also St Ruffin; St Wulfhad
Stoneleigh 164, 220
Stone sculpture 9–10, 94–110, 141–8, 150, 153–5, 252
  Cropthorne Group 97, 100, 107, 142
  Dove Valley Subgroup 106–7, 109, 138, 147
  Lichfield Angel 97, 100, 115–6, 119, 154
  Peak Group 96–9, 100, 142–3
  Pennine Fringes Group 101, 106–7, 138, 143, 148, 252n116
  Sandbach Group 97–100, 103, 143–4, 146, 154
  Trent Valley Group 101–9, 135–6, 138, 143–4, 146–8, 153, 252
  Wirral Group 101
  see also Bakewell; Breedon-on-the-Hill; Coventry; Derby; Eccleshall; Over; Overchurch; Repton; Sandbach; Wilne; Wroxeter
Stori 66, 75, 233
Stowe 111, 122–3, 134
  see also Lichfield; St Chad
Subkingship 23, 26, 28, 32, 36, 48–9
  see also Overkingship
Sugnall 65
Superior churches 87, 144, 168, 176, 219–24, 229
  see also Ecclesiastical landscapes; Mother churches; Mother parishes
Sussex 23, 25
  see also Ælle; Chichester, diocese
Sutton (Denbighshire) 66, 68, 74
Synod of Whitby 50n14, 55
Synods see Church councils

Tamworth 62n70, 78, 133, 200, 222n27
  see also Mercian royal councils
Tarvin 66, 73, 76–7, 79–80, 146, 192, 229, 239
Tatenhill 101n45, 147–8, 151–2, 179
Taxatio Ecclesiastica of Pope Nicholas IV 2n10, 61, 172n84
Tegeingl 191
Tettenhall 168–9, 220, 224
Textual communities 12, 20–1, 38–40, 60
Theodore, archbishop of Canterbury 9, 19–26, 46, 60, 159, 255
  encounters with Chad 49, 54, 56–60, 156
  involvement in division of the Mercian see 28–9, 32–3
  see also Church councils
Thingferth, abbot of Evesham 167
Thomas of Marlborough 129
Thored 76–80, 220–1, 223
Threekingham 125
Thurvaston 79
Tiberius Group 100–1, 153
Tilston 66, 72–3
Tithes see Ecclesiastical tributes
Tithing 237
Tomsæte 62n70, 241
Tomtun see Tamworth
Tonna 66, 75
Torhthelm (alias Totta), bishop of Leicester 15, 31, 35, 80–1
Tostig, earl of Northumbria 204
Totta see Torhthelm
Town fields see Field systems
Trent, battle 27
Tribute payments see Ecclesiastical tributes; Regnal soke; Regnal territories
Trumberht 51, 60
Trumhere, bishop of Mercia 15, 17
Tuda, bishop of Northumbrians 56

Uhtred, ealdorman in Mercia 143, 145, 147, 221
Uttoxeter 78

Vikings 2, 40
  invasions 87, 97, 110, 125–6, 130, 136
  see also Danish polities; Stone sculpture
Vita Sanctae Werburgae see Goscelin of St Bertin

Wales 61–2, 138, 150, 191, 243n87, 260
  see also Anglo-Welsh borderland; Barrog; Gruffydd ap Llywelyn; Place-names, Brythonic
Wall (Leek) 235–6
Wall (Lichfield) 191
Walsall 165
Waltheof, earl 79
Wantage 146
Wardpenny see Regnal soke

Index

Wardsilver; *see* Regnal soke
Warmundestrou *see* Hundreds
Warwick 67
Water 181–2
   minster sites 151–2
Waterfall 235n65, 236
Weald of Kent and Sussex 196, 201
Weaverham 198
Weedon 92, 125
Weeford 122,
Welbatch 72
Wellington 150
Werenberht, bishop of Leicester 31
Wessex 23, 41–2, 56, 108, 145, 258
   Greater Wessex 41, 251
   see also Æthelwulf , ealdorman of Berkshire; Æthelwulf, king of Wessex; Anglian genealogies; Cædwalla; Ceawlin; Ecgberht; Ine; St Eadgyth; Tiberius Group; Winchester
West Kirby 144
Westbury-on-Trym 248
Westminster 141
Whitby 30, 133, *see also* Synod of Whitby
Whithorn 117
   diocese 14
Wigferth, priest 123n133
Wigheard, archbishop elect of Canterbury 25
Wiglaf, king of Mercia 129
Wigmund, king of Mercia 129
Wilfrid, bishop 15, 28, 48, 54–61, 80, 205, 255
   bishop of Leicester 30–2, 34
   Lichfield estate 190–1
   see also Hexham; Lastingham Narrative; Northumbria, diocese; Ripon; Stephen of Ripon, *Life of Bishop Wilfrid*; York, dicoese
Willaston 70
William I, king of England 206, 220, 237n67
William of Malmesbury 12, 37, 38n113, 38n116
William Malbank 220, 238–9
William, son of Nigel 220, 239n71
William, son of Corbucion 67n88
Willibald, *Life of St Boniface* 85
Wilne 66, 146, 150–1, 229
   stone sculpture 99–100, 106, 108, 146, 150
Winchester 146
   diocese 23, 30n74, 85, 160
   New Minster 91, 251, 258
   Old Minster 44
Wine, bishop of Winchester and London 19, 56, 59n59
Winfrith, bishop of Lichfield 15, 17–18, 26, 28, 49, 52–4, 58–9
Wirksworth 96, 97n32, 128, 142–3, 150
Wirral 101, 144
   see also Burton in Wirral
Wistanstow 129
Wolfhamcote 164
Wolseley 65n79
Wolston 164
Wolverhampton 108, 144–6, 168–9, 173, 188, 220–1
Woodcote 72
Woodland countryside *see* Agricultural landscapes, settlement dispersion
Worcester 153, 161–2, 167, 173, 248
   archive 1, 34, 60–1, 69, 74, 81–3
   diocese 11, 15–6, 26–8, 30–4, 38, 42–4
   diocesan bounds 61
   episcopal leases 160–1
   in Domesday Book 69, 81–3, 163
   see also Calendars; John of Worcester, Chronicle; St Milred
Worthenbury 71, 222n27
Wotenhull 70
Wrekin *see* Wreocensæte
Wrentnall 66, 72
Wreocensæte 241
Wrockwardine 80, 150
   see also Hundreds
Wroxeter 77, 79–80, 141–2, 165, 176, 220–1
   stone sculpture 97, 100, 141–2
   see also Wreocensæte
Wulfgeat 239n71
Wulfgeat of Donington 145
Wulfhere, king of Mercia 17–18, 25–7, 53, 58, 80, 191–2
   see also St Wærburh; St Wulfhad
Wulfred, archbishop of Canterbury 47, 121, 247
Wulfric Spot 176, 221, 229, 234
Wulfrun 144–5, 221
Wulfwin 76
Wybunbury 66, 75, 78, 229–30, 239

York 37
  see also York, archbishopric; York, diocese
York, archbishopric 14, 18, 20, 39, 42, 90n12
  see also Ecgberht; Oscytel
York, diocese 14, 19, 23, 26, 54–8
  see also Lindisfarne, diocese; Northumbria, diocese
Yorton 66, 72